PERSONALITY AND ADJUSTMENT

PERSONALITY

AND ADJUSTMENT

William L. Patty, PH.D.
DEPARTMENT OF PSYCHOLOGY, LOS ANGELES CITY COLLEGE

Louise Snyder Johnson, PH.D.
DEPARTMENT OF PSYCHOLOGY, UNIVERSITY COLLEGE
RUTGERS UNIVERSITY

New York   Toronto   London

McGRAW-HILL BOOK COMPANY, INC.

1953

PERSONALITY AND ADJUSTMENT

Library of Congress Catalog Card Number: 52–13011

PREFACE

All of us get perplexed at times about ourselves and others. The employee wonders why he does not get greater satisfaction from his job. The employer is concerned about human elements which hamper production. The parent worries about the behavior trend of his child. Teenagers brood about their popularity. And partners in marriage complain about lack of sympathy from each other. All such questions call for better understanding of human personality and its varying adjustments.

Both authors realize that many forces in the development of personality are as yet unidentified and unmeasurable. Nevertheless, they believe that a systematic study of growth and the problems of adjustment will contribute to improved understanding of all human behavior, be it complex or profound. The authors have experimented with different teaching approaches in their own university, college, junior college, extension, and adult-education classes. They have also worked closely with individuals as psychological counselors in educational, industrial, and clinical situations. From these experiences this text has grown.

The needs and interests of both students and laymen have been foremost in the minds of the authors as they prepared this text. It is especially designed for an introductory course in the psychology of personality which can be given a mental-hygiene slant. It might be used as a second-semester text, following an initial semester of general psychology, or it might be used as a first-semester text in which emphases match the phases of psychology which students typically wish to study first.

Parts of this book should serve well as reference material for a variety of other courses in psychology, education, personnel management, family relationships, writing and dramatics, group leadership, etc. Recent researches, clinical data, and illustrations from everyday life have been woven together in a way which the authors hope will be meaningful to diverse readers. Practical application will be encouraged by use of the questions at the end of each chapter. The suggested readings are drawn from many disciplines so that student interests may be guided through further explorations.

The general arrangement is in five parts, each introduced by a brief summary-transition designed to assist the reader's feeling of continuity of subject matter. Part One sketches several important but general problems of mental health, outlining international, national, and samples of local programs. Part Two analyzes four of the fundamental aspects of personality, namely, psychosomatics, motivation, culture, and perception. In Part Three these aspects are amalgamated into discussion of the development of personality through the life cycle. Various methods of assessment are examined as they contribute to an understanding of the many facets of personality. In Part Four the process of adjustment is magnified and highlighted as growth in relationship to four sample critical areas, *i.e.*, courtship, the family, handicaps, and delinquency. Part Five discusses some of the techniques available for helping inadequately adjusted personalities toward more healthy growth trends. Emphasis here has been on improving the reader's insight into the processes of adjustment. Based upon the earlier discussions, Part Five in its latter half develops a list of "criteria" which seem in the experience of the authors to suggest viewpoints holding positive relationships to healthy growth of personality.

Very many students, colleagues, and friends have contributed to the development of this book through the years. Their frank criticism of some concepts and approaches as well as their enthusiasm for others have deeply influenced both authors. They wish it were possible to list all to whom a debt of gratitude is felt.

William L. Patty
Louise Snyder Johnson

LOS ANGELES, CALIF.
NEW BRUNSWICK, N. J.
FEBRUARY, 1953

CONTENTS

PREFACE   v

Part One MENTAL HEALTH
AND PERSONALITY ADJUSTMENT

CHAPTER 1 The Need for Mental Health   3
The Meaning of Mental Health; Maladjustment—An Individual View; Maladjustment—A Societal View

CHAPTER 2 Approaches to Mental Health   21
International and National Spearheads of Attack; Community-level Facilities; Study of Personality

Part Two FUNDAMENTALS OF PERSONALITY

CHAPTER 3 Motivation   43
Motives Are Causes; Motives Are Biosocial; Motives and the Person

CHAPTER 4 Psychosomatics   62
The Digestive System; The Respiratory System; The Cardiovascular System; The Musculature; Nervous Systems; Emotion

CHAPTER 5 Culture   98
Cultural Patterning; Characteristics of United States Culture; Applications of Cultural Understanding

CHAPTER 6 Perception   123
How Perception Works; How the Study of Perception Is Used

Part Three PERSONALITY AND GROWTH

CHAPTER 7 The Growth of Personality   149
The Study of Personality; The Process of Growth; Experiencing the Life Cycle

CHAPTER 8 Learning and Personality 173

Learning; Modes of Action

CHAPTER 9 The Structuring of Personality 191

Dimensions of Personality; Trait Analysis; The Architecture of Personality

CHAPTER 10 The Adjustments of Personality 203

The Concept of Adjustment; The Mechanisms for Maintaining Selfhood; Wellsprings of Neuroticism; Patterns of Deviate Behavior; Perception and Neurosis

Part Four AREAS OF PERSONALITY ADJUSTMENT

CHAPTER 11 Courtship and Marrying 243

Readiness for Courtship; Courtship; Engagement

CHAPTER 12 Home and Family 274

The Family Life Cycle; Goals of Home and Family; Influences That Shape Family Goals

CHAPTER 13 Handicap 299

The Meaning of Handicap; The Emotional Handicap; The Physical Handicap; The Mental Handicap; The Social Handicap; The Handicap of Age

CHAPTER 14 Delinquency 335

Past and Present; Delinquency and Personality Structure; Prevention and Treatment

Part Five PERSPECTIVE FOR MENTAL HEALTH

CHAPTER 15 Readjustment 359

The Goals of Readjustment; Resources for Readjustment; Psychotherapeutic Techniques

CHAPTER 16 The Criteria 381

Understanding Oneself (Criterion 1); Techniques of Integration (Criterion 2); Philosophy of Work (Criterion 3); Social Participation (Criterion 4); Life Perspective (Summary of Criteria)

NAME INDEX 391

SUBJECT INDEX 397

Part One MENTAL HEALTH AND
PERSONALITY ADJUSTMENT

The title of this book, *Personality and Adjustment,* suggests the interdependence of the individual and the media in which his personality is expressed. Part One discusses some of the ways in which personalities show the quality of their adjustment. Opposite ends of the continuum from good mental health to mental illness serve to point up the definition of the healthy personality. Types of maladjustment appearing in our society and statistics on mental illness develop the picture of present-day mental health in the United States.

With the pressing need for improved mental health clarified, some constructive approaches to the problem are listed. Examples cited are from actual attempts being carried on by neighborhood groups and by national or international organizations to increase the numbers of personalities with healthy adjustment. The part that the study of personality can play in this crusade is suggested so that the reader can define his present goals as a responsible member of society.

CHAPTER 1 *The Need for Mental Health*

Mental health has to do with everybody's everyday life. A study of the contemporary scene brings to light unmet personality needs in the same way in which market research unearths unsatisfied consumer desires. Personalities show their inadequacies in all varieties of inability to get on with the business of living. Insecurities and hostilities are evidenced in cultural patterns by such tendencies as unwholesome reliance on magic, on father figures in government, and on dreams of escape.

Understanding of health often comes from the study of disease. In the same way, prophylaxis for mental health can be based in part upon improved insight into the crippling effects of poor mental health. To set the stage for this understanding, this chapter will develop the meaning of mental health and describe maladjustments in individuals and in society.

THE MEANING OF MENTAL HEALTH

Every day each one of us is adjusting to himself, to his fellows, and to all the other aspects of his world. From the time of birth every human being faces a succession of changing circumstances in his various areas of living. The way in which he reacts to these situations determines the pattern of his personality and the quality of his mental health.

Mentally Healthy Individuals

People designated as physically healthy are commonly visualized as rosy cheeked, well proportioned, and vigorous. What is the parallel concept of mentally healthy individuals? The shortest way to describe these people is to say that they are *emotionally mature*. They

3

have learned how to adapt themselves in such a way as to find happiness and effectiveness in living. Their desires and satisfactions are adequately synchronized into well-integrated personalities.

Mentally healthy people feel comfortable about themselves and their abilities. They do not expect to be able to do everything perfectly, nor do they underestimate their powers. They tackle college work, office work, or housework as a challenge to their strengths and weaknesses. They use the gaps between their ideals and their accomplishments as spurs to constructive improvement. Feeling sorry for themselves, blaming others, or escaping by means of narcotics is not part of their repertory. Instead, they grapple with situations as they arise.

They shape their environment if it is possible; if not, they adjust to it. If they decide that an employer is unfair, they take the matter up with the appropriate authority or look for another job. If they believe that their representatives in Washington are not working for their interests, they write letters of protest or try to elect more trustworthy candidates. They do not turn to crime or to anti-American activities to "get even."

These individuals have generally satisfying relationships with other people. They do not have inner needs which make them bow to everyone nor do they feel impelled to dominate others. They are not driven to buy attention by overplaying their relationships with friends and business associates. They do not suffer from inner feelings which must be assuaged by hurting their wives and children or by attacking minority groups. In short, they are able to consider the interests of others and to feel part of a group.

These mentally healthy people are characterized by a positive state of well-being. To the degree that it is possible in the real world of today, they are happy, confident, and satisfied. They are able to stay with a job, to live effectively within the codes of their society, and to adjust to new or emergency situations. They have attained a high degree of personal adjustment, and this is reflected in their daily life.

Maladjustment as a Continuum

Those who falter or fail in the adjustment process may be considered emotionally immature, maladjusted, or mentally ill. They might be visualized on a continuum extending from minor emotional problems to serious mental illness. Their difficulties may show in attitudes toward themselves such as lack of confidence or guilt feelings. Their poor adjustment may come to light in relationships with

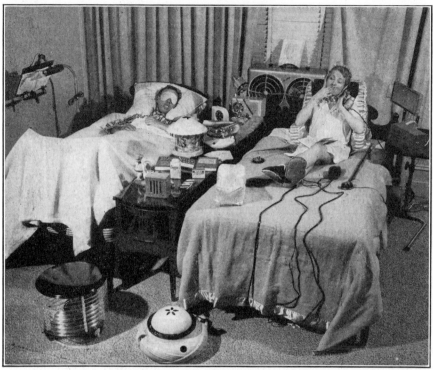

Fig. 1–1. Widespread insomnia mirrors maladjustment. Americans have a tendency to look for gadgets to solve all their problems. Here are 40 of those designed for inducing sleep. They are Sheep Rotators, Lullipines, Metronomic Lullers, Yawn-inducing Pendiculation Plaques, Ear Stoppers, Pulsating Relaxers, Sleep Shades, and Relax Records. (*Reprinted by permission from Look Magazine.*)

thcir fellows. They may sulk, act huffy, or fly into temper tantrums when they cannot have their own way. They may join the ranks of revolutionists rather than evolutionists. They may be unable to adapt to the world of work and be continually blocked by indecision, inability to concentrate, or overdependency. As by-products of their tensions they may suffer headaches, insomnia, eczema, fever, or other disorders. The emotionally induced anguish of such individuals may be as painful as illness caused by germs or injury, but to many laymen they appear merely lazy, queer, inclined to "show off," difficult, or prejudiced. Because of lack of understanding of these difficulties, many people suffer them in silence and without adequate help.

When a person is mentally or emotionally ill, it is understood that he suffers from a "neurosis" or a "psychosis"; either may vary greatly in intensity. "Insanity" is a term which should only be used in cases in which a court of law adjudges an individual unable to carry responsibility for himself and for the natural results of his actions.

"Neurosis" and "psychoneurosis" are terms applied almost interchangeably to emotional illness involving less personal and social danger than psychosis. The reactions are within the accepted limits of social living. There is distortion of reality, but there is, usually, no break with it.

In psychosis there is an almost complete loss of contact with the surrounding world, a withdrawal from reality. This characteristic makes it difficult or impossible for the psychotic to manage his life in the world of reality and may also be a source of danger to himself or to others. Thus he may need a special world created for him such as an institution provides.

Extent of Mental Illness

Various estimates have been made of the number of people who are mentally and emotionally ill to an extent that interferes with normal living. Conservative estimates range around 10 per cent of the population.[1] This figure seems less startling when broken down into various categories. Whenever journalists mention that help for emotional problems is available, they are besieged by requests for more information. One such writer turned over to the National Committee for Mental Hygiene several thousand letters from all parts of the country. These gave evidence of real distress and begged for aid on personal problems. This avalanche was precipitated by a line in her column stating that there was a national organization working toward improvement in mental health.

[1] William C. Menninger, *Psychiatry: Its Evolution and Present Status,* p. 98, Cornell University Press, Ithaca, N.Y., 1948.

Millions of people in the U.S. are under emotional strain due to fears, tensions, anxieties and frustrations. Many require hospitalization and psychiatric treatment. Lack of trained personnel is a problem in mental hospitals. Psychiatrists are giving more time to early treatment or prevention of mental disorders.

1 OUT OF 16 ARE *MENTALLY ILL

It is estimated that there are 1.5 million people in the U.S. suffering from mental illness, and 7.5 million suffering from other personality disturbances—about one in every 16 people.

*(*Including personality disturbances)*

ANNUAL COST OF MENTAL ILLNESS

$1,750 Million

Total $2.8 Billion
1950

Patients' Loss of Potential Earnings

$548 Million

Federal

$560 Million

State

Mental illness costs the public about $1.1 billion a year in state and federal taxes.

This cost does not include private mental hospitals or visits to psychiatrists.

FIG. 1–2. Mental illness is a No. 1 problem. (*Courtesy of Chicago Sun-Times, based on Facts & Figures, 1952, National Association for Mental Health, Inc.*)

ALMOST HALF OF ALL PATIENTS

Mental   Other
Hospitals   Hospitals

Patients in mental hospitals make up almost half the total patients in hospitals in U.S.

MENTAL HOSPITALS PUBLIC AND PRIVATE

In U.S. there are about 680 mental hospitals and 240 institutions for the mentally deficient and epileptic.

State   County,   Private
Hospitals   City   Hospitals

MENTAL HOSPITALS ARE OVERCROWDED

Beds Occupied

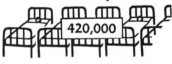

420,000

New Beds Needed

330,000
(State)

Mental hospitals have 41 per cent of hospital beds, while mental patients make up 47 per cent of all patients.

PATIENT COST IN MENTAL HOSPITALS

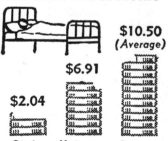

$10.50
(Average)

$6.91

$2.04

State   Veterans   Private
Hospitals   Hospitals   Hospitals

This is the daily cost of maintaining a mental patient.

Fig. 1–3. Hospital facilities are inadequate. (*Courtesy of Chicago Sun-Times, based on Facts & Figures, 1952, National Association for Mental Health, Inc.*)

Some indication of the immensity of the problem is afforded by the national statistic of 100,000 attempts at suicide annually.[2] Alcoholics are estimated at more than 3,000,000 in the United States. The emotionally ill individual projects his inner conflicts onto those around him. Some of this shows in the 7,000,000 citizens who have criminal records.[3] Other indications are found in divorce statistics. In 1945 there was one divorce for every two marriages in urban areas and one for every three in the country at large.[4] During World War II one out of every eight men examined for the draft was turned down because of personality problems. Fifty-one per cent of all separations from the military services were due to maladjustment.[5]

From certain points of view, the mentally ill persons in mental hospitals present the more serious aspect. There can be no absolute separation of these two phases of the problem, however, because the number of those respectively in and out of hospitals depends on the facilities for this type of hospitalization available in the various parts of the country. The trend toward increased care for the aged is also adding to the hospital lists. Admissions accumulate much faster than institutions can be built and staffed. In 1947 the Surgeon General reported that there were 8,000,000 Americans in need of treatment for mental disability.[6] Such statistics as these clearly indicate the important fact that America needs to improve its mental health.

MALADJUSTMENT—AN INDIVIDUAL VIEW

Maladjustments reveal themselves in the form of antisocial behavior, pain, or general inability to accept oneself or others. These

[2] Kenneth E. Appel, Mental hygiene for the adult in the world today, p. 67, in W. B. Terhune (ed.), *Living Wisely and Well: A Discussion of Techniques of Personal Adjustment,* E. P. Dutton & Co., Inc., New York, 1949.

[3] Leon J. Saul, *Bases of Human Behavior,* p. 7, J. B. Lippincott Company, Philadelphia, 1951.

[4] B. L. Jenkinson, *Marriage and Divorce in the United States 1937–45, Vital Statistics,* Bureau of Census, Special Report, 1946, 23:9.

[5] *The National Health Assembly Official Report: America's Health: A Report to the Nation,* p. 298, Harper & Brothers, New York, 1949.

[6] R. M. Dorcus, The psychoses and the psychoneuroses, p. 265, in L. A. Pennington and Irwin A. Berg (eds.), *An Introduction to Clinical Psychology,* The Ronald Press Company, New York, 1948.

difficulties are accented under stress. In the average case they are present during an individual's entire life span, but not until they are intensified by a particular environment does the person realize that something is wrong. Some of the more common pressures are war, employment problems, and various types of personal frustration.

Maladjustment in Military Life

Every major war has been followed by the appearance among veteran groups of a type of illness which has seemed clearly a result of war experiences. This illness has always incapacitated the individual to some extent. In earlier wars there was a preponderance of battlefield experience for almost every member of the armed forces. Descriptions of this peculiar type of illness seemed to indicate a relation to the main characteristics of the battlefield situation. Some veterans of World War I were presumed to have experienced more intense shellfire, hence to have suffered shock to their bodies from air-pressure concussions. Explanations of this "shell shock" were attempted by physiologists and physicians along every conceivable line, but for many cases no organic basis was found. Some explanations of a psychological type were suggested, but public and professional interests were not yet ready.[7]

World War II had no single characteristic such as the exploding of shells to serve as scapegoat. The term "combat fatigue" became the handy label. But combat fatigue soon appeared in a surprisingly large proportion of men for whom there was no record of combat activity. From more careful study it became evident that the newer understanding of mental illness in civilian situations could be applied to these cases. The term "psychoneurotic" thus began to appear in the reports pertaining to Selective Service procedures, receiving centers, and hospitals. This unwieldy term soon achieved simplification and became, in the language of the noncommissioned man, "psycho." Recognition of the true character of "shell shock" or "combat fatigue" places it as one segment of the whole problem of mental health. Public attitudes are veering away from the older

[7] William H. Burnham, *The Normal Mind: An Introduction to Mental Hygiene and the Hygiene of School Instruction*, p. 135, Appleton-Century-Crofts, Inc., New York, 1924.

tendency to make accusations of laziness and lack of personal integrity toward a better understanding of maldevelopment of personality.

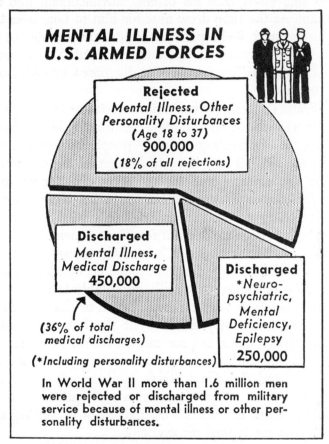

MENTAL ILLNESS IN U.S. ARMED FORCES

Rejected
Mental Illness, Other Personality Disturbances
(Age 18 to 37)
900,000
(18% of all rejections)

Discharged
Mental Illness,
Medical Discharge
450,000

(36% of total medical discharges)

(*Including personality disturbances)

Discharged
*Neuro-psychiatric,
Mental Deficiency,
Epilepsy
250,000

In World War II more than 1.6 million men were rejected or discharged from military service because of mental illness or other personality disturbances.

FIG. 1–4. Rejections and discharges reflect unhealthy personalities. (*Courtesy of Chicago Sun-Times, based on Facts & Figures, 1952, National Association for Mental Health, Inc.*)

Neurosis in Occupational Difficulties

Unemployment compensation and social-security legislation provide situations in which the civilian problem of psychoneurosis is highlighted. The following illustration will help to clarify the way in which psychoneurosis leads to absenteeism and, commonly, to the resultant dismissal and unemployment.

Frank had always been a loyal worker, and he knew his drafting. When the plant was enlarged, he was offered the position of supervisor at a higher salary. His first reaction was most pleasant. His family was impressed with his coming advancement and made a fuss over him. As the time drew near for him to take over the new position, he began to feel a paralysis in his arm. Physicians tried to locate the organic cause of the difficulty, but X rays and tests showed nothing. Finally a psychiatrist diagnosed Frank's trouble as a form of neurosis.

Behind Frank's seemingly enthusiastic exterior lay much anxiety and fear. He was sure of his ability on the drawing board, but whenever he thought of directing so many people he became panicky. What if he should fail and have to bring that news home to his family? He also remembered his unhappy experiences in school when he was considered the teacher's favorite, and he feared the same sort of thing would happen when his working companions found that he had been singled out for advancement. This is merely one example of the innumerable behind-the-scenes dramas which can be accounted for by the fact that much occupational maladjustment cannot be explained in socially acceptable terms.

Supervisor anxiety is very common. Much of the total energy of employees goes into worry about what the boss will think. The real, or underlying, cause is poor mental health of either or both parties. Unemployment resulting from other causes, but still involving mental and emotional illness, is commonly observed. Dismissal for refusal to accept supervision and quitting for lack of interest in the work or because of difficulties in getting on with other employees are typical illustrations.

Neurosis in Physical Illness

Frank's difficulty illustrated one type of psychosomatic problem. Psychiatrists estimate that from 40 to 60 per cent of all human illness is a consequence of, or is seriously complicated by, unresolved emotional conflict.[8] Many of the sufferers do not seek professional help, so that there is no easy way to identify them.

[8] *The Mental Health Programs of the Forty-eight States: A Report to the Governor's Conference*, p. 216, Council of State Governments, Chicago, 1950.

Many emotional tensions are discharged through peptic ulcer, colitis, asthma, arthritis, skin eruption, hypertension, fatigue, insomnia, and migraine. Hatreds, longings, and desires for attention act upon the body system, disturbing normal physiological activity. Weiss and English [9] mention three general classifications of patients: Group I, those with no organic disease to account for their sickness; Group II, those with both organic and emotional symptoms; Group III, those with disorders generally considered wholly within the area of physical disease. Each group comprises a third of the total of those who consult physicians.

Maladjustment Reflected in Accidents

There appears to be a distinct relationship between an individual's emotional stability and his accident frequency. Accidents seem to cluster around certain types of maladjusted people; unknowingly they are using this behavior to injure themselves or others. In the case of some individuals, accidents serve as the punishment required by an inner sense of guilt; in such cases psychological investigation frequently unearths emotional reasons why the accidents occur at a particular time. With remarkable consistency such accidents seem to follow a period of emotional tension.

A typical illustration is the case of Mr. M., who could not understand why he had bumped into a car at a stop light, smashed his fender getting out of a parking lot, and broken his glasses, all in one morning. Inquiry revealed that among other things he had a very upsetting phone call from his divorced wife just before he started off that morning. Mr. M. had a long record of accident proneness. He was a very neurotic person, and one of the ways his personality balance was maintained was through self-punishment in the form of accidents.

There are psychological aspects of industrial-accident compensation. The term "industrial accident" refers to bodily injuries sustained at work. Insurance payments usually amount to only a part of the regular earning power of the employee for the period of time involved. Nevertheless, certain persons seem to be chronic accident

[9] Edward Weiss and O. Spurgeon English, *Psychosomatic Medicine: The Clinical Application of Psychopathology to General Medical Problems,* pp. 1–2, W. B. Saunders Company, Philadelphia, 1943.

repeaters. More and more these accidents are being traced to personal rather than mechanical difficulties.

FIG. 1–5. A child suffers from parental maladjustments. Immature parents have upset the emotional climate of this home. Surrounded by material pleasures and luxury of every type, this little girl still longs for warm affection. (*From Child of Divorce, RKO Radio Pictures, Inc.*)

The Second-line Sufferer

Much of the suffering caused by maladjustments is in the second line. Difficult personalities multiply emotional upsets in an office, just as a contagious disease disseminates itself. Tensions and stresses are characteristic of families containing a psychoneurotic personality. At the very least, the loved ones of those suffering from mental illness are deprived of the support of and much of the potential for human relationships.

To the extent that a person is ill, his productivity is impaired. Someone has to carry his load of self-support and community responsibility; in addition, aid must be provided for the ill person. In some instances the other members of the family circle are denied necessities because of the drain on the budget to provide care for the sufferer.

The diverse chain reactions set in motion by mental illness can easily be envisaged as affecting families, fellow workers, and neighbors. It is unlikely that anyone can escape being touched by the problem. Everybody has a stake in mental health.

MALADJUSTMENT—A SOCIETAL VIEW

Turning the spotlight from the individual to society discloses a mass of evidence of immaturity. Cultural patterns reflect escapism, unwholesome cravings for various types of magic, and interpersonal and international tension. Some experts have diagnosed the contemporary social scene as characteristic of a sick society. Illustrations of these danger signs will be evaluated.

Pseudosolutions as Mirrors of Maladjustment

Pseudosolutions are two-way mirrors of the emotional disturbances of our times. Those who offer them actually exemplify a mild form of mental illness. Those to whom these short cuts appeal are certainly revealing their own instability. Since their personality needs are not being met in actual life situations, they attempt to fulfill these needs by offering or by using magic. From early times, whenever insecurities have been especially upsetting, men have resorted to magic.

Characteristic of the personality which has been weakened by mental and emotional illness is a tendency to feel that the burden of living is very heavy. The sufferer becomes prey to exploitation; almost any panacea is acceptable which can be made to look quick and easy, unusually certain, and beyond the powers of ordinary explanation. The purveyors of magic used by these troubled people reflect their own weakened personalities. Usually the means of communication between these two varieties of mentally ill people are forms of pseudoscience, pseudoreligion, pseudoengineering, or pseudopsychology. Supersalesmen, for a fee, advertise to teach the secrets of inevitable social success and irresistible popularity. Newspaper, magazine, and radio columns, syndicated to appear throughout the nation apparently in answer to widespread demand, offer advice to the lovelorn, formulas for success deriving from numerology, astrology, and psychology. For the business executive there are purchasable schemes for increasing production and profits. Such improvements can always be made in an organization, but not by the magical methods offered by these self-styled "personnel engineers," "management engineers" or "sales psychologists." With these short-cut methods the emphasis is too much upon the possibility that someone from the outside will quickly and surely bring about rapid success.

Illustrations of Magic Short Cuts

Who cannot recall having seen "personals" columns in newspapers and journals? From one such column these paid advertisements were selected as typical.

WE CAN BUILD SUCCESS INTO YOUR LIFE

Our Counselors integrate and focus ALL your qualities, and prove that you are worth more than you think.

A STRANGELY GIFTED MAN

SPIRITUAL ADVISOR

Geo. Blank—HELPS AND ADVISES you on all affairs of life.
Solves every human problem.
Sad hearts gladdened.
Many weary lives made bright through the timely advice of this remarkable man.
Nos. 3, 4, or Beverly bus to ——— Avenue.
[Address]
Hours: 11 a.m. to 5 p.m. Daily and Sunday.
Thursdays till 9 p.m. [Phone]

WORRIED—TROUBLED

CONSULT FAMOUS READER

I have helped thousands, why not you? I read your life like an open book. Give help and advice on all affairs. Hours: 12–10 p.m. Daily and Sunday. [Address]

These advertisements typify the most common claims made by exploiters of the mentally and emotionally ill. The troubled person tends to feel, upon reading such advertisements, that here is someone whose rare powers will be adequate to the lifting of his overwhelming burden. In addition to the rareness of the talents offered and the unusual positiveness of the results promised, he is impressed by the technique of supplying the needed information or problem solution, which is mystical and unexplainable. These three characteristics are found, in varying degrees, in almost all the remedies that appeal to the various types of maladjusted persons.

Common Escape Offerings

Mental ill health is also evident in the increase in popular facilities for escape. There is an almost endless roster of unusual "religions" promising mysterious and overwhelming power to each and every follower. One self-styled religious leader built up a considerable following by offering that all problems would be placed in writing on an airplane which would be flown up to heaven nightly. The troubled individuals after paying for this service could then relax, since they had referred their problems on high. There are many cults in which the practice is to turn one's life over to the direction of a leader. Similar examples demonstrating the great need of some individuals to escape from reality are constantly appearing.

Soap operas and their counterpart in popular books, movies, and comics relieve the troubled personality of the necessity of grappling with reality. Likewise, the desire to escape responsibility by turning decisions over to radio commentators, newspaper columnists, or government figures is everywhere evident. In fact, many political leaders seem to succeed by wearing a kind of psychological armor which makes them appear the essence of power, capable of taking over all responsibility. Demagogues capitalize upon this situation to their own advantage and wreak havoc upon the machinery of democracy. They take advantage of the feelings of dependence, the hunger for boss-manship. Unscrupulous individuals can manipulate masses of emotionally ill people to a degree which may be dangerous to democracy. Hitler capitalized upon the frustrations of people, particularly young people, in his rise to power. Sick nations seem to choose psychopathic leaders.[10]

The Larger Scene

The social scene may absorb, deflect, or encourage hostilities. At times in the past the stage seems to have been set for healthfully absorbing more insecurity and hostility than can be absorbed today. Some large events have served to reduce the evidence of psychoneuroses. Major economic depressions, except in their early stages, show a statistical reduction in such evidence. Fortunately, some observers point out, the people of the United States have had the advantage of great safety valves through much of their history. Cited as examples are the ever-advancing frontier, lure of free Western lands, and the gold rushes to California and Alaska. It is likely that these phenomena minimized the amount of personality illness.

Antithetically at present there are many cases in which insecurities are projected as hostility. Thus mental and emotional illness is jeopardizing our culture. In some instances this hostility takes the form of turning on one's nation, for example, by joining anti-American groups or by violating security regulations. Some brilliantly capable scientists show evidence of emotional instability, and authorities are afraid to trust them lest they turn out to be traitors. In such cases personal insecurity turns into hateful aggression against the society which, in the view of the anxious individual, is responsible for his unhappiness. Hostilities are also being projected by those politicians whose denunciations of their opponents stem more from their own inner needs than from factual evidence. Editors and columnists in certain instances use newsprint as a form of catharsis for their own antagonisms. Some of these who rave against powerful leaders may be unknowingly fighting a father figure.

Great numbers of individuals join together to make common cause with their tensions, conflicts, demands, and hates. Insecurities and frustrations can create all types of group and national stresses. These tensions are channeled into aggressive behavior or intergroup

[10] George W. Kisker (ed.), *World Tension: The Psychopathology of International Relations*, p. 96, Prentice-Hall, Inc., New York, 1951.

distrust. Illustrations are myriad in employer-employee disputes and in interdenominational strife in the form of denunciations of the beliefs of others. Collective insecurity is one of the influences precipitating war.

Summary

Whether looked at from the individual or from the group viewpoint, maladjustment is a number one problem. The statistics are appalling. The lost potentials in individual effectiveness and happiness are staggering. These individual immaturities are taking their toll from society's health. Generally upsetting conditions and mounting personal tragedies spread before us a sordid panorama. To report on possible approaches to the problem will be the next order of business.

QUESTIONS FOR DISCUSSION

1. List some of the reasons why many people do not like to consider the problems of mental illness.
2. How do most people label mental illness?
3. Describe some of the effects of poor mental health on business and industry.
4. Suggest ways in which accidents resulting from poor mental health might be lessened.
5. What, if any, has been the increase in hospital facilities for the mentally ill in your community in the past few years?
6. Give some examples of organizations characterized by hostility.
7. Why do most people try to cover up any history of mental illness in their families?
8. What proportion of the people you know rely on pseudosolutions for their problems?
9. Find some examples of advertisements of pseudosolutions in the press.
10. List some of the contemporary pressures which may be increasing mental illness.
11. Do you think that most people you know feel so insecure that they need father figures in politics?
12. To what extent do you believe that the advertisements you see make you feel frustrated? Give an example.
13. Why would most people rather find physical than emotional causes for their illnesses?
14. Inquire of several people you know as to how they react to the term "psychoneurosis."

15. Do you believe that lack of understanding of the characteristics of psychosis increases the community's problems? Explain your answer.

ADDITIONAL READINGS

Alexander, Franz: Mental hygiene in the atomic age, *Ment. Hyg., N.Y.*, 1946, 30:529–544.

Bane, Frank: The Governors' study on mental hospitals, *Ment. Hyg., N.Y.*, 1951, 35:10–13.

Burtt, Harold Ernest: *Applied Psychology*, Chap. 3, Prentice-Hall, Inc., New York, 1948.

Hymes, James L., Jr.: Maturity: What is it? *Childhood Ed.*, 1950, 27(1):2–3.

Landis, C., and Farwell, J. E.: A trend analysis of age at first-admission, age at death and years of residence for State Mental Hospitals, *J. Abnorm. Soc. Psychol.*, 1944, 39:3–23.

McLaughlin, James T.: Normality and psychosomatic illness, *Ment. Hyg., N.Y.*, 1950, 34(1):19–33.

Niederland, William G.: *Man-made Plague: A Primer of Neurosis*, pp. 1–85, Renbayle House, Inc., New York, 1949.

Overstreet, Harry A.: *The Mature Mind*, pp. 119–143, W. W. Norton & Company, New York, 1949.

Rees, John R.: International amity begins at home, *Ment. Hyg., N.Y.*, 1950, 34:1–10.

Rennie, Thomas A. C., and Woodward, Luther E.: *Mental Health in Modern Society*, Chap. 5, Commonwealth Fund, Harvard University Press, Cambridge, Mass., 1948.

Saul, Leon J.: *Emotional Maturity: The Development and Dynamics of Personality*, pp. 3–22, J. B. Lippincott Company, Philadelphia, 1947.

Steiner, Lee R.: *Where Do People Take Their Troubles?* Houghton Mifflin Company, Boston, 1945.

Thorman, George: *Toward Mental Health*, Public Affairs Pamphlet No. 120, New York, 1946.

CHAPTER 2   *Approaches to Mental Health*

The possibility of further misguided leadership by mentally ill men and women in this atomic era has moved thoughtful people everywhere to call for action. Strategy moves forward on three fronts: (1) widening public awareness of the problem, (2) promoting research into causes and diagnoses, and (3) improving techniques of treatment and prevention. The most important of all goals is the promotion of healthy mental and emotional maturation.

The plan of this chapter is to start at the outer boundaries and work inward. A digest of the global approaches will be given as a backdrop for the mental-hygiene stage. National organizations and governmental supporting legislation which have been instrumental in furthering this cause will be described. Illustrations will be given of some of the most productive of the local approaches. With this background, the importance of the study of personality in the battle for mental health can be presented.

INTERNATIONAL AND NATIONAL SPEARHEADS OF ATTACK

The problem of mental health is being attacked from many angles. Boundaries between the social sciences are breaking down. Helpful insights are being culled from psychiatry, physiology, sociology, anthropology, and psychology. Studies of the inner physiological and psychological processes and evaluations of the cultural climate in which the personality grows are helping to improve the outlook for the future. Various implementations of the findings of these many disciplines are appearing on the international and the national horizons. In these and other privately and publicly sponsored approaches lie our hopes for an emotionally sounder world.

International Congresses on Mental Health

The first International Congress on Mental Hygiene was held in Washington, D.C., in 1930. The second such congress convened in Paris in 1937. The next met in London in 1948; its theme was "Mental Health and World Citizenship." The fourth international congress convened in Mexico City in 1951. The agenda included the following: mental health in education, occupational and industrial mental health, mental health of the immigrant, transplanted and homeless persons, problems of psychiatric treatment and prophylaxis.

Each of these conferences has involved much more than a brief coming together of experts from various nations. For example, the London meeting was the culmination of the work of three hundred subsidiary commissions. These employed the talents of some five thousand members in twenty-seven countries, representing many fields, including psychiatry, education, social work, law, anthropology, and clinical psychology. Each commission conferred for about a year before submitting its report to the general conference.

Other International Organizations

The purpose stated in the Articles of Association of the World Federation for Mental Health, now located in London, is as follows: "To promote among all peoples and nations the highest possible level of mental health (which term wherever used in these Articles shall be deemed to include mental health in its broadest biological, medical, educational and social aspects)." [1]

The activities planned are to establish and maintain effective collaboration with governments, government agencies, professional groups, corporations, organizations, or individuals which may be appropriate; to propose conventions, agreements, and regulations and make recommendations with respect to mental health; to develop informed public opinion among all peoples on mental health; to promote cooperation among scientific and professional groups which contribute to the advancement of mental health. [2]

---

[1] World Federation for Mental Health, *Annual Report 1948–49,* p. 84, London.

[2] Articles of Association of the World Federation for Mental Health, *Ment. Hyg.,* N.Y., 1949, 33:490–500.

Some of the suggested implementations are: to collect suggestions for improving world mental health, to analyze these with committees representative of various cultures of the world, as well as the various disciplines within these, to make recommendations regarding these suggestions to UNESCO. This type of approach is growing. Some work along the same line is being done by the International Council for the Mental Health of Children.[3] A survey has been made of the present status of mental-health activities for children in various parts of the world. The Council collaborates with authorities in each country to plan needed facilities. It disseminates information among laymen and professional workers in all matters concerning the mental health of children.

There are visions, not yet even in the blueprint stage, of setting up an international institute for mental health to work on the mental-hygiene phase of international tensions. One group of social scientists from various countries brought together by UNESCO has already worked out a detailed study consisting of analyses and suggestions. One paragraph in their joint statement reads: "While men vary greatly in their capacities and temperaments, we believe there are vital needs common to all men which must be fulfilled in order to establish and maintain peace; men everywhere want to be free from hunger and disease, from insecurity and fear; men everywhere want fellowship and the respect of their fellow-men; the chance for personal growth and development."[4]

National Associations for Mental Health

The seeds of international cooperation were probably planted some forty years ago by an American, Clifford Beers. This hero of the war for mental health was once so depressed that he attempted suicide. This episode, which occurred soon after his graduation from Yale, was followed by considerable experience with diverse therapies and mental institutions. Motivated by his own suffering, he set up the National Committee for Mental Hygiene. This organization was

[3] International Council for the Mental Health of Children, Mental health of children in the world of today, International Reports, *Nerv. Child*, 1950, 8:409–451.

[4] Hadley Cantril (ed.), *Tensions That Cause Wars: Common Statement and Individual Papers by a Group of Social Scientists Brought Together by UNESCO*, pp. 17–18, University of Illinois Press, Urbana, Ill., 1950.

a pioneer in the promotion of widespread programs for the prevention and treatment of mental illness. It launched the two magazines *Mental Hygiene* and *Understanding the Child,* both of which combine a multidiscipline approach toward personality problems. More recently the Mental Health Foundation was organized by a group aware of the terrible conditions in the mental hospitals of this country and determined to keep as many individuals as possible from unnecessary suffering. They pushed the use of mass media for alerting the public. They furnished sound recordings dealing in dramatic fashion with anxieties, insecurities, and many other phases of mental hygiene for use in radio stations, clubs, and schools. Certain key members of the American Psychiatric Association joined with some outstanding lay people in the field of mental hygiene to form the Psychiatric Foundation in 1946. Another group of psychiatrists has prepared an outline which may be used by laymen as a guide for evaluating and improving existing community mental-hygiene programs.[5]

Such organizations have served as nuclei in the mental-hygiene movement. They deserve much credit for lending stability and strength to a cause which was to capture public imagination only after prolonged effort. By mid-century the time was ripe for the amalgamation of these three organizations, the National Committee for Mental Hygiene, the National Mental Health Foundation, and the Psychiatric Foundation, into a single unit, the National Association for Mental Health. Its stated purpose is "to bring some few central truths of mental health to the attention of every person in the country; to see that psychiatric services are available at whatever level needed—mental hospitals, clinics, psychiatrically oriented teachers; to facilitate research on the whole problem of improving emotional health." [6]

The American Psychological Association is another organization vitally concerned with helping people to use psychology in making life better and happier. Committees from the APA work with governmental agencies, the armed forces, industry, schools, and or-

[5] *Outline for the Evaluation of a Community Program in Mental Hygiene,* Group for the Advancement of Psychiatry, Topeka, Kans., 1949.

[6] Oren Root, Basic aims of the National Association for Mental Health, *Ment. Hyg.,* N.Y., 1951, 1:1–4.

ganizations of all kinds to find answers to the many problems of human relations.

National Mental Health Act

Various pressures finally converged upon government policy makers, with the result that they took action to assist the movement for improving mental health. In 1946 the National Mental Health Act became an official part of the United States Public Health Program. At that time, it was appreciated by Congress and by many other supporters that the Act was only a beginning. Its aim was action in the fields of research, training of personnel, and improvement and expansion of community health services.

On the research front, grants were given to universities, hospitals, laboratories, and other public and private institutions and individuals approved by the National Mental Health Council, which the Act established. This council is selected from leading scientific and medical authorities. The National Institute of Mental Health, likewise established by the Act, has a full-time staff and advanced students. It is equipped with a hospital unit for clinical observation of patients selected on the basis of studies being made.

Training of personnel has been furthered by funds to provide adequate postgraduate training specialists, to improve undergraduate psychiatric training for medical students, and to interest more medical students in the field of psychiatry. That such legislation was overdue was indicated by statistics released the year the National Mental Health Act was passed. Only one-fourth of the required number of psychiatrists, clinical psychologists, and psychiatric nurses was available and only one-fifth of the needed psychiatric social workers. These estimates doubtless were conservative, since the public is slow to realize the potentialities of such services.

The third aim listed in the Act referred to community health services. An annual appropriation up to 10 million dollars was earmarked for grants-in-aid to the states for their development of mental-health programs at the community level, plus demonstrations by the United States Public Health Service if requested by individual states. Two such demonstrations are institutes on the latest psychiatric techniques arranged for physicians and on the use of mental-hygiene clinics as therapeutic service.[7] Another example of the working of the Act is the financial aid granted to public schools to provide for psychological testing. While the original appropriation was large, it did not seem so to those closely informed about the need. They pointed out other national spending patterns in that same year. A glance at these may put the figure in the proper perspective.[8]

Gambling on sports	$15,000,000,000
Education	2,500,000,000
Social security	593,123,600
Slum clearance	118,750,000
Cancer research	4,832,000
Venereal-disease research	1,000,000
Research on mental illness	300,000

Source: Notes and comments, *Ment. Hyg., N.Y.,* 1947, 31:506.

COMMUNITY-LEVEL FACILITIES

International and national organizations are important for focusing attention on the serious world-wide mental-health problem and laying foundations for large-scale improvements. However, an acceptance of the philosophy that mental health is everybody's business is evidenced by the emergence of many small grass-roots movements. Community organizations are evaluating their own area's strengths and weaknesses as to emotional and cultural climates and are experimenting with measures designed to create conditions leading to better mental health.

Present Trends

The expressed opinions, attitudes, and viewpoints of leaders in the mental-health movement add up to emphasis on the need for more prevention. This means more attention to the nurturing of healthy personalities. Experts have found that small amounts of prevention, or aid with the earliest symptoms of maladjustment, are much more effective than greater efforts later on. The preschool child who withdraws from people can be helped to confidence much more easily

[7] James V. Lowry, How the National Mental Health Act works, *Ment. Hyg., N.Y.,* 1949, 33:30–39.

[8] *Illinois Society for Mental Health Newsletter,* Chicago, 1947, 3 (6).

and with much less expense than his counterpart in middle life, who may withdraw from the world to such an extent that he must be protected by the specialized environment of a mental institution. Better still would be the development of preventive measures to the point where each child would grow in a mentally healthy atmosphere

Fig. 2–1. Nursery schools are a step in prevention. They help both children and parents toward better mental health. Help to parents in understanding the importance of health growth is a basic service of every good nursery school. (*Courtesy of Berkeley Nursery School, affiliated with Bryn Mawr College.*)

so that withdrawal tendencies might never appear. Thus the utopian situation would seem to be one in which good mental hygiene is so common that the creation of emotional problems is minimal.

Second only in value to keeping the utopian situation in sight as a goal for the future is the present triple-pronged attack of (1) locating early signs of difficulty, (2) having available the necessary resources for handling these, (3) being able to secure the acceptance of such help. Treating maladjustment before it has reached the stage of a full-blown neurosis may save years of suffering and ineffectiveness on the part of the individual and also cost far less in mental-health resources. To accomplish this requires a great degree of awareness of initial symptoms of personality warping on the part of those who come into personal contact with youth. Parents, nurses, teachers, ministers, lawyers, physicians, youth leaders, personnel workers, and police officers are in key positions to spot incipient difficulties. They must, however, have facilities available for early treatment. This means more private and public treatment resources for all income groups. It entails cooperation on the part of the client. Many ill individuals have suffered so much through the misunderstanding of family and friends that they fight any professional help. A curious commentary on the prejudices and preferences of the public is that many like to boast about their own or their children's so-called "nervousness" but few seem willing to secure help. More widespread understanding of mental hygiene may someday make people feel as matter-of-fact about seeking expert help in this field as they do about having a sprained ankle strapped.

Many of those working toward improved mental health have found conditions surrounding the ill individuals blocking recovery and even contributing to maladjustment. They have suggested the importance of surveying the stresses and strains produced by the cultural climate. Specifically, it has been suggested that the mental-hygiene aspects of material used in advertising, comic strips, movies, radio, and television should be studied. Many of these appeal to snobbery, exploit fear, and arouse feelings of shame; all these methods may affect emotional health. Economic security and wholesome recreational facilities are specific ingredients for healthy personal growth. Cultural patterns which give the individual an opportunity to feel important and enjoy living are preventive aids. Implanting the idea that there are various kinds of success—*e.g.*, family, friendship, citizenship, and other—would be a boon to individual security.

Coordinated Efforts for Mental Health

Public awakening to the appalling need for alternatives to institutional care has had far-reaching results. Church, social, business, and other groups are featuring discussions on mental health. Cleveland has twenty-five groups organized into a council for mental health which conducts monthly forums.[9] Many organizations are visiting

[9] Samuel Whitman, The responsibility of the local community for a mental health program, *Ment. Hyg., N.Y.*, 1949, 33:51–60.

and evaluating their present resources and developing needed ones. An interesting two-year study of selected communities in Texas was made to ascertain how well they were meeting mental-health needs and to serve as a basis for developing improvements.[10] Some of the constructive activities were in-service training of local community leaders by roving consultants, holding of family-life conferences and institutes, as well as collecting suggestions from all types of people familiar with incipient mental-health problems. As a result of this study, one community decided to extend its program of teacher education in child development to include parents. Another decided to work out a program to bring its foreign-born parents closer to their native-born children. These communities developed leadership to find ways and means of providing healthier atmospheres in which their youth could grow.

Even small communities, alerted by meetings of mental-hygiene groups, have found ways to make a start by combining efforts. In some of these enterprises the school system, the hospitals, and certain personnel departments of businesses have cooperated to share a psychologist or other mental-hygiene worker. They have thus brought aid to their town which no one group alone could afford. Combined efforts from various sources have resulted in more nursery and play schools. Besides helping youngsters to grow under good mental-health conditions most of these groups also aid parental understanding. Directed observation, discussion, and individual counseling in these nursery schools help parents to start their children off with sufficient emotional sturdiness to withstand modern pressures.

The Louisiana Society for Mental Hygiene and experts from the ranks of psychiatrists, pediatricians, psychologists, social workers, nurses, teachers, and educators have combined forces with lay groups in a pioneer undertaking. They have developed a clever series of prenatal and postnatal pamphlets written for the average parent.[11] These are sent out monthly by some ten states to prospective or actual parents at the appropriate time. They describe and

---

[10] Bernice M. Moore and Robert L. Sutherland, *Family, Community and Mental Health: Profiles of Community Action,* The Hogg Foundation, University of Texas Press, Austin, Tex., 1950.

[11] *Pierre, the Pelican,* The Louisiana Society for Mental Hygiene, New Orleans.

illustrate with gay cartoons the special problems which go with parenthood. They give reassuring and practical suggestions on subjects like the following: "Helping the baby to have friends," "Do you think that he will feel guilty too often?" "Comparing the first and second child." In an informal, chatty way parents are helped to understand their own feelings and to develop good emotional health in their infants.

The American Theatre Wing has collaborated with professional workers in mental hygiene to create dramatic sketches for parent meetings.[12] Fathers, mothers, and children by acting out these scripts and audiences by watching and discussing them are helped to understand the implications of parent-child relationships.

Many states and cities have committees surveying local programs as they contribute to the need of the alcoholic person. There has been considerable cooperative activity in developing branches of Alcoholics Anonymous, an important nationwide organization whose purpose is to substitute constructive programs for alcohol in the lives of these emotionally ill people. The Laboratory of Applied Physiology at Yale University has offered industrial plants a service which surveys the extent of the alcoholic problem, helps in developing constructive personnel policies, and provides educational information service for workers. Some industries have cooperated with this group and have worked out prophylactic programs.

Hospitals and Clinics

It has been estimated by the United States Public Health Service that all-purpose clinics should be available for each 100,000 of the population.[13] Such clinics, designed to serve all ages, usually consist of psychiatrists, psychologists, and social workers, who confer on each diagnosis and plan for treatment to be carried out by one of the staff. General hospitals are adding psychiatric out-patient clinics to their resources. Some of these have started discussion groups in connection with obstetrical departments to ensure a better atmosphere for the coming child. Sometimes these include fathers, since their attitudes toward pregnancy and birth are an important part of the

[12] *Temperate Zone,* National Committee for Mental Hygiene, Inc., New York.
[13] James M. Cunningham, Factors in the development of state mental health programs, *Ment. Hyg., N.Y.,* 1947, 31:220–228.

child's environment. A few have developed various group therapy facilities for neurotics and for people recovering from more serious difficulties.

Juvenile courts, domestic-relations courts, and veteran centers have added mental-hygiene facilities. Child-guidance clinics are being developed in many schools and communities. Some of these clinics are becoming coordinating in-service educational agencies for child and family agencies. The Judge Baker Foundation in Boston, for instance, has both students and workers in allied fields attending its regular conferences.[14] This is one of the many cases in which the findings of research in mental hygiene are supplemented by laboratory evidence. In some instances these clinics have gone further, endeavoring to detect underlying conditions in the community which contribute to maladjustment. The concept that lies behind all these necessary new services is that mental ill health is a *psychocultural* phenomenon.

Private Resources

Most cities have a mental-health society which keeps lists of reputable psychiatrists and psychologists. Departments of psychology in many colleges and universities have clinics and act as referral agencies. The American Psychiatric Association and the American Psychological Association have directories of their members. Possibilities for individual therapy vary all the way from a few conferences to daily sessions over a period of several years. All types of psychotherapies are being used in groups. These are led by trained group leaders, who may be psychiatrists, psychologists, or psychiatric social workers.

Because of the great gap between the number of qualified practitioners available and the widespread need for help, some who are far from expert are tempted to pose as qualified. For the protection of the public it is well to popularize the essential qualifications of the dependable psychotherapist and counselor. The American Board of Psychiatry and the American Board of Examiners in Professional Psychology certify their members. Specialists often work in teams; for in many cases members of the American Association of Psychi-

[14] George E. Gardner, Appraising the contribution of the mental hygiene clinic to its community, *Amer. J. Orthopsychiat.*, 1951, 21:74–82.

atric Social Workers evaluate the setting in which the client lives, psychologists do the clinical or diagnostic testing, and psychiatrists give the medical examinations. Treatment is carried through by one or more of this team.

The best therapists are those who have developed mature personalities. They are not overprotective; they are neither too paternal nor too critical. They have an appreciation of the various cultural pressures, so that they do not see abnormal symptoms in the behavior of groups different from their own. Their training has inculcated in them a broad understanding of feelings, motivation, the process of learning, physiology, and other related fields. They are equipped both to deal with problems falling within their scope of treatment and to recognize those which should be referred elsewhere. Further discussion will be found in the chapter on Readjustment.

STUDY OF PERSONALITY

International, national, and community approaches thus far have done little more than scratch the surface of the tremendous problem of mental health. To define and to secure an adequate program which will prevent mental and emotional illness *before* specialized treatment of a medical, psychiatric, or psychological nature is required means the harnessing of all possible resources. An important approach is the study of personality. Just as physical health has been greatly improved over the last decades by a more widespread understanding of physical hygiene, so mental health can be improved by increased insight into the growth and adjustments of personalities.

Public Hunger for Psychological Understanding

Public attention focuses more and more on psychology. Novels, motion pictures, radio, and television feature psychological themes. An increasing number of popular psychology magazines and books on personality reflect consumer demand. In one recent year, 1948–1949, more than one hundred books in the field of mental health were published for lay readers.[15]

[15] Luther E. Woodward, Mental health is for all, *The Booklist,* American Library Association, Chicago, 1949, 46:109–111.

A group of experts recently found reflected in the literature of mental hygiene an enormous public interest in the psychology of everyday life.[16] These researchers read all the material listed in library catalogues under the headings of mental hygiene, psychiatry, personality, abnormal psychology, and marriage. They surveyed book reviews and publicity from private and public agencies as well as references in texts and articles. From this body of material they selected those authors who had a "right to be heard" on the subject being discussed. From their writings they classified 2,394 mental-hygiene suggestions; of these they found that 42 per cent covered ideological and attitudinal orientation and 43 per cent gave advice on situational adjustment, the rest being miscellaneous. Overwhelmingly, the material dealt with the psychology of everyday adjustment. More and more people understand the laws of physical hygiene and they seem to crave a like facility with mental hygiene and emotional first aid.

Information alone does not necessarily lead to insight; there is a great deal more to understanding and learning than the mere reading of facts. Some people have developed an antagonism that blocks any insight into themselves. Their own insecurities make it too painful to take inventory of the stuff of which their life patterns have been misfashioned. Others have a fixed idea that textbook writers and teachers are unfamiliar with life. Still others have built up a strong antagonism to the word "psychology" because they fear it or have continually heard it used in a derogatory way or have acquired superficial notions of it from popular books or movies. Still others have placed psychology on a pedestal and expect miracles of it; when these do not happen, they are through with psychology in any form. One young man in a class on personality was disgusted when he found that it did not provide a list of ways in which he could quickly become a financial success. A young woman expected this class to give her the answer as to which of two men she loved.

To gain the most from a study of personality one must be able to clear away misconceptions like the ones just mentioned. He must approach the subject with an eye to learning to understand his prejudices. Then he can evaluate the material as it is rather than as he wants it to be. Readiness to develop insight depends upon the

[16] Robert Tyson, Current mental hygiene practice: an inventory of basic teachings, *J. Clin. Psychol.*, 1951, 7:1–90 (Monograph Supplement, No. 1).

individual's personality, including his social and value concepts. The International Congress on Mental Health describes this situation as follows: [17]

Education in mental health appears to be most successful if it reaches people at critical periods in their lives, e.g., when they are young and impressionable; when they are in trouble; when they are seeking advice, as for example, mothers of infants; during convalescence; and during periods of transition, such as adolescence, or at the later stage of choosing a career.

Study of Personality for the Young

In keeping with the trend to start therapy as early as possible is the effort to apply the study of the psychology of personality to the early years. One child psychologist says, "I propose that the study of child psychology, designed to promote understanding and acceptance of self and understanding of others, should be a planned feature of the education children receive from nursery school onward." [18] He underscores this proposal with the following idea: A large proportion of children will go into adulthood troubled and unhappy, with irrational fears, hostility, etc., carried over from unresolved childhood struggles. The answer cannot be found in offering treatment after people are already on the rocks. Instead of waiting until there is need for clinical psychology, which is largely to help individuals who have failed to make a comfortable adjustment to the conditions of life, why not help the growing person while he is in the process of adjusting to these conditions, including conditions within himself?

A psychiatrist expresses a similar idea in these words: "Why should the child have to pick up here, there, and everywhere all the age-old misinformation, worn out beliefs, and decaying concepts concerning what motivates people, what brings them together, what breaks them down, what makes for stable families, the facts of fear and stress, of guilt, of recreation, and of hostility?" [19]

[17] The International Congress on Mental Health, August 11 to 21, p. 12, London, 1948. (Mimeographed report.)

[18] Arthur T. Jersild, Self-understanding in childhood and adolescence, Amer. Psychologist, 1951, 6:122. By permission of the journal and American Psychological Association.

[19] D. Owen Cameron, Life Is for Living, p. 54, The Macmillan Company, New York, 1948. Quoted with permission of the publisher.

These ideas are being translated into action in some areas.[20] A pioneer project was started in Delaware by Col. H. Edmund Bullis, an executive officer of the National Committee for Mental Hygiene. In a sixth or seventh grade a problem for discussion is introduced by the teacher reading a stimulus story. One example is a narrative of the very unsocial actions of a photographer.[21] His lack of skill in human relations opens up a wide area for group discussion. In a later story some of the early incidents in this man's life are narrated to show the development of his hostile attitude. The discussants speculate on the motivations lying behind the behavior and bring up parallel situations from their own personal experiences. The chance to relate problems which would otherwise be kept secret and the demonstration of the universality of human problems are both constructive forces from the standpoint of mental health. Along the same line, many new textbooks for these grades deal with problems of both physical and mental health.[22]

Another project is being developed by Ralph H. Ojemann at the State University of Iowa. His aim is to inculcate in students certain principles of psychology which will always be ready for application to daily life. He believes that the basic psychological concepts should become a body of common knowledge comparable to the fundamentals of mathematics. He has developed, for use in social studies, guidance, and home economics, materials which humanize all content dealing with behavior. Motivations underlying behavior as studied in history or current social problems are stressed. Each social institution, each civilization is examined to ascertain how it meets human needs. Through "room councils" students are encouraged to use their knowledge in interpersonal relations with adults and other children both at school and at home.

The Canadian National Committee for Mental Hygiene has sponsored a program through an interdisciple group at the University of Toronto. Social work, education, psychology, and psychiatry have

---

[20] *Promotion of Mental Health in the Primary and Secondary Schools: An Evaluation of Four Projects,* Report No. 18, Committee on Preventive Psychiatry of the Group for the Advancement of Psychiatry, Topeka, Kans., 1951.

[21] H. Edmund Bullis and Emily E. O'Malley, *Human Relations in the Classroom,* Course 1, p. 18, Delaware State Society for Mental Hygiene, Wilmington, Del., 1947.

[22] For an example see Helen Shacter, Gladys Gardner Jenkins, and W. W. Bauer, *You're Growing Up,* Scott, Foresman & Company, Chicago, 1950.

combined forces to improve personality formation by furthering
the process of emotional maturation so that the child can capably
meet the ordinary stresses of life. Human-relations classes are given
in grades 6 to 12 under trained leadership. In these the children
are encouraged to discuss any topic they feel to be problematic at
the time. The topic and manner of dealing with it are group-deter-
mined. The children participating in these free discussions can
secure help individually from closely associated school counseling
and psychiatric teams. There has been a noticeable relieving of
anxieties through this free participation, which sets the stage for
improvement in emotional development.

The Interpretation of Personality in Other Settings

Personality is becoming more and more a subject for study. The
military services of various countries have harnessed mental hygiene
for orientation and therapy purposes. In helping raw recruits to
adjust to military life they use lectures and discussions based on
mental-hygiene interpretations of fear, hostilities, and frustrations.
This understanding of what is happening to them emotionally affects
their mental health much as inoculations do their physical health.
It makes them less susceptible to neuroses. On the home front there
is much clamoring for "know-how" in psychology. Some industries
have tried out group discussions on psychological problems; these
seem to help morale and cut down absenteeism and turnover. The
United Service Organizations has pressed experts on psychological
counseling into service in a nationwide training program to help
develop in its hostesses and many other workers an insight into
mental hygiene.

Many human-relations centers throughout the country have developed a combination group-therapy, mental-hygiene teaching
plan. In one of these, 100 leaders in labor, industry, government,
education, and community service meet in a summer session to
help clients to change their patterns of functioning to more effective
ones. They work through small discussion groups on various problems of group and personality dynamics.[23]

[23] Ronald Lippitt, Group dynamics and personality dynamics, *Amer. J. Orthopsychiat.*, 1951, 21:18–31.

Psychology of Personality in This Text

The aim of this book in discussing the psychology of personality is to take the student behind the scenes for a better understanding of just how his and other personalities have developed. By using his own experiences as a laboratory the student can test the soundness with which the processes have been described. Sometimes information dispels myths which interfere with the acceptance of self and others. Anxieties often hover about the mistaken ideas that mental illness is inherited, that children are naturally wicked, that mind and body are two separate entities. The psychologically literate person is better prepared for living.

An understanding of the ways and means of adjustment in the various areas of living sometimes brings to light ineffective or energy-wasting mechanisms. Some of the illustrations used may call forth unhappy echoes from the past or seem to the reader like painful caricatures of himself. "Bull sessions" or class discussions will probably show that most people labor under the mistaken belief that their difficulties are unique. In such discussions the student becomes aware for the first time of the great percentage of people struggling with their times. This should lead to healthier thinking. Insight into one's motivations, into the tie-up between one's mental and physical processes, into one's cultural patterning, and into one's conceptualizations of life comprises a sort of personal blueprint with which to build a more healthy personality structure. Such increased understanding should make one a better spouse, parent, neighbor, friend, worker, and citizen.

Summary

The many approaches to mental health described above are wholesome beginnings. More and more people both in high places and at the grass roots are realizing that the problem of mental illness must be tackled by everyone. Some individuals will be in a position to make international bodies more aware that many of the world's ills can be cured by cultivating an increasingly constructive approach to human relationships. Others will be able to push national legislation or organizations designed to create conditions making for more wholesome growth. Everyone can help cut down the incidence of maladjustment by more understanding of himself and his neighbor. In these and other yet unknown steps lies the hope of an emotionally sounder world.

QUESTIONS FOR DISCUSSION

1. List several organizations in your community which are working toward the improvement of mental health.
2. Do your local library's available material and reader borrowing reflect interest in mental health?
3. Do you believe that international organizations for mental health will improve relations between nations?
4. Has any organization to which you belong made a recent survey of community mental-health facilities?
5. What percentage of the members of the organizations of your community would be interested in discussions of mental health?
6. Do you think most people you know want to understand more about psychology?
7. What are the facilities for parent education in child psychology in your community?
8. Give some reasons why the amounts spent on mental health are so low.
9. Can you suggest ways in which more people can be interested in mental health?
10. How does your community rate in regard to adequate mental-hygiene facilities?
11. Can you suggest ways in which your community can do a better preventive job in mental hygiene?
12. Are there ways in which the cultural environment of your community could be made more conducive to mental health?
13. Do you think that movies and novels on psychological themes interest and educate most people?
14. What are some of the reasons why people do not seek psychological aid?
15. What specific suggestions would you have for carrying out the aims of the National Association for Mental Health?

ADDITIONAL READINGS

Beers, Clifford W.: *A Mind That Found Itself: An Autobiography by Clifford Wittingham Beers,* Doubleday & Company, Inc., 1933, New York.

Binger, Carl A. L.: Public education in psychiatry: is it possible? is it desirable? *Amer. J. Psychother.,* 1951, 5:4–15.

Brinton, Crane: Individual therapy and collective reform: a historian's view, *Amer. J. Orthopsychiat.,* 1950, 20:453–465.

Caplan, Gerald: Mental hygiene work with expectant mothers: a group psychotherapeutic approach, *Ment. Hyg., N.Y.*, 1951, 35(1):41–50.

Chisholm, George Brock: Social responsibility, *Science*, 1949, 109:27–30, 43.

Hertzman, Jack: School mental hygiene—a public health approach, *Amer. J. Orthopsychiat.*, 1950, 20:529–544.

The Hogg Foundation: *Ten Years of Mental Health Work in Texas*, The Hogg Foundation Reports, University of Texas Press, Austin, Tex., 1950.

Menninger, William C.: *There Is Something You Can Do about Mental Health*, National Association for Mental Health, New York, 1949.

Mental Hygiene and Public Health, 1951 Report of the Second Session of the WHO Expert Committee on Mental Health, *The Bulletin of the World Federation for Mental Health*, 3(1):27–31.

Pratt, Dallas, and Neher, Jack: *Mental Health Is a Family Affair*, Public Affairs Pamphlet No. 155, New York, 1949.

Spock, Benjamin M.: Schools are a fertile field for mental health efforts, *The Child*, 15(1):10–11, 39.

Torrance, Paul: Getting mental hygiene practices into action through a college class, *Ment. Hyg., N.Y.*, 1951, 35:88–95.

U.S. Department of Labor, Children's Bureau: *Helping Children in Trouble*, Publication 320, 1947.

W., William: The Society of Alcoholics Anonymous, *Amer. J. Psychiat.*, 1949, 106(5):370–375.

Part Two FUNDAMENTALS OF
PERSONALITY

The lack of mental health has been shown to be one of the foremost problems of modern society. Continual alarms sound in the form of mental illness, emotionally induced physical symptoms, and widespread longing for escape. Too many people are unhappy, anxious, and worried. Personality difficulties are being worked out in occupational maladjustments, psychologically caused accidents, alcoholism, divorce, and many types of antisocial behavior. The psychologically oriented person hears these alarms in his own life and his neighbor's as well as in his country and the world.

Many forces have been combining in an effort to retard the increase in emotional ill health. The various disciplines of psychology, psychiatry, sociology, anthropology, physiology, and education are building a more comprehensive understanding of personality. International, national, and local forces are integrating their resources. Many new services are being organized for prevention and treatment. Courses and textbooks such as the present one make each student a participant in the larger mental-hygiene program.

An understanding of mental hygiene must start with a clear conception of the fundamentals of personality. Personality is an amazingly complex phenomenon. It has as many sides as a finely cut diamond. There is no technique by which one can obtain a capsule type of understanding. There is no personality digest available. To simplify the study of the foundations of personality as much as possible, Part Two will offer the student a view of its four main components. *Motivation* is the compass which guides the course of personality. The *basic systems* of the body are the machinery for effecting relationships between people and things. The social scene is

41

a *culture matrix* which provides the environment in which the individual interprets and evaluates his world. *Perception* is the process through which the individual works out a meaningful relationship with his environment. An understanding of these four interacting fundamentals is basic for further insight into oneself and others.

CHAPTER 3 *Motivation*

No other single topic of psychological study can be said to be so basic as motivation. Here the continuity of animal and human behavior is appreciated most fully. Here the individual organism's immediate future is most accurately anticipated. And here, too, the personal integrity of the individual can best be estimated. For study of the personality, either in its typical or in its deviate manifestations, the study of motivation offers the most suitable point from which to start.

As has been pointed out in preceding chapters, the person with a problem, or the person who is troubled with emotional disturbance, often acts neurotically. The person who lives the life of a parasite, exploiting others, is also acting as a neurotic. In such deviate types of behavior the psychologist seeks to find the same fundamental motivations as are present in the healthy, or normal, types he has studied so intensively. Psychologists approach unhealthy specimens of behavior as distortions of the healthy. Sometimes, but not always, the deviate behavior is merely a magnification of the normal to undesirable proportions, as is suggested in most books on abnormal psychology. In any event, the psychologist's problem is to consider the two processes of distortion and magnification as *growth* phenomena.

Growth comes to mean the chain of motivations which lead to the present behavior. This chapter is concerned primarily with the various meanings of motivation and with the choice of one meaning as most fruitful for the study of personality. Later, in chapters bearing more directly on personality theory, motivation as growth will be elaborated.

MOTIVES ARE CAUSES

Meaning of Motivation

Motivation is a term which, to the psychology student, soon comes to mean *psychological causation*. It refers directly to the fundamental scientific concept of *sequence* or *continuity*, the only basis upon which modern science has been able to develop. This basis assumes that all events grow out of the past and will lead on into the future. It is referred to by philosophers as the "continuity of nature." Its roots are in the continuity of human experience. When one event is responsible for another, there is a relationship of *causation*. In this sense, the motive always precedes the particular act; and insofar as it is possible to find predictable repetitions of the motive-act sequence, it is possible to claim that some fundamental description of human behavior has been achieved. If such a description were of very wide applicability, it could be called a "law" of psychology.

In everyday language the motive-act sequence can be briefly summarized: No cause without an effect; no effect without a cause. There is never a motive without some effect, and there is never a response or effect which has not been preceded by a motive. Sometimes the tracing of a motive-effect sequence is extremely difficult, requiring from months to years of careful exploration into the background of experience and ways of thinking of the individual. This lengthy process is illustrated in psychoanalysis. There are other, newer ways of carrying on explorations which achieve similar results in less time. These will be discussed later.

Specific versus General Motives

The areas in which human motivation operates range from the simple *act*, in which the motive is obvious, to the complex and prolonged *career*, in which it is not possible to define all the detailed aspects of the motivation. Investigations in the laboratory have been extremely helpful in establishing a firm foundation for the study of motivation; experimental methods are replacing traditional theories based on untested hypotheses. For example, under carefully controlled laboratory conditions the comparative strengths of certain specific motives in the white rat have been determined. Food hunger has been shown by the Columbia Obstruction Box apparatus to be stronger than sex hunger in the laboratory rat.[1] Whether conclusions drawn from studies of the rat can be applied to humans is, of course, debatable. But the exacting techniques of these laboratory studies of rats can well be applied to the study of human motivations.

To date, there is mounting evidence for the conclusion that human motivation is highly complex and very seldom follows the simple and direct process of satisfying tissue requirements such as the need for food, oxygen, etc. Most human activity seems to be "purposive" and goal-oriented at the same time that it revolves around getting the tissue needs satisfied. Today students of normal human behavior lean to the conclusion that *only the general pattern* of human behavior can be understood or defined. People will eat, but when and what and how they eat is going to vary with time and place and conditions. In another way, Smith may be known to be accident-prone, *i.e.*, very likely to have an accident of some sort soon. However, it will be impossible to predict the exact nature of the accident.

Prescientific Motives

It is always interesting to compare psychological teachings with the beliefs of the man on the street. If one were to ask the man on the street what is meant by "motivation," his answer might be anything from a medieval to a modern psychological interpretation. For instance, in medieval times it was customary to give motivation a supernatural emphasis. Motives were then believed to be the workings of spirits. In this vein it is only reasonable to believe that evil spirits would manifest themselves in undesirable behavior while good spirits would show themselves through desirable behavior. A child or an adult who misbehaved was described as "possessed of the devil," and it was the custom to punish or frighten the devil out of such a person. In some cases this procedure was probably an expression of a psychosis rather than an attempt to help the individual being punished! The ingenious means of inflicting pain were often so vicious as to cause invalidism or even death.

[1] C. J. Warden *et al.*, *Animal Motivation*, Columbia University Press, New York, 1931.

Even today primitive interpretations of motivation are encountered. National news services occasionally report instances of "hexing" or the casting of a "spell" upon a person. Astrology is devoted largely to discussion of "good and evil" planetary influences. Frequently it is reported that people have interpreted hypnosis as a form of spirit "possession" or domination by means of "black magic." (In this sense, the motivation of the person would be the spirit of the hypnotist!) These are vestigial forms of primitive man's attempts to understand the world around him. Much of the exploitation of troubled people today is possible only through these medieval interpretations. Interpretation of motivation as a state of being possessed by an outside spirit was not conducive to scientific understanding or measurement.

Political Motives

Another historical illustration of motivation is shown in certain *political* interpretations. About the time that the Constitution of the United States was being developed there was much interest among leading thinkers in the *fundamental nature of man*. It is obvious that the fundamental nature of man is one way of referring to his basic motivations. These were thought to include such items as raising a family, building a home, pursuing happiness, owning property, worshiping in his own way. And somewhere in, or perhaps underneath, these motives would be found a fundamental tendency to be *competitive*, or *individualistic*. Such a political approach to motivation contributed to the growth of freedom in the Western world, and thus in a sense may be said to have made modern psychology possible. The political approach did not, however, produce an adequate basis for the scientific study of motivation. It must nevertheless be recognized that the political interpretation of motivation today forms the basis of the differences between the social philosophies and governments of the leading nations of the world.

Physiological Motives

Still another attempt to understand motivation developed during the years ending with the great depression, although it had its beginnings early in the Industrial Revolution. It is not necessary to trace the historical development of this viewpoint. The term "mechanistic" brings out its essential character. With the over-powering emphasis upon the new and wonderful science of mechanics, a major branch of physics, which occurred as a result of the Industrial Revolution, it was only natural that philosophers interested in the mind, and other students interested in human behavior, should try out mechanical interpretations. Therefore, the psychologies which today are called "mechanistic" were the ones which developed before 1930.

Animal and human behavior were considered to be built up from "elements" which should be studied in isolation so that elemental cause-effect relationships could be determined. The conditioned reflex and the inherited reflex were considered such elemental units. These two reflex types are, without doubt, important to our modern understanding of behavior. But, like a machine, the reflex requires an outside, or additional, motivation or power supply. An explanation of the motivations underlying reflex behavior was sought from physiologists, who, incidentally, had first described it.

. Physiological studies have certainly made it evident that there are processes which are necessary to physical survival. The needs, upon first inspection, might seem to be few and simple, including no more than food, clothing, and shelter. More careful observation makes it obvious, however, that other processes are also indispensable. The living organism must have oxygen; it must have moisture in some form; it must reproduce itself if the species is to continue. Thus the farther the investigation goes, the more items have to be added. A list commonly used is as follows:

Food (highly complex)	Elimination
Water	Oxygen
Temperature	Activity
Sex	Rest or sleep

These are all "needs" which must be satisfied if the organism is to continue to live. The organism is thus said to be "driven" to satisfy such needs, and it is common to refer to the organism's attempt at satisfaction as "drive behavior." Sometimes such drive behavior is termed "primary." A large portion of everyone's lifetime is directly or indirectly devoted to satisfying these basic needs or carrying on these physiological processes.

Habit as Motive

To such a list as the above it is necessary to add at least one other item: *habit*. Many illustrations might be given of habit behavior, which seems to supply its own tendency to repeat itself. Habitual smokers are fully aware that the smoking is not really necessary to their living. And yet the smoker is driven to smoke almost as powerfully as he is to eat. Many people find it impossible to sit at a table without "doodling," or making some kind of markings on the table top or on paper. They will go to much trouble merely to maintain an established habit. Thus, habit, or well-established learned behavior, is added to the list of drives. Often it is described as "secondary" drive behavior. Conditioned-reflex behavior is of this type. It is fortunate that habits are so automatic, for this permits the individual to do many things without making a special effort to organize his routine activities.

Wish and Desire as Motive

Somewhat different is the *empirical* approach. This can best be illustrated by the methods of William I. Thomas, a welfare worker who for many years specialized in dealing with delinquent girls and women.[2] Thomas found that he was unable to explain their behavior by means of any of the then better-known theories of drive and motivation. He therefore collected a large quantity of information and later studied it to see what conclusions could be drawn therefrom. It was almost a process of letting the research evidence draw its own conclusions. Thomas asked many thousands of girls and women what it was that they really wanted in life. The answers seemed to fall very neatly into four classes:

Security: the wish to avoid uncertainty; to know what to expect; to be safe from suffering and deprivation
New experience: the wish to be free from boredom; to have changes in one's way of living; to do new things; to experience adventure
Response: to have people respond to the person for no other reason than that they liked her; to be wanted and liked; to be worth liking
Recognition: the wish to be looked up to by other people; to stand out in the group as somehow more noticeable than the others

[2] W. I. Thomas, *The Unadjusted Girl*, Little, Brown & Company, Boston, 1923.

These *four wishes* form the basis of a highly convenient technique for analyzing behavior. They contribute to the psychology of motivation. They do not, however, make it possible to develop a really adequate understanding of the *processes* of motivation.

Still another type of list was drawn up by Knight Dunlap, based upon his many years of psychological study and interpretation of human behavior.[3] His list of *nine desires* stems from observed behavior but also takes account of physiological drives or needs:

1. Alimentary desire
2. Excretory desire
3. Protective desire
4. Activity desire
5. Desire for rest and relaxation
6. Amorous or erotic desire
7. Parental or philopedic desire
8. Desire for preeminence
9. Desire for conformity

Dunlap's list has the advantage of being brief but not oversimplified and of being compatible with the physiological processes. Other lists or interpretations have been developed by such writers as Freud, Adler, Jung, Woodworth, Mc Dougall. Murray has offered an especially interesting one.[4] There is little agreement among the various lists, however, and present-day tendencies seem to be in the direction of finding some other approach to the study of motivation. Doubtless the various lists of motives have served a purpose in encouraging the understanding of all forms of behavior, the ability to see life's motives in full perspective.

MOTIVES ARE BIOSOCIAL

The Charting of Motives

A more recent approach to the study of motivation is the "topological" one first used extensively by Kurt Lewin.[5] This viewpoint

[3] K. Dunlap, *Civilized Life*, p. 64, The Williams & Wilkins Company, Baltimore, 1935.

[4] Henry A. Murray (ed.), *Explorations in Personality*, pp. 80–89, Oxford University Press, 1938.

[5] K. Lewin, *Principles of Topological Psychology*, McGraw-Hill Book Company, Inc., New York, 1936.

made extensive use of *field theories,* by means of charts showing arrows (vectors) symbolizing "behavior tendencies" or "pressures." Such charting is probably more valuable in describing behavior than in explaining it. But an extremely important fact was thus emphasized: The organism is always behaving in relation *to* a particular situation. Thus a switch from the physiological theories was accomplished and the *interdependence* of the organism and its environment was acknowledged. Study of the combination of the organism with the environmental situation has become the favored approach.

"O" for Organism

The changed emphasis derived from the topologists and similar leaders has added new meaning to an older set of symbols. The traditional diagram of stimulus-response psychology had been

(Stimulus) S———R (Reaction)

In its revised form it has become

$$S \to O \to R$$

S indicates the *stimulus,* the beginning of the particular act or unit of behavior. It may be in the environmental situation or within the body of the organism itself. The arrow shows the sequence or cause-effect relationship. O indicates the *organism* in its particular condition or state at the time it is affected by the stimulus. R is the particular *response* made by the organism following the stimulation. R is always a form of *behavior* carried on by the organism which has been stimulated. The symbol S might also be the stimulus situation *as it is understood or interpreted by the organism.*

An example of this relationship is the following: Mr. S. is driving to work in his car. He notes the traffic signal ahead shifting from red to green as he approaches. As he is in a hurry this morning, he presses the throttle to gain speed. Yesterday morning he was not in a hurry and in the same situation he merely held the throttle steady. On these two mornings the S, namely the shift of the traffic signal, was much the same but the O was different. One morning O was hurried; the other morning O was not hurried. Hence the R was quite different on the two mornings. Had the traffic situation involved a police car, the S, R, and O might have varied considerably, although O was the same organism. In a very real sense, the *state of the organism is the motive.* This interpretation of motive is probably better than earlier ones, but it is still less than adequate.

"O" for Outlook

To continue the discussion of the topological charting of behavior, one additional symbol is required. A vertical line | is used to indicate a barrier which thwarts the organism as it attempts to achieve the sought-after R.

$$S \rightarrow O - | R$$

The organism is pictured in this way as unable to make the response. But the organism has received the stimulus and must do something. When the thwarted organism is repeatedly stimulated but cannot make the response, complications occur. A characteristic known as *frustration* becomes part of the organism's reaction to the particular stimulus. Such a diagram as the following might be used to indicate this frustration reaction:

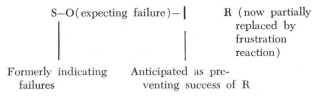

This form of behavior is illustrated by the case of a man seeking employment during a period of depression. In the morning he sees his family and realizes their need for income from his labors. He goes out to seek employment. On many previous days he has applied and been rejected, *i.e.,* his previous responses to the stimulus of employment opportunity have been fruitless or unsuccessful. This morning when he applies for a job, he does so in a hopeless and half-hearted spirit, without putting real effort into his attempt. He feels that it is of no use to try for the job. Such a response to the stimulus might even lead to nervous breakdown if this man were pressed sufficiently. At times experiences of frustration lead to intensified efforts or even to exaggerated restriving, but frustration reactions typically appear as discouragement and escape or running away. Studies of rats and other animals in the psychological laboratory show such behavior to be typical of them as well as of humans.[6]

The topological approach to the study of motivation proves itself to be very convenient for describing motivated behavior. It stresses the fact that animal behavior seems to maintain a sense of direction in a complex situation. Its weakness lies in the difficulty, if not the impossibility, of describing behavior in sufficient detail by means of the available symbols.

Characteristics of Motivated Behavior

To date the most adequate understanding of motivation seems to be provided by the *biosocial* approach, which combines in a single theory most of the earlier knowledge, empirical as well as physiological, and which uses the topological charting techniques effectively. The biosocial theory recognizes three general and readily observable characteristics of motivated behavior: *persistence, exploratory variation,* and *emotional energization.*[7] These characteristics are of especial importance to the discussion in later pages and should be carefully noted.

Persistence as an observable characteristic of motivation is especially evident in the presence of barriers or obstacles. Under such conditions as described above for frustration ($S \rightarrow |R$), the organism develops a state of agitation or tension which leads it to make increased efforts to accomplish its goal. The more hungry a person is, the more persistent will be his food-seeking behavior—until weakness sets in or he "learns" that the effort is futile. Persistence of effort is the chief index of the strength of the motive. The persistence itself forms a sort of *direction* or *pattern* which holds the various parts of the behavior together, giving a sense of direction toward the goal. Unmotivated behavior is goalless, patternless, directionless.

Exploratory variation, as a characteristic of motivated behavior, is best observed when failure has resulted from the first attempt to achieve the goal. Given such initial failure (if it is not overwhelm-

[6] Norman R. F. Maier, *Frustration: The Study of Behavior without a Goal,* McGraw-Hill Book Company, Inc., New York, 1949.

[7] Adapted from Ross Stagner, *Psychology of Personality,* 2d ed., p. 260, McGraw-Hill Book Company, Inc., New York, 1948.

ing and if the organism continues to exert efforts toward the goal),
variations of the initial effort will be attempted.

Variations in behavior may be like those that a small child exhibits upon moving into a new neighborhood and encountering
strangers. In his attempt to strike up an acquaintance with the new
children he may simply walk up to the group and say "hello." If
this fails, he will usually explain that he lives "over there in that
house." Failing still, he may run home and return promptly with a
football or some other attractive toy and offer to play. Failing again,
he will have recourse to one childhood technique after another until
he has established a relationship with the neighborhood group—or
decides to give up temporarily. (Adults behave in these ways too.)
The degree of variation of behavior is proportionate to the strength
of the motive (just as with persistence) and similarly to the intelligence or mental capacity of the individual. Bright people will automatically think up more variations than will dull ones. When the
limit of conceivable variation is reached, the persistence and variation normally end. Other motives come into operation, leading to
other lines of activity, or perhaps to apathy or inactivity.

Emotional energization takes place only in strongly motivated
instances. When there is delay or resistance present in the goal-
directed effort, the organism's behavior will show increased energy
in some such form as anxiety, anger, crying, explosiveness, aggression, or some other emotionally tense reaction. Success feelings following the achievement of the goal after emotionally energized effort
are especially satisfying. More will be said later about the physiology
of emotional energization.

Motivated Behavior Shows Direction

With the three general characteristics of motivated behavior in
mind, it is possible to recognize motivated behavior as *organized
behavior which shows a direction of effort.* A motive is a sort of
compass which indicates to the organism, and at times to observers,
where the organism is trying to go or what it is trying to do. A single
observation may suffice to indicate the motive. Then again the
persistence, the exploratory variation, and the emotional energization may have to be observed extensively if the given behavior is to

be understood as motivated. From the outside, motivated behavior looks "purposive." From the inside, it feels like "tension"—*i.e.*, that *something is starting to happen.*

"Whoever finds those ten dimes can keep them!"

Fig. 3–1. Strong motivation gets work done happily and quickly. (*Cartoon by Henry Boltinoff. Courtesy of The American Magazine.*)

Motives Imply Tensions

All motivated behavior can be traced to some form of tension. Every student is familiar with the feeling described ordinarily by the remark "I just can't wait any longer." Sometimes it is evidenced as a sense of being high-strung or "jittery." Such feelings as the latter indicate the presence of more than the usual amount of tension. Underlying such subjective feelings is a physiological basis. A person aware of food hunger will, if he is observant, note himself watching bakery windows. He may be especially conscious of appetizing odors from the coffee shop or delicatessen, or he may find himself thinking how enjoyable it would be to go out to dinner. If a person in this frame of mind were taken to the laboratory for study and subjected to measurement of stomach contractions, it would become evident that the so-called "hunger pangs" felt subjectively correspond with constrictions of the walls of the stomach. Changes in the walls of the stomach are, in turn, related to cell metabolism and to blood chemistry. The tension, however, is not merely the physiological process of muscular contraction or of cell metabolism or of change of blood chemistry. Rather, *the tension is a tendency to become active in a certain way*—in this instance it is to become active in getting food.

Speaking subjectively again, a person who is hungry and is faced with a plate of appetizing food not only feels hunger pangs but finds it difficult to leave the food alone. He must start eating! As part of this feeling that he must start the actual intake of food, there will be small muscular contractions which sometimes are quite observable in the hands and arms and even in the facial muscles. The hands reach for a knife or fork or spoon; the lips are moistened and the throat is active. These little muscular contractions are important parts of the tendency to act, or the *tension*. Such a condition is sometimes called the "set" of the organism. Doubtless it could also be described as the "wish" pattern. The collective noun by which reference is made to all these little tendencies as they contribute to the given end is "hunger."

The Organization of Tension

The process of developing a motive is essentially one of organizing the many little tensions into a unified and dynamic system, or pattern. Thus the motivated behavior is a form of behavior which necessarily involves the *management* of these many tensions. The management of tension plays an extremely important part in all human behavior, especially in the kind involving intelligence. In addition to tensions deriving from the physiologic needs, there are tensions traceable to the social culture and to the habit patterns of the individual. These represent social standards and fashions. In the social system there is a carefully observed pattern of behavior laid out for each child to grow into and for each adult to follow. The individual organizes his tensions so as to be "proper" or "good"—or perhaps "bad." The pressure to conform to or to resist the social pattern can be very productive of tension.[8] Tensions must also be

"This new incentive plan works wonders. I called up each one's wife and offered her a new fall outfit if her husband's production doubles from now to October."

FIG. 3–2. Desire for approval is an important motivation. (*Copyright 1951 by the Curtis Publishing Company.*)

recognized as maturational phenomena. The social motives will be discussed later; it must suffice here to note that they form part of the tensional management processes of the individual.

Homeostasis

Although the bodily tensions are the deeply buried bases of motivated behavior, there is a general underlying pattern of the moti-

[8] John J. Honigmann, Culture patterns and human stress: a study in social psychiatry, *Psychiatry*, 1950, 13:25–34.

vational processes. This underlying pattern is the process of *homeo-stasis, i.e., the maintenance of dynamic equilibrium within the total organism.* Physical activity is always a manifestation of energy. This is true in terms both of the biological concept and of the concept used by physicists. Energy is convertible from one form to another, and the biological organism survives through a structure which is continuously converting energy from food and oxygen into activity and body heat.

The greater the need for heat to maintain body temperature or the greater the need for energy to carry on activity, the more rapid must be the process of energy conversion. Hence there is a fundamental process within every animal organism which assures the stabilizing of behavior and bodily temperature. This stabilizing process is the homeostatic process. It is evident in the maintenance of internal body temperature at approximately 98.6° (as measured by mouth), in spite of the fact that external atmospheric temperatures constantly vary.

Body temperature and food assimilation are the easy illustrations of the homeostatic process, but it is necessary to remember that this process is characteristic of the total personality, including bodily, social, emotional, and ideational activities. A person strives vigorously if not desperately to maintain appearances and other indications of social status whenever such status has been lost. When there is a loss of economic status, the individual normally attempts to save face by returning to his former status through increased effort, or perhaps he strives to maintain the appearance of such status through more exacting dress or a more carefully chosen car or house, or perhaps through cultivating friends on the desired economic level. Thus an ancient Cadillac may be chosen although a newer car in the small class might cost the same amount and provide better transportation. A threadbare but originally expensive suit may be preferred to a new but low cost one.

Politically a similar process of homeostasis is evident. A man will argue vigorously to defend his political party in the midst of a period of obvious fraud or weak management if he believes the party is showing a loss of status which may lessen his own importance. On the other hand, during successful times there seems no need for argument that all is normal. Equilibrium, as seen by the party member, has been restored. People who are bored when variety of activity is less than normal may seek adventure. Some turn rebellious if pressed into subjugation, and tend to revolt. When active too long without periods of rest, people become fatigued and seek diversion or relaxation.

MOTIVES AND THE PERSON

Motives and Needs

The total personality is the actual unit in which the pattern of motivation must be observed and studied. To get below the surface of personalities and discover what was propelling them, Henry A. Murray made a two-and-a-half-year study of fifty-one males of college age who had no knowledge of psychology. They were selected by the Harvard University employment office and were paid for their time. Tests, interviews, conferences, and other techniques were used by a staff of experts in the fields of physiology, psychology, and sociology to explore the forces motivating these young men.[9] A great deal of information concerning the organization of needs and their relationship to patterns of personality was uncovered.

There may be small, or "specific," motives in an individual's behavior in limited instances such as dating or the purchase of a pair of gloves. These smaller motives become understandable only as they can be seen to fit into the fulfillment of larger goals sought by this individual. Smaller motives contribute to the individual as he seeks to be the kind of person he feels he has to be.

Motive Hierarchies

Motives group themselves. Some contribute to each other directly; for example, the exploratory walking through the market at the time of food hunger contributes to the choice of foods and also contributes to the feeling of right living. This tendency of motives, or of needs, to cluster together will be discussed later as the formulation of *personality traits*.

Motives cluster together in another way. Some motives are more encompassing than others; they apply to more numerous and to larger segments of behavior. Maslow has referred to this process as

[9] Murray, *op. cit.*

the tendency of motives to form hierarchies which express levels of importance of needs.[10] The motivational life of each individual thus has a kind of organization of structure which provides a pattern for his personality.

Motives and Adjustment

The problem of managing the variety of motives requires a truly remarkable balance of power between abilities, ideals, and possibilities in this world. This managing is so important that the organizing of behavior is actually the adjustment process of each personality. Motives definitely affect one's perception. Needs act as magnets in bringing into perceptual focus those interpretations which will satisfy them. Prejudice and fear often prevent a person from seeing clearly. Relationships of this kind between needs and perceptions are today readily explored by projective tests such as the Thematic Apperception Test.

Sometimes an individual's various motives are confused. They are disoriented, or out of gear with the real world in which he lives, or in conflict with each other. Some individuals seem to grow into a personality struggling to fulfill motives which cannot be satisfied. These people seek to satisfy impossible needs at times and relatively impossible needs at other times. They crave perfection, to have the world at their feet, or to outdistance all competitors. They are never fully successful, since they strive for the impossible, and so they are forced to make unhealthy changes in their own personalities, which today are commonly called "neuroses." These neurotic behaviors will be considered more fully under the headings of adjustment in the discussions both of personality and of selected critical areas such as courtship, family, handicap, etc.

Summary

In capsule form, motivation can be defined as a complex of bio-social tensions or needs which (1) are organized into general and specific goal orientations, (2) pervade the entire personality, (3) trace the growth continuity of the individual, and (4) follow the homeostatic principle in all commerce between the organism and

[10] A. H. Maslow, Some theoretical consequences of basic need-gratification, *J. Person.*, 1948, 16:402–416.

its environment. Since motivation is such an important fundamental of personality, it will be a recurrent theme throughout this book.

QUESTIONS FOR DISCUSSION

1. List some of your motivations for attending college.
2. Can you think of some examples of your own changes in motivation?
3. Do your specific motives contribute to the fulfillment of your larger goals?
4. What do you think are the strongest motivations of youth today?
5. Do you believe that most people understand their own motives? Why?
6. Give some examples of possible motivations for choosing certain careers.
7. What diverse motives might be behind the desire to run for political office?
8. Is it important to understand the motives of friends, fellow workers, candidates for office?
9. Is it safe to assign motives for the behavior of those you do not know well? Why?
10. Give some examples of political parties using the process of homeostasis.
11. In what ways might the popularity of certain movie or television themes illustrate the process of homeostasis?
12. Do you believe that most people expect others to have motivations identical to their own?
13. Do you believe that people in some countries have nobler motivations than those in others? Why?
14. How can propaganda affect motivation?
15. Give some examples of common frustrations of motives.

ADDITIONAL READINGS

Allport, Gordon W.: Motivation in personality, *Psychol. Rev.*, 1940, 47:533–554.

Anderson, John E.: *The Psychology of Development and Personal Adjustment,* Chap. 10, Henry Holt and Company, Inc., New York, 1949.

Beaumont, Henry, and Macomber, Freeman G.: *Psychological Factors in Education,* Chaps. 2, 3, 5, 10, McGraw-Hill Book Company, Inc., New York, 1951.

Berrien, Frederick K.: *Comments and Cases in Human Relations,* Chap. 4, Harper & Brothers, New York, 1951.

Brown, Warner, and Gilhousen, Howard C.: *College Psychology,* Chaps. 9, 10, Prentice-Hall, Inc., New York, 1950.

Diserens, Charles M.: Motivation, Chap. 15, in Charles E. Skinner (ed.), *Readings in Psychology,* Farrar & Rinehart, Inc., New York, 1935.

English, Horace B.: *Child Psychology,* Chap. 4, Henry Holt and Company, Inc., New York, 1951.

Garrett, James F., and Myers, Julian S.: Motivation and rehabilitation, *Occup. Ther. & Rehab.*, 1951, 30:296–299.

Keller, Fred S., and Schoenfeld, William N.: *Principles of Psychology: A Systematic Text in the Science of Behavior*, Chap. 9, Appleton-Century-Crofts, Inc., New York, 1950.

Langer, Walter C.: *Psychology and Human Living*, Chaps. 3, 4, 5, Appleton-Century-Crofts, Inc., New York, 1943.

Lewin, Kurt: Psychology of success and failure, *Occupations*, 1936, 14:926–930.

Maslow, A. H.: A theory of human motivation, *Psychol. Rev.*, 1943, 50:370–396.

Snygg, Donald, and Combs, Arthur W.: *Individual Behavior: A New Frame of Reference for Psychology*, Chap. 4, Harper & Brothers, New York, 1949.

CHAPTER 4 *Psychosomatics*

The preceding chapter, on Motivation, introduced an emphasis upon wholeness of personality which will continue throughout this book. The present chapter begins a discussion of the machinery of behavior. It should be kept in mind that the wholistic emphasis need not be lost in the investigation of detailed physiology. During recent years this emphasis has found expression in the study of organic functions as they group themselves while at work. These groupings are called *functional systems*. Popular books on medicine, as well as some highly technical ones, present the psychosomatic viewpoint, combining psychic (mental) with somatic (bodily) functions into the single unit referred to as the "patient." Psychologists made a similar shift approximately two decades ago.

Physiological studies by W. B. Cannon and others prior to 1930 initiated an emphasis upon the total body which was an early stage in the wholistic approach to the psychology of personality.[1] Such concern for the larger patterns of behavior was not really new. From the times of the early Greek philosophers this approach to the human being was well known, if not always so popular as it has become recently. Cannon's reintroduction of the concept of homeostasis provided a basic principle for the interpretation of behavior. Psychoanalysts and psychiatrists have been demonstrating, through actual laboratory and clinical evidence, the profound relationship between the mental and the physical condition of the sick.[2]

There is an inescapable connection between the physical and mental phases of a person's experience. An axiom for the psycho-

[1] W. B. Cannon, *Bodily Changes in Pain, Hunger, Fear, and Rage*, 2d ed., D. Appleton & Company, Inc., New York, 1929.
[2] J. S. Perry, Emotions as functional factors in the etiology and prognosis of disease, *Med. Rec., N.Y.*, 1934, 1939:643–645.

logical observer might well be: Discover the most characteristic forms of equilibrium in the individual, and you will have found the key to his motivations. Because bodily activity is all that is readily observable by man's sense organs, the axiom applies directly at the physiological level. Large segments of individual experience tell of physiological phenomena. The bodily behavior of friends and neighbors gives cues to their goals and motives. For this reason the study of personality requires much attention to the bodily aspects of behavior. The human body is a fascinating combination of interlocked organic functions, each organ carrying on its own individual work at the same time that it cooperates with all the other organs. There are various ways of grouping the organic functions; the following list of nine will serve present purposes:

Digestive—ingestion of food and excretion of waste solids
Respiratory—inhalation of oxygen and exhalation of waste gas
Cardiovascular—circulation of the blood
Musculature—bodily movement and support
Nervous—communication between bodily parts and organs
Endocrine—hormone production
Lymphatic—temperature control and assimilation of fats
Urinary-perspiratory—elimination of waste liquids
Reproductive—birth of the young organism

Of the nine functional systems listed, only the first five will be discussed. This is partly to save space and partly because these five illustrate the relationship between mental and physical processes sufficiently to make this clear for the total personality. By means of all the functional systems, the individual personality expresses its meanings, its purposes, its choice of tactic, and its own past in its commerce with the world.

THE DIGESTIVE SYSTEM

The Structure

Commonly called the *gastrointestinal system,* this functional grouping of organs serves the needs of digestion, including ingestion and excretion. A one-celled animal, Paramecium, illustrates this process well. It is merely a tiny hollow tube, floating in a liquid environment containing particles of food. This liquid environment flows in at its front end and leaves its tubelike body at the back end. Some particles of food stick to the inner walls of the tube and soon are resorbed into the very substance of the paramecium. It moves through its liquid environment by means of hairlike cilia which act like the fins on a fish. When the paramecium wishes to increase the flow of liquid through itself, it waves the cilia and speeds the movement of its body. If the cilia stop moving, the body comes to a standstill.

In the human body the tube structure has become highly complex. It has lengthened to some 35 feet and, as a space saver, has been curled around, forming the stomach, the small intestines, and the large intestine, or bowel. Nevertheless it is a continuous tube through which the food mass is passed. In place of the cilia moving the entire body over the food, there are muscles in the human digestive tract which force the food through the body. Added convenience is achieved by the stomach's capacity to store food, which eliminates the need for the continuous eating that is necessary in the case of the paramecium.

Peristaltic action, the forcing of food through the entire digestive tract from mouth to rectum, is a process in which the ring muscles contract in rhythmic alternation. A number of doughnuts piled on top of each other and fastened together would illustrate the way in which the intestinal tract is composed of ring muscles. These rings are of different sizes, some being larger in diameter and much more powerful than others. The rectum itself is merely a very powerful ring able to close itself completely. The muscles at the top and bottom of the stomach are similar, all being *sphincter* muscles. In the throat, as in the lips of the mouth, there is also a muscular closing, which can prevent the entrance of foreign substances. Throat closing, or "gagging," is a familiar process to everyone.

When a paramecium is confronted with a substance, such as acetic acid, which is unacceptable if not actually dangerous, it stops short by holding its cilia rigid. This is a kind of *general tension* throughout its body. In such a situation the human being merely gags. Both paramecium and human have *evaluated* the situation or substance as unacceptable to such a high degree that it must be refused admission. The paramecium can reject only in a simple way, but he does it with his entire body. Humans can reject in many ways, the more extreme ones involving the entire body, the minor ones only portions of the body.

The Functions

Besides the gagging process which occurs at the entrance to the digestive tract, there are supplementary processes which are psychologically significant organic evaluations. Under pressure of inadequacy or guilt the flow of saliva will be reduced. When an individual is faced with an appetizing dinner or a desirable love-making situation, an increase in the flow of saliva occurs, indicating willing acceptance of this portion of the universe. There is an ancient story that an Oriental despot at one time was unable to determine who had stolen some valuables from his palace. Displaying wonderful understanding of psychosomatics, he called the suspects to his court and required each one to chew a mouthful of dry rice. After a few minutes he instructed them to spit out the rice. The dry mouthful then indicated the guilty one! The consequences of failing this test were well known to every suspect, hence guilt feelings were dramatically present only in the suspect who had reason to fear.

Additional evaluations are carried on by the stomach, an organ which is composed of the largest ring muscles in the entire digestive tract. Vomiting is a rejection of the idea as well as of the material. Small children, particularly, will regurgitate an entire series of meals if they become emotionally upset soon after eating or if an emotional upset is intensified at mealtimes. Most parents' manuals suggest cuddling and fondling the infant for a while after each feeding, and stress the fact that the eating situation, as well as the food, should be appetizing. "Burping," or rifting, is a common form of regurgitation of psychically objectionable ideas and situations.

In extreme situations, regardless of the age of the subject, it has been found that the individual's own judgment of acceptability is highly important.[3] Children forced during feeding periods are less able to thrive on an "ideal diet" than children who choose their own foods with almost no restriction. The experiences of occupants of concentration camps indicate that adults, like children, have to want the food they eat in order to maintain normal digestion. Strangely,

[3] C. M. Davis, Self-selection of diet by newly-weaned infants, *Amer. J. Dis. Child.*, 1928, 36:651–679.

some prisoners were able to thrive on the very scanty diet of thin soup made from rice husks left after the military police and officers had eaten the rice, whereas other prisoners starved to death on this same diet. The dividing line seemed to be between those who, through worry, resisted the camp situation and those who learned not to worry but to adapt themselves to the camp life.

Further along the digestive tract, such difficulties as spastic colon, chronic constipation, loose bowels, and gaseous conditions in the lower intestine are very closely related to the psychic aspects of living. These are, in fact, unfavorable evaluations if not actual rejections of the general way of living that the individual faces. Service men who have known actual combat know well that in times of extreme stress their digestive-tract muscles act (out of control) to eliminate. In a milder form this kind of elimination would be considered a psychosomatic illness.

The muscular contractions involved in such bodily behavior may be carried on over a long period of time and with such extreme spasms as to produce actual tissue lesions. Peptic ulcer, duodenal ulcer, gaseous pains around the heart, and other gastrointestinal ailments may be traceable to a life situation which the patient has been unable to accept. Parents' attitudes toward the very young infant often seem to be the beginning of inability to "stomach the world." [4]

The effectiveness of the gastrointestinal system is at all times in significant measure determined by the psychological life of the individual. Since digestion is the means of nourishing the body, the maladjusted individual will be undernourished or given to excesses of certain kinds of food and deficiencies of others. Dietary excess or deficiency has a direct effect upon the supply of energy available to the individual and thus affects his attitudes and morale. Organic reactions seem to be sensitive in turn to the general attitudes of the individual.

Roughly, three types of gastric disorders seem associated with personality structure: (1) overactivity in elimination with an attitude of aggressive riddance of an unwelcome world; (2) ulcer or dyspepsia with a tendency to worry along with a trouble-laden

[4] Edward Weiss and O. Spurgeon English, The gastro-intestinal system, Chap. 7, pp. 189–251, in *Psychosomatic Medicine,* W. B. Saunders Company, Philadelphia, 1943.

world; (3) underactivity in elimination with a tendency to hold on to what few good things do happen to come along.[5] These personality types show behaviors which are inadequate to the needs of the individual in the commerce of living, thus evidencing mental

"What gets me is his having ulcers and being a failure."

Fig. 4–1. Indigestion and a feeling of failure may be symptoms of maladjustment. (*Reproduced by permission, copyright 1951 by The New Yorker, Inc.*)

and emotional illness through physical symptoms. Such persons seldom secure real or enduring relief from medical treatments, hence become easy prey for the exploitations described earlier.

Summary

The digestive system is one of the mechanisms whereby the psychological life of the individual becomes evident. Physiological

[5] F. Alexander, C. Bacon, *et al.*, The influence of psychological factors upon gastrointestinal disturbances: a symposium, *Psychoanal. Quart.*, 1934, 3:501–588.

functions and malfunctions express the individual's basic attitudes toward his world and his life status in this world. These evaluations or attitudes constitute his deep-seated motivations. They express his attempt to live a certain type of life, albeit he may be totally unconscious of the exact pattern of that type. Maintenance of an inadequate digestive state may be homeostatic normalcy for this individual, and he thus may seek to continue his unhealthful life or habit patterns. At the same time there will be a tendency of his physical structure to register complaints, suggesting the unhealthful life practice. The motivational striving becomes intensified, emotionalized, with a general increase in the tendency to seek greater variation of activity in ways which may seem meaningless if not fantastic.

Illustration of this evaluative function of the gastrointestinal system is found in the case of Kate, a first-semester freshman in college. Kate lived in a rooming house near the campus, although her father and stepmother lived in the same city. Her first few weeks on the campus were normally satisfying. Midsemester grade reports, however, destroyed an illusion she had built up. It was thereafter unavoidably clear that in chemistry she was just barely passing. Her father, a salesman hard-pressed by rugged competition, and by a family background of marked sternness, had said with his well-known finality, "A single D and Kate will have to drop out of college." The stepmother offered no encouragement.

Kate became worried but did not know where to turn. She soon evidenced a general drop in scholarship in subjects in which she had previously found easy success. Rapid gain in weight made her clothes unbecoming and her face expressionless and puffy. Self-consciousness and fidgeting developed. Her class attendance became weak and her scholarship dropped lower. Brief counseling, opened up through discussing her poor attendance, brought to light the fact that instead of studying she was sitting in her room, eating chocolates by the pound and worrying about her general situation, particularly her father's reaction. The candy "sweetened" the otherwise unappetizing campus situation. Her digestive tract expressed her wish for a "sweeter" world. Kate cooperated well with the counselor and it was not long until she was guiding her own life independently from a much more mature viewpoint.

THE RESPIRATORY SYSTEM

The Organ Structure

The second functional system to be discussed, respiration, is in many ways analogous to digestion. Prenatal development of the respiratory tract is indistinguishable from that of the digestive tract until the embryo is rather well formed; both grow from the same type of cells. Not only in this embryological sense, but also in a psychological one, breathing is closely tied to digestion. The respiratory system is united structurally with the cardiovascular system, which in turn is integrated with the digestive system. These three carry on the process of providing the ingredients of bodily energy production, of metabolism.

The respiratory system is simple: air is normally inhaled and exhaled through the nasal passages; the throat leads into the bronchial tubes, which in turn branch out into the various areas of the right and left lungs. In addition, there is the machinery of the rib muscles and the diaphragm. The muscles internal and external to the ribs force these bony structures to expand outward or to contract inward. When the ribs expand outward, the diaphragm coordinates by pulling downward. When the ribs contract inward, the diaphragm extends upward. Thus the capacity for expansion and shrinkage of the upper body cavity is remarkably great. These bellowslike movements adjust to minimum and maximum need for breath in the body.

Air taken in by inhalation contains oxygen in different amounts, depending upon the situation in which the organism exists. It also contains varying amounts of moisture. Tremendous areas of lung tissue, loaded with capillaries carrying portions of the bloodstream, absorb from the freshly inhaled air available oxygen and perhaps some moisture. In reverse fashion, the carbon-dioxide waste which must be released from the blood through the lungs, along with some moisture, is exhaled as part of the used breath. Both the taking in of oxygen and the elimination of waste carbon dioxide are necessary parts of respiration. This rhythmic reflex activity of breathing, or respiration, is a matter of common knowledge. But there is more to respiration than just the reflex physiological process.

Psychological Functions

Respiration is highly complicated at the psychological level. This derives in part from the importance it bears for an individual's remaining alive, an importance expressed in early historical times by belief that the breath is part of the soul or essence of life itself. Such primitive interpretations may gain little credence today, but it is a fact that few, if any, humans can face disorders of the respiratory organs without a deep sense of fear. Breathing is *vitally* important; it signifies life itself.

In addition to the simple reflex rhythms and their continuance, certain adaptations of the general breathing pattern must be noted. A worried individual, by quickened breathing, demonstrates to himself and to others his evaluation of his position as fearful for himself and his valued possessions. Labored or restrained breathing suggests fear of taking a free breath. The special freedom of a few breaths taken at the moment of success in performing a physical task, such as climbing a mountain, is a healthy expression of strength. This is the exhilarating strength *left over,* a superabundance beyond the demands of the task.

Usually, voluntary control of inhalation or exhalation is found only when needed to supplement a particular activity. Swimmers, singers, orators, athletes, yogi practitioners, etc., use voluntary breathing to establish habitual modifications of their reflex breathing patterns. These are either emergency or specialized examples and of less psychological importance than the normal adaptations.

Semivoluntary modifications of the breathing pattern may develop in an individual whose anxiety becomes chronic, *i.e.,* whose life is habitually fearful. Since the individual is usually unaware of the deviation, some method of measurement is needed to ascertain its existence. Such a measurement record can be obtained through the *pneumograph,* the *spirogram,* or the *respiratory tracing,* each a graphic record of the breathing pattern of the individual. Experience with such records has indicated that there are three types of breathing patterns deviating from the usual or normal: abnormal *level, depth,* and *rate.*[6] Psychoneurotic persons commonly evidence "shallow" breathing, *i.e.,* breathing of less than normal depth as shown on the respiratory tracing.

[6] Weiss and English, *op. cit.,* pp. 398–399.

Shallow breathing subjectively feels like "shortness of breath," a common complaint of the psychoneurotic person. "Difficulty in getting the breath" is also a universal complaint which accompanies any one of the above irregularities.

Effects upon Personality

Bronchial asthma is one condition in which difficulty in breathing is usually recognized to be involuntary. It is certainly not under the control of the afflicted individual. But there seems to be good evidence that it is one of the semivoluntary deviations from normal breathing resulting from long periods of emotional upset and thus of respiratory evaluations of danger. Asthma attacks are spasmodic contractions of the muscles in the bronchial tubes. These contractions interfere with both inhalation and exhalation. They lead to great discomfort and fright. The feeling of fright is a cue to the origin of the ailment, for anxiety seems to be a central condition in the personality of the asthmatic.[7] Thus the asthmatic spasm as a part of the breathing pattern is semivoluntary. It is in the class of the conditioned reflex, so well known to laboratory psychologists. *Hypoventilation* is the so-called "smothered feeling" characteristic of the labored breathing which accompanies worry and anxiety. These reductions in breath quantity indicate that the individual's attitude toward life is that living is a great effort because the struggle is intense. Such a person often feels that his burden of responsibility is unduly heavy and craves opportunities to explain or describe this burden.

It is more important to recognize the symptomatic meaning of labored breathing than it is to designate it as abnormal. Everyone has his moments of labored breathing, moments when bodily structure is acting normal in the face of surprise, disappointment, or anger, or of great effort of mind or body. The individual who acquires a long-lasting respiratory pattern such as labored breathing, however, has a chronic symptom.

Oxygen starvation and failure to eliminate carbon dioxide in adequate amounts have marked general effects upon the health and vigor of the individual. In addition, specific effects are probable. It is known that oxygen deficiency at high altitudes results in forget-

---

[7] T. M. French and Franz Alexander, *Psychogenic Factors in Bronchial Asthma*, Psychosom. Med., Monogr. 4, 1941.

fulness and increased difficulty in shifting from one way of thinking or acting to another. La Paz, Bolivia, has been dubbed the "city of forgetfulness" because its high altitude causes newcomers to experience an almost shocking degree of forgetfulness.

Although it has not been proved to be the result of hypoventilation, neurotic personalities typically have trouble in making changes in their behavior [8] and are notorious for their tendency to forget their appointments or to be overly careful about appointments as if in fear of missing them. Other characteristics of lack of oxygen in the body are general irritability, poor emotional control, excessive feeling of effort or of having to force oneself, general mental apathy, or what people commonly call "chronic fatigue." [9]

Summary

When anxiety develops in a life situation, the breathing patterns of the individual express this anxiety; if the anxiety continues over a prolonged period, the abnormal breathing patterns may become chronic, or permanent. The body now must react to the affected respiration, finding itself in somewhat weakened condition and thus more anxious about consequences. Many secondary adjustments are related to this anxiety.

Because of its prompt expression of the deeper evaluations an individual makes of his environment, respiration is one of the obvious indications of the health of the personality. Respiration can bring anxiety to light if the meaning of the various breathing patterns is understood. Normal breathing suggests that an individual is in normal mental as well as normal physical health. It is only one of many signs, but it must not be overlooked.

THE CARDIOVASCULAR SYSTEM

The Cardiac Muscle

A system of supply called the "cardiovascular system" extends into every part of the body. Its central part is popularly called the

[8] Robert R. Blake and Glenn V. Ramsey, *Perception: An Approach to Personality,* pp. 393*ff.,* The Ronald Press Company, New York, 1951.

[9] S. H. Bartley and E. Chute, *Fatigue and Impairment in Man,* pp. 87–89, McGraw-Hill Book Company, Inc., New York, 1947.

"heart" and more technically the "cardiac muscle." Also there are the systems of arteries, of capillaries, and of veins. The cardiac muscle is unique within the body, since it is composed of a kind of tissue which *pulsates* of its own accord. This fact was first brought to light by Dr. Alexis Carrel when he kept a slice of chicken heart alive for several years in a test tube after it had been completely isolated from the remainder of the body. This slice continued not only to live, but to pulsate, even to grow! Basic activity of the heart, therefore, is recognized as not being caused by neural impulses, as is almost every other bodily activity. Its beating is automatic, although variations in rate or pulsation do result from neural impulses to be discussed later.

For the present it is sufficient to understand that by the pulsations of the cardiac tissue, and because of the shape of the heart, a pumping action *transfers* blood from the auricles (inlets) to the ventricles (outlets). Some hearts beat very regularly, others with considerable irregularity. The rate of beating will slow down as the individual grows from infancy to old age. Temporary variations will appear in illness and infection, in emotionalized behavior, and in physical effort.

The following diagrams illustrate graphically the differences between rest, work, and recovery as expressed in heart action.

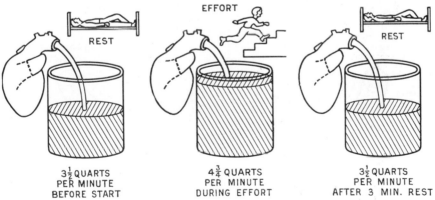

Fig. 4–2. The heart in rest, work, and recovery.

Under calm conditions of rest, called "normal," the heart transfers about 3½ quarts of blood per minute. This quantity becomes a standard of measure which is readily estimated by counting the pulse rate.

During violent exercise in which no fear or rage is present, such as square dancing or playing tennis for pure enjoyment, the heart will transfer about 4¾ quarts of blood per minute. This is 65 per cent over normal. After exercise is stopped and the individual has relaxed for about three minutes (if he is in reasonably good health) heart activity will return to its normal rate. On the other hand, if this same activity were emotionalized by rage or terror, there would be a 2 or 3 per cent greater transfer of blood and output of energy. Recovery of normal heart action in this event would take a *very much longer* time. Variations of the rate of blood transference through the heart are important indications of the bodily health, of the general effort of the individual, and of his emotional condition.

The Vascular System

Just as the chief function of the heart is to transfer blood from intakes to outlets, so it is the general function of the vascular system to carry blood to all parts of the body and then back again. Each living cell within the body must have its blood supply in order to stay alive. Circulation of blood generally is from the heart into the arteries, next into the arterioles or branches, and then into the capillaries; the blood proceeds into the venules or branches which merge into the veins which return the blood to the heart for further trans-

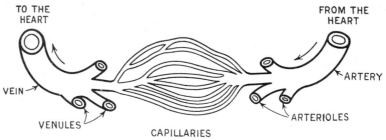

TO THE HEART

FROM THE HEART

VEIN

ARTERY

VENULES

ARTERIOLES

CAPILLARIES

Fɪɢ. 4–3. Blood vessels of the vascular system.

fer. The diagram in Fig. 4–3 shows schematically the relations between the various types of blood vessels that comprise the vascular system. Arterial blood is normally loaded with the necessary supplies

of nourishment, oxygen, hormones to stimulate or modify cellular reactions, and a variety of other substances needed by the many types
of cells within the body. Venous blood is loaded with carbon dioxide,
waste products, excess hormones, and other substances which the
cells could not absorb.

The Controls of Circulation

Arteries, capillaries, and veins are not inert pipes through which
blood is pumped. They are living organs, carrying on individually
important functions, reacting to stimuli while maintaining their own
living structures. The arteries assist the heart to force the blood
through the entire vascular system, doing considerable work which
sometimes is mistakenly credited to the heart. This transporting is
performed by means of muscles within the walls of the arteries
which, like the heart, contract rhythmically, urging the blood along
much as food is forced through the intestines.

Arteries and arterioles govern the amounts of blood provided to
specific areas of the body. This controlled distribution is accomplished by enlarging (dilating) or shrinking (constricting) the inner
diameter, particularly of the arteriole. In this way blood can be
supplied to the skeletal muscles in great quantity whenever the individual runs or dances or otherwise uses skeletal muscles vigorously.
At other times great quantities can be circulated around the small
intestines to absorb nourishment more quickly, or to draw especially
enriched and purified blood from the liver to forestall muscular exhaustion. Or again, larger amounts of oxygen can be secured by increasing the flow of blood through the lungs. These three examples
highlight, in fact, the three general subdivisions of the vascular
system.

The Vascular Subdivisions

Oxygenation is the function of the *pulmonary* segment of the vascular system. This segment starts at an outlet of the heart as an
artery, branching again into the lung capillaries, which merge into
the venules and then into the large vein which returns the now
oxygen-rich blood to the heart for redistribution. Lung tissues
stretched by inhalation expose their many capillaries to the inhaled
air. The deeper the breath, the more of these capillaries are exposed.

Through the walls of these tiny vessels oxygen is absorbed by the blood as it flows along. At the same time, waste carbon dioxide is released to the breath for exhalation. These two processes are of equal importance to the life of the individual. The pulmonary segment of the vascular system is therefore recognized as vital, particularly because the body has no equipment for storing oxygen in the way that it can store food.

Two other vascular subdivisions are necessary. One of these collects nourishment from the small intestine and is called the *hepatic*. It also transports blood to the liver for storage and purification. This segment follows much the same sequence as the pulmonary, except that it concentrates itself in the abdominal areas of the body. During sleep and rest following eating, this hepatic system is especially busy. During vigorous exercise it is much slowed down.

The third and last subdivision of the vascular system is the *systemic* segment, which supplies the many skeletal muscles of the body, as well as some of the muscles necessary to digestion, respiration, and circulation. During muscular effort this segment is especially active, as is the pulmonary. But all three segments must work in perfect coordination for good health.

The Control of Blood Pressure

General activity must be maintained within the limits of safety to the total body structure. To accomplish this end, a process of self-regulation controls the blood pressure. *Presso-receptors* are little nerve structures which register variations in blood pressure. These are located at two strategic points—one in the large artery near the heart and the other in the neck, to assure control of the blood supply to the brain. The heart is thus able to speed up or to slow down as pressure drops or builds up in the arteries. These changes in blood pressure are caused chiefly by the dilation or constriction of the capillaries. Capillary dilation permits more blood to pass through these vessels and thus lowers arterial pressure, indicating a need for more blood to be sent this way to meet local needs. Capillary constriction reduces, perhaps even stops, the passage of blood in the local area, causing pressure to build up in the arteries and arterioles. This process conserves the richly valuable blood, and thus is important to good health. But it also raises a hazard.

As pressure in the arteries increases, the presso-receptors register the increase and the heart slows down somewhat. If this were not the case, pressure would build up and produce *high blood pressure.* Extremes of this pressure would either strain the heart to the point of injury or cause a blood vessel to burst. Failures in this adjustment of blood pressure are well known to the general public as a burst blood vessel, cerebral hemorrhage, or "stroke." Failure of the cardiac muscle is popularly described as heart attack. Some of these failures are crippling, others fatal.

Vasoconstriction and Vasodilation

Under normal operating conditions each capillary has an internal diameter just sufficient to permit blood cells to flow along in single file. These cells can thus do full duty, wasting none of the rich arterial blood supply. When a person is relaxed and resting, about nine tenths of his capillaries are constricted, *i.e.,* closed, to prevent passage of blood. The remaining tenth is all that is needed to supply surrounding muscle tissue and to keep it alive. Because the capillaries take turns in constricting, and then dilating (opening), this rotation by tenths comes to mean that each muscle fiber is nourished during bodily relaxation only about a tenth of the time. Heart action, too, is greatly slowed down.

When any particular part of the body becomes extremely active, all *local* capillaries dilate to provide maximums of supplies and to carry away waste carbon dioxide. Local blood supply may be increased in two ways: first, by opening additional capillaries; second, by dilating all capillaries to maximum diameter. Normal tasks or efforts require only the bringing into service of additional capillaries. Drastic effort, such as emergency attempts to save a life, require greater blood supply for the muscles, regardless of long-term efficiency. In such emergencies, local capillaries dilate to as much as 2½ diameters. Service to local cell tissues can vary from *one* to *eighty* times the minimum blood supply.[10]

Death from "natural causes" results when the capillaries are unable to pass blood corpuscles which have become enlarged owing to other breakdowns in the person's health. To a lesser extent the

[10] M. H. Knisely, E. H. Bloch, T. S. Eliot, and L. Warner, Sludged blood, *Science,* Nov. 7, 1947, 106:432.

close relation between the capillaries and general health becomes evident. The tremendous variations in blood pressure which result from dilations and constrictions of large numbers of capillaries can be seen to explain much of the problem of pressure adjustments for the heart and arteries.

Fortunately, normal behavior requires only a few muscle groups to be active at one time. While walking, for example, the individual ordinarily relaxes in large measure all the unused muscles. In most activities, as in walking, there is a rhythmic alternation of rest and effort for each muscle group. This specialized use of certain muscles in any one activity, and the rhythmic use of almost all muscles in rotation, allows for an averaging out of the arterial blood pressure so that the heart does not suffer undue strain. Following prolonged emotion, however, these conditions do not prevail within the body. Fear and rage call for great expenditure of effort, and the heart, arteries, and arterioles promptly go to work. If the capillaries are at this time constricted, and remain so for very long—which is their characteristic reaction in fear—the resulting increase in blood pressure will be troublesome. Likewise, in rage blood is drawn from the storehouse of the liver to fill the dilated vessels, and the remaining supply of rich emergency blood is reduced. In both fear and rage the hepatic segment of the vascular system is slowed down by general vasoconstriction, a process which, at least for the time being, reduces the replacement of food elements into the liver. These emotionally organic processes of the blood vessels are necessary to the lives of humans, but they can be misused.

Vasoconstriction may have immediate or prolonged effects, notably reduced activity of the muscles or inadequate recovery from fatigue in the given local area. A superficial illustration is the experience of "turning white"; this is a blanching of the face and perhaps other body surfaces caused by extreme vasoconstrictions in and immediately under the skin. Blushing, or flushing, is local vasodilation provided by nature to allow for cooling the body at times of high body heat or high atmospheric temperature. But this same condition appears in the anticipation of enraged activity, suggesting that the body is preparing itself for vigorous struggle. Sexual excitement involves a similar process of adjusting blood circulation. In all these cases, the original stimulus to both vasoconstriction and vasodilation is psychological. It suggests impending actions or modifications of actions already in progress.

Prolonged states of either fear or rage affect not only the body in general but the mental health and personality of the individual. It has been found that in the earlier stages of psychoneurosis there frequently appears a considerable imbalance or disturbance of prolonged nature in the cardiovascular system, especially in cases marked by worry or anxiety.[11] Similarly, many worried people suffer from functional heart disease, or perhaps essential hypertension, both conditions being expressions of emotion through the cardiovascular system. The common cold illustrates the relation of this functional system to organic illness. During strong fear the membranes in the nasal passage become excessively dry; during great rage they become engorged with blood (caused by vasodilation). In these states they are unable to resist infection carried by the virus or germ life always present in the air. Thus, following great rage or fear some people typically develop head colds. The frequency of colds about the time of final examinations in most colleges is a vivid example. Psychosomatic specialists now trace many illnesses to the cardiovascular processes. Sometimes these illnesses eventually become fully organic, while in other instances they merely aggravate existing illness.[12]

In the following illustration, some of the many relationships between cardiovascular behavior and the individual personality are shown.

Gertie was about sixty-five years old at the time of this observation. She suffered serious limitation in her activities as a result of dangerously high blood pressure and a weakened heart. Her age made recovery unlikely. Management of Gertie's cardiovascular condition required careful medication and diet. Her personality was almost painfully direct. Slight differences in opinion expressed conversationally would promptly lead her to flush and become tense. She frequently had simple head colds. Her ideas on most topics were

[11] Ross A. McFarland and James H. Huddleson, Neurocirculatory reactions in the psychoneuroses studied by the Schneider-method, *Amer. J. Psychiat.*, 1936, 93:567–599.

[12] Cf. Weiss and English, *op. cit.*, pp. 57–63, discussions of "cardiac neurosis" and "neurocirculatory asthenia."

inflexible, conventional, and usually overly simple. Details of her housekeeping were immaculate; she had a place for everything. Her work history showed some evidence of kleptomania, but she apparently used the stolen items as gifts, probably to avoid spending money, which she was inclined to handle with great thrift.

Gertie's attitude toward herself was one of rigorous discipline. She chose to do the right thing in the right way rather than to enjoy life. Her standards of rightness were, like most of her other ideas, shallow. She had not married, saying that she had never known a man who was "not trying to take advantage of her." Her conversation was frequently punctuated with, "I would have done it this way." She insisted there could be no relationship between her views upon her own life and the illness she suffered.

Gertie's personality illustrates the long-term result of very many years of rigorous self-discipline, aggravated by an equally long period of struggle against the pressures of living in a world which apparently was not made according to her simple and rigid standards. Such a long struggle, with its emotional involvements, could not but affect the cardiovascular system.

THE MUSCULATURE

Bodily movements are performed by those parts of the organism composed of the specialized tissue called *muscle fibers*. This kind of tissue has a particularly marked capacity to shorten by contracting and to lengthen by relaxing. By systematic arrangement of these muscle fibers, all movement, both internal and external, can be performed. In the process of contracting and relaxing, heat is given off in rather large quantities, a phenomenon obviously related to perspiration during vigorous activity. Body temperature and muscle activity are in this way closely interrelated. In order that certain muscle fibers can work rapidly, some means is necessary to stretch and hold them in place. This means is found in the rigid bones which group together to form the skeletal system. The combination of bones and attached muscle fibers forms the *musculature*. Sometimes this word is used to include also the nervous system, but for present purposes it is used in the narrower sense.

Internal Movements

Preceding sections in this chapter have described functional systems which are in each instance composed of *smooth muscle fibers*. These systems are vital in that they serve directly the continuation of life itself. The fact that they are internal often results in their movements going unnoticed, except during times of illness or injury. The greater part of the vital, or life-maintenance, functions, including reproduction, are carried on internally by these smooth muscles arranged in tubular structures such as blood vessels, glands, intestines, etc.

External Movements

Movements of the obvious kind are produced by those muscle fibers attached to the skeleton. External movement is thus a process of skeletal muscle activities. The laborious movements of a crawling worm, gracefully efficient movements of skilled acrobats, and smoothly flowing leaps of the family cat over the garden wall are all produced by skeletal muscles. Some of these movements are faster than those of the eye muscles, therefore are "faster than the eye can see."

Most skeletal muscles are attached to two different bones. Some, like the facial muscles so important to the expressions of feeling, are attached to a bone at one end and to a segment of skin at the other. When the muscle contracts, it shortens toward its *point of origin*, the end fastened to the bone, which remains stationary. Contraction of the muscle therefore moves the other bone, or the skin segment, to which its other end is attached as its *point of insertion*. The biceps muscle, really a large group of muscle fibers, is a very good illustration, and the student should observe it carefully. Located at the front of the upper arm, its point of origin is near the shoulder end of the upper arm bone. As it contracts, it pulls the forearm upward, bending the elbow. At the opposite side, or back, of the forearm are the triceps muscles. These likewise originate at their upper end. At their lower end they are attached to the extreme end of the forearm bones. Thus as the triceps contract they pull the elbow straight.

Biceps and triceps oppose each other; one relaxes as the other contracts, and the forearm moves down or up accordingly.

Although the elbow is one of the simplest joints in the entire skeletal structure, it illustrates well the manner in which skeletal muscles are arranged in *opposing pairs* throughout the body. Some skeletal joints are able to move in more than one axis; an example is the shoulder, which can move in almost every direction. Nevertheless, the muscle groupings are arranged in opposing pairs. As long as one group relaxes whenever its opposite contracts, and as long as the relaxation exactly balances the contraction effort, a smooth flow of external movement takes place. If both members of the pair relax at the same time, the given member is limp. If both contract at the same time, the given member is rigid and tense.

Muscle Tonus and Performance

In addition to relaxation and contraction, there is a third muscle condition, known as *flaccidity;* this is a state of complete inactivity, with no tension in the muscle. This condition is normally undesirable for skeletal muscles and probably does not exist in good health. In healthy muscular behavior the skeletal and smooth muscles of the body are in some degree of contraction at all normal times. What is popularly called a "relaxed" muscle is evidencing *tonus*. This is a state of readiness for action which requires that about 10 per cent of the muscle fibers contract at a given moment. Various fibers take turns at contracting and relaxing, the larger group not contracting unless work is being performed. Tonus is therefore a kind of muscle pulsation corresponding to the capillary process as described in the preceding section. The nerve process corresponding to this tonus activity will be discussed below. Each muscle fiber is in continuous activity, alternating between its *contracting phase* and its *restitution phase*. In the smooth muscles this alternation of phases provides the pulsations which carry on the functions for which the muscles exist. Thus the peristaltic action of the digestive tract, for example, is essentially alternation of muscle phases. Generally speaking, smooth muscles follow a much slower rhythm than do skeletal muscles.

Individual muscle fibers follow the "all or nothing" law as they alternate between their two phases; they are always either fully in contraction or fully in restitution. This principle is based upon the demonstrated fact that the heart muscle contracts always to its fullest extent or not at all, regardless of the strength of nerve impulse. Variations in the strength used in any single effort of a group of muscle fibers, such as the biceps, are explainable as the percentage of the total number of muscle fibers which are contracting in a particular effort. If only 10 per cent contract at a given time, the muscle is merely ready for action. If all fibers contract at the one time, the muscle will be exercising its maximum strength.

All muscles appear to expend energy during contraction and to accumulate energy during restitution. Their more important work is thus carried on while the muscle group is relaxed. When the individual muscle fiber's store of *phosphagen* is diminished to a certain point, fatigue sets in; this will be offset only as the phosphagen is restored, during restitution. Thus the muscle is an accumulator, much like the electric storage battery which starts an automobile. Energy is accumulated slowly during the charging, or restitution, phase, and it is released freely during the work period. Proper balance between these two phases is vitally important to muscle health. In the skeletal muscles, where contractions are not automatic in rhythm except for tonus periods, it is possible to upset this process and to produce fatigue.

Learning and "Mass Activity" of Muscles

Voluntary or skeletal muscles depend upon nerve impulses to initiate contractions. But readiness to contract, or accumulated energy ready to be released, depends upon conditions surrounding the particular muscle fibers. Chemical conditions are of especial importance. For example, adrenin from the endocrine gland system will speed restitution to some extent, making the muscle more easily stimulated to contract. This heightened stimulability for contraction is evident during emotional upset as muscles throughout the entire body tend to react to the extra adrenin provided. During emotionalized activities the individual becomes tense all over. He is unable to limit his activity even during attempted use of well-known skills requiring small coordinations. This is *mass activity*.

General activity of the entire muscle system appears not only during emotion but also in new situations. The individual feels he must do something but does not know which muscles to use since he has no previously acquired habit skills, so he tries "to do everything at once." A beginning swimmer thus splashes around, uselessly wasting effort in mass activity. A child first learning to print letters shows this generalized behavior in the pervasive tension throughout the body.

Mass activity appears in three interrelated instances. During early infancy it is especially common. Infants lack both physiological maturity and preestablished habits. The young baby reacts all over, kicking its legs, waving its arms, arching its back, tightening its throat muscles, and making gurgling noises as it breathes. In all later stages of the life cycle mass activity continues to appear at the start of a learning activity, appearing as an integral part of emotionalized behavior. The opposite of mass activity is found in the highly developed skill of the acrobat, who uses only those muscles necessary to the specific stunt and keeps other muscles in a relaxed tonus condition. Every muscular skill is of this nature, using only a few muscle fibers and groups rather than a widespread and poorly coordinated activity of many muscles. Economy of muscular effort is a real accomplishment, evidencing confidence, training, and good health.

Fatigue

Enough has been said to suggest the general nature of muscular fatigue as resulting from inadequate restitution. It is an exhaustion of the particular muscle fiber's store of latent energy. During fatigue the muscle either cannot be stimulated to contract at all, or else it requires a nerve stimulus of perhaps 500 to 600 times the usual strength before it will contract. This condition can be called *physical fatigue*. There is, however, a great increase in susceptibility to physical fatigue whenever the person experiences *mental fatigue*. When an individual is tired, he makes mistakes in his performances, whereupon he promptly feels even more tired. In unpleasant situations most people become fatigued quickly. In hopeless situations it is normal to feel tired even before effort begins.

In a thorough study, Bartley and Chute concluded that there is no objective criterion available to discriminate between physical fatigue and mental fatigue. Even the traditional theory of depletion of blood sugar does not form such a criterion.[13] It is common knowledge that the mere thought of certain activities or tasks will evoke marked feelings of fatigue and that on the other hand after a day of hard physical labor a person may feel anxious to go dancing!

The factor of interest or motivation cannot be disregarded in considering behavior in any form. We all express dramatically our attitude toward the tasks we face. When a task is obnoxious, we usually express our reaction by letting our shoulders slump as in fatigue. Our facial muscles sag in a similar reaction. This relaxation of certain muscles indicates that we are made to feel "tired all over" by this task, that enthusiasm for this phase of living is absent. About the only way to tell whether the fatigue is genuinely physical or a dramatic role is to offer us a highly desirable task when we are tired. Even during physical fatigue we will experience a surge of energy if interest is aroused. This is evidenced in every student's life; he gets "awfully tired" reading one subject, but forgets his fatigue when he turns to some other subject or activity equally dependent upon the use of the eyes!

Muscles and Moods

Muscles must be appreciated as the highly integrated machinery of the body for carrying out a certain portion of the individual's total behavior. They may be necessary to all behavior, but they do not initiate behavior, except in relatively minor details. Some activities are adaptations of the individual to his internal or tissue needs. Muscle processes permit each person to bend or to straighten only in those ways permitted by the skeletal-muscular structure. The speed and frequency of these acts are likewise determined by the limits possible to these structures. Physical fatigue in a group of muscles will require a variation of the individual's activity until that fatigue is overcome. Heightened stimulability of muscle fibers and illness or injury will change the form as well as the extent of the individual's reactions.

Under ordinary conditions the general form and extent of activity derive from the organized effort being carried out by the individual. His purposes, interests, enthusiasm (or lack of it), and his mood are

[13] Bartley and Chute, *op. cit.*, pp. 398*ff.*

the more usual determiners of the behavior of his muscles. He plays a role which his muscles dramatically fulfill. The man who says to himself, "I am determined," must dramatize this role by means of his muscles. He finds himself gritting his teeth or setting his jaws, perhaps stiffening his back or crouching slightly in readiness to spring into combat. The opposite of this behavior appears as he dramatizes his feelings of sociability and congeniality. He relaxes his jaws, loosens his back muscles, even lessens the depth of his breathing. Likewise, his fears and angers must appear in muscular expressions, tensions of readiness for escape or struggle. Each role the individual plays must become concrete as muscular activity. This process follows a vicious circle, for as physical fatigue increases, the body slumps in discouragement. As the individual feels himself slumping in fatigue, he recognizes that his strength is becoming limited and he becomes discouraged and further fatigued. Good morale depends upon a combination of energy and success.

The importance of role playing as a muscular dramatizing of one's attitude or interpretation of oneself is illustrated in the case of Miss S., a social-service worker. In this type of work much responsibility must be carried over prolonged periods, and unless adequate and frequent vacations are provided, a feeling of chronic discouragement tends to develop. Miss S. found herself in this state, and upon the advice of her colleagues began a series of conferences with a psychotherapist which was to continue for almost three years. After the first year and a half, her fatigue diminished greatly, even though her work continued without change. She then began to see herself more objectively, noting that her mirror showed her looking more tired than she felt, that her personal grooming falsely suggested near exhaustion. To bring her appearance into line with her own feelings about herself, she consulted a stylist. A new hair-do soon compensated for a slight deformity at the base of her neck. Practice and coaching enabled her to learn to walk with head high and back erect. Improved posture soon eased foot fatigue and made it possible for her to wear a more stylish shoe. These and similar devices assisted her musculature to express more effectively the person Miss S. really was coming to be. With her handicapping habits lost, she now could dramatize herself in a genuine and healthy manner.

NERVOUS SYSTEMS

Two Nervous Systems

The physiology of living things allows both for variety of reactions and uniformity of function. The given type of cell reacts only in its own particular way. Muscles contract and relax. Bones remain rigid. Glands produce appropriate secretions. Nerve cells pass impulses from one end to the other. The nerve cell is thus responsible within the organism for communication, each impulse being figuratively a message. By means of these communications the various areas and segments of the body can be coordinated. Instead of many separate cellular reactions, or several distinct functional systems, the living organism can behave as a unified whole.

Not all communications within the body are carried on by means of the nervous systems, however. The blood carries nourishment, toxins, hormones, waste products, disease germs, and many other substances. These originate in one place and are carried to other points, instigating reactions there. Such communications by way of the blood stream, and all other fluid movements in the body, are primitively slow. They match the tempo of nature in the crude state of plants and simple animals which can survive only slow changes in their environments. The speed of man's movements must match that of his friends' if he is to cooperate with them and must exceed that of his enemies' if he is to survive. The higher animals, including man, are therefore equipped with a functional system for the integration of high-speed activities.

Two nervous systems serve the higher animals: the *sensory-motor* and the *vasomotor*, or autonomic. The sensory-motor integrates activities of the many skeletal muscles which move the musculature. In addition this nervous system maintains contact with the external environment through reactions of the sense organs. The vasomotor system integrates the body's internal functions, which sustain life. The latter activities are, compared to those of the musculature, relatively slow in movement and adapt only within a very limited range. Once changed, they are equally slow to return to their earlier patterns.

The difference in speed of reaction of the two nervous systems is frequently observed. The case of a person who is almost run down by a truck while crossing the street will serve as an example. He notices the approach of the truck, jumps quickly aside, and in a confused manner gets back to the curb. There he nearly collapses; he is in a state marked by irregular breathing, perspiration, and a general feeling of weakness and fright. The speed with which he jumped aside indicates the rapid reaction of his sensory-motor nervous system. The slower reaction of the vasomotor system is indicated by the longer time which elapsed before the change in the breathing pattern, for example, appeared, when he was at the curb. This longer reaction time is also indicated by the even longer period that elapsed before the changed breathing returned to its normal pattern.

Another evidence of the difference in reaction times is the speed of learning new muscle movements as compared with the slowness with which vital functions adapt, for example, to a change of meal schedule or a marked change of altitude. The two systems necessarily must work together for greatest efficiency.

Peripheral and Central Divisions

A distinction has already been pointed out between the vasomotor and the sensory-motor systems. Now a division must be noted between the central nervous processes and the peripheral nervous processes. This division is one of importance both to structure and to function. Vasomotor nerves and sensory-motor nerves are distinguishable in the peripheral system. But in the central system they seem to merge, frequently serving the same organs jointly and connecting to common areas in the brain. This is to be expected, since both vital functions and musculature must function always in close coordination.

The peripheral division of the sensory-motor system branches outward from the brain and spinal column to attach to every sense organ and to every voluntary muscle fiber throughout the body. Peripheral fibers of the vasomotor system branch out almost as extensively, but go to the capillaries of the vascular system, to the sweat glands, to various muscles connected with breathing, etc. The major functions of the sensory-motor system seem to be oriented to external adjustments, particularly emphasizing relationships between the organism and its environment. The vasomotor functions tend to be internal to the body, concerned largely with the continuance of life itself. Both, however, are responsive through nerve impulses passing through the brain and integrated in the central nervous system.

The brain itself is largely sensory-motor, so far as mere size is concerned. It and the spinal column, plus the chain ganglia, comprise the central nervous system. Most students are familiar with the branching out of the various nerve trunks from the central nervous system. Recent interpretations of the brain suggest that the inner parts are largely nerve fibers radiating outward from the center to the surface or cortex. Thus the function of the cortex is to transfer nerve impulses from some radial fibers to others so that neural arcs may function. This transfer seems to take place through coordinator neurons which have many dendrite endings and branches. Such complexity of transfer exists that a general diffusion of impulses takes place, particularly in the frontal regions.[14] The telephone switchboard analogy fails at this point.

Brain studies today tend to chart the cortex into areas identified by numbers, *e.g.*, "area 17." Electroencephalograph, or brain-wave, studies of these areas, plus surgical investigation of animal nervous systems, are accumulating some very decisive evidence. Reflex arc circuits are giving way to brain-area relationships. Many functions formerly assumed to reside in the cortex are now known to reside in other parts of the brain; of particular importance among these areas are the thalamus and the hypothalamus.

The Thalamus-Hypothalamus

Roughly at the center of the brain, the *thalamus* is the great relay station through which the most important nerve impulses seem to pass on their way to and from the cortex. The thalamus serves as a unifying center for the highly complex peripheral nervous system, both sensory-motor and vasomotor, and the cortex. Visual and auditory processes are dependent upon this structure to relay nerve impulses to the cortex. Recent studies of the cortex also demonstrate that certain areas are both sensory and motor. Electrical

---

[14] D. O. Hebb, *The Organization of Behavior: A Neuro-psychological Theory*, Chap. 4, John Wiley & Sons, Inc., New York, 1949.

stimulation of these areas of the cortex under laboratory conditions gives the subject both an artificial sensory experience and a muscle-contraction or activity experience. Certain other areas or "bands" of the cortex inhibit muscular reactions.[15] Nerve impulses traveling to and from the cortex are routed through the thalamus-hypothalamus.

For our present purposes the hypothalamus is more significant than the thalamus. It lies somewhat below the thalamus and serves as a control center for the autonomic nervous system. It does not originate nerve impulses, but relays them and reroutes them.

The central integrations which are carried on in the hypothalamus may be described as follows: [16]

Body temperature is crucially dependent upon this center. Whenever it is necessary for the body to lose heat, the hypothalamus causes vasodilation, increased sweating, increased respiration, and a lowering of metabolism. Through converse effects it causes heat to be conserved, and in addition, by inducing shivering, the body temperature to be raised. As the primary neural center regulating endocrine secretions, the hypothalamus plays a major role in regulating metabolism, particularly of fats, carbohydrates and water. It is there, too, that the control of blood pressure and thus of the distribution of blood to the brain is mainly, though not exclusively, vested. Sexual functions, which include complex autonomic effects as well as certain somatic reactions, depend upon the hypothalamus. Furthermore, physiological conditions associated with hunger and thirst are dependent in an important degree upon the activity of the hypothalamus . . . it is also a center for emotional behavior.

This list of physiological integrations is most impressive when considered in the light of the preceding discussions of the functional systems and their relation to many of the same functions as are controlled through the hypothalamus. Cortical areas may receive nerve impulses from both sensory nerves and the corresponding nerves of the vasomotor system. Just as an electrical needle applied to certain areas of the cortex gives both sensory and motor reactions, so also will this give vasomotor reactions such as change of blood

[15] Heinz Werner and Seymour Wapner, Sensory-tonic field theory of perception, *J. Person.*, 1949, 18(1):93.

[16] Clifford T. Morgan and Eliot Stellar, *Physiological Psychology*, 2d ed., p. 45, McGraw-Hill Book Company, Inc., New York, 1950.

pressure, pulse rate, body temperature, etc.[17] Ordinarily behavior involves neural impulses, not artificially introduced electrical ones, but nerve pathways can be explored by electrical impulses.

If the posterior part of the hypothalamus is stimulated electrically, *sympathetic* segments of the vaso motor system will be activated. These nerve trunks leave the spinal column of the human body largely between the top of the hips and the center of the shoulders. Such stimulation results in dilation of the eye pupils, heart acceleration, elevation of blood pressure, and lowered stomach and intestinal activity. If the anterior part of the hypothalamus is stimulated, the *parasympathetic* segments become active. These include the cranial, or upper, end of the vasomotor system and the sacral, or lower, end. In this case, eye pupils contract, heart action lowers, blood pressure drops, blood sugar lowers, and, in extreme instances, sleep is induced.[18]

Nerve impulses coming from autonomic areas of the cortex stimulate either posterior or anterior parts of the hypothalamus which in turn stimulates the sympathetic or parasympathetic segments of the vaso-motor nervous system. At the same time, sensory-motor neural arcs integrate skeleto-muscular activities. Integration of the various functional systems has thus taken place in the central nervous system.

EMOTION

Emotional Illness

Although emotion is not one of the functional systems, it is a physiological function and important because it takes in all the functional systems. Adequate information is available to describe not only specific infections and injuries affecting a functional system but also the processes involved in many chronic illnesses. Even the accidents which result in burns, broken bones, and poisoned stomachs are commonly explored today to discover which may be directly or indirectly related to the place and time of the accident. Suicide, which ranks tenth from the top in the list of most frequent

[17] Werner and Wapner, *op. cit.*, 88–105.
[18] Martin L. Reymert (ed.), *Feelings and Emotions*, pp. 22*ff.*, McGraw-Hill Book Company, Inc., New York, 1950.

causes of death, is carefully distinguished from accident. It is considered by health experts to be the result of mental illness.[19]

Alcoholism, too, is considered a psychosomatic illness. Since World War II there have been about two thousand deaths per year from alcoholism in California alone. In the San Francisco area the average alcoholic was arrested forty-seven times—an "expensive revolving door." [20] These and other chronic ailments now respond in varying degrees to treatment which is in whole or in part comprised of psychotherapy. Frequently no physical administrations are given in connection with this therapy.

Illness which responds to psychotherapy is commonly described as "emotional." Psychosomatic studies make it abundantly clear that these and many other illnesses do involve emotional factors. The problem of understanding personal adjustment thus revolves around understanding emotion. Preceding sections of this chapter have stressed the way in which structural limits of each functional system assure bodily survival within a range of environmental conditions relating to digestion, respiration, etc. Slowing or speeding of the rhythms within one system soon is adjusted to by the others until some compromise is reached which represents homeostatic equilibrium within the total organism. Emotion is the process of rapidly energizing the entire organism. Sometimes when emotion gets out of adjustment with the basic equilibrium, illness appears.

The concept of emotional illness seems to grow from the above-noted presence of emotion whenever certain illnesses appear. Conversely, treatment of the emotional adjustments of such an ill person seems to relieve the individual's poor health. This is called "clinical" evidence, *i.e.*, it is concluded that emotion is the cause of the illness because treatment in the emotional sphere brings beneficial results. In view of these aspects of emotion, it becomes a problem to explain how healthy personalities can ever experience emotion, as indeed they do. The present section attempts to clarify the emotional process and thus to give the term clearer meaning.

[19] Oliver E. Byrd, *Health Instruction Yearbook,* p. 26, Stanford University Press, Stanford University, Calif., 1948.
[20] Robert E. G. Harris, Alcoholism: California's expensive revolving door, *Search Magazine,* July, 1951, p. 7.

Changing Concepts of Emotion

Years ago it was customary to describe emotions as feelings of fear, rage, joy, jealousy, excitement, depression, and the like. Studies of photographs of actors portraying these various emotions were often exhibited to groups of judges for the purpose of having them guess at the emotion which the actors had in mind in each case. Guesses were generally unsuccessful. In one important experiment hypnotized subjects were instructed to feel happy and then to judge photos of emotional expressions. When "happy," the subjects would judge the photos one way, but when instructed to be anxious they judged the same photos quite otherwise.[21] Specific emotions seem to be recognizable only when the subject and the situation are both known to the judge. This conclusion opens the way to the study of some more fundamental process of emotion as underlying specific emotional expressions.

Watson's observations of infant behavior led him to conclude that rage, fear, and love (sex) are inherited emotions.[22] Other writers have suggested that only two emotions can be listed, namely rage (anger) and fear; rage is attack or approach to the stimulus, while fear is retreat or escape. The former destroys the stimulus and ends an unpleasant experience; the latter eliminates further contact with it. This simple twofold classification fails to account for experiences of emotion which seem to have neither fear nor rage in them. When the laboratory subject is given a small injection of adrenaline, he feels "about to be upset" but cannot decide why, or whether by rage or by fear. Similar reactions occur in everyday life.

A more fundamental approach has suggested that emotion is basically simply excitement. This may be channeled by the culture pattern to become rage or fear. These two emotional reactions are expressed differently by various cultural groups. Some people talk loudly and carelessly when enraged; others become reserved and silent. Both are demonstrably excited. Fear, too, can be expressed in two ways: by running and by freezing to one's tracks. Under this theory of combining bodily reflex reactions, which are integrated

[21] C. Leuba and C. Lucas, Effects of attitudes on descriptions of pictures, *J. Exper. Psychol.*, 1945, 35:517–524.

[22] John B. Watson, *Psychology from the Standpoint of a Behaviorist*, 2d ed., J. B. Lippincott Company, Philadelphia, 1924.

autonomically, with learned expressions or adaptive reactions, the varieties of emotional behavior can be explained. Even such deviate behavior as sadism, masochism, egocentrism, etc., becomes explainable. The emotion is thus not a separate process or functional system. It is either a physiological process or a characteristic way of behaving and is best described as *emotional behavior*.

Physiological researches discussed in the preceding section on the nervous systems define processes of intensifying sympathetic and parasympathetic nervous functions and thereby producing behavior which shows rage, fear, or mixtures of the two. Emphasis today seems to be upon defining emotion as such autonomically intensified reactions. Often the subject has learned to react with fear or rage to a certain type of stimulus before he has become aware of learning this. The slowness of recovery from emotional activity, as compared to recovery from other types of activities, is accounted for by the way in which this autonomic process changes the blood chemistry which affects the heart action. The delayed recovery described in connection with the cardiovascular system is thus indicative of emotionalization of the original behavior. Many older interpretations with longer lists of specific emotions have given way to this concept of an autonomically integrated process.

Evaluation and Emotion

Why does an organism react with emotionalization to certain stimuli to which other organisms do not? Emotion is, psychologically speaking, a *massive* experience. It sets in motion a generalized activity involving the entire individual. The list of hypothalamic integrations quoted above indicates how general this action is. The intensity of the emotion corresponds directly to the organism's anticipation of safety or danger. His intensified activity in a safe situation will be best called "interest." It will differ physiologically from emotion. A paramecium "freezes" into immobility when it comes into contact with the fatal acetic acid. Similarly, when man becomes emotional he is completely emotional. He may react with greater or lesser intensity, becoming more or less disorganized in his coordinations, but he reacts "all over."

The problem is to predict whether his growing excitement will become rage or fear. If he has learned to run away, hide his head, or change the subject, he will try one of these reactions. Or he may merely stand still and tremble all over. If he has learned to attempt to destroy the stimulus by striking at it, or by calling it names, he will use one of these methods of asserting his superior strength or status over the irritating stimulus. If he judges his strength to be inadequate, he may react with fear or resort to fear after trying rage. What he does will be determined by his evaluation of the situation and of himself. Strong emotional excitement discourages the repetition of formerly unacceptable relationships, even preventing repetition of the line of thought which leads up to such relationships.[23]

The Darwinian concept of emotion seems to be compatible with modern psychology. It holds that emotionalized behavior is always an emergency reaction, indicating the organism to be reacting to a serious threat of some kind. The threat may be either to one's immediate self, or to something very dear to this self. The mother tiger will become as emotional in response to a threat to her young as to herself. Humans are just as prone to become emotional in reaction to a threat to their social status as they are to a threat to their bodily or spiritual welfare. If it is known what a man likes, and what he requires of himself, it will be possible to predict his definition of a threatening situation.

Because emotion seems so readily defined in terms of a general mobilization of the organism as it anticipates danger or threat, the problem becomes one of accounting for rage and anger. Studies of maladjusted persons as well as mentally ill persons find anxiety the basic or underlying psychological condition. This will be discussed in a later chapter, but for the moment it should be pointed out that anxiety is chronic fear. Sometimes the anxiety is expressed directly as fear; sometimes it is converted into anger as if in accordance with the axiom "The best defense is an offense." In discussing essential hypertension, a common cardiovascular ailment, one authority on psychosomatics described persons evidencing this converted fear as follows: [24]

[23] Hebb, *op. cit.*, p. 254.

[24] H. G. Wolff, Life situations, emotions, and bodily disease, Chap. 24, p. 309, in Reymert, *op. cit.*

From the standpoint of attitudes as well as circulatory physiology they were mobilized for combat but did not engage in it against the pertinent adversary. Under a façade which was designed to imply that they were affable and easygoing, they were tense, wary, suspicious. . . . They felt a need to show prowess without exhibiting aggression and continually feared that they would not succeed in doing so.

Having evaluated the world as a hostile place in which to live, these patients used their autonomically integrated body mechanisms to carry out activities fearfully or with rage.

The understanding of emotion thus requires understanding of the process of perceptual evaluation. Psychosomatics has been helpful in describing the machinery of behavior, in many of its normal aspects and in ill health. The diffused excitement of the infant eventually becomes in adult men and women the culturally channeled expression classed as rage, fear, or a mixture of these. The presence of such emotional adaptations inevitably connotes fear as the underlying evaluation. Emotion is the reaction to threat, its intensity in direct proportion to the degree of weakness felt, albeit the organism presents his reaction publicly as the offensive protective reaction of anger.

QUESTIONS FOR DISCUSSION

1. Give some of the reasons why most people do not like to accept the psychosomatic viewpoint.
2. When a doctor explains an illness as real but without organic cause, what does he mean?
3. Give some examples from your own experience of the effect of emotional stress on digestion.
4. What types of growth experiences are usually behind the finicky appetite?
5. How would you explain the meaning of the term "Wall Street stomach"?
6. Give some examples of respiratory difficulties experienced under emotional stress.
7. What might be the basis for the claim of some physical education instructors that teaching one to breathe correctly will develop poise?
8. How can fright increase the rate of heartbeat?
9. Why do executives with stressful lives seem to be especially subject to fatal heart trouble?
10. What might be a psychological explanation for the fact that hypertension is unknown in some simpler cultures?

11. Is there any truth in the statement that long lives are due to lack of worry?
12. What might be the psychological causes of awkwardness or poor posture?
13. When people are tired does it always mean that they have worked too hard? Explain.
14. Give some examples of the different ways in which anger is expressed by people from diverse cultural environments.
15. Give an example of the same experience causing fear in one person and not in another. What accounts for this difference?

ADDITIONAL READINGS

Gilbert, Jeanne, and Weitz, Robert D.: *Psychology for the Profession of Nursing*, Chap. 3, The Ronald Press Company, New York, 1949.

Guthrie, Edwin R., and Edwards, Allen L.: *Psychology: A First Course in Human Behavior*, Chap. 5, Harper & Brothers, New York, 1949.

Harris, Irving D., Rapoport, Lydia, Rynerson, Mary Ann, and Samter, Max: Observations on asthmatic children, *Amer. J. Orthopsychiat.*, 1950, 20: 490–505.

Kraines, S. H., and Thetford, E. S.: *Live and Help Live*, Chap. 11, The Macmillan Company, New York, 1951.

Jost, H.: Some physiological changes during frustration, *Child Develpm.*, 1941, 12:9–15.

Mohr, George J.: Psychosomatic problems in childhood, *Child Develpm.*, 1948, 19(3):137–142.

Riess, B. F., and De Cillis, Olga E.: Personality differences in allergic and non-allergic children, *J. Abnorm. Soc. Psychol.*, 1940, 35:104–113.

Ripley, Herbert S., and Wolff, Harold G.: Life situations, emotions, and glaucoma, *Psychosom. Med.*, 1950, 12:215–224.

Rose, Annelies A.: Menstrual pain and personal adjustment, *J. Person.*, 1949, 17:287–302.

Saul, Leon J.: Physiological effects of emotional tension, Chap. 8, in J. McV. Hunt (ed.), *Personality and the Behavior Disorders: A Handbook Based on Experimental and Clinical Research*, Vol. 1, The Ronald Press Company, New York, 1944.

Tuttle, Harold S.: *Dynamic Psychology and Conduct*, Chap. 16, Harper & Brothers, New York, 1949.

Young, Paul T.: *Emotion in Man and Animal: Its Nature and Relation to Attitude and Motive*, John Wiley & Sons, Inc., New York, 1943.

CHAPTER 5 *Culture*

The individual does not grow in a vacuum. He is born into a group whose members show much uniformity in perceptions, motivations, and behavior. This social setting will affect his indoctrination into life. It will shape his expectations of himself and others.

For many years there seemed to be a gulf between the psychologists and psychiatrists, who explained personality in purely individual terms, and the sociologists and anthropologists, who considered the social group as the fashioning agency. The two points of view are now converging to stress the dynamics of individual-society relationships. Group patterns are shown to reflect individual emotional adjustments and individual behavior to mirror the group's culture. Interaction is the catchword of today. Each individual makes an imprint on the community; his beliefs·and conduct are in turn shaped by society. The growth of personality is a complicated process which will be discussed in more detail in Part Three. The present chapter will examine the area of cultural phenomena surrounding the individual. This will include the ingredients of culture, the characteristics of United States culture patterns, and certain subculture patterns.

CULTURAL PATTERNING

Culture patterns might be thought of as the traditional ways of living in a particular society. They show great diversity but nevertheless can be discussed on the basis of common functions and processes. This section will define some of the elements in patterning and prepare the way for a more comprehensive analysis of the particular variety encountered in the United States.

Definition of Culture

Culture, in the social-science use of the term, has none of the evaluation characteristics of popular usage, in which its use is lim-

Fɪɢ. 5–1. Feelings soon are channeled into culturally acceptable patterns. (*Collier's.*)

ited to an interest in so-called "highbrow" activities. Instead it refers to the way of life of any group, *e.g.*, a tribe of Indians or a social clique. Strictly speaking, it includes both material (tools and machines) and nonmaterial components. The nonmaterial part of culture consists of commonly accepted and expected ideas, attitudes, values, and habit patterns. These are expressed in folkways (ways of behaving) and mores (codes for proper conduct including both dos and don'ts). Laws and ordinances might be thought of as a crystallization of certain mores. Some cultural indoctrination is easily recognizable by eye and ear, *e.g.*, gestures, gait, intonation of voice, manners of eating, styles in clothing. Much cultural patterning is more subtle, being made up of intangible social forces not easily identified. These influence motivations, perceptions, the expression of feelings, and attitudes toward people and institutions. They prescribe patterns of courtship, marriage, child rearing, occupational life, and all phases of group interrelationships. Some traditional attitudes represent adjustments to situations which no longer exist. When this is true there is a culture lag. New patterns have not been developed to meet changes. All in all, culture is a limiting factor from the point of view of personality growth.

The college student need not look beyond his own campus for examples of cultural phenomena. Every college has a culture complex—a group of customs, values, and behavior patterns which have had their origin in the history of the college and in the various culture groups from which its students come. Many European students have been shocked to find American college men and coeds working with their hands to earn their way through school, since they have built up from their own cultural heritage a stereotype of a student as one who works only with his head. Another common cultural phenomenon is the social pattern which dictates the amount of studying considered proper. On some campuses group pressures are strongly in favor of the so-called "gentleman's C." Many frown upon any association between professors and students. In certain groups any student who converses with the faculty outside of class is regarded as an "apple polisher," or worse. The student's actions are in some cases initiated and in others hamstrung by mores.

Dating at a college is surrounded by definite dos and don'ts peculiar to the particular campus. It is very important to be seen with the "big wheels" and in the right "coke joints." On some campuses custom dictates that senior men must date freshmen women. Others encourage dating of off-campus women. This was true at Stanford University when the percentage of women was kept so small that the men, perhaps as a defense, built up the tradition that Stanford women were unattractive.

The English anthropologist Geoffrey Gorer considers American dating a strange and unique cultural pattern. He describes it as a "highly patterned activity or group of activities comparable in some

Fig. 5–2. Colleges have colorful traditions. The Junior Cane March of the University of Pennsylvania has been a long-time tradition. Generations of third-year Penn men accept this behavior pattern each fall. (*Courtesy of The Sunday Bulletin, Philadelphia.*)

ways to a formal dance, in others to a very complicated competitive game." [1] He comments that it is designed to enhance the self-esteem and assurance of both parties. Conversation on a date is different from all other conversation; it is a mixture of persiflage, flattery, wit, and love-making. It is now commonly called a "line" but each generation dubs it with a new name. Because this pattern is peculiar to America, it has given rise to misunderstandings. Foreign women, unfamiliar with United States mores, have often misinterpreted the American man's "line" by taking it literally.

[1] Geoffrey Gorer, *The American People: A Study in National Character*, p. 109, W. W. Norton & Company, New York, 1948.

Culture Carriers

Culture patterns are learned through example and indoctrination. Groups develop goals and create institutions to carry them out. In primitive societies a direct line can be traced from the common aspirations of the group to the individual's education for his role in that group. The whole tribe is the communication system by which the younger member is indoctrinated into its folkways and mores. There is no division into smaller groups (subcultures). There are no currents or crosscurrents of regional, class, or national subcultures. The direct process of the one common (unicultural) patterning system is clearly visible to all. The new member is continually shaped into the type of individual desired by the unified tribe. This one definite pattern of expectation simplifies adjustment for the growing personality.

In the United States instead of one tribal system we have many. Primary face-to-face units consist of family, neighborhood, and other groups operating by word of mouth and example. Influences in secondary groups have a more indirect means of communication. Some of these secondary groups are schools, religious bodies, play groups, business or industrial corporations, associations of employers or employees, art and scientific societies. Some of their means of communications are books, magazines, radio, television, movies, and direct-mail advertising. The culture carriers of the college are the upperclassmen.

Success—A Group Definition

Group goals mirror the value system of any culture or subculture. The emphasis may be on social success, on the acquisition of material possessions, on development of some specific ability, or on service to the group. Selected criteria will form the accepted yardstick for measuring success. Each individual will acquire status according to his rating on this prestige scale. He will be successful to the degree that he fits culturally.

At some campuses unusual prestige is attached to campus queens, athletes, or members of particular organizations or social classes. When leaders of one campus meet with those of others in regional or national conferences, they realize that differences have been operating in the various groups. The epitome of success in an engineering college may be quite different from that in a teachers college. The qualities found in the person at the top of the hierarchy in an Ivy League college may not fit the leader-stereotype of a Middle Western state university.

Some Hollywood movie stars rate each other's status purely on the basis of weekly salary. In certain academic circles the criterion is pages of published research. Among radio personalities it may be Hooper Ratings; among salesmen, volume of sales; among campus coeds, dates per week. It is said that at one time a social clique in Bar Harbor, Maine, rated its members according to miles hiked during the summer season. In every group the one who best epitomizes the group ideal is the most successful. Sociometry has been discovering that the key to influencing groups is to secure the cooperation of those who most nearly fit the group ideal. Thus the type of person who can rally a woman's club around a cause may be quite different from the one best suited to secure the cooperation of a labor union. Much of the success of any new idea depends upon the backing it receives from those who are the embodiment of the group's ideals.

Individual Reaction to Status Systems

Hierarchy ratings affect the individual goals of all members of the group. The coed may neglect everything but her development of popularity characteristics. The professor may slant his every thought toward the accomplishment of research. The salesman may overlook all values except high-pressuring for sales. Sometimes when an individual is not able to obtain sufficient success in one particular hierarchy system, he tries for it in another group. This explains some of the popularity and the holding power of secondary groups; they give status to individuals who have been undernourished in this respect in other circles. Fraternal orders, luncheon clubs, and various hobby groups may offer such opportunities for status. An artist's niche in his occupational group might be a low one, but socially he could be at the top. Many people play much more important roles in their avocational than in their occupational life, and vice versa.

At times individuals find themselves compelled to accept a different status from that to which they have become accustomed. A young man from the South who had never appreciated the difficult position of those in a minority group found himself in such a position as the result of being one of the last comers to an Army aviation-repair station overseas. This group had developed values and attitudes based on the premise that the best people joined up early and only dregs could be so late. For the first time in his life he found himself definitely in the minority bracket, at the bottom of the status system.

A dramatic example of reversal of roles is portrayed in James Barrie's play *The Admirable Crichton*. An upper-class English family and their butler are shipwrecked. The family, having no experience in practical things, is helpless in this situation. The butler steps into the role of leader, and the members of the family are necessarily in a subservient position. When they return home and the old setting calls for a reversal of roles, the butler finds it impossible to revert to type.

Many students have this type of experience when they come to college from a small high school in which their place in the hierarchy was at the top level. The new role as an insignificant freshman seems impossible to fulfill. Later on, the college honors student often finds it most difficult to embrace the part of a beginner after graduation. Hollywood stars sometimes find box-office returns affecting their status overnight. These drastic changes in status place great strain on the personality.

In-group versus Out-group

Sometimes one changes color like a chameleon in response to group standards. Members of certain fraternities show the effect of group conditioning very clearly. Men long versed in service clubs like Rotary or Kiwanis have in common certain attitudes and actions of informality which they share. An attitude of "we-group," or "in-group," versus "others-group," or "out-group" develops. When an individual is emotionally tied up with a group, loyalties become very strong. One student boasts that his fraternity is the best. Another points out that his college is second to none. This man speaks with pride about the superiority of his union. Another is sure that his sect alone is qualified to interpret the Bible. This type of energetic adherence to the we-group may involve hatred and antagonism to the opposing group, or out-group. In its extreme form this attitude stereotypes members of one's own group as superior to any other. Other groups are then judged by the standards of one's own. This stereotyped thinking may develop such rigidity as to become overt prejudice toward all outsiders. This ethnocentrism if carried into other realms of life can play havoc with the relationships between individuals, subgroups, and even nations. Such manufactured antagonism provides a great hostility potential, ripe for demagogues to use.

Reaction to Cultural Pressures

The more a person is in need of group status to bolster his own confidence, the greater will be his conscious motivation to model himself after the cultural ideal. Because of the student's desire for the approval of his compeers, the cultural patterns of the campus can be really tyrannical. Continuation of this process is reflected in the "keeping up with the Joneses" attitude so common in many life situations. Even though they do not subscribe to the group goals, many people abide by them for the greater goal of rating or belonging. When individuals are asked to make lists anonymously of the social mores and taboos which they follow unwillingly, some interesting results appear. College women have cited such taboos as not asking men for dates, being considered unwomanly for excelling in math, not being able to run because it is not "ladylike." [2]

There will always be those who, because they have developed either unusual assurance in themselves or inner antagonism toward all restraints, will defy cultural patterns. These may be the inventors of better ways of living. New social inventions are often made by those for whom conformity entails suffering. Or they may turn into idol smashers, disparaging the values of the group within which they live. Expression for this kind of hatred is often found by joining forces with an out-and-out revolutionary group. Those who rebel to the point of becoming delinquents will be described in the chapter on Delinquency. In some cases cultural expectations lead to so many frustrations that the individual gives up trying to adapt to them. He may find a utopian group to which he can adjust, or he

[2] Stuart Henderson Britt, *Social Psychology of Modern Life*, rev. ed., p. 78, Rinehart & Company, Inc., New York, 1949.

may become a hobo or a recluse. If he retreats too far into the world of unreality, he may become mentally ill. Thus in many ways individuals can be *in* a culture but not *of* it.

CHARACTERISTICS OF UNITED STATES CULTURE

The living framework within which the growth process of the American child takes place is most complicated. An attempt will be made in this section to analyze some of the larger cultural configurations, which are nationwide in scope, as well as those pressures emanating from some of the many subcultural groups.

Diversity of Patterns

It is difficult to describe the almost innumerable aspects of the cultural milieu into which the infant is born in the United States. If he is pictured at the center of a large circle representing the national culture pattern of the United States, he will also be within the bounds of many smaller overlapping circles representing subgroups. Different sets of circles may also have to be drawn for father and mother to represent cultural pressures arising from ethnic, religious, regional, occupational, social class, and organizational sources, among others. Thus a conglomeration of patterns makes up the cultural milieu in which the individual must live and grow.

The family is an integrating force and can emphasize, neutralize, discount, or reverse these cultural conditioners in early life. It may subscribe to all or to only a portion of the outside pressures. In order to picture the potential of culture as a factor in the development of personality, each of several circles will be described in more detail. It will be seen that some of the circles reinforce each other, while others conflict. As the individual's development proceeds, certain circles will become more and more influential through direct contact and through lessening of family influence. The family's role will be discussed in more detail in the chapter on Home and Family.

Generally Accepted Goals

The traditions and institutions of a culture develop into a matrix that molds the type of individual who epitomizes the goals of the group, its scheme of values. Thus to describe United States culture one must summarize the values inherent in the national goals. Listening to the types of thought and behavior considered un-American by radio and television commentators becomes confusing. Lists of so-called Americanisms have been drawn up by diverse groups, sometimes reflecting their own particular subcultural slants rather than the national majority's. In a country as large as this, with multiethnical backgrounds and strong regional feelings, it is most difficult to agree upon common goals. Also, in a growing and nonstatic country like America customs and mores are always being evaluated to determine which should be preserved, which reformed, which discarded. This diversity of ideologies and trends is one of the outstanding features of the culture of the United States. However, some culture concepts do penetrate many areas, forming a sort of national culture pattern. A list of top values to which Americans would give priority might run something like this:

Great generosity
Strong emphasis on things mechanical
Importance of speed and progress
Belief in the value of mass education
Pressure for children to reach greater success than parents
Emphasis on activity, aggressiveness, and competition
Great value of prestige and possessions

Success Motive

In an adjustive society like the United States, most people are dreaming of improved hierarchical roles. This is in strong contrast to the older caste system of India, to the Victorian class concept, or even to the culture of early New England and the South, where everyone's role was established by family and class when he was born. In the old Japanese tradition a person's success was measured by how successfully he could live up to the code of his predecessors. In the United States it is based upon how successfully he can outdistance his predecessors. To be successful is probably the most widely heralded common goal. One cult of success reflecting the traits common to the United States culture constellation is the rating and dating complex found on many college campuses. Another reflection is the popularity of the "rags to riches" philosophy and of biographies of the "self-made man." Judgments of success and failure are an important part of Americana. Many conflicts between adolescents and parents can be traced in part to parental attempts to bring this American dream to reality. Often parents have such a narrow interpretation of what constitutes success that youths whose ability does not warrant professional status are made to feel themselves failures. There is a widespread belief that the golden age is located in the future and that everyone's ship will come in. Many people never give up their belief that great things are just around the corner, that success has no limits.

The portrait of a successful person highlights aggressive and competitive action. The contemplative life is considered idleness. The contributions of thinkers, artists, and other less aggressive types are not so much admired. There is an overwhelming fear of being considered a "sissy" or a coward. The emphasis is on the muscular, aggressive male.[3] This restricts men's interests because in order to prove that they are not sissies, they must be identified only with pursuits which are considered masculine. Masculine-feminine standards thus are culturally determined.

Tension-producing Tendencies

Tensions result from discrepancies between desire and gratification in society. Do you believe that most people see through the particular variety of consumer psychology being developed by each new campaign to increase popular desires? Many media of communication directly inflate common expectations. Over radio and television, in the headlines, and on the billboards, the American people's desires are enlarged to mammoth proportions. Some advertising guides frankly stress the need to develop fears and frustrations to such a degree that the consumer will be ripe for suggestions as to how to handle these. Then the product can be offered as a solution to these developed frustrations, such as lack of glamour, of sex attraction, of prestige, or of great business success. This technique builds on the attitude of keeping up with the Joneses, a feeling that life can be made complete only by more purchases.

[3] Marian E. Breckenridge and E. Lee Vincent, *Child Development: Physical and Psychological Growth throughout the School Years*, 2d ed., p. 219, W. D. Saunders Company, Philadelphia, 1949.

Glittering and impossible ideals are built up as necessities to happiness. Marriage is pictured as a continual honeymoon and the good life as one surrounded by all possible gadgets. At the same time possibilities for the gratification of these inflated desires are definitely limited, so that it is actually impossible for most people to

"I don't like television any more than you do, but we don't want people to think we can't afford it."

FIG. 5–3. Some people feel compelled to keep up with the Joneses. (*Copyright 1951 by the Curtis Publishing Company.*)

achieve them. Thus the wide gap between craving and fulfillment expands, and this results in increased tension.

Another tension-producing phase of United States culture is the uncertainty and indirectness of routes to the commonly accepted goals. There are no adequate signposts. It is more difficult to learn the routes than in some less complicated societies. More than this, many of the routes taught seem to be incorrect. A dramatic example of the tendency of discontinuous routes is the encouragement in many quarters for the child to learn the route of docility while at the same time the ultimate goal is aggressive independence. In this competitive society one must try to be at the same time both friend and rival, to live in antagonistic cooperation. The most heralded routes to success are hard work and education, but in many cases these turn out to be blind alleys. Motion-picture stars, for instance, receive twenty times as much income as college professors.[4] Some routes appear to lead to goals inconsistent with common cultural expectations. The great gap between the professed ideals and the actual behavior of some of the map makers confuses those searching for routes. On the one hand honesty is held up as a necessary virtue, while on the other hand the racketeer and gangster are continually glamorized by radio, television, and movies. Standards of consideration and cooperation conflict with much of the aggressive competitiveness that is highly valued. Widely publicized examples of short cuts, such as oil gushers, gambling, etc., sidetrack many into hopeless situations. In these numerous ways, maps for reaching the cultural destination show a need for greater clarity. The gulf between ideals and reality lacks ready-made bridges.

Ethnic Patterning

The national and racial backgrounds of grandparents and parents of American children are mirrored in life values and customs. Certain groups have worked out techniques for continuing some of the folkways of their former culture constellation. For example, the Swedish Americans have their Vasa Order of America. This has a membership of more than fifty thousand organized in lodges throughout the United States for fraternal and cultural purposes. This group's aim is to enhance and improve the knowledge of those cultural values that are the joint heritage of all Swedes and descendants of Swedes. Some groups' customs have been well integrated with the larger stream of United States culture, while others' have been partly merged and come to the surface only in festival patterns invoked for weddings, funerals, etc. Thus the old national traditions keep their nostalgia-provoking quality and make for greater conflict during the process of becoming acculturated into the new patterns.

[4] Kenneth E. Appel, Mental hygiene for the adult in the world today, p. 72, in William B. Terhune (ed.), *Living Wisely and Well: A Discussion of Techniques of Personal Adjustment*, E. P. Dutton & Co., New York, 1949.

When a considerable portion of the subgroup culture differs from that of the larger stream, what difficulties are encountered? Because of the tendency in the United States to believe that variants from the widely accepted goals and folkways are wrong, critical attitudes often develop. Then the subcultural group may lean more heavily on its distinctive patterns for support by insisting upon its own ways of living. These may interfere with its youth's social relationships. Some parents, *e.g.*, have not yet accepted the United States folkways of dating or other recreations, while others cling to parent-domination patterns to the point of appropriating their children's wages. When the cultural expectations of parents are too different from the peer patterns of a youth, personality problems arise. In certain instances even small differences in table manners or entertainment patterns will so affect the young that they are ashamed of their parents. It has been suggested that the high value Americans attach to education springs from its great efficiency as a means of indoctrination into the United States culture patterns. Also, in the minority groups the outside influences seem to play a more important part as culture carriers than the families. Thus many youths are trying to grow into the United States culture configuration and away from the patterns of their elders. This situation is fertile ground for difficulties in family relationships. More problems arising from minority patterning will be discussed in the chapter on Handicap.

Occupational Patterning

An occupation more or less automatically assigns an individual and his family to a subgroup. The cultural stereotype of this group will then influence the personalities of all its members. This will come about as a result of the constancy of the group's pressures on the individual and of the role expectations of this membership, with which the out-groups have been indoctrinated.

Some of the specifics which will influence personalities are the advertised requirements of this occupational group. The higher and higher standards being set up for entrance into a medical career add to every doctor's prestige. Types of work are more or less arranged in a hierarchy of importance. In the United States most people would agree on a common rating of job prestige. This would not necessarily correspond to dollar income. "White-collar" work, even though often lower in earnings, would come ahead of so-called "labor" on most lists. This hierarchy of occupations is peculiar to United States culture. In England, for instance, the politician enjoys much more prestige. In some countries those who work with their

Man sometimes feels wife and company gang up

Fig. 5–4. Occupational and social groups exert pressures. (*Courtesy of Michael Ramus, Life Magazine.*)

hands are more valued than those who write or talk for a living.

Because of the trend toward job specialization, urbanization, and the growth of occupational associations, individuals are thrown more and more on their occupational groups for social life. This intensifies attitudes of in-group versus out-group. Each member more or less unknowingly finds his attitudes toward members of other groups and situations molded by the conversation he constantly hears and the occupational journals he reads. Reading educational journals and talking over the school lunch table expose one to attitudes differing from those of the businessman. The individual who wishes to rate with his own occupational group must necessarily adopt certain common attitudes. As has been shown, one's success in a group correlates with his exemplification of the group values. Vocational tests are in part based upon this principle.

Thus stereotypes have been built up in the public mind. The lawyer is considered somewhat rigid and verbalistic. The industrial tycoon is depicted as aggressive and impatient of restraints, while the artist is expected to be temperamental. Whether these expectancies are fact or fiction, they are an important aspect of the cultural climate in which an individual and his family live. Thus through specific in-group pressures, and through the ready-made halos or horns commonly attributed to the members of the out-group, occupational patterning becomes a real force in the development of personality.

Regional Variations

The regional variations in community mores are very marked in the United States. One anthropologist describes New England as influenced by the Old World point of view, the South by an even greater veneration for the past, the Middle West by a third-generation emphasis upon conformity to what is believed to be the American way, and California by a zeal for newly manufactured solutions.[5]

As one drives across the continent, he can almost watch the customs change with the miles. As the West is reached, there's a rise in anti-Oriental sentiment. In parts of the South, this type of attitude is shown toward the Negro. On the Eastern seaboard the person who is making use of prevailing cultural attitudes to climb upward in the status hierarchy finds that detrimental remarks about South Europeans strike a responsive chord. A Westerner who thought Italian food a great delicacy found clerks in conservative Eastern shops bragging that only stores on the wrong side of the tracks carried Italian foodstuffs. These regional mores are reflected in the warmth or coolness made manifest toward certain movies or books echoing these sentiments. Contrasting attitudes toward coeducation are in general found in the South and West. Speakers

[5] Margaret Mead, *And Keep Your Powder Dry: An Anthropologist Looks at America,* p. 101, William Morrow & Company, Inc., New York, 1942.

have discovered that the same story can make friends in one region and enemies in another!

Folkways also show regional variations. Fraternity secretaries report many examples of regional differences within their own groups. In one section women are never allowed in the fraternity house without chaperons, while in another it is considered perfectly good taste for them to stay late without chaperonage. A dean of women described the embarrassment that lack of appreciation of this geographical difference caused her. Having transferred from an Eastern to a Western college, she made a rule requiring chaperons for all cars driving mixed groups to a distant game. Students and parents alike became incensed at this "absurdity," as they termed it. The dean then realized that she was unsuccessfully attempting to use a cultural pattern transplanted thousands of miles from its source.

If the regional culture has been protected by a rigid in-group attitude and is undiluted by that of other subgroups, its indoctrination may act as a serious handicap. Much of the difficulty that individuals experience socially in groups far from home is the result of such early conditioning. Some individuals are so dependent upon the props of one specific learned pattern that they feel ill at ease in other groups. This bothers them when they find themselves in a position to deal with people of other regional patterning. In large cities one may be confronted by a great variety of converging culture configurations. These pressures tip the scales in personal balance sufficiently to force some individuals to return to the comfort of those more rigid patterns which they have learned. Others escape into some type of bromide, be it cult, alcohol, or dream world.

Social Class Patterning

Membership in a social class is derived from social heredity, principally through the status of the individual's family. Social classes are more elastic in United States culture than in many others. There is vertical mobility by way of the paths of education, money, talent, skill, occupation, and marriage. Probably education is the route most often attempted. There are fewer distinctions in class culture patterns in some regions than in others. In certain communities the old family elite is socially dominant. This might be termed the "upper-upper." Below this in order of rank are the "lower-upper," which consists of society but not old families, and "upper-middle," leaders in civic affairs. These three strata constitute the segment of society above the so-called Common Man.[6] Below these rank the "lower-middle," "upper-lower," and "lower-lower." In some communities there are fewer clear distinctions of level. Students of these phenomena in American life believe that the divisions are not based entirely upon economic factors. The members must behave in ways which conform to the group's scheme of values. For the most part, qualifications in regard to friends, organizational contacts, hobbies, periodical reading, and political opinions are indigenous to the group. Some people choose the hobby of orchid growing because it is identified with the elite. The followers of radio commentators seem to be divided along social class lines. Soap operas slant their characters, plot, and values to the lower groupings.[7]

After studying the social-class influences on adolescents in a Middle Western town, researchers came up with some interesting differences in values. The so-called upper class placed more importance on the family's past history and esthetic interests. The middle class stressed responsibility to community. In contrast, the lower classes appeared to restrict loyalty and responsibility to family, neighbors, and friends.[8]

Many students of social patterning have pointed out the middle-class pressures on American children. These include a great emphasis on discipline, early control over bodily processes, and pressure to advance. Some authorities believe that the American middle-class child is surrounded by stiffer pressures to conform to rigid patterns than the youth of most other cultures.[9] In many ways there is much less appreciation of originality and flexibility than in the class on either side of the middle.

[6] W. Lloyd Warner, Marchia Meeker, and Kenneth Eells, *Social Class in America: A Manual of Procedure for the Measurement of Social Status*, pp. 13–32, Science Research Associates, Inc., Chicago, 1949.

[7] W. Lloyd Warner and William E. Henry, Radio daytime serial: a symbolic analysis, *Genet. Psychol. Monogr.*, 1948, 37:3–71.

[8] Robert J. Havighurst and Hilda Taba, *Adolescent Character and Personality*, p. 31, John Wiley & Sons, Inc., New York, 1949.

[9] W. Allison Davis and Robert J. Havighurst, *Father of the Man: How Your Child Gets His Personality*, pp. 76–85, Houghton Mifflin Company, Boston, 1947.

Membership in a social class more or less definitely endows individuals with the attributes by which that particular class is known. This affects personality styling by ensuring a certain amount of acceptance or rejection by those of other social classes. This ready-made attitude is illustrated by a study of children's ratings of individuals on the basis of looks, leadership, friendship, etc. The children in the upper and upper-middle classes were rated high by all others, while those of the lower classes were ranked low.[10] In this instance membership in a social class rather than inherent qualities appeared to be the yardstick. This halo effect of automatically attributing all good qualities has been noted often. It can work just as effectively in the other direction, with youngsters making fun of the clothes and manners of a child who may be conforming to a higher-class pattern. There is a sort of stereotyped evaluation based upon the rater's class values. This would certainly be a powerful factor in personality development. Many adolescents seem to be definitely conscious of this type of class stratification process. Some studies find that this identification is higher with girls than with boys of the same stratum.[11]

The antithesis of this showed itself in the isolated atomic research towns of World War II, in which for security reasons strict secrecy cloaked the names and all other identifying features of inhabitants. In an almost laboratory manner these towns exemplified the American ideal of social equality. Housing was uniform and work activities highly compartmentalized. The wife of a physician living at Los Alamos reports that she did not know whether her neighbor's husband was the leader of a scientific work team or was engaged in some menial service task. Only after the project's purpose and achievements were announced to the world did the individuals in this unique community begin to sift themselves out into a typical American hierarchy of social classes.

Culturally minded observers of these towns noted that personality insecurity soon manifested itself in people moving into these towns

[10] Bernice L. Neugarten, Social class and friendship among school children, *Amer. J. Sociol.*, 1946, 11:305–313.

[11] Richard Centers, Social class identifications of American youth, *J. Person.*, 1950, 18:290–302.

where social-class structure was pulled out from under human relationships. Many personalities whose structure had been largely
based upon social-class props found themselves completely on their
own for the first time in their lives. They had to develop new patterns of interrelationship which would fit the new classless culture.
There was no other path to popularity and status except that won
by the individual through his own competence.

There are forces which lessen the power of class distinctions.
Part of America's heritage is a denial of social class ideology in
speeches and writings. This is demonstrated in the emphasis on
individual responsibility for achievement. Also, among some groups
there is a tendency to avoid class identification. Individuals who
are interested in moving from one group to another are especially
apt to keep themselves aloof.

Regional pressures are more influential in certain areas. Membership in the upper-upper class in the Middle West, for instance,
would not necessarily give one a similar high rating among the
"proper Bostonians." Certainly these forces make for a fluidity not
found in many cultures.

APPLICATIONS OF CULTURAL UNDERSTANDING

As has been pointed out, culture colors one's preferences and
views. It is a way of life buttressed by custom and propriety. It
might be thought of as the prescription for life adjustment supplied
by the group. It would be as difficult to assign certain characteristics to cultural influences and others to biological or psychological
conditions as it would be to say which part diet and which rest
can play in physical well-being. These cultural patterns become
permanently incorporated into personality structure.

Results of Cultural Myopia

Exposure to a restricted way of life without experience with other
patterns may result in a sort of cultural myopia. This is doubly true
when one has a strong emotional need to be propped up by the
group. Cultural patterns are likely to seem changeless to those who
live them. Most individuals are not conscious of the elements of

their way of life, which they have incorporated into their value system and behavior syndrome without any critical evaluation. In most instances they do not realize where they acquired their standards but merely accept them as the proper design for living. Blind loyalty to these as the only correct way of life usually engenders a critical attitude toward different patterns, whether found in other individuals, other subgroups, or other nations. Rigid adherence to specific patterns hampers personal relationships with those who have grown up in other cultural climates.

This ethnocentrism may lead to repercussions in strife between groups such as capital and labor, AFL and CIO, or fraternity and nonfraternity students. In some cases those who have been rigidly indoctrinated in one subculture denounce those who hold other values as un-American, demanding that everyone adhere to their own particular pattern. Cultural boundary lines have been known to increase international tensions and frustrate attempts to bring about better relations between nations. Some authorities believe that they are the greatest stumbling blocks to peace.

The Price of Cultural Ignorance

A lack of appreciation of the significance of cultural patterning is evident on many fronts. Much stress and strain could be eliminated by a better insight into this phenomenon. The child entering school must cope with new culture patterns. Instances have been reported in which diverse ways of eating spaghetti have given nursery-school youngsters a feeling of inferiority. Married partners often are graduates of different schools of culture. A young woman coming from a family constellation in which men cooperate in all family activities may think her husband uncooperative when he is merely carrying over his group's indoctrination that it is "sissified" to do household tasks. The worker is likely to find that his coworkers have folkways and mores different from his own. The success of a new employee often depends upon his studying the group codes before he acts. In certain instances failures of college presidents have been to a great extent based upon their lack of appreciation of the mores and folkways of the college. Any newcomer to a region may be confronted with "foreign" ways. Everyone who travels abroad has the experience of being upset by what seem to him personality traits but should really be labeled as mores. Surely a realistic preparation for life should include expectations of meeting new culture patterns.

Even words take on different meanings in different culture patterns. A young American woman who had always been the life of the party in her home town, married an Englishman and settled in England, where she made a very conscientious attempt to continue her popularity. To her amazement her husband reported to her one day that the story was going around that she had insulted Mrs. X. at a tea. He realized that some cultural variant was at the root of this and asked her to reenact the whole afternoon's experience. "Oh, that's it," he exclaimed as she repeated that she had said, "No, thank you, I don't care for any more cake, Mrs. X." It seemed that in the particular mores of that group the word "care" implied that one wouldn't "touch it with a ten-foot pole."

At one time much of the United States treatment of Indians was based upon a lack of appreciation of the implications of cultural patterning. Despite the fact that the Indians' whole indoctrination into their way of life had been surrounded by ceremonials, the youths in certain schools were forbidden to continue their well-intrenched patterns of attending native rites.[12] As was to be expected, with their cultural props removed, they showed much anxiety. As soon as they could escape from the school they reverted to their old folkways and mores.

The missionaries who work in foreign countries within the framework of the native culture patterns are much more successful than those who try to implant new ones. Groups cannot have cultural patterns grafted onto them as can trees. Personalities are much more complex than trees.

Economists for the United Nations recently cautioned that new technological aid for economically backward countries must be adapted to the customs of the people involved.[13] People are so deeply rooted in their own cultural backgrounds that help offered in the wrong way appears like pressure or force.

[12] Dorothea Leighton and Clyde Kluckhohn, *Children of the People: The Navaho Individual and His Development*, pp. 64–68, Harvard University Press, Cambridge, Mass., 1947.

[13] *The New York Times*, May 5, 1951, p. 30C.

Cultural Insight and Maturity

These lines from Dr. Henry Stack Sullivan are appropriate: [14]

What anyone can discover by investigating his past is that the *patterns* of tensions and energy transformations which make up his living are to a truly astonishing extent matters of his education for living in a particular expected society. If he is clever, he can also notice inadequacies in his educators' expectations; he finds that he is not any too well-prepared for living in the groups in which he has come to be involved.

As one becomes aware of the cultural conditioning that he has received from the various groups and subgroups with which he has been associated, he is able to achieve a certain psychological separation from it. From this vantage point he can more realistically evaluate the strengths and weaknesses of his indoctrination. Detachment also removes some of the blinders which have kept him from understanding those trained in other cultural curriculums. He will not expect all his associates to have his own particular cultural patterns any more than he will expect them all to know physics, if this subject is his major. Furthermore he will be better equipped to strengthen those of his culture patterns which contain fewer tension-producing potentials and contribute more to personality growth.

Summary

An important area of the psychology of personality is that concerned with cultural phenomena. Individuals are in part shaped by the expectations of the groups to which they belong. From birth they are surrounded by culture carriers in the guise of parents, nurses, and teachers. Beyond the borders of their homes they are influenced by neighborhood customs. Each step of growth introduces new groups with specialized attitudes and behaviors. In order to rate in school, college, church, vocation, or nation, individuals must to some extent fit the pattern which expresses the particular group's common goals.

Culture patterns in the United States offer an extensive laboratory for study. Certain common emphases are on an almost national

[14] Henry Stack Sullivan, Tensions interpersonal and international: a psychiatrist's view, in Hadley Cantril (ed.), *Tensions That Cause Wars*, p. 83, University of Illinois Press, Urbana, Ill., 1950.

basis. However, there are many subcultural patterns which wield considerable influence. A few examples of these are ethnic, regional, occupational, social class, and organizational. Each of these has a hierarchical status system with certain more or less accepted paths to its goals. Sometimes those who are unable to fit into one group culturally transfer their interests to another. Success and failure are merely indications of place in the particular status system.

The effects of cultural myopia are widespread. Many personality difficulties are closely tied up with ignorance of cultural expectations and evaluations. Reflections of we-group, others-group attitudes are observed in many of the interpersonal and intergroup strivings so prevalent today. Individual personalities must be interpreted against the backdrop of the culture patterns by which they have been surrounded. Understanding of one's own personality entails an evaluation of the cultural environments in which he has grown.

QUESTIONS FOR DISCUSSION

1. Make a list of your college mores and folkways. Do you think any of them have changed in the last few years?
2. Give some examples of in-group versus out-group strife on your campus.
3. In what ways does the hierarchy rating system on your campus differ from that of your home community?
4. Give some examples of diverse culture patterns with which you have had experience.
5. List the various culture carriers which have been influential in your life.
6. List the ethnic culture patterns of your community.
7. Could you list the specific steps necessary to reach the most important goals of our culture?
8. Do you consider national origin or social class in choosing your friends? Why?
9. Do you believe that certain patterns of culture are right and others wrong?
10. Do you think that most people are trying to climb higher on some imaginary social ladder? Why?
11. Suggest ways and means which might increase understanding of the culture patterns of other nations.
12. Give some examples of differences in occupational subgroup patterns.
13. Give some examples of misunderstandings between friends which can be traced to differences in cultural indoctrination.
14. Do you believe that most people prefer to associate with those indoctrinated with the same cultural patterns as they themselves have been?

15. List some frustrations stemming from cultural patterns which might affect mental health.

ADDITIONAL READINGS

Bossard, James H. S.: *The Sociology of Child Development,* Chap. 6, Harper & Brothers, New York, 1948.

Burgess, Ernest W.: The family in a changing society, *Amer. J. Sociol.,* 1948, 53:417–425.

Folsom, Joseph K., Vance, Rupert, Cavan, Ruth Shonle, and Haynee, Norman S.: Regional family patterns, *Amer. J. Sociol.,* 1948, 53:423–434.

Goldschmidt, Walter: Social class in America: a critical review, *Amer. Anthrop.,* 1950, 52:483–498.

Gyr, John: Analysis of committee member behavior in four cultures, *Hum. Relat.,* 1951, 4:193–202.

Hartshorne, Edward Y.: Undergraduate society and the college culture, *Amer. Sociol. Rev.,* 1943, 8:321–332.

Hollingshead, August B.: *Elmtown's Youth: The Impact of Social Classes on Adolescents,* John Wiley & Sons, Inc., New York, 1949.

Kelly, Janet Agnes: *College Life and the Mores,* Columbia University Press, New York, 1949.

Kluckhohn, Clyde: *Mirror for Man: The Relation of Anthropology to Modern Life,* McGraw-Hill Book Company, Inc., New York, 1949.

Labarre, Weston: The cultural basis of emotions and gestures, *J. Person.,* 1947, 16:49–68.

McGuire, Carson: Family backgrounds and community patterns, *Marriage and Family Living,* 1951, 13:160–164.

Mead, Margaret: *And Keep Your Powder Dry: An Anthropologist Looks at America,* William Morrow & Company, Inc., New York, 1942.

———: The impact of culture on personality development in the United States today, *Understanding the Child,* 1951, 20:17–18.

Plant, James S.: *Personality and the Cultural Pattern,* Commonwealth Fund, Harvard University Press, Cambridge, Mass., 1937.

Report of a preparatory commission for the Fourth International Congress on Mental Health: Interaction between culture and mental health in industry in the U.S.A. and Canada, *Bull. World Fed. Ment. Health,* 1951, 3:233–237.

Wessel, Bessie, Campsi, Paul, and Jones, Robert: Ethnic family patterns, *Amer. J. Sociol.,* 1948, 53:435–452.

Young, Kimball: *Personality and Problems of Adjustment,* Chap. 7, George Routledge & Sons, Ltd., and Kegan Paul, Trench, Trubner & Co., Ltd., London, 1947.

Much of behavior serves the tissue needs of the body. Habits, ways of solving problems, deciding which problems are worth solving, and standards for everyday behavior derive from the social context. But in addition to these two determinants of behavior, or rather as an organization of these two, there is a third approach to the study of personality. Today, this third approach is of special importance to psychological research and to the psychological clinic. It is the study of *perception*, or perceptual processes in the individual.

Early Greek philosophers found much to think over in the evident differences between their own perceptions and those of the people around them. These very differences today claim the attention of research psychologists. Methods of investigation have changed greatly; objective techniques and factual materials have brought theories of perception out of the armchair and into the clinic and the laboratory. This area of research in psychology has become the gateway to the understanding of personality.

The present chapter will describe some of the more recent interpretations of perception, with emphasis on visual perception, because this aspect has the most research behind it. Other sensory processes are known to follow the same steps. The uniqueness of the individual's personality is expressed through his perceptual processes, and his purposes become more clearly evident from a study of these processes than from observation of his day-to-day behavior. Even his hidden motives become evident through a study of his perceptions, in part because he is bound to see his own motives in his own contemporary situation.

HOW PERCEPTION WORKS

Incomplete Figures

Macroscopic, or global, studies of perception carried on by a British psychologist, F. C. Bartlett, illustrate an approach to re-

FIG. 6–1. Some distortions in perception are measurable. It is difficult to believe that these two ladders are of equal height. Perception is influenced by judgments based upon past experience. (*Courtesy of the Franklin Institute Museum.*)

search in this important area of psychology. He asked university students to reproduce freely a picture vaguely resembling a man's face. In most cases the reproductions looked like a conventional drawing of a man's face. Even the printed titles became conventional.[1]

Bartlett also noted that when the university students were asked to reproduce their drawings from memory, successive reproductions

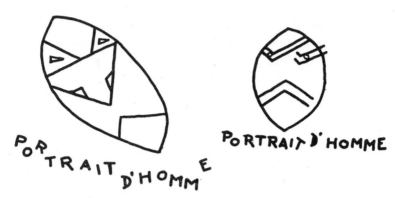

Fɪɢ. 6–2. Reproduction of drawings. Memories are not photographs but tend to be remembered as conventionalized forms.

became increasingly conventional. He observed, too, that incomplete figures were usually seen as completed. A common illustration of this is found in normal reading, but usually goes unnoticed: a person

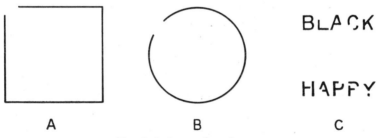

Fɪɢ. 6–3. Incomplete figures.

often reads errors by correcting them. The figures in Fig. 6–3 illustrate this phenomenon.

College students typically find no difficulty in naming A as a "square" even though aware that a square is defined as a closed figure having four equal sides or angles. *A* does not have four angles, nor four equal sides, nor is it a closed figure. Similarly, *B* is commonly identified as a "circle." The two words of *C* are not perfect, but, as with the geometric figures, they are correctly named "black" and "happy."

Almost as typical as the answers described above are certain student reactions which follow. When attention is directed to the fact that *A* is really not quite a square, students reply, "We knew that, but we felt we *had* to say it was in order to answer your question." Given misspelled words, badly printed signs, and even slightly misdirected highway markers, most people still get the correct word meanings, understand the signs, and travel the correct routes.

Ambiguous Figures

Certain types of figures have two or perhaps more different pictures within them. These are called "ambiguous" figures. There are many of these, some known as "traditional illusions" and a few known as "miracle pictures." An example of the latter is the "holy picture" in which, as you stare at the apparently closed eyes, they "open." *D* in Fig. 6–4 illustrates an ordinary ambiguous figure which has become a classroom tradition. Look at the figure in a normal manner and then name it. Most observers will consider it either a vase or a pedestal of vase-like form. Or, they will consider it a pair of faces in profile. Now look at the figure again, but focus your eyes upon it at a central point about the level of (*a*), then shift to the central point at about the level of (*b*). This shifting back and forth between these two points usually changes the figure from vase to faces and back again.

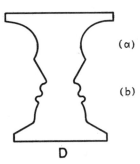

(*a*)

(*b*)

D

Fig. 6–4. Ambiguous figure.

Once in a while a student will be found for whom it is impossible to achieve this shifting even in meaningless ambiguous figures. When such inability is general, it is referred to as poor "lability" of perception, indicating presence to some extent of personality rigidity or limited adjustment powers. When this inability is present in relation to specific figures only, the indication is quite different. One student, for example, was quite unable to see the vase figure, although he had no trouble in seeing the faces. After considerable effort he managed to see the ambiguous figure as faces-pedestal. He was still unable to see the vase. A little free-association exploration made it clear that when he thought of a vase the next step in his habitual thought pattern was to the word "flowers." At the mention of this word he

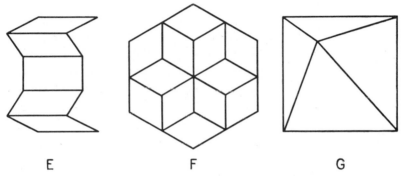

E   F   G

Fig. 6–5. Geometric ambiguous figures.

showed considerable tension, for he was acutely allergic to the pollen of most flowers and went to great care in his living to avoid them. There seemed to be a clear "avoidance reaction" in his behavior which made him perceptually avoid the vase figure!

The phenomenon of the ambiguous figure is mechanically explainable by the different points of focus. At which part of the figure is the perceiver looking? The presence of two pictures is obvious. If they are equally obvious, the shift is rapid and easy. They then are said to have equal "potency." As the eyes focus upon the figure, they tend to "wander" slightly. Eye wander is a phenomenon both useful and entertaining. Primarily it explores the visual environment in the same general way that a dog explores the neighborhood with his nose, stopping to investigate more fully those points which catch his interest. Eye wander also responds very readily to suggestion— a reaction which is important to classroom teaching as well as to every coed who emphasizes her good points and distracts from her defects by the application of cosmetics.

Eye wander thus serves many purposes besides playing a part in the perceptual phenomenon of ambiguous figures. The three geometric figures in Fig. 6–5 are all ambiguous, with about equal potency in their respective instances. Can you identify the focus points which shift the figures?

Perceptual Set

The phenomenon becomes especially interesting when another small experiment is attempted. Forcing the shift from the one ambiguity to the other, by shifting the point of focus as from (a) to (b) in Fig. 6–4, may be mechanically explainable. Nevertheless, in that experiment, why was it that the imaginative set seemed to result in the regular movement or fixation of the eyes? What has the thought or the imagination to do with the printed figure? Could it be that perception is not a *passive* reaction which, like an "electric eye," merely reacts? Or is it that in this form of perception the mechanics of the eye serves some other governing influence? These questions reach too deeply into the study of psychology to be answered in a few simple words, but the following experiment suggests their answers.

Look at D just long enough to focus the eyes on it in a general way. Then without moving the book or changing the eye focus, close the eyelids and imagine two young lovers sitting on a park bench with only their heads visible across the back of the bench. Open the eyes suddenly to D. Note the eye level as either at (a) or at (b). Usually students find that they were looking at the figure at (b) level. This phenomenon is not merely accidental, as may be demonstrated by varying the experiment. This time let your imagination picture a lovely bouquet of your favorite flowers. The eye level will now favor strongly the (a) level. Why do the eyes *pull* to the particular focal point, or bring out the particular picture when other pictures are equally present in the stimulus situation?

Some interesting answers can be given, but first it should be noted that this phenomenon is not merely a phenomenon of the laboratory. It is not a mere trick. One group of experimenters took a whole series of uncompleted figures mixed with ambiguous figures and applied them to students in statistical quantity. Suggesting one possible name for each sketch led the students to see the suggested object. If another possible name was given. that appropriate object would be seen in the sketch.[2]

A more recent experiment explored the opposite kind of evidence, namely, the individual's *failure to see* ambiguous situations as having more than one interpretation. Like the student mentioned earlier who could not see the "flowers" because of his habitual avoidance of them, resulting from his allergic reactions to pollens, the subjects in this experiment showed a remarkably consistent failure to see two sides to contradictory experiences. The experimenters concluded that such consistency evidences a basic perceptual process of "repression" or "inhibition" which goes on without the individual's being aware of it.[3] Each individual seems to have a relatively permanent "perceptual set" which in some very profound sense is involved in his personality.

Perception—An Active Process

The individual who, for example, cannot seem to see A as a square must have something in his personal or subjective make-up that makes him see it differently and also makes him unable to see it as a square. He may be a geometrician, so pedantic about geometric figures that he simply *has* to see this figure as "an open figure, with three angles and four parallel sides." The *subjective organization* originates in his own past experiences and familiarity and is *imposed upon* the *primitive* stimulus figure. The geometrician is unusually concerned with specific details and with the mathematical definitions. Most observers will settle for a quick naming of the figure as a "square" so that they may go about their other business.

This reaction of a person to his needs is so completely automatic that he is not aware that his needs enter in and will even deny that they do. Many recent studies of perception, using scientific tech-

[2] L. Carmichael, H. P. Hogan, and A. A. Walter, An experimental study of the effect of language on the reproduction of visually perceived form, *J. Exp. Psychol.*, 1932, 15:80.

[3] H. A. Witkin, The nature and importance of individual differences in perception, *J. Person.*, 1949, 18(2):145–170.

niques, bring out this relationship between perceptions and needs or interests. One experimenter presented a series of "good" tasks along with a series of "formless" tasks to a group of subjects. The good tasks were structured, *i.e.*, the subjects could see an organization in them which made them into unified, complete wholes. The formless tasks were repetitions of small items, over and over again. The subjects were carefully observed for tendencies to return either in actions or in memories to the particular tasks at which they were working when the experimenter interrupted them.

Eighty-two per cent of the returns were to the good tasks, and only 18 per cent to the formless tasks.[4] Clearly, these results indicate that, in general, action arises from a need to see or perceive a completed whole. The subject may not know why his mind keeps returning to some topic or task. All he knows is that he wants to get back at it. Our being exposed to a picture hung askew on a wall leads us to straighten it, just as hearing but one shoe dropped in the room above catches our attention and makes us wait to hear the other shoe. These compulsions of attention are as real as are the individual's needs for the tissue satisfactions provided by food, sex, and rest.[5]

That the perceptual needs express themselves without benefit of the individual's deliberations or consciousness is attested by experiments with the tachistoscope, a slide projector with an attached shutter which controls the length of time of each exposure. Subjects are shown a list including both ordinary words and words that commonly arouse strong reactions of fear, guilt, or prejudice. If the exposure time for each word is reduced to the very minimum needed for recognition, the common, or ordinary, words take longer than do the uncommon. If exposure time is reduced below the amount needed for recognition of the uncommon words, the subject will still give evidence measurable by a polygraph. He exhibits emotional reactions to the words evoking fear, guilt, or prejudice.[6] Such words seem to stimulate the individual to defend himself. He perceives

[4] Jane W. Torrey, Task completion as a function of organizational factors, *J. Person.*, 1949, 18(2):192–205.

[5] David Krech, Notes toward a psychological theory, *J. Person.*, 1949, 18(1):83.

[6] Robert A. McCleary and Richard S. Lazarus, Autonomic discrimination without awareness: an interim report, *J. Person.*, 1949, 18(2):171–179.

these words at high speed because through them he anticipates a need to defend himself. He fails to perceive the ordinary words at such high speeds because they have no special significance for him. This perceptual reaction is referred to as "subception" because it is usually unconscious. He perceives actively, not just passively, according to his organized needs.

Objects versus Fantasy

Organizations of perception are familiar to most students in the following three ways:

1. *Habits:* Objects, situations, and people are perceived as being cues for habitual actions whenever special caution is not exercised. Resemblances are "spread," or generalized upon, to include much more than can be proved to be similarity; things change but continue to serve as cues or stimuli for old or habitual actions. Symbols become cues for habitual actions and feelings which get "read into" unsuitable situations.
2. *Needs:* Food-hungry organisms see and investigate every stimulus situation as possibly productive of food, while well-fed organisms fail to notice foods. Lovelorn swains see each new acquaintance as a possible partner in romance. Three bridge players see any unoccupied person as a possible "fourth." Desperately thirsty prospectors on the desert see mirages of cool spring waters, while hot and baked desert travelers see mirages of sky-blue lakes and shady pools.
3. *Interests:* Needs and interests are very closely related, being distinguishable chiefly on the basis that needs are less flexible, more limited in possibilities of satiation. Alert scientists see everything as potentially related to their current research projects; artists see situations in their "art angles." Nature-loving hikers see a campfire as a desirable experience, but the forest ranger sees this fire as the potential start of a catastrophic forest fire.

Incomplete or slightly incorrect figures will be *filled in* automatically as the perceiver brings to the stimulus object or situation his own subjective organizations. He literally forces the object or situation into his own habits, needs, and interests. Some objects and situations will not stand much forcing; others are very amenable to forcing or interpreting. These two extremes can be fitted onto a scale as follows:

Objects ←———————————————————→ Fantasy

| Primitive organizations ("insistent" or relatively unamenable to "forcing") | Subjective organizations (can be changed "at will" but not ignored completely) |

H

The left end of the scale might be called "primitive," while the right end might be called "subjective." Fantasy will be at the extreme right end of the scale. Most perceptions will range centrally.

Frequently experience draws from both ends of the scale, fitting the primitive and subjective organizations together harmoniously. The perceiver feels in this event that he knows what he is doing, that his actions are right and readily verifiable. He can say to himself, "Anyone can see that this is so-and-so." He then *anchors* upon the particular organization at which his perception has arrived.[7] Thereafter he will find difficulty in perceiving this stimulus object or situation in any other way.

"First impressions" of people are hard to correct even though all later experience with these people is in contradiction to those impressions. First impressions of activities such as playing a musical instrument or swimming are inclined to remain with a person for a very long time. This is one reason why a small child's experiences are so important to his later growth.

Perception and Motivation

The tachistoscopic experiments noted above suggest that before the stimulus object has been "seen" it has been evaluated as to its potential effect upon the observer. It is not uncommon to hear people say, "I don't know why, but I feel worried." Often this feeling is traceable to the kind of prerecognition experience that the tachistoscope reveals. Perceptual set precedes the appearance of the stimulus in many cases. But the stimulus produces a change in this perceptual set which takes place before the stimulus object is "seen." Postman, Bruner, and McGinnies have suggested that this early stage of perception includes a *selective sensitization* to positive needs of the individual, a *perceptual defense* against threats to the

[7] Gardner Murphy, *Personality: A Biosocial Approach to Origins and Structure*, p. 346, Harper & Brothers, New York, 1947.

individual, and a *value resonance* in which satisfactions to the individual are accentuated in his perceptions.[8]

This early stage in the individual's perceptions corresponds to the interpretation of motivation in Chapter 3. In the complete act the early stage is what is normally considered the cause or the motive.

"I'll bet the paint alone cost $20—not to mention what he was getting paid by the hour"

Fig. 6–6. Perceptual evaluations grow out of personal experiences. (*Courtesy of The American Magazine.*)

The term "subception," as used above, brings out the fact that the motives are noted in the earliest stages of the complete act.

Perceptual defenses are evident also in the failure of the perceiver to notice or even to react to certain stimuli which are known to register in his sense organs. When the perceiver's expectations are violated by his environment, he must resist by failing to see, or by distorting what he sees, or by changing his own plan of action. Usu-

[8] Leo Postman, Jerome Bruner, and Elliot McGinnies, Personal values as selective factors in perception, *J. Abnorm. Soc. Psychol.*, 1948, 43:142–154.

ally the perceiver must make a compromise between what he wants to see and what he wants to avoid seeing. His motives must adapt to what his environment will permit. This compromise is present in his perception of his environment.

Sometimes it is forgotten that perception continues on into the response, or reaction, to the stimulus. A brief introspection will suggest that as the individual takes note of his progress in realizing his plans, he enjoys a feeling of achievement which resonates through his entire personality. On the other hand, a feeling of failure tends equally to pervade him. Values are merely the goals which a person seeks over a long period of time. Hence his value resonance is expressive of his motives over this long time.

HOW THE STUDY OF PERCEPTION IS USED

Projection

Studies of sensation, including the structure of the sense receptors and the neurons attached to them, serve to define some of the limits and tendencies of the individual's behavior. Color-blind people do not become naval officers. Anosmic persons do not become coffee tasters or perfume chemists. These limits and tendencies are like all other anatomical factors in behavior, for the individual's modification of the physical world is carried on through his bodily mechanisms. Similarly, the sociocultural molding process is carried on through relations between people. *Perception is the dynamic organizing process within behavior, uniting organism with environment in meaningful relationships.*

Gap filling, figure completing, error correcting, figure-ground organizations, and a host of other perceptual phenomena can be lumped together under the single term "projection." Perception includes much more than projection, but in all perception there will be some projection. In the earlier example of the geometric figures the fourth corner of A is *projected* onto the incomplete figure so that it actually appears to the observer as if it were a *real* part of the "square." Proofreaders see misprinted words as correct whenever they let themselves respond to the meanings of the words, *i.e.,* to the printed words as meaningful figures.

Projections as Need Indicators

But projection does not stop at simple gap filling. Details which are projected onto the stimulus in its primitive organization are drawn from the subjective organizations which represent the individual's habits, needs, and interests. The individual who persistently perceives campfires as enjoyable, regardless of the fire hazard created by a particular fire, forces perceptual relationships to take on the pattern most satisfying to his own needs or requirements. This is positive projection as much as is gap filling. The ancient precept "There are none so blind as those who will not see," is folklore recognition of this "selective," or inhibiting, phase of perceiving. Such selection is partly by means of the attention being attracted to some things but not to others, and partly by defensive structuring. Sometimes the individual's needs prejudice his perceptions to such a large extent that he "cannot afford to see" certain things.

In its more positive aspects, the selective phase of perceiving is a simple and direct illustration of the fact that all behavior is motivated, is drive-satisfying. Perception, like all other forms of behavior, must provide satisfaction of motives and drives. "The molding of perception . . . in the drive-satisfying direction follows directly from the satisfying or frustrating quality of past perception; one learns to *behave* this way or that because such behavior is satisfying. All cognitive processes are apparently continually shaped in greater or lesser degree by the pressure of wants." [9]

Problems which seem confusing and insoluble at one moment will suddenly *restructure* relationships, and the solution becomes obvious. This *insight* experience is, of course, a form of learning. It results from the *changed perspective* brought about by shift in the needs or interests of the perceiver. The situation remains much the same, but the individual's perception of it takes on a different organization, reflecting his changing needs. As hunger, thirst, boredom, love, pity, or hate become dominant in the individual's state of being, his perceptions restructure around this dominant need or interest. Three young graduate students, accustomed to preparing their own meals, were charged with cooking, dishwashing, and shopping, in rotation. Whenever class schedules required that the stu-

[9] Murphy, *op. cit.*, p. 365.

dent charged with shopping do his purchasing (which implied menu planning) *after* mealtime, it was common experience for him to feel absolutely barren of ideas for the next meal. But if he shopped *before* mealtime, while he was hungry, he would see endless possibilities in every store window. He would see his needs in the showcases! His menu problems would solve themselves.

Even breadth or narrowness of perspective will be determined by present state of being. Moments of rich or broad experience set the stage for later moments of similarly rich and broad experience. In reverse, narrow experiences set the stage for further narrow experiences. People who have had broad experiences such as travel, cosmopolitan living, nature study, and the like, actually perceive more broadly.

Development of Projective Tests

Because the quantity, quality, and specific content of perception involve so much the projection of the personality of the perceiver, there has developed a testing technique based upon this phenomenon. Such testing is called "projective"; it provides a major nucleus in the study of the psychology of personality. Clinical psychology would be a very different form of activity without projective testing.

The history of projective testing began in 1879, when Francis Galton performed the first formal experiments with free association. He was his own subject, reading the stimulus word to himself and then recording his first thought in reaction to it. His findings were prophetic, for he observed that "associations which recurred several times, over a four month period, could be traced largely to his boyhood and youth, and associations which occurred only once stemmed from more recent experience. The diagnostic power of this method did not escape Galton." [10] He noted that his own experiment was too limited for scientific evidence. But he concluded that records of free associations "lay bare the foundations of man's thoughts with more vividness and truth than he would probably care to publish. . . ." [11]

[10] Silvan S. Tomkins, *The Thematic Apperception Test: The Theory and Technique of Interpretation,* p. 1, Grune and Stratton, Inc., New York, 1947.
[11] *Ibid.*

Following Galton's lead, but not until 1907 and 1908, researches were reported by two school psychologists. Brittain studied imagination by means of nine pictures, concluding that some fundamental relationships existed between physical activity, affective life, and imaginal activity.[12] Libby investigated similarly the feelings as well as the imaginations of school children, noting some of the characteristics of the adolescent's subjective behavior.[13] By 1932, particularly in the progressive schools, children were commonly encouraged to project their feelings through creative art, music, or literary means. At the college level, students also projected their needs creatively into "planned economies" and "planned cities" and plans for houses in the modern world of technology. John Dewey's use of the "project" as the basis for the curriculum was not without understood connections between the projection of perceptual patterns and the projection of personality into purposeful achievement as the major form of learning. *Readiness* for a particular learning experience was known to consist in possession of proper experiential background to structure perception of the problem to be solved.

Projective Tests in Therapy

In the therapy tradition, there were many uses of projection applied to the patient, some of them closely approximating the projective test. In 1925 a psychiatrist at the Clinic for Juvenile Research in Detroit developed and used the Social Situation Picture Test. It was less a test, in the technical sense of this word, than a rough tool which helped shorten the interview period for each new registrant at the clinic. Eight pictures represented situations commonly encountered by typical delinquents. The technique of using the pictures was little more than to ask the subject to imagine himself in the situation portrayed. As he talked he would "tip off" the therapist as to his own reactions and behavior tendencies. These tips could be followed up in the usual psychiatric conference.[14] This instrument was never standardized or subjected to carefully controlled experi-

[12] Horace L. Brittain, A study of imagination, *Ped. Sem.*, 1907, 14(2):137–207. For this and the following reference, credit is due to Tomkins, *op. cit.*

[13] Walter Libby, The imagination of adolescents, *Amer. J. Psychol.*, 1908, 19:249–252.

[14] Louis A. Schwartz, Social-situation pictures in the psychiatric interview, *Amer. J. Orthopsychiat.*, 1932, 2:124–133.

mental verification. However, it made use of a technique which has become very popular with psychotherapists. Some of its forms are asking the patient to complete unfinished stories, to answer questions as if still an infant, to interpret cloudlike formations and ink blots, and to act out dramatically some of his own and related roles on an ad-lib basis.

The TAT

Educational psychologists favoring the "wholistic," or global, psychologies took as their central theme the "creative experience of the whole child." This emphasis led directly to several theories of personality which recognized the "creative experience" as centrally perceptual and projective. The general trend of interest in psychology's largest field of application, education, doubtless had much to do with the rapid development of projective studies of personality, commonly called "depth psychology." The need was for an easily administered and yet valid instrument which could X-ray the personality, uncover the deeply hidden but powerful forces at work within the individual. Such an instrument appeared in preliminary form in 1935 as the Thematic Apperception Test, devised by Morgan and Murray. This test was literally a set of ambiguous picture situations, like *D*, the vase-faces picture. Scenes portrayed in the TAT, as this test has come to be called, typically arouse more than one figure or meaning. Part of their ambiguity derives from the fact that they are printed slightly out of focus, thus leaving much detail to be filled in by the testee. Additional ambiguity is achieved by careful choice of subject matter, usually representing an activity which could move toward several possible endings from the scene pictured.

Morgan and Murray maintained that their test "was based on the well-known fact that an individual confronted with an ambiguous social situation and required to interpret it was likely to reveal his own personality in this process. While interpreting the objective situation the individual was apt to be less defensive, less aware of the scrutiny of the examiner, and consequently more likely to reveal much of his own inner life." [15] Success of this test in psychodiagnos-

---

[15] Tomkins, *op. cit.*, p. 3.

tic work has taken it out of the experimental class; its general applicability has been well demonstrated.[16]

Projective techniques have developed to include many other approaches besides the picture series, since it has been recognized that

FIG. 6–7. A card from the Thematic Apperception Test. (*Reprinted by permission of the publishers from Henry A. Murray, Thematic Apperception Test, Cambridge, Mass.: Harvard University Press, copyright 1943 by the President and Fellows of Harvard College.*)

projection is an ever-present part of perception and that *the perceptual pattern is a direct expression of personality pattern.* Some

[16] Tomkins, *op. cit.,* pp. 3–4, reports that the "TAT was employed in the study of a wide variety of psychopathological syndromes: hysteria, anxiety hysteria, and obsessive-compulsive neurosis, schizophrenic psychosis, head injury, psychopathic delinquency, stuttering, and mental deficiency."

of these other techniques include the Gestalt Completion Test, the Rorschach ink-blot test, psychodrama and sociodrama, finger painting, clay modeling, and cartoon completions. The simplest to describe, although not the simplest to learn to use, is the TAT.

Two Illustrations

The TAT is composed of thirty cards—twenty-nine pictures and one "blank" card. The following stories were written by a college student as a part of a classroom demonstration intended only to illustrate the phenomenon of perceptual projection as a subtle but accurate revelation of personality. Only four picture cards were used, and these not in official testing sequence. Watch for similarities between the stories.

Card 13B, a small boy sitting on a cabin doorstep: Dale is sitting on the doorstep of his home in Oklahoma. It is an old, weather-beaten clapboard house with only one room. He went fishing today, with four of his pals. He only caught one fish, but it was a nice one and he felt very proud when he showed it to his mother. Dale is now sitting in the doorstep thinking of the fun he had fishing and enjoying the savory odors of his fish being fried for his supper. It will be a wonderful supper!

Card 4, a young man pulling slightly away from a young woman: Bob and Jane have returned home from an evening of entertainment together. They have been married about six months and this was a celebration. They had an especially good dinner at a restaurant that they used to like and were pleased with their whole evening. Bob wants to re-enlist in the army, because of his belief that war is coming. Jane is now pleading with him to wait, at least not to spoil their lovely evening with such unpleasant thoughts.

Card 8GF, a lady sitting with chin in hand, staring into space: Mrs. Riley has been working hard all day scrubbing the stairs and hallways in the tenement in which she lives. Her husband works regularly, but doesn't earn much money. So she pays their rent by scrubbing. She is thinking now of what to get for their supper that will make a good meal without costing too much. Her thoughts are interrupted by the sound of the front door closing and she says "Oh, I must hurry" and she jumps to get busy.

Card 9BM, several men in rough clothes, sleeping on the ground: These men are sleeping after their lunch for a few minutes. Soon their boss will blow his whistle and they will all return to their work. They are building an electric power line, way out of town, or maybe this is a track-working gang.

Each card serves to bring out a different facet of the testee's perceptual patterns; thus these four stories cannot serve in lieu of the entire test.

Several scoring techniques are applicable to the TAT, and all bring out surprising quantities of information which the testee is unaware of having revealed. The important point is not how subtle the test may be but how adequate it is. The four stories quoted indicate the way the test works. In these four stories there is a single *thema* running throughout: *food.* The writer seemed to see food-taking in every picture, although no picture showed any food objects or food-taking activities. Moreover, food is always appetizing, satisfying in more ways than mere nourishment. At this point it will not be surprising to learn that the young man who authored these stories was at that time forty pounds overweight, even though his parents had spent considerable money on medical treatments and diets to reduce his weight and relieve his high blood pressure. Further exploration into his perception of himself and his world (by means of more formal TAT applications) brought to light the fact that his growth had not carried him beyond some fundamentally infantile attitudes. His stories reveal this to some extent through their emphasis upon food-interest projections. But his attitudes toward his parents were infantile, too. His overeating was literally "compulsive behavior" evidencing mild personal maladjustment which should respond favorably to psychotherapy.

Another set of four stories illustrates projection in a somewhat different personality. The first three cards are the same as those used above, but the fourth is different.

Card 13B, a small boy sitting on a cabin doorstep: The picture shown is of a little boy who has been severely reproved for having done something considered by his parents to be disgraceful and he is sitting down covering his mouth with his hands to help control his grief. He had been caught pulling a girl's dress up and was given stern punishment. However, he sits here more grief-stricken by the actions of his parents than by the beating he received, as he does not understand why he was punished.

Card 4, a young man pulling slightly away from a young woman: The haunted expression in the man's eyes portrays some great grief or sorrow caused by a crime which the man committed. In retrospection the scene turns back to the home of the man's mother, who is pleading with her son to desist from his idea, for it involved premeditated murder. However, all her entreaties were in vain, for the man committed the murder, the shock of which killed the aged, infirm mother. He is shown being comforted by his sister, who, although she doesn't like what he did, is trying to comfort him in his hour of greatest tragedy.

Card 8GF, a lady sitting with chin in hand, staring into space: The woman is projecting herself back in her mind to the grim tragic past, when, through an oversight on her part, she caused the death of her only child. It had all come about one afternoon, when having brought her child with her downtown, to do some shopping, she met with an old acquaintance outside the main entrance of the store, near a busy intersection. She became so engrossed in conversation with her friend that she forgot all about her child, who meanwhile had strayed away from her and was pushed by the crowd into the path of a car. Hearing the shouts of the excited crowd, she glanced up and saw her little boy struck down. Here she is shown recollecting the past and again envisaging the horrible accident.

Card 15, a gaunt human figure, palms together, pointing downward, standing in a cemetery: The man stands before a tombstone and wrings his hands in grief, because it is the fresh grave of his own son, who, having been driven mentally ill by the great musical goal his father set for him, committed suicide. His father now stands there, almost overcome with grief at the death of his son, and failure of accomplishing the irrational goal he had set for his son. He had been living a new life in this goal towards which his son was progressing. It had been denied himself while a young man, so he was living again through his son.

The obvious *thema* appearing throughout these four stories is a very tense relationship between the boy (the student) and his parents. He has been clear in describing the early stage of his relationship as at that time beyond his understanding and in indicating that he was being pressured by his parents in an extreme manner. Later this vague, incomprehensible feeling of being pressured takes the form of being in a hopeless situation. The final story reveals the hostility or hatred he feels toward his father, who has merely used him to satisfy his own selfish dreams. These vague feelings of hatred—it could have been love had the parent-child relationships been different—are so deeply buried in this young man's personality that he vigorously denied the revelations of his stories.

Much as Francis Galton had anticipated, the young man was not anxious to expose to the public the inner life bared by the TAT. He felt his effort to hide the disrespectful father hatred deeply within himself had failed. His scheme of values exposes itself through his perceptions in this way.

Other Projective Testing Devices

The TAT draws upon visual perceptions as it reveals the foundations of the testee's thoughts and feelings. Other sensory media have also been studied, *e.g.*, in the tautophone, a sound record of partially heard conversations. The listener fills in gaps and thus structures the incompleted conversations or sounds. The same selective sensitization was found in connection with auditory perceptions studied experimentally as with the selective sensitization to visual perceptions.[17] Parallel studies of felt body temperature would be interesting in this same connection, as would studies of body tension and tension release.

The personality reveals itself through all forms of the perceptual process to be an active and dynamic process of unifying experience into itself. It is difficult to say whether this unifying is performed in the perceptual process itself, or if there is some other. At any rate, through the study of the individual's perceptions it is possible to learn of his inner personality organization. It is this use of the projective test which in recent years psychology has found so dramatically useful.

QUESTIONS FOR DISCUSSION

1. Can you offer an explanation for the fact that errors occur even when printed material has been proofread by several experts?

[17] James M. Vanderplas and Robert R. Blake, Selective sensitization in auditory perception, *J. Person.*, 1949, 18(2):252–266.

2. Give an example from your experience illustrating how a perceptual set affects one's evaluation of a situation.
3. How might perceptual set be related to the importance of publicity for a public speaker?
4. On the basis of this discussion, explain Margaret Mead's statement in *The American Dream* that Americans abroad often say that there are no slums in the United States.
5. What help does this chapter give in explaining the saying "Love is blind"?
6. In the light of this chapter, explain why some individuals notice a difference in attitudes toward them after changing their names.
7. What might be behind the strong dislike of some individuals for modern architecture?
8. A study of causes of unemployment based upon interviews showed certain causes clustering in the cases reported by certain interviewers. How might this be explained?
9. If two people give entirely different reports of the same incident, is one necessarily lying?
10. Explain of what use projective tests might be in industry. In marriage counseling.
11. Would it be possible to "cheat" in a projective test? Why?
12. Explain the connection between perception and habits.
13. Explain the relation of the perceptual pattern to the personality pattern.
14. What handicaps might interfere with perception? Explain.
15. Might a "visitor from Mars" have difficulty in interpreting the expressions on the faces of actors in our movies? Explain.

ADDITIONAL READINGS

Aleck, Adolph W.: Perception, Chap. 18, in Charles E. Skinner (ed.), *Readings in Psychology,* Farrar & Rinehart, Inc., New York, 1935.

Anderson, Harold H., and Anderson, Gladys L. (eds.): *An Introduction to Projective Techniques,* Prentice-Hall, Inc., New York, 1951.

Asch, S. E., Block, Helen, and Hertzmen, M.: Studies in the principles of judgements and attitudes, I: Two basic principles of judgement, *J. Psychol.,* 1938, 5:219–251.

Beaumont, Henry, and Macomber, Freeman J.: *Psychological Factors in Education,* Chap. 6, McGraw-Hill Book Company, Inc., New York, 1951.

Blake, Robert R., and Ramsey, Glenn V. (eds.): *Perception: An Approach to Personality,* The Ronald Press Company, New York, 1951.

Bruner, Jerome S., and Krech, David (eds.): *Perception and Personality: A Symposium,* pp. 66–87, Duke University Press, Durham, N.C., 1950.

Cantril, Hadley: *The Why of Man's Experience,* The Macmillan Company, New York, 1950.

Combs, A. W.: The use of personal experience in Thematic Apperception Test story plots, *J. Clin. Psychol.*, 1946, 2:357–363.

Frank, Lawrence K.: *Projective Methods*, Chaps. 1, 4, Charles C Thomas, Publisher, Springfield, Ill., 1948.

Haggard, Ernest A.: A projective technique using comic strip characters, *Character & Pers.*, 1942, 10:289–295.

Hallowell, A. I.: Cultural factors in the structuralization of perception, Chap. 7, in John H. Rohrer and Muzafer Sherif (eds.), *Social Psychology at the Crossroads*, Harper & Brothers, New York, 1951.

Hastorf, A. H., and Knutson, A. L.: Motivation, perception and attitude change, *Psychol. Rev.*, 1949, 56:88–94.

Kelley, Harold H.: The warm-cold variable in first impressions of persons, *J. Person.*, 1950, 18:431–439.

Krech, David, and Crutchfield, Richard S.: *Theory and Problems of Social Psychology*, Chap. 3, McGraw-Hill Book Company, Inc., New York, 1948.

Pepitone, Albert: Motivational effects in social perception, *Hum. Relat.*, 1950, 3:57–76.

Postman, Leo, and Solomon, Richard L.: Perceptual sensitivity to completed and incompleted tasks, *J. Person.*, 1950, 18:347–357.

Snygg, Donald: Maze-learning as perception, *J. Genet. Psychol.*, 1936, 49:231–239.

Weingarten, Erica M., A study of selective perception in clinical judgement, *J. Person.*, 1949, 17:369–406.

Part Three PERSONALITY AND GROWTH

Part Two described the fundamentals which might be thought of as the raw materials from which personalities develop. Motivations constantly push from within. Physical processes and cultural patterns continually affect thoughts, feelings, and behavior. Perception merges these influences into an individual conception of others and of situations.

Part Three sketches how these materials are used in the architecture of personality. It interprets the development of the self-concept through the stages of life. It explains the part which learning plays in the structuring of personality. It will suggest the wide range in possibilities of healthy and unhealthy adjustments and evaluate the various potentials for removing imperfections in this growth of personality.

Anticipating future actions of other people is not only interesting, it is critically important. Earliest history tells of difficulties men faced when they tried to anticipate what might be forthcoming from rulers and from enemies. Large portions of the major works of religious literature devote themselves to the task of putting specific acts and personalities into the perspective of understanding. These problems are still among the greatest problems of mankind. They are the same difficulties that psychologists face, both in themselves and in their subjects, as they attempt to predict specific behavior and to make past behavior understandable. Man's greatest puzzle is indeed his own personality.

THE STUDY OF PERSONALITY

Background

Analysis of behavior has been a concern of psychologists for the past century. The study of conditioned or innate reflexes contributed greatly to man's knowledge of his own habitual ways of living. But the attempt to put these reflexes back together again has been as futile as the effort to reconstruct Humpty Dumpty. As one writer put it in 1928, psychology has been "explanatory" in its listing of sequences of acts; there must also be developed an "understanding psychology" which will help in dealing with values and attitudes.[1]

Two general sources of information have been very helpful to the growth of the scientific study of personality. First, a large body of evidence has been collected and some very important concepts have been developed in therapeutic work. Psychiatry, the treatment of

---

[1] Wilhelm Dilthey, quoted in Robert S. Woodworth, *Contemporary Schools of Psychology*, rev. ed., p. 250, The Ronald Press Company, New York, 1948.

psychic disorders, has contributed its experience. The new clinical psychology has offered highly important evidence and concepts. Second, personality has been subjected to research by statistical and laboratory methods using projective techniques.[2] Through their common interest in personality, therapeutic and scientific researchers find a basis for cooperation and agreement.

There has developed a general recognition that the study of personality is concerned with *behavior in its totality*. Psychologists therefore put studies of the individual-as-a-whole under the heading of "personality," treating it as primarily unified.[3] These studies delve into the individual's behavior to find the ways in which his many and various acts are linked together. The *linkages*, as distinguished from the specific acts themselves, are the subject matter of personality studies.

Behavior has an underlying pattern, as is well known to every thinking being. On many occasions a student expresses himself in recitation in one way, only to feel an instant later that that was not what he meant to say, not what really represented his belief. Sometimes the situation is reversed, as is suggested by remarks like, "Jim is not really like that." Specific acts, taken by themselves, do not reveal the true personality. One incident from a story will seldom disclose the underlying plot. Personality exposes itself only through a series of *related* incidents or acts, much as the plot of a story reveals itself as various related incidents unfold.

People normally are aware of the fact that they formulate purposes, are aware of their feelings, and even at times experience self-consciousness. Traditionally these forms of experience have been grouped together under the heading of "mental phenomena." At times, too, the word "mental" has been used so narrowly that it could have no importance and its user felt obliged to apologize.

But in his day-to-day life the individual commonly attaches high importance to his mental experiences. They must be dealt with, then, by any treatment of the science of personality. For it is the goal of this science to give understanding to *all* experiences as they relate

[2] Gordon W. Allport, *Personality, a Psychological Interpretation*, Henry Holt and Company, Inc., New York, 1937; Kurt Lewin, *Principles of Topological Psychology*, McGraw-Hill Book Company, Inc., New York, 1936.

[3] Woodworth, *op. cit.*, pp. 251–252.

to the unified behavior of the individual, Just as contemporary physics has had to give new and more exact form or definition to the ancient concept of atom, so the scientific approach to personality must give more specific form to the ancient concept of "persona." Personality once was merely the name for the dramatic type or role indicated by the mask worn by players in the Greek theater. The scientific study of personality must be more inclusive.

Every science is in part pragmatic. One proof of adequacy for the new concept of personality will be its ability to produce results when applied to such important tasks as guiding learning, personal counseling, facilitating group leadership, and carrying on psychotherapy.

The Constancy of Personality

The inner dynamics of the individual can be discovered by the familiar scientific method of *hypothesis and verification*. The basic information from which these hypotheses are drawn is already familiar, being known by such common and synonymous terms as "character," "long-term viewpoint," "style of life," "temperament," "pattern for living." Each of these terms indicates a quality of constancy or stability, something about the individual which can be summarized and predicted. To have a personality, if this means anything at all, means substantially that it is the same from day to day and even from year to year.

Habits have the same constancy, or stability, as do other phases of personality. They may be depended upon to repeat themselves. For the past three quarters of a century it has been commonplace to explain habit behavior on the basis of combined neural arcs which unite sense organs with effectors such as muscles or glands. These anatomical interpretations of habit certainly emphasize constancy. In addition to constancy of habit, there is also constancy in the physiological reactions to the world at large that take the form of adaptations in the functional systems, *e.g.*, abnormal breathing and digestive patterns.

A broader constancy than the physiological and habitual may also be observed directly in human behavior. This is evident in perceptual behavior of laboratory subjects presented with partially audible sounds. As has been pointed out, these controlled sounds will be

heard differently by subjects according to the different value interest or emphasis of each.[4] Thus Grandpa Smith, when asked to pay
one of his many small debts, would reply, "What was that you said?
I don't hear very well." But if someone offered him in the same
tone of voice a repayment of $3 when the exact amount due him
was $3.10, he would hear correctly the first time! Hearing sensi-
tivity, like sensitivity of other types, seems to be improved when
aligned with the individual's value interests.

The stability of habit patterns is probably due less to the physiology of neural pathways than to the stability of an individual's
scheme of values.[5] Values—actually value interests—are learned.
They range from momentary techniques exercised to satisfy tissue
needs to long-term and lifetime goals or ways of living. An individual's behavior organizes itself almost entirely around the values
which he has learned or accepted even though he has thought little
about them. Values are organizing factors within the personality
and within perceptions.[6]

Illustration of Constancy

The following case illustrates how the scheme of values can be
seen to be more fundamental to the stability of behavior than is the
neural pathway.

Tommy, aged six, was a persistent bed-wetter. He had been described by several people as "lazy" and by others as having inherited
a "weak bladder." Some thought the trouble was that he drank
too much water after supper. The psychological consultant to whom
he was taken because of his inability to get along with the other
children in school found that his bed-wetting fitted in with other
aspects of his behavior and with certain environmental factors.
Tommy's father was constantly teasing him, carrying on a subtle
persecution. Only on rare, usually public, occasions did the father
display affection toward him. The bed-wetting was Tommy's equally
subtle assertion of his own independence. It was also an under-cover

[4] James M. Vanderplas and Robert R. Blake, Selective sensitization in auditory
perception, *J. Person.*, 1949, 18(2):252–266.

[5] Cf. E. R. Hilgard, *Theories of Learning*, p. 338, Appleton-Century-Crofts, Inc.,
New York, 1948.

[6] J. S. Bruner and C. C. Goodman, Value and need as organizing factors in perception, *J. Abnorm. Soc. Psychol.*, 1947 (42):33–34.

retaliation for the persecution and denial of affection, as well as a manifestation of his general fear of punishment by his father. Tommy, of course, was too young to understand his own actions. His father was too immature emotionally to realize what he was doing. Following the consultation, the father refused to cooperate with the psychologist. He employed "his own psychologist," who forced the issue by using a technique for "reconditioning" Tommy. This consisted of Tommy's sleeping on an electrified pad which gave an electric shock whenever the pad was moistened. After three weeks of this, Tommy stopped his bed-wetting. Shortly thereafter, however, he began to "tell lies" indiscriminately and to indulge in "breakage" or destructive behavior based on no reason except the satisfaction it seemed to give him.

The behavior pattern continued to express the same hostile scheme of values, even though neural pathways had been overpowered by modern technology!

Dynamic Nature of Personality

Behavior can best be understood as the individual's attempt to adjust his *internal* activities to his *external* environment, or to unify the two. Such adjustment between internal and external is continuous. It maintains a general homeostatic equilibrium of personality through the scheme of values, which is in part the physiological homeostasis. Thus behavior is an organized, adaptive series of motivated acts. The organism is at all times actively following out its *general pattern*.

This is a markedly different interpretation from that which assumes a *passive* organism awaiting stimulation into action. Students of all ages must decide whether they are *dynamic* organisms attempting to build and to express themselves, or are passive organisms waiting for the instructor to make lessons and lectures so stimulating that learning will take place without effort. The theories of child psychology which held sway in the period from 1915 to about 1935 erred greatly in this respect: they considered the child essentially a passive organism. The more recent theories are oriented to the whole child as a dynamic and purposefully integrated organism. Even the newborn infant is encouraged by up-to-date parents, pediatricians, and psychologists to eat, sleep, and exercise in accordance with his own dynamics.

Observing the Personality

To understand the individual personality, it is necessary to observe behavior in its entirety and in its widest variety. Such observation is directed at the formulation of a hypothesis or interpretation of the *underlying and unified pattern of behavior.* By means of this pattern the individual personality maintains itself in its own characteristic and unique equilibrium. Around the personal values of an individual his more specific motives cluster. Thus the observer first notes the surface, or overt, behavior; he then notes the underlying motivations. Lastly, he formulates his hypothesis for the central scheme of values. Personality can be understood most simply as *the total organization of values symbolic of experiences previously assimilated.*

The dynamic character of this organization of values appears in the valences of the perceptual field. Like the pull of the magnet upon iron filings, some objects exert a "pull" upon the perceiving organism. They instigate a relationship with this organism which is based upon having *worth* to the organism; *i.e.,* desiring this object or goal, the organism is willing to sacrifice and struggle to achieve it. Negative value is merely avoidance or repulsion, its chief significance being the fact that the positive values are withheld. Positive or negative, the evaluation is in large measure perceptual, showing the various symbolic objects and situations which indicate the individual's hopes and wishes and unrelieved tensions. The purpose of projective test studies and of case-history studies is understanding of the ways in which values are combined, organized within the individual personality to achieve and maintain its dynamic equilibrium.

THE PROCESS OF GROWTH

The Life Cycle

How can one ever understand anything so endlessly complicated as personality? Probably no one can grasp all the details that make even one personality, but the general pattern can be understood by another approach. The present section approaches the personality by sketching how it comes to be what it is today. In brief, there is only one way known whereby the personality has come into itself— *it has grown.*

Growth is recognized to be a process which is *continuous,* absolutely without interruption although marked by variations in tempo. It is so much a part of life itself that interruption would mean the death of the individual organism. Growth follows a biological pattern, commonly understood as the organism's "life cycle." Life cycles are much the same for all members of each species, but they are entirely different when the various species are compared with each other. Special conditions of diet, weather, or accident change the life-cycle pattern for the individual. Other special conditions such as X rays and beta rays have been found to change the life cycles even of offspring of parents exposed to these rays in sufficient intensity.

Case-study Investigations

The individual's growth pattern is dealt with as a *case study,* describing what are known to be the more important facts of his biography to date. One of the most commonly accepted hypotheses in present-day study of personality is that the contemporary behavior of any individual can be best understood by *inventorying* his background of heredity and experience. "Heredity versus environment" makes a good argument, but "heredity versus experience" is more useful. Interpretation of an individual's background suggests the hypothetical pattern of personality which may be used in the guiding of his later learning experiences, in counseling, employing, or promoting him, or in the treatment of his personality maladjustments.

Present-day case studies are widely diversified. Social welfare workers, for example, are seldom able to make the type of case study that would be required by a clinical psychologist. Emphasis upon certain types of information and the ways various facts are put together into a unified interpretation, marks the difference between needs of case-study workers. The clinical psychologist will want particularly information of a psychometric nature, such as scores on standardized psychological tests and scales, projective-test summaries, and some form of interest inventory. The fundamental approach of psychosomatic medicine, as well as of some types of psychotherapy, is the case study. All case-study investigators will need data on health, home and parental background, manner of living (married, single, type of housing), social habits, economic situation, and religious habits. All case-study investigators strive for a unified interpretation of the personality.

Beginnings of Personality

It has been found through biological study that two valuable generalizations can be made about the life cycle. Primitive forms of life are relatively simple and fixed both in their physical structures and in their ways of behaving. This fixed pattern obviously can be successful only if the conditions for life and growth of these organisms or plants are consistently favorable. In the primitive forms of life, offspring depend little, if at all, upon the parents after the initial hatching or birth. The life cycle of primitive organisms thus starts with a remarkable independence, and growth is little more than the unfolding of a fixed pattern.

Given a slow-moving or relatively static environment, a fixed pattern of growth can be highly successful, as has been demonstrated in earlier geological periods when such organisms predominated the earth.[7] Application to the individual personality of this idea of the automatic unfolding of a predetermined life cycle suggests the fatalistic concept of the inheritance of all personal characteristics. Most psychologists consider this a dangerous generalization.

At the other end of the scale of complexity a different pattern is found. The least primitive, the most complex, form of life is the human personality. The obvious incompleteness and inadequacy of the human infant at birth are the greatest evidence of its promise. It is just this incompleteness and inadequacy which comprise true *infancy*. This is the period of life in which *an organism is best able to adapt to contemporary conditions, which may be different from those which prevailed when the parents themselves were infants.*

In one sense, infancy stands in opposition to heredity. In another sense, infancy makes possible sociocultural heredity, the *molding* of the individual to fit the standards set for him by society. Physical

[7] Cf. Lecomte du Noüy, *Human Destiny*, pp. 55–80, Longmans, Green & Co., Inc., New York, 1947.

heredity assures the human organism of a prolonged infancy as part of his life cycle. From then on, the human parents and the social groups of which they are part are chiefly responsible for the personality which develops. This personality will, as a result of its infant modifiability, be able to *adapt* itself to more *variable conditions* and to more *complex levels* of living than can primitive forms of life.

Growth Channels

Adaptation of the personality decreases as the individual grows through his life cycle, being greatest in infancy and least in adulthood. This must follow if the earlier experiences in the individual's lifetime are recognized as the foundation of all later attitudes. Consider the case of a small infant who suffers much discomfort from lack of adequate bathing and changes of clothing, is forced to follow a clock schedule of feeding with the result that he experiences food hunger (known to be excruciatingly painful to the young infant), and is handled abruptly by some adult. Such an infant is impressed with the external world as being an uncomfortable situation. Since this has been his first and strongest impression of the world, in all later evaluations he will be inclined to rate contact with the world as undesirable. Generalizing in this way upon the experience available is uncontrolled and untempered. Such infant evaluations start his core values.[8]

The trend of growth of the personality is determined very largely through the *moods* evoked in the infant by the "nest situation" created by his parents. These moods might be technically classified on the basis of frequency, intensity, and duration of fear, rage, and joy. Some very clear illustrations of this are given by Margaret Mead in the anthropological studies in which she gives evidence indicating that temperament derives from early experience.[9]

Another influence on the trend of growth takes in the extremes of *overstimulation* and *understimulation*. Not only during infancy

---

[8] Core values are the general feeling of being wanted or respected by the world at large or segments of it. They are the infant's primitive generalizations about his place in the world.

[9] Margaret Mead, *Sex and Temperament in Three Primitive Societies*, William Morrow and Company, Inc., New York, 1935; Margaret Mead (ed.), *Cooperation and Competition among Primitive Peoples*, McGraw-Hill Book Company, Inc., New York, 1937.

but also during childhood and adolescence these two extremes play important parts in forming the individual's general evaluation of or attitude toward the world about him. A child about a year old who is left alone (understimulated) much of the time tends to develop habits of thumb sucking.[10] Seemingly, at this approximate age the infant needs to watch people. A warmly human environment supplies the external stimulations which distract him from his own internal sensations. Understimulation in infancy starts a trend of growth which is introspective and characterized by habitual overconcern with internal sensations and feelings. Conversely, overstimulation, too much shifting of the external environment, sets a trend toward feelings of instability and a habitual overconcern with self-protection.

Behavior patterns such as continued thumb sucking, or its equivalent finger sucking and, at later ages, object sucking, are not necessarily undesirable. Rather, this form of "oral activity" cannot develop normally if it is supported at the early age by fixed conditioned reflexes. The individual should be actively seeking new cues for action, such as games to play, or new aspects of curiosity to satisfy, instead of escaping by means of self-stimulation.

Self-evaluations

As soon as the individual becomes mentally able to evaluate himself even crudely, *finding his environment unacceptable means that he is as unacceptable to the environment as it is to him.* This stage of development is usually not reached until the child has gained some slight facility in talking.[11] The personality develops as a result of commerce with the world, each person incorporating into himself the meanings that he derives from these encounters. But meanings can be built only through the experiences the individual is *capable* of having at the exact moment, that he is then *ready* to have. Incidentally, it is not necessary that he be aware or conscious of all that happens to him. Much learning takes place quite unconsciously

[10] Mary S. Kunst, A study of thumb- and finger-sucking in infants, *Psychol. Monogr.,* 1948.

[11] Florence Goodenough, The use of pronouns by young children: a note on the development of self-awareness, *J. Genet. Psychol.,* 1938, 52:333–346.

from background experiences which do not immediately appear important to his evaluation of himself. Yet, no part of his growth into personality is as important as his attitude toward himself.

Fig. 7–1. Interests tend to represent ages and experiences. (*Cartoon by Bill Gay. Courtesy of The American Magazine.*)

EXPERIENCING THE LIFE CYCLE

At any given time in a life a particular form of experience seems to be dominant. In fact, the life cycle of the human being would appear to be divisible into periods on this basis. It follows that a list of these periods would outline the biography of most individuals. Probably such a sequence of periods is in part the manifestation of physiological maturation, but it also must be related to the socio-cultural environment. It might be in point to quote here an amusing but not documentary biographical sequence expressed in terms of the ambitions of a lifetime.

To be a circus clown
To be like Dad
To be a cowboy
To make All-state
To get rich
To make ends meet
To get the old-age pension

The development of a personality during each period will set the later trend, as, for instance, the nesting situation lays the foundation for all later personality trends.

The Steps in Outline

The findings of documentary studies on the subject agree in presenting a ladderlike series of phases through which the individual passes in his life cycle. These studies are descriptive rather than explanatory and combine information from such areas as the physical, sociocultural, and psychometric.

In the beginning there is the *prenatal period,* in which the organism has a slight ability to learn in a very generalized manner. During this period, the behavior is nonspecific, consisting largely of *mass activities.* Although considerable evidence is available in this area of investigation, conclusions have not as yet quite "jelled," particularly in relation to the effects upon the unborn infant of ill health and nervousness in the expectant mother. It appears that mental ill health in the expectant mother affects the development of the child in ways which may appear later as anemia, nervousness, underweight, and other equally general conditions. Experiences involving sense receptor, motor, or glandular reaction probably are lacking.[12]

The next period is roughly defined as *early infancy;* this lasts from

[12] K. C. Pratt, A. K. Nelson, and K. H. Sun, *Behavior of the Newborn Infant,* Ohio State University Graduate School Series, Contributions in Psychology, No. 10, 1930; Arnold L. Gesell in collaboration with Catherine S. Amatruda, *The Embryology of Behavior: The Beginnings of the Human Mind,* Harper & Brothers, New York, 1945.

birth (parturition) until the infant learns to walk, at about twelve months. During this period experience tends to be very general and subjective. *Late infancy* takes the child up to the age of about thirty-six months; it is characterized by increasingly specific experiences and the beginnings of distinguishing between self and not-self. This period is followed by *early childhood,* the "peewee period" of slow body growth, which lasts for nearly three years and leads into *late childhood.* Late childhood is physically hard to distinguish from its sequel, *early adolescence,* which is indicated with increasing clarity as growth continues, showing both in the physical and in the intellectual phases of development.

Because of factors of racial, dietary, and emotional pressure, the onset of adolescent development tends to vary greatly from one individual to another. Thus birthdays are not accurate indicators of the beginning of "puberty." Very roughly, early adolescence is thought of as the period from about age seven until the onset of late adolescence. During early adolescence pubertal hair, mammary development, change in voice, and change in bodily proportions make their appearance, and there are incipient changes in gonadal functions.

Late adolescence announces itself formally by the start of menstruation or of night emissions. These are, of course, merely overt evidence of the glandular changes which were taking place gradually during the preceding life period, and which in subtle ways affected the individual's sensory and intellectual life during that period. Late adolescence continues until psychological growth and physical growth have approximated their limit of expansion.

Youth is the period roughly defined as from eighteen until twenty-two but more exactly lasting from physical maturity until the age at which the economic and social processes in society can accept the individual into *early adulthood.* This period of early adulthood is the "getting started" age in respect to both marriage and economic activity, an age of semirealistic ambitions and much hope for future progress. At about twenty-seven it gives way to *full adulthood,* which continues until the period of the *climacteric,* or "change of life." This in turn initiates the span of years for which there is as yet no more suitable name than the out-moded term "old age."

This last span of years is composed of the interesting and useful *post-climacteric,* and the term might well be used to denote this period. For a small number of people this would be followed by the condition indicative less of age than of health—*senility.* There is a great lag in both public understanding and scientific information regarding the post-climacteric personality, owing chiefly to the fact that only in recent years has it been at all normal for people to live such long lifetimes.

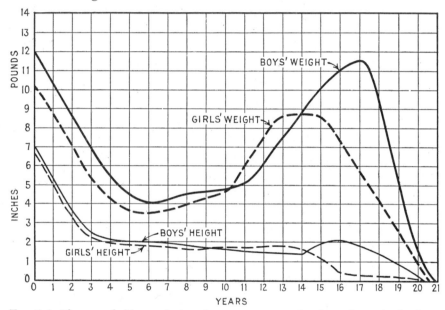

Fig. 7–2. The remarkable regularity of average gains in height and weight for boys and girls each year illustrates the fact that an individual's behavior is predictable. The chart shows the tempo of physical growth, *e.g.,* boys gain less weight during their second year than they do in their first. The increased speed of growth during the adolescent years is present for both boys and girls, although important differences develop. (*Birth to age 3, adapted from Baldwin, Davenport, Stuart, Burgess, as quoted in Sidney L. Pressey and Francis P. Robinson, Psychology and the New Education, rev. ed., p. 14, Harper & Brothers, New York, 1944.*)

In the preceding sketch of the ladder of life, the human growth sequence can be seen in familiar perspective. At each period there will appear not only certain predictable physical activities but also certain interests of intellectual and of social importance. Further, there is a tendency for certain worries or problems to be experienced most frequently at certain periods of life. Although growth is continuous, its tempo will vary according to a schedule governed largely by glandular maturation. Figure 7–2 indicates this tempo on its vertical axis.[13]

Living and growth constitute a one-way street. Experiences are irrevocable. Each period of life forms the setting within which the experiences of the next period will take place. Each period prepares the individual for the next period incorporating previous ones.

LIFE PERIODS AND VALUE STAGES

Life period	*Value stage*
Early infancy (parturition to toddling)	Start of core values in affection-security Mouth-centered sensitiveness Interest-excitement versus frustration-rage Exteroceptor-enteroceptor balance
Late infancy (toddling to walking)	Affection-security more varied and active Auditory-visual-tactual sensations added to mouth sensitiveness Self-concept beginning to organize newly assimilated experiences around core values Playmates start second-level sociocultural values Awareness of boy-girl bodily differences; comparison with self as a standard Toilet training and self-feeding establish core values related to "cleanliness" and "full acceptance" Verbal symbols indistinguishable from objects
Early childhood (about age three to five, inclusive)	Affection-security now largely reassured through experimentally independent actions and temporary regressions to "nest situation" Self-concept begins to show contrast between "self" and "other" Awareness of bodily differences leads into start of male or female role values Exploratory abilities result in rapid increase in contacts with material and sociocultural worlds Verbal symbols become moderately distinct from referents, but with limited dependability
Late childhood (about age five to eight, inclusive)	Affection-security now largely assumed, but requires occasional verification Self-concept now orienting to sociocultural at "pal" level, experimenting with privacy Self-other distinction fairly clear Boy-girl differences now central values; some heterosexual explorations Verbal symbols becoming distinct from referent objects in imaginative sense also

[13] Sidney L. Pressey and Francis P. Robinson, *Psychology and the New Education,* rev. ed., p. 14, Harper & Brothers, New York, 1944.

Fig. 7–3. Affection-security requires continuous verification. This child shows satisfaction all over. New shoes from America through the American Red Cross convince this Austrian orphan that he is fundamentally acceptable even though the present situation is unfavorable. (*American Red Cross photo by Gerald Waller.*)

Life Periods and Value Stages—(*Continued*)

Life period	Value stage
Early adolescence (about age eight to thirteen, inclusive)	Affection-security now mostly "approval"
	Self-concept now in "gang" stage, with need to be different from earlier behavior standards and reactions to authority
	Self-other distinctions sharp, sometimes painful and hidden by "fads"; your adult world versus our world versus baby things
	Boy-girl differences rapidly becoming man-woman differences, although awkwardly
	Verbal symbols now gain abstractness, making possible start of thought or worry about religion, fair practice standards, morals
	New emotional experiences puzzling if not prepared for by earlier knowledge

Life period	*Value stage*
Late adolescence (about age fourteen to seventeen, inclusive)	Affection-security now a mixture of approval and adult love, with many habit regressions or infantilisms
	Self-concept now adding adult appearance and freedom values, with some evidence of self-responsibility
	Self-other distinction now almost complete, applied to parents also
	Boy-girl differences now man-woman relationships but with limited scope, experimental
	Verbal symbols adequate to most abstract thinking, overgeneralization of ideals and heroes
	Adult emotional experiences such as man-woman love, parental love, adult love of own parents beginning to take form
Youth (about age eighteen to twenty-two, inclusive)	Affection-security now centered in career plans or ambitions, with man-woman love meshing into plans
	Self-concept now includes vocations and social mannerisms, standards of comparative ability, secondary group affiliations, and some philosophy of life
	Man-woman relationships adult except for economic and parental aspects
	Verbal symbols now losing some of the tendency to be overgeneralized, but skill in dealing with abstractions still increasing through usage
	Adult emotional experiences achieve more definite form, although still somewhat experimental
Early adulthood (about age twenty-three to twenty-seven, inclusive)	Affection-security now centers in husband-wife relationships, with home maintenance, career advancement, social acceptability as contributors
	Self-concept integrates with affection-security processes
	Man-woman relationships become adult as self-concept incorporates spouse and offspring into itself. Love as giving as well as receiving becomes the specific "love emotion"
	Verbal facility increases chiefly through continued increase of alertness—with improved abstract thinking
Late adulthood (about age twenty-eight to climacteric)	Apparently little change in values listed above, except for some loss of alertness and compensation through greater background of experience. Security factors of career emphasized more than "toehold" factors
Climacteric (about age forty to sixty, but not well defined)	Somatic changes, appearance of organic weaknesses not noticed earlier; psychological problem of change of family pattern from parenthood to grandparenthood, loss of ambition due to limitations on future progress, acceptance of self as is rather than as expected to be in the future; facing of old age and stepping aside for youth to progress

Several researchers have defined the growth trends of infancy; others have similarly analyzed childhood.[14] When growth trends are physiological, they can be discovered more easily than when they are mixtures of the social and the cultural, the emotional and the perceptual. The enormous quantity of literature pertaining to the measurement of intelligence is concerned with definition of growth trends; it antedates considerably the physiological research. The growth trend which is primarily organization of personality, *i.e.*, personality growth itself, is the important one for present purposes.

The Case of Pearl

Studies of personality at all periods, from infancy to death, are achieving important insights. Some of the more interesting generalizations appear in the following case study, which should be read with frequent reference to the preceding chart. It should be kept in mind, *e.g.*, that (see first item on the chart) *core-value* development has its basis in the affection-security relationships of the *nesting situation*.

Pearl was the first-born child of her family. Her very busy father was an engineer, generally opposed to child psychology although willing to read specific techniques such as how to bathe the baby. He wanted to be sure that his child would grow up "able to compete." Pearl's mother had been an only child and was the kind of person who needed more than the average amount of attention from other people in order to feel secure. Her moods ranged from periods in which she could bestow affection to periods in which she had no affection to give and could only receive it. Thus Pearl experienced affection at certain times but at other times was denied it. She reacted in the usual way—fought for the needed affection or attention by showing off or by misbehaving. Sometimes she hurt the feelings or bodies of her playmates or destroyed their toys to gain within herself the feeling of superiority or worthiness of attention.

A show of affection for other children, which at Pearl's present age of four should be free and genuine, is made only when she can thereby gain the notice or approval of adults around her. Her feelings of affection are thus shallow; her feelings of competition are

[14] Arnold Gesell, Frances L. Ilg, *et al.*, *Infant and Child in the Culture of Today: The Guidance and Development in Home and Nursery School*, Harper & Brothers, New York, 1943.

intense. Her confidence in her own ability to compete successfully is slight.

Appearance of a new baby brother in her family, although anticipated by Pearl, has multiplied all these tendencies to a point which has made her even more troublesome to her parents and has affected her physical health. The pediatrician describes the condition as "emotional in origin and due to the presence of the new baby." He prescribes much-increased affection for Pearl, with carefully regulated diet and rest.

It is doubtful whether Pearl's parents possess sufficient affection-security to carry out the prescription. They may not have enough affection, beyond their own personal needs, to meet Pearl's requirement.

Interpretation of the Illustration

The term "sibling rivalry" is properly defined in psychology as the inability of one child to share affection with a brother or sister, regardless of respective ages. When the total amount of affection available to Pearl has been so limited, sharing it with the baby brother becomes possible only at the cost of self-starvation. This is a price which infants and small children are quite unable to pay or to understand. It is too abstract. As she finds her world refusing to give her what she needs, in her infantile way, Pearl feels unwanted—rejected. Hence she fights the whole situation desperately and with her entire personality.

As Pearl grew from early infancy to late infancy, she organized her original core values into a definite pattern. Encountering the characteristic problems of late infancy, she adapted these new experiences to fit her previous feelings of unacceptability. She was accustomed to thinking of her parents as having one baby, namely herself. When the new baby brother arrived, the old idea of one baby could mean only that she, Pearl, was even less needed in that family. Proof of this appeared all around her, in simple facts such as Daddy choosing to be with the baby, Mommy having no time to help Pearl, the whole house having to be quiet because "Baby is sleeping."

Other new experiences, too, had to be assimilated. Feeding oneself at the age of three or four is at times an overwhelming task. At best it is hard work. If the situation in which food is taken is not a happy one, the carry-over of feeling from the general situation to the very difficult task of self-feeding is complete. Mealtime is a time of such close contact between parent and child that it symbolizes the deeper parent-child relationships in especially clear form. As was pointed out in an earlier section, food taking means to the individual child acceptance of the environment into himself. Thus the mealtime *situation* as well as the food is evaluated as totality. Food taking, strange as it may seem, may even come to be perceived as a stimulus or cue for the organism to fight to defend itself!

Pearl failed to gain weight when upset by the sibling rivalry not because the meals were any less tasty or nourishing but because the general situation had become unappetizing, unacceptable. The controlled diet and scheduled rest periods prescribed were intended as means for making the whole experience more palatable. But here again these prescriptions served only to burden the parents with added inconvenience, with additional feelings that Pearl was a peck of trouble and not deserving of their affections. Aggressive parental feelings commonly arise when the affection is weakened.[15]

Unless some drastic change in the home situation takes place soon, Pearl may organize her later experiences around a core of evaluations based on the conviction that life can be accepted only with cynical reservations, that she must defeat her contemporaries before she herself is defeated. Or she may go to the other extreme and believe that she cannot possibly succeed although she must force herself to try. Her affections will continue to be shallow, perhaps merely serving as a tool for her to use in her struggles.

The pattern of growth charted above applies to all the growth trends. The toilet-training process frequently becomes involved with the affection-security core values during late infancy, determining the individual's attitude toward himself in regard to cleanliness or uncleanliness. During childhood and adolescence it will additionally involve abstractions such as *moral* purity and related guilt feelings. Often these feelings stand in the way of the development of healthy attitudes toward sex. Especially may those surrounded by unwholesome reactions that sex is "dirty" attach their attitude toward uncleanliness to the whole subject of sex. The central nature of cleanliness values is obvious.

Near the start of early childhood, Pearl will have to cope with the

[15] Goodwin A. Watson, A comparison of the effects of lax versus strict home training, *J. Soc. Psychol.*, 1934, 5:102–105.

task of formulating a more complete interpretation of herself. By that time her self will be much more complex than it was at four. At age six or seven she will know and wonder much more about the physiological sex differences, will be much more able to sense the specific worries of mother and father. She will want to have a friend "all her very own" and not chosen by the family.

This friend will also have to fill Pearl's need for security in limited ways. Perhaps this friend will be inferior in age or ability to an extent which will encourage Pearl to domineer. Without the support of strong bonds of affection to her parents she will find that the characteristic fears and uncertainties of her childhood are stronger than those faced by average children. Her efforts to manage these fears and uncertainties will then get her into trouble at school as well as at home. Her cynical attitudes, started in infancy, will keep her from acquiring skill in securing the help she will need so desperately.

Somewhere along the line, at age eight, nine, or ten, there is a strong trend of interest in sociocultural standards. Cultural influences tell a person how he *ought* to behave, *i.e.*, how to behave correctly. People who feel themselves to be members of a group, such as a family, tribe, or neighborhood, typically behave according to the standards of that group. Sometimes they interpret this group membership as permanent and unalterable. Or perhaps the group itself defines this membership as unchangeable. Some religious organizations and nearly all minority "races" consider their memberships as permanent. The personality which has core values of inadequacy or insecurity will seek the needed additional security through *obvious* adherence to some sociocultural group. Such a group membership becomes a substitute for the fundamental security. This hunger for belonging sometimes leads to the strange choice of a closely knit but socially unacceptable group such as a criminal gang or even the Communist party.

Pearl will find a social group which harmonizes with her own scheme of values and which provides opportunity to express the feelings which she must vent. She will also be governed by her set of values through the larger sociocultural system of folkways, mores, and ideals. Insecurity within her core values may then be expressed in terms of class distinctions, racial discrimination, religious intolerance, or perhaps social reform movements. As she progresses up the ladder from late childhood, her *self-concept* will become more and more fixated by the way of life she has designed. The following chart shows the age at which certain major attitudes take shape.[16]

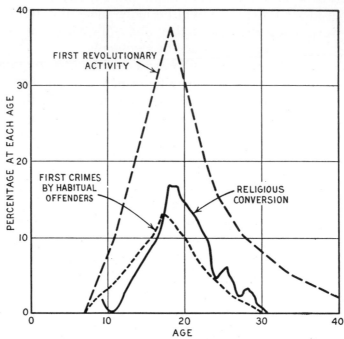

Fig. 7–4. Attitude changes with growth. Like physical growth, attitudes change predictably. As the years pass, certain periods of the life cycle are accompanied by rapid change or by rapid "jelling" of attitudes which thereafter serve as the larger motives of living. The chart shows the frequency among adolescents at each age of religious conversion, first revolutionary activity of Russian political leaders, and first crime of habitual offenders in England. (*From data of Cyril Burt, as summarized by F. K. Shuttleworth, The Adolescent Period, National Research Council, New York, 1938, Fig. 370, and E. T. Clark, The Psychology of Religious Awakening, The Macmillan Company, New York, 1923, as quoted in Sidney L. Pressey and Francis P. Robinson, Psychology and the New Education, rev. ed., p. 272, Harper & Brothers, New York, 1944.*)

QUESTIONS FOR DISCUSSION

1. Give an example from your own experience which illustrates that a personality is not revealed by one act alone.
2. Give some examples of the effect of the individual's value interests on his sensory acuity.
3. Do you believe most students consider themselves passive organisms in class? Why?

[16] Pressey and Robinson, *op. cit.*, p. 272.

4. Do you believe that an instructor who treats students as passive organisms in the learning situation is more popular than one who treats students as dynamic organisms?

5. How might the attitude of a student who considered himself a dynamic organism express itself in regard to collateral reading?

6. Why do many people tend to pigeonhole personalities according to types rather than to use the concept set forth in this chapter?

7. Do you think that most people would be able to describe their own unified pattern of behavior? Why?

8. From the point of view of the present discussion would you think the work record of an individual useful to employment officers? Why?

9. How does the idea that many people hold that they like or dislike people on first acquaintance fit in with the concept of personality presented in this chapter?

10. Trace the unified pattern of behavior of some (unnamed) friend.

11. Explain possible effects of understimulation in childhood on the growth of a personality.

12. What are some common reasons for a prolonged need for finger sucking? Pipe smoking?

13. Show how your choice of vocation has changed during your life cycle.

14. Do you believe that most adolescents understand what is going on in their growth? Would it help them if they did?

15. What type of experience affects the growth of personality in such a way as to turn individuals toward groups hostile to the majority? Explain.

ADDITIONAL READINGS

Abbate, Grace McLean: The middle-aged child steps out, *Child Study,* 1950, 28(1):9–11.

Blair, Arthur Witt, and Burton, William H.: *Growth and Development of the Preadolescent,* Appleton-Century-Crofts, Inc., New York, 1951.

Breckenridge, Marian E., and Vincent, E. Lee: *Child Development: Physical and Psychological Growth Through the School Years,* rev. ed., W. B. Saunders Company, Philadelphia, 1949.

Dearborn, Walter F., Rothney, John W. M., *et al.: Predicting the Child's Development,* pp. 311–340, Sci-Art Publishers, Cambridge, Mass., 1941.

Doll, Edgar A.: *Your Child Grows Up,* John Hancock Mutual Life Insurance Company, Boston, 1939 (pamphlet).

Dysinger, Wendell S.: Maturation and vocational guidance, *Occupations,* 1950, 29:198–201.

Fry, Clement C.: *Mental Health in College,* Chap. 4, Commonwealth Fund, New York, 1942.

Ginsburg, Sol W.: Adolescence is hard on everyone, *Child Study,* 1950, 28:12–14.

Jenkins, Gladys, Shacter, Helen, and Bauer, William: *These Are Your Children: How They Develop and How to Guide Them,* Scott, Foresman & Company, Chicago, 1949.

Lambert, Clara: *Understanding Your Child—Ages 6 to 12,* Public Affairs Pamphlet No. 144, New York, 1948.

Macnaughton, Dorothy: The inner world of the preschool child, *Child Study,* 1950, 28:6–8.

Meek, Lois Hayden: *Your Child's Development and Guidance Told in Pictures,* J. B. Lippincott Company, Philadelphia, 1940.

Preston, George H.: *The Substance of Mental Health,* Rinehart & Company, Inc., New York, 1943.

Redl, Fritz: Pre-adolescents—what makes them tick? *Child Study,* Winter, 1943–1944, pp. 44–49. (Also reprint by Child Study Association of America.)

Thompson, Helen: Physical growth, Chap. 5, in Leonard Carmichael (ed.), *Manual of Child Psychology,* John Wiley & Sons, Inc., New York, 1946.

Moment-to-moment experiences show endless variety. No two people will experience the same event in quite the same way. This variety is obvious, but not more so than the similarity which exists between personalities. In seeking to explain similarities between people, sociocultural channels and standards become important. Physiological differences are equally important. The individual's own unique biography needs to be understood, too. The life cycle is so much a process of learning, and of refusing to learn, that the present chapter is given over to description of the learning process.

Learning is a way of growing. Humans, like plants, can grow into healthy specimens or into deformed and stunted ones. Modern psychology has so linked together perception and motivation in the individual personality that doubt no longer exists as to the deforming and stunting effects of unhealthy motives upon growth. A further point needs to be stressed, namely, that learning can be unhealthy in degree as well as in direction. The degree to which learning is refused can be considered as a measure of the threat of damage to his personality felt by the individual.

LEARNING

Assimilation

Food assimilation and "psychological assimilation" are much the same in process. Both are going on all the time automatically. No foods are wholly and immediately ready to enter the bloodstream without stomach and intestinal processing. New situations or experiences are like kinds of food, *i.e.*, none is ready for immediate and literal usage. Assimilation is a whole series of acts whereby the entire organism makes selected portions of its environment into integral parts of itself.

As every new stimulus is encountered, it is evaluated subceptively, or perceptually. The organism sees itself in relation to this new situation. It then plans various actions suggested by current motives. Some portions of the situation may serve as *cues* to indicate the use

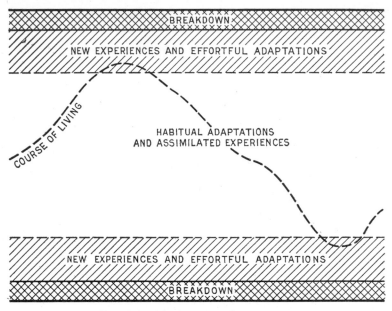

Fig. 8–1. Adaptations as homeostasis.

of established habits and known techniques. Other portions of the situation may be new to the organism, suggesting that older behavior patterns are not adequate to them. The organism will, in the face of a strange situation, have to predict probable effects of the various projected actions. It becomes responsible for control of both actions and situation. Otherwise its motives or purposes get lost in aimless and random actions. This is always the problem when the future is faced. Somehow the strangeness of the new situation must become familiarity; uncertainty of outcomes must become motivated and purposeful *control* of results. This *shift* from strangeness to familiarity, from uncertainty to control, is the general character of all psychological assimilation. When the once new situation becomes part and parcel of the individual's characteristic way of experience, *he has assimilated it into his personality.*

Adaptability in Learning

Obviously, assimilation as described above is *learning.* People unfamiliar with "eating" in its fullest sense think of it as merely the putting of food into the mouth. They do not see that this is only the first step of the total assimilation process. And so it is that learning is misconceived as the simple acceptance, the "swallowing," of new facts or ideas. Between the initial swallowing and the final understanding, there is the complex process of assimilation into the personality's scheme of *values.*

All education and learning—including perceiving, thinking, and feeling—can be understood best as the building process through which the personality takes form. By their individual backgrounds of education and learning, some personalities develop a greater capacity to assimilate new experiences. They develop a higher rate of "personality metabolism." They are able to maintain their dynamic integrity in spite of chaotic environmental pressures. Their assimilation is highly efficient: new ideas and sudden events are faced adventurously as learning proceeds, with practically no fear. This capacity for efficient internal organization and for easy adaptation to new situations is found only in the personality able to take an adventurous attitude toward new situations.

But then, the failure of a given personality to face adventurously toward new situations is a familiar one. It is indeed doubtful if any one personality could be adventurous in all possible situations. Every individual lives within a set of limits beyond which it cannot survive. As Fig. 8–1 indicates, its most nearly normal living is within the central area, in which habits take care of the many adaptations. Habits follow the individual's pattern of living as established through previously assimilated experiences. Sometimes new situations arise which require a little more adaptation but do not suggest serious hazard. These new experiences present to the healthy personality an *invitational character* which is genuinely a part of the individual's perception of the world.

Beyond the limits of new experiences which are inviting there is a kind of experience which implies destruction of the personality, the body, or the individual's faith in himself. At the outer extreme of the range of experience, these are indicated in Fig. 8–1 as resulting in a failure to adapt and thereby in damage to the individual. Nervous breakdown is a failure to adapt. In persistent nonadjustive reactions, the individual just holds tight onto himself and does nothing but let time pass. If the personality suffers serious damage it is unable to return under its own power to its normal homeostatic equilibrium.

There is thus a set of limits to the adventurous possibilities even in the learning process. For some personalities these limits are close to day-to-day living, while in others they are so far apart as seldom, if ever, to threaten his adaptive powers. The distance between these limits suggests the extent of the individual's ability to learn broadly.

The Process of Learning

Complete acts of learning show a simple formula: from the general to the specific. The learning cycle of a single habit or unit of learning is a change from inefficient, emotional, and inattentive behavior to efficient, unemotional, and attentive behavior. Put more simply, as the individual organism suddenly faces a strange situation it becomes tense throughout its entire body.[1] This tension also pervades the perceptual field. It is labeled *mass activity* by physiologists and psychologists alike. As discussed in Chapter 4, above, mass activity is the normal *first reaction* to a strange situation. It means that the organism, if now beyond infancy, is "ready all over" for almost any form of action that will appear necessary. If no action is started, and if time is short but pressure for action is great, the delay will result in an intensified mass activity which is recognizable as *emotion*. If this general state of mass activity were to continue it would indicate that learning was not taking place.[2] The problem aspects of the new situation would remain unsolved.

On the other hand if the organism launches into some course of activity, particularly if this activity results in the general tension being suddenly or even gradually reduced, learning is taking place.

[1] Arthur T. Jersild, Emotional development, Chap. 15, p. 762, in Leonard Carmichael (ed.), *Manual of Child Psychology*, John Wiley & Sons, Inc., New York, 1946.

[2] Norman R. F. Maier, *Frustration: the Study of Behavior without a Goal*, Chap. 4, McGraw-Hill Book Company, Inc., New York, 1949.

Once the organism has tried one or several ways of acting, it learns which specific actions will not work and which will produce de-

"I just write the unimportant things in my diary. The important ones, I remember!"

Fig. 8–2. Memory is aided by emotional involvement. A person cannot help but remember important experiences, although it is not always possible to recall them. (*Cartoon by Kate Osann. Courtesy of Collier's.*)

sirable results. Each one of these actions will help to clarify the organism's specific interpretation of the situation. This new interpretation becomes the perceptual pattern which automatically thereafter will lead into those specific actions. The learning process in this way is a *transition from general tension to specific or localized action*. Perceptually, attention narrows from the broad and unclear field to specific cues or figures. Learning which follows this formula is sometimes distinguished from the "conditioned-reflex type" of the laboratory by being called *perceptual learning*. Probably all human learning is largely perceptual.[3]

Learning to ride a bicycle is a good illustration of the typical learning process. At first the whole body is tense. The initial awkwardness of a learner is evidence of his general tension. His fear of sudden catastrophe expresses itself through this tension and through a lack of detailed perception. As learning progresses there is a gradual reduction of many little tensions until, at the final and skillful stage, only the minimum of muscle tension is needed. Leg muscles pump automatically and brake with equal ease. Even while going around corners, arms steer and mid-back muscle adjustments compensate for unbalance with but limited and local tensions. At this stage the rider has come to perceive the bicycling situation as no longer a threat of catastrophe. Now the bicycle is under control. Only in face of an emergency will there be a return of the general tension.

The Entire Organism Learns

There is no doubt, from contemporary studies, that the learning process involves the entire body and not just the nervous system. Almost three quarters of a century have passed since it became established that in addition to the *mental* phases of learning there is always a *sensory-motor* phase. Only recently has it been recognized in psychology that in addition to the sensory-motor there is also a *visceral* phase. At the level of everyday observation everyone has experienced visceral changes, such as restricted breathing, which have become permanent parts of the learned reaction. Public speakers often report that they have never been able to overcome the "pit of the stomach" form of visceral tension at the start of a speech, a reaction acquired as a result of their first awkward public appearances. Acknowledgment of the existence of mental, sensory-motor,

[3] E. R. Hilgard, *Theories of Learning*, pp. 331ff., Appleton-Century-Crofts, Inc., New York, 1948.

and visceral phases of learning means acceptance of the fact that the entire personality is involved in the learning process.

Because visceral reactions indicate so directly the *evaluations* within the act as it was originally learned, they are important to

Fig. 8–3. Real interest compels attention. Mind wandering and mental blocks do not interfere with attention when the topic fits the needs of the personalities. (*Photo by Ruth Orkin.*)

understanding that learning is psychological assimilation. Briefly, learning is less the memorizing of isolated bits of subject matter than it is the developing of the entire personality so that it can function in different situations or with different motives or values. Each act of learning, as it becomes an integral part of the growing personality, contributes to the growth or change of this personality. Learning is the internal process of personality growth.

Students rightfully expect theory of learning to have practical values. Their difficulty arises when they fail to take note of the *complete learning act.* Subject matter can be interesting to the individual only as it harmonizes with his motives, as it contributes to his growth of personality. The early stages of learning therefore must promise to *him* some furtherance of his personality growth, not merely in the abstract but in the concreteness of this individual's own understanding of himself. When the subject matter, or the activity, contributes in this manner, the student feels *interest, i.e.,* he wants to accept and assimilate. Learning thus combines his motivations and perceptions. The practical approach to learning is to develop first a recognition of the growth opportunities offered by the assignment or the new situation.[4]

Resistance

Feelings of apathy or antagonism to the learning are properly called *resistance.* They indicate that the individual's way of living is threatened by the subject matter or activity or viewpoint in question.[5] Each individual has a unique self-concept, wholly and exclusively his own. Thus the feeling of resistance is understandable only in terms of the individual student. From the individual's viewpoint, resistance means that the learning is inconsistent with his own concept of himself. *He would not be himself* if he accepted and assimilated the things in question. Because it is the fundamental nature of personality to grow through learning, resistance to learning is always a form of self-defense against threat, a sheltering of the self. Obviously this sheltering impulse is diametrically opposed to the adventurous spirit of learning.

Strange as it may seem, psychological resistance can become so generalized that the individual will resist (*i.e.,* refuse to accept and assimilate) entire subject areas. He may resist in this way certain teachers or preachers or physicians. Students who by their own acknowledgment are "poor spellers" typify this phenomenon. Their misspelling will be consistent in terms of the percentage of the total number of words tried, rather than in terms of the difficulty of the individual words! The below-average or failing student often

[4] Hilgard, *op. cit.,* pp. 348–349.

[5] Elliot McGinnies, Emotionality and perceptual defense, *Psychol. Review,* 1949, 56:244–251.

illustrates this attitude even in quizzes which are unusually easy or unusually difficult. The evidence becomes even more convincing when it is learned that often the poor speller can be successfully treated through counseling directed at bringing about a *changed*

"She could learn much faster if she wanted to."

FIG. 8–4. Resistance to learning represents individual motives. Refusing to learn may be a self-defense, or it may be habitual and chronic. In any case, the avoidance of learning is directly related to the individual's self-regard. (*Courtesy of Ladies' Home Journal.*)

attitude toward spelling skill. Frequently the student will show sufficient spelling ability after this has been effected to keep up with the average of the class and in addition to make up for the former weakness without need of additional tutoring or time! "Two of the poorest spellers in the High School of Clifton, N.J., were used to demonstrate this method before a university class in psychology. Given twenty words to spell, one missed all twenty and the other nineteen. The school counselor, continuing the use of the method (of developing change in attitude), reports that both are now excellent spellers and have taken up spelling as a sort of hobby." [6]

It is an interesting sidelight that the poor student often shows apathy toward the instructor at first, then antagonism, declaring that he should have been "made to learn." This well-entrenched interpretation of teaching puts the student into a passive role which is completely inconsistent with the dynamic and purposive nature of learning. Such a passive attitude appeals greatly to the student with a personality already on the defensive, already resistant. The common experience of being unable to recall something in class and remembering it as soon as the threshold of the classroom door has been passed on the way out demonstrates the well-established difference between recall and memory. This inability to face by means of recall, in certain types of situations, particular bits of information, or perhaps certain unassimilated experiences such as childhood fears, hatreds, adult prejudices, and aggressions, is the most common way for psychological resistance to appear. The psychotherapist deals with it in the more extreme form, but the student and teacher must cope with it more frequently. Inability to learn may not be evidence of inadequate intelligence; instead it may be a system of a self-concept defending itself against some perceived threat.

MODES OF ACTION

When the living organism is faced with a new stimulus situation, three *modes of action* are possible, either singly or in combination: *assimilation, resistance, reconstruction.* Where assimilation is possible, it is the fundamental nature of the organism to proceed to assimilate the new stimulus situation and its appropriate reaction into parts of its own growing personality. Assimilation in the broader sense seems to be part of the nature of protoplasm itself. Enough has been said to clarify the meaning of the term "resistance" in its psychological usage; further details will be given later under the heading of Adjustment. *Reconstruction,* the third mode of action,

[6] Prescott Lecky, *Self-consistency: A Theory of Personality,* rev. ed., p. 248, Island Press Co-operative, Inc., New York, 1951.

is the most frequently used of the three. It serves the organism in many situations which require effortful adaptation.

Reconstruction

If reconstruction is the mode of action, *both* the organism itself and the perceived situation will have to be reconstructed or compromised. A common campus situation will serve to illustrate. Jim has asked Ruth to go to a school dance. But Ruth has already made a commitment to go to the movies with her friend Sue. Jim, because he is interested in Ruth, immediately interprets her "previous engagement" as a thinly veiled admission that she has a date with his "competition." This would mean that Jim was being threatened, in so far as he has wanted to think of himself as a special friend of Ruth's. So he is upset. As he sees the total situation, it is unassimilable in important ways. Ruth, however, *reconstructs* the general situation by getting him to perceive it differently and hence to respond to it less as a threat. She explains that she is going to the movies with Sue and adds that if he had asked her earlier she would have preferred the dance date with him. This is different! Jim understands. His reconstruction puts him back into his previous concept of himself even more securely. Thus both the situation and Jim's self-concept have undergone a process of change, or a reconstruction. Thinking and insight constitute this reconstruction process.[7] That is why thinking is today considered to be *problem solving.* Through this reconstruction it results in conclusions which resolve all the original complexity and uncertainty. It opens the door to action.

Threat Reactions

Sometimes it is impossible, at least within the available time, to reconstruct the situation. And yet the situation cannot be resisted or avoided. Reconstruction is then limited to the personality of the individual; he must reconstruct, or adapt, *himself.* This is the kind of situation in which action is required but goal achievement appears impossible. Maier has described this type of situation as producing *frustration* in animals and humans alike.[8] Here is an

[7] Hilgard, *op. cit.,* p. 346.
[8] Maier, *op. cit.,* pp. 93–100.

occasion which calls for holding defensively to one's established self-concept and way of living and at the same time requires surrender and loss of self. If this situation is utterly hopeless, all goal-oriented or purposeful activity is useless and the organism is forced into the frustration or purposeless activity commonly described as "nervous breakdown" and "traumatic neurosis." Thinking no longer organizes behavior.

Normally the organism resists the impending failure by using additional energy. This added energy is largely without an adequate activity outlet so long as the behavior is disorganized. Therefore it must express itself at least in part as *general tension,* as *emotion.* Bruner and Postman have found that when an individual's expectations from his environment are violated he develops a resistance to perceptions which indicate the existence of unexpected or incongruous objects or conditions. Among these resistances is the tendency to be stubborn about some one interpretation which seems capable of preventing the unexpected or incongruous. This is a tendency to establish the incongruous as utterly inconceivable and impossible. When these responses fail to achieve their aim, the individual's perceptions become disrupted.[9] This disruption of the perceptions will cause the figure to appear ambiguous or unclear and confused. In either case the individual's activity is equally unclear and confused.

Modern physiology describes the organic aspects of emotional behavior in sufficient detail. At the psychological level the popular interpretation still follows antiquated theory that there are several specific "emotions." Another popular belief is that emotion is a separate "force" within the personality. The more scientific contemporary psychologies, however, consider emotion as a characteristic of behavior. It is the increased energization of behavior which takes place only when energy is drawn from the reserves of body and mind to meet situations *which threaten to get out of hand.*

Fear and threat in some form seem always to underlie the emotional state. But it is the organism's perception of the situation which holds the threat which results in the fear. Emotion can be very well described as an *emergency or threat reaction.* Rage then

[9] J. S. Bruner and Leo Postman, On the perception of incongruity: a paradigm, *J. Person.,* 1949, 18(2):206–223.

becomes merely fear on the aggressive, as distinct from retreat. Lust, joy, grief, and the other specific emotions are merely situation reactions combined with the fundamental emotional reaction of fear.

As was pointed out above in connection with the cardiovascular system, intense activity can be distinguished from emotional activity by the difference in the period of time required for heart action to return to normal. Emotion depletes the organism; for instance, under emotional stress the organism loses much of its planning ability and refinement of coordination. It also loses much of its efficiency in perception, perceptual relationships becoming disrupted even though there is a temporary increase in sensory acuity.

Generally speaking, emotion is a *crashing through* sort of behavior which serves its purpose best when more civilized techniques have been exhausted. Blind power and crude strength are substituted for skill, insight, and adaptiveness. In emotional activity the most stereotyped habits lose least of their precision and regularity but even they are somewhat affected. Military training develops rigorously certain forms of stereotyped behavior which will be needed by service men in emergency situations, it being well recognized that the nonhabitual activities will become completely disorganized in the extremely emotional reactions of the battle.

Nonlearning Reactions

The disorganization which appears during emotion, and which continues after the emotional episode for a considerable time, is *general disorganization.* The whole personality crumbles to a degree and will remain in this state until either the threat is removed or the personality has achieved a reconstruction of itself or of its situation. This is commonly recognized in cases of *amnesia,* or major loss of memory. The memory loss is never complete and it seems to apply only to those activities of the individual which are related to certain unassimilable experiences. When these experiences have been reconstructed so as to become assimilable, the full memory returns. The individual now dares to know who he is because he now feels able to be himself again.

The degree of intensity of emotionalization usually indicates the extent to which the threat has penetrated into the personality and its self-concept. This suggests also the extent of self-reorganization that the individual judges to be necessary to make possible the acceptance of the threatened consequences. Extreme inability to remember, covering large segments of the individual's behavior, indicates that the threat has penetrated deeply, demanding partial reconstructing of core values.

The following case illustrates the reaction to threat involving a breakdown of personality adjustments in relation to the individual's self-concept.

Mr. L. was discovered by the police wandering around, unable to remember either his name or his address although able to talk and to take care of himself in immediately personal ways. Routine police investigations revealed that Mr. L., who was a vice-president of a local bank and an active church member and civic worker, had shown signs of worry for several months. His wife was well known for her brilliant hospitality and club leadership. Review of Mr. L.'s financial status indicated that he was facing bankruptcy, a process which would involve the loss of his position in the bank. Mrs. L. was unaware of this situation. Mr. L. was placed in a private rest home, for his own safety and for psychotherapeutic treatment of his amnesia condition.

The impending situation was not assimilable to Mr. L. He could not face the prospect of ceasing to be the socially admired Mr. L., whose attractive wife gave wonderful parties. He could not bear the possibility of becoming the *formerly* successful Mr. L., who now showed less financial ability than most of his former patrons. So he simply failed to remember the two central facts: that he was Mr. L. and that he lived at the address where the attractive Mrs. L. lived. He did not, of course, do this by simple fiat of will. In fact, the decision to cease remembering took place at what would be called the "involuntary level," termed "unconscious" by some therapists. Amnesia is a "conflict reaction" to threat and represents the breakdown of normal behavior patterns in both animals and humans.

Because learning is normal to both animals and humans, it takes place automatically. It needs no effort of will. It is, in fact, as fundamental to the life and growth of the organism as is the assimilation of food and oxygen. The feeling of effort which sometimes accompanies learning is like the parasite on a migrating fish: it serves its own purposes but is totally unnecessary to the movement from place to place. Feelings of effort point to the presence of resistance by the organism as it faces its environment. This resistance is the struggle of self-defense. It fights the enforced environmental situations to which it must orient itself through understanding. If it accepts this new situation it will be forced to give up some of its present and precious values.

To remain or not to remain one's precious self—that is the question forever faced by the personality in its advancing experience. The feeling of effort is merely the "squeaking" which accompanies the straining for self-consistency. Many psychotherapists have recognized this phenomenon, including Freud and his followers. "If there is any teaching which has come from Freudian psychology it is that motives are organized in some sort of hierarchy within the individual, resulting in a value-system expressed as behavior. This system may go by such names as 'character-structure' or 'ego,' but whatever it is called, it becomes very important for the learning of that individual." [10]

Conflict and Learning

Conflict, the inability of the organism to integrate itself in relation to the particular situation or environment, forms the early stage in every act of learning. As this conflict is resolved, restructuring of perceptions and of the personality takes place. The ability and willingness of the individual personality to restructure itself somewhat in an efficient manner are its only means for avoiding emotional breakdown. Studies of people who cannot seem to adapt to situations which are beyond their control suggest that prejudice is a refusal or inability to adapt. They perceive the world as composed of extremes, with no middle ground. Hence their decisions must be extreme ones. Such people frequently suffer emotional difficulties because of the great difficulty of living in a world of extremes. They not only need, says Gardner Lindzey's study, better means for reacting to their frustrations but also need to become less vulnerable to frustration experiences. [11] Such people need to reconstruct them-

[10] Hilgard, *op. cit.*, pp. 348–349.
[11] Gardner Lindzey, Differences between the high and low in prejudice and their implications for a theory of prejudice, *J. Person.*, 1950, 19(1):16–40.

selves to the point where they perceive the world differently and less frustratingly.

It is the ability of the personality to work its way through the conflict stage of new experience that marks it as strong. The strong personality is able to take a chance, to make a *provisional try*. Kurt Lewin's genius, as evidenced in psychological research that reorganized the entire field of psychological inquiry in America, can be attributed to his deep faith in just this willingness to make a provisional try. His trials were the formulation of hypotheses which were not evident to other scientists more in need of the security of traditional interpretations.[12] Convert the feeling of conflict through learning, and the positive feeling of competence arises to give the individual that faith in himself which fosters the further adventure of learning.

Summary

The integration of personality is the end result achieved by means of adventures in learning. The individual reaches out through new encounters with his environment, finding at first some degree of conflict between himself and this new experience. The resolving of this initial conflict is normally an assimilation of the new evidence into the individual personality or self. Through new experiences the personality grows around its self-concept as a nucleus. The richer the experience, the better able is the personality to resolve further conflicts and the greater is its self-confidence and feeling of adequacy. The integrated personality is able to perceive opportunities for growth in a cool and relatively unemotional manner—thus to learn efficiently.

QUESTIONS FOR DISCUSSION

1. Describe an instance in which you found it difficult to assimilate new learning.
2. Give an example of an adventurous attitude toward learning.
3. Explain how the range between an individual's learning or adaptive limits would affect his college work.

[12] Cf. David Krech, Notes toward a psychological theory, *J. Person.*, 1949, 18:70.

4. List some examples of well-known personalities who seem to illustrate narrow and wide ranges of adaptability, with reasons for your choices.
5. Explain the steps by which the "jittery" feeling before examinations might develop.
6. Explain the way in which the development of a D student might take place.
7. Give examples of how the lack of adventurous attitudes toward new learning might affect the choice of a career.
8. Is there any relation between the ability of the people to assimilate new ideas and governmental processes?
9. Is continual drill the best way to improve poor spelling? Explain.
10. Give an example from your own experience of using each of the three modes of action in facing new experience.
11. Why is the attitude that all emotion is bad based upon misconceptions?
12. What are the psychological bases of military training?
13. Give an example of the effect of emotion on memory.
14. What is the psychological explanation for a feeling of effort in learning? Can anything be done about this?
15. What new reasons have you discovered in this chapter for any difficulties in learning that you may have experienced?

ADDITIONAL READINGS

Alper, Thelma G.: Memory for completed and incompleted tasks as a function of personality: correlation between experimental and personality data, *J. Person.*, 1948, 17:104–137.

Beaumont, Henry, and Macomber, Freeman G.: *Psychological Factors in Education*, Chap. 4, McGraw-Hill Book Company, Inc., New York, 1951.

Dewey, John: *Experience and Education*, The Macmillan Company, New York, 1938.

Dollard, John, and Miller, Neal E.: *Personality and Psychotherapy*, Chaps. 3–5, McGraw-Hill Book Company, Inc., New York, 1950.

Gouldner, Alvin W. (ed.): *Studies in Leadership: Leadership and Democratic Action*, Part I, Harper & Brothers, New York, 1950.

McCaul, R. L.: The effect of attitudes upon reading interpretation, *J. Educ. Res.*, 1944, 37:451–457.

McKinney, Fred: Certain emotional factors in learning and efficiency, *J. Genet. Psychol.*, 1933, 9:101–116.

Meltzer, H.: Individual differences in forgetting pleasant and unpleasant experiences, *J. Educ. Psychol.*, 1930, 21:399–409.

Missildine, W. H.: The emotional background of thirty children with reading disabilities with emphasis on its coercive elements, *Nerv. Child*, 1946, 5:263–272.

Mowrer, O. H.: Anxiety-reduction and learning, *J. Exp. Psychol.*, 1940, 27:497–516.

Muenzinger, K. F., and Vine, D. O.: Motivation in learning, IX, the effect of interposed obstacles in human learning, *J. Exp. Psychol.*, 1941, 29: 67–74.

Prescott, Daniel A.: *Emotion and the Educative Process, A Report of the Committee on the Relation of Emotion to the Educative Process*, Chap. 8, American Council on Education, Washington, D.C., 1938.

Shaw, Franklin J.: Two determinants of selective forgetting, *J. Abnorm. Soc. Psychol.*, 1944, 39:434–445.

CHAPTER 9　*The Structuring of Personality*

The biography of any given personality may be considered the longitudinal approach to an understanding of this person. To highlight and summarize such a biography a case study would be needed, particularly in connection with the problems being currently faced by the individual. So much material exists, however, in every biography that time and cost seldom permit the complete understanding of an individual by this means. Some quicker way to the answers must be found if such functions as education, counseling, job placement, and therapy are to proceed efficiently.

The classification, or typing, of personalities is an age-old practice. It tends in the wrong direction when used with prejudice and awkwardness, but in the hands of objective and skillful operators it can be very helpful. Recent studies in psychology have developed cross-sectional, or latitudinal, interpretations which provide a good foundation for classifying. These cross-sectional interpretations will be explored in the present chapter. Doubtless latitudinal and longitudinal studies of personality will both continue to present their own respective advantages and the two will continue to supplement each other.

DIMENSIONS OF PERSONALITY

The Concept of Dimension

Cross sectioning is implied in a technical term which has recently come into wide usage, *dimensions of personality*. Security-insecurity, for example, might be placed upon a scale as follows. On the far right hand, at *C*, would be the "Feeling of extremely great insecurity." At the far left hand, at *A*, would be the "Feeling of extremely great security." The distance between these two would describe the gradations of feelings from one extreme to the other. Each person would be rated as commonly fluctuating between the two extremes on the scale, as *B* suggests a small variation in feelings from day to day.

Feeling of extremely   Feeling of extremely
great security   great insecurity

A   C

B

Probably most personalities could be placed at the more central locations on the scale rather than at one of the extremes. But there would be some ratings at one or the other extreme. Personality and temperament tests frequently use this scale concept of personality dimension.

Similarly, dimensions can be found for other commonly recognized characteristics by measuring their range on other linear scales, such as competition-cooperation, social-antisocial, affectionate-reserved, stable-unstable, high-low energy, and high-low intelligence. All that is necessary to find a personality dimension is a measuring scale of validity and reliability. It is not necessary to assume that personality dimensions are forms of behavior determined through hereditary means. They are concerned with the individual as he is in the present, allowing for growth relationships from past into future.

Well-known Dimensions

Leadership-followership demonstrates the interpretation of personality dimension. It is an acquired competence which, in large measure, is of the nature of skill.[1] Some individuals are able to assume the leadership role in a group, to carry the responsibility of this role in ways which permit the followership roles to work effectively. Aggression, which is usually an emotionalized form of behavior, is sometimes contrasted with submission to form an aggression-submission scale. Sometimes individuals mistake aggres-

[1] Alex Bavelas, Morale and the training of leaders, pp. 143–165, in Goodwin Watson (ed.), *Civilian Morale*, Second Yearbook of the Society for the Psychological Study of Social Issues, Houghton Mifflin Company, Boston, 1942.

sion for leadership; however, few college students will be so deceived as to become followers of mere aggression.

Incidentally, there is as much ability required for good followership as there is for good leadership—a good leader works *within* the group, not ahead of it, and he realizes that the credit due him is no greater than that due any competent follower. This rather subtle concept of leadership is lost sight of whenever aggression is part of the personality of the leader.

Another dimension that has been commonly used is found by means of the introversion-extroversion scale. This is based on an ancient interpretation of behavior which was given systematic form in the writings of Jung.[2] He believed that the extrovert is inclined to perceive the external or objective conditions, while the introvert tends to perceive his own reactions predominantly. American psychologists have not followed Jung's emphasis; instead they have applied this approach more commonly to the study of the social interests or activities of the individual. This confusion in meanings, plus strong statistical evidence that most people are "ambiverts," is sufficient reason for avoiding any major usage of the introversion-extroversion scale as a basic dimension of personality.

Other recognized dimensions of personality, and any that may in the future be devised in addition to these, must be added to the known physiological dimensions. The latter might include biochemical balance scales such as were studied by Eysenck.[3] There probably should also be included any of the valid psychosomatic body types as dimensions.[4]

Most students of Freud seem to agree upon the pleasure-pain principle. The views of Alfred Adler might also be expressed in a scale, with "feelings of inferiority" and the "feeling of mastery or power" at opposite ends. Although these concepts of Freud and of Adler may now be thought of as scale concepts, or dimensions, their originators apparently did not think of them in quite this way.

[2] See Carl G. Jung, *Psychological Types: Or the Psychology of Individuation,* pp. 417, 472, Harcourt, Brace and Company, Inc., New York, 1923, for definitions of extrovert and introvert.

[3] Hans J. Eysenck, *Dimensions of Personality,* George Routledge & Sons, Ltd., and Kegan Paul, Trench, Trubner & Co., Ltd., London, 1948.

[4] William H. Sheldon, *The Varieties of Temperament: A Psychology of Constitutional Differences,* Harper & Brothers, New York, 1942.

In the study of personality by means of testing or statistical applications the concept of dimensions is very useful. It lends itself well to graphic representations such as charts and profiles. Final selection of the most fundamental dimensions, however, awaits the future.

TRAIT ANALYSIS

A somewhat different method of studying personality is found in the analysis of *traits*. Early studies tended to overgeneralize and oversimplify personality. Even today there are many pseudopsychological approaches to the study of personality which do this. Emphasis on measurements, based on the assumption that personality will necessarily express itself in bodily proportions or in facial dimensions, represents the perennial tendency to overgeneralize.

Nevertheless the concept of the personality trait has its valid uses. A trait is *a group of specific acts which have been organized into a pattern of behavior showing consistency in recurrence.* Traits, as thus defined, are subject to measurement. They serve to further the understanding of personality by simplifying the endless complexity which daily observations present. And they serve to emphasize the consistency or stability of a personality over relatively long periods of time.

The Constancy of Traits

An interesting example of trait measurement demonstrating the constancy of personality is found in a study of a group of college students measured on two occasions 6½ years apart. The questionnaire used both times was designed to measure neuroticism, considered as a combination of several traits. On both occasions 82.8 per cent of the questions were answered in an identical manner.[5]

Long-term constancy of traits is also shown in comparisons between child-guidance records of children and later records of their adult psychotic symptoms. Unquestionable evidence of this kind has been found in mentally ill persons.[6] Both normal and abnormal

---

[5] M. N. Crook, Retest correlations in neuroticism, *J. Gen. Psychol.*, 1941, 24:173–182.

[6] J. E. Birren, Psychological examinations of children who later became psychotic, *J. Abnorm. Soc. Psychol.*, 1944, 39:84–95.

personalities show constancy of trait behavior. Studies of intelligence also demonstrate this constancy. The study of personality by means of trait analysis, given adequate methods, holds much promise of success. Floyd Allport, who has been one of the leaders throughout much of the history of recent personality study, defined traits in 1924 as "groups of characteristic reactions based upon native constitution and systems of habit and selected for observation as exhibiting the typical adjustments of the individual to his environment."[7] He considered that a fairly adequate list of traits would include intelligence, motility, temperament, self-expression, and sociality. Today several additional ones could be noted, for further research has brought out new information and new interpretations. But Allport's list is remarkably comprehensive as it stands.

The Cattell Study

One of the most complete studies of personality by means of trait analysis is Cattell's elaborate survey of ratings. Rating technique usually requires the appraiser to fill out a list in which each trait is judged upon a *continuum* ranging from much to little, or upon a *scale* showing opposing traits at opposite ends. Cattell secured a tremendous quantity of ratings, representing almost all conceivable activities. These ratings were handled statistically in such manner as to form combinations which represented the actual grouping of the original activities.

The combinations Cattell finally reported are important evidence of the way acts are related to each other. Research has moved in this way toward a more modern concept of personality as an integration of activities. Cattell listed 121 "phenomenal clusters," or surface-level acts which tend to appear together as commonly observable behavior. These clusters were usually observed in certain relationships which he described as 50 "nuclear clusters." The latter showed sufficient interrelationships to justify a final listing of 20 "sectors of personality" which summarized all the many activities originally observed.

[7] Floyd H. Allport, *Social Psychology*, pp. 102–103, Houghton Mifflin Company, Boston, 1924.

Stagner's adaptation of Cattell's table of sectors of personality is presented in the following chart, which simplifies, or "boils down," the behavior of entire personalities into these relatively few traits.

PRINCIPAL SURFACE-TRAIT "SECTORS" OF PERSONALITY

1. Fineness of character　　　　　　vs. Moral defect, nonpersistence
   a. Integrity, altruism　　　　　　vs. Dishonesty, undependability
   b. Conscientious effort　　　　　　vs. Quitting, incoherence
2. Realism, emotional integration　　vs. Neuroticism, evasion, infantilism
   a. Realism, reliability　　　　　　vs. Neuroticism, changeability
   b. Practicalness, determination　　vs. Daydreaming, evasiveness
   c. Neuroticism, self-deception,　　vs. Opposites of these
      emotional intemperateness
   d. Infantile, demanding self-　　　vs. Emotional maturity, frustration toler-
      centeredness　　　　　　　　　ance
3. Balance, frankness, optimism　　　vs. Melancholy, agitation
   a. Agitation, melancholy,　　　　　vs. Placidity, social interest
      obstinacy
   b. Balance, frankness, sportsmanship　vs. Pessimism, secretiveness, immoderate-
      　　　　　　　　　　　　　　　ness
4. Intelligence, disciplined mind,　　vs. Foolish, undependable, unreflective-
   independence　　　　　　　　　　ness
   a. Emotional maturity, clarity of　vs. Infantilism, dependence
      mind
   b. Gentlemanly, disciplined　　　　vs. Extroverted, foolish lack of will
      thoughtfulness
   c. Creativity, self-determination,　vs. Narrowness of interest, fogginess
      intelligence
   d. Intelligence, penetration, general　vs. Lack of general ability
      talent
5. Egotism, assertion, stubbornness　vs. Modesty, self-effacement, adaptability
6. Boldness, independence, toughness　vs. Timidity, inhibition, sensitivity
7. Sociability　　　　　　　　　　vs. Timidity, hostility, gloominess
8. General emotionality, high-strung-　vs. Placidity, deliberateness, reserve
   ness, instability
9. Gratefulness, friendliness, idealism　vs. Sadism, slanderousness, suspiciousness
10. Liveliness, instability, verbal expres-　vs. Reserve, quiescence, naturalness
    siveness
11. Imagination, intuition, curiosity, care-　vs. Thrift, inflexible habits, smugness
    lessness
12. Bohemian, disorderly　　　　　　vs. Persevering, pedantic
13. Esthetic, thoughtfulness, construc-　vs. Absence of these
    tiveness
14. Physical strength, endurance, cour-　vs. Physical inactivity, avoidance of dan-
    age　　　　　　　　　　　　　ger
15. Amorousness, playfulness　　　　vs. Propriety

16. Alcoholism, rebelliousness, careless-   vs. Piety, reverence, thrift
    ness
17. Curiosity, wide interests   vs. Limited interests
18. Hypochondriacal, taciturn retrover-   vs. Eloquence, interest in future
    sion
19. Asceticism, eccentricity   vs. Comfort-loving conventionality
20. Inflexibility, wandering   vs. Adaptableness, ease of settling down

SOURCE: From Ross Stagner, *Psychology of Personality*, pp. 149–150, McGraw-Hill Book Company, Inc., New York, 1948, as adapted from R. B. Cattell, Principal trait clusters for describing personality, *Psychol. Bull.*, 1945, 42:129–161.

THE ARCHITECTURE OF PERSONALITY

The structure of a house is the basic arrangement of walls and beams which underlies the finished detail of interior as well as exterior decoration. In a similar way the structure of a personality is the basic framework upon which specific details of moment-to-moment behavior are built. With the finished house, the structure is commonly hidden by the detail work. With the personality, the deeper structure is not ascertainable by direct observation. But personalities are like houses in that some show their structural characteristics more clearly than others.

Certain people "wear their hearts on their sleeves." To the competent architect the structure of a building is readily apparent because he knows how buildings come into being and how the stresses and strains are counteracted within the structure. Competent psychological observers are able to perceive personality structure in much the same way. In both cases the arrangement of details and the general outlines indicate the important stresses and strains that the structure is meeting, as well as its general reaction to them.

In personality the foundation members of the structure will be the *core values*, observable only indirectly through several "layers" of behavior. Figure 9–1 expresses this concept graphically.

At the center are the *core values*, largely the feelings of security-insecurity. The layer next to the center is composed of *source traits*, first-level expressions of the core values, consisting largely of the hostility-friendliness feelings. Fanning out from these source traits are the *trait sectors*, the expressions of the source traits as actual experience has formed the individual's behavior. Cattell's twenty items describe this level of behavior very adequately.

Then there is the outer layer, which includes the commonly observed behavior of the individual. This behavior is illustrated by such simple specific acts as a man's hat tipping, a woman's hair tossing. Each of these, by itself, is meaningless and contributes nothing

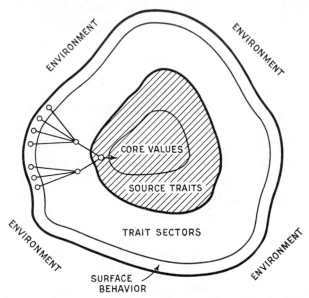

Fig. 9–1. Schematic diagram of structure of personality. The shaded area includes the motives which are nonspecific, *i.e.*, merely general and diffused tendencies toward action. This would be illustrated in the feeling of hunger, which may be interpreted as depression or discouragement, loneliness, homesickness, need for alcoholic beverage, or need for food. The original feeling must be expressed in relationship to surface behavior such as noting the time of day, or the social situation, before the motive can become specific. Because most conscious or attended behavior is *specific*, owing in part to the individual's background of experience in paying attention to specific figures of perception, he is ordinarily not aware of the portions of his personality structure indicated by the shaded areas. These probably coincide with much of the so-called "unconscious," although no duplication in meaning is intended by the authors.

to an explanation of the individual's behavior. But put these acts into the proper combination with other acts, and then put these combinations into the proper perspective as relationships between a person and his environmental situation, and the original acts begin to reveal the underlying motives and patterns of the inner layers of personality structure.

Motivation and Structure

Because motivation exerts its influences from the center outward, like the spokes of a wheel, the more consistent behavior in every individual tends to indicate which are the more central layers of values, *i.e.,* what the individual really wants. Surface acts are always *compromises* with the environment, hence they take on much of the variety and inconsistency of moment-to-moment environments. Similarly, the more central the source of the motive is, the more general its expressions in activity will be—the more different acts and perceptions it will motivate.

A man tipping his hat to the woman who lives next door may serve as a simple illustration of the structural levels in personality. The actual tipping of the hat is an act at the level of surface behavior. It "tells us nothing" about the man or his intentions. It merely serves as our starting point for observing him. Usually the observer notes some additional behavior, such as the man's smile or the lack of one, the generous or restrained manner in which he makes the hat-tipping gesture, and perhaps also the way in which he utters his greeting.

By combining, or grouping, various bits of behavior it is possible to discover something of the man's attitude toward his neighbor and the motives behind the hat tipping. He may be a "wolf" making overtures to his neighbor's attractive wife. Or he may feel really friendly toward his neighbor and get genuine enjoyment from this meeting. Or, again, he may have hopes of selling his neighbor a used car—or a mansion at the bottom of the sea.

Motives cannot be deduced in the course of a mere passing on the street. But the trait sectors do become apparent as behavior is observed broadly and over a period of time. The outer layer of surface behavior is utilitarian and always serves the deeper-lying purposes or motives. It is the nature of motives to produce concrete results, which become available for inspection. The hat-tipping man will sooner or later reveal his motives by attempting to get results. But also, as he tips his hat he will be much inclined to recite to himself his hoped-for accomplishments. This self-recitation is so much a part of behavior that he cannot completely avoid acting it out—as is commonly done on the dramatic stage. Overly sweet intonations do not completely hide the leer in the voice of the Wolf as he addresses Little Red Riding Hood. Trait sector 1 (moral defect, dishonesty, and undependability) would become evident as the surface behavior of the Wolf dramatically expressed his aspirations.

If the hat-tipping man felt genuine friendship and his surface behavior had no other purpose than to express his satisfaction at this moment of companionship with his neighbor, his trait sector would probably manifest no such *ambivalence* of motives as did the Wolf's. His motives might be complex, but they would not be in conflict, *i.e.*, of double valence. Instead, his expression of purpose would be "genuine" and express his integrity, or integration of personality. His sociability would not be in conflict with his purpose of deceiving a prospective customer.

Deeper Motives

At a deeper level, the source trait tends to represent an even broader or more generally influential tendency. *Hostility* is the approach to situations in a warlike, or "destroy before I am destroyed," manner. It indicates a dominant tendency to perceive other people as a threat. Its opposite, friendliness, is expressed through both trust and self-confidence. At the source-trait level there is little more than a general attitude which inclines all outer-level behavior to evidence either its hostility or its friendliness. One person might express his friendliness in a reserved but utterly truthful manner. Another might express it outwardly by much cordial gesturing and speaking. On the other hand a person might express his fear of not being accepted by fighting hard to *force* his acceptance. This would properly be called *hostility behavior*. Again, a person's fear of not being accepted might keep him from being as sociable as he really would like to be, and so he would use *rejection behavior*. Thus hostility and rejection both arise from much the same core values.

Core values, lying at the very center of the personality structure, stem from the earliest experiences of the individual. They are his infantile and unlimited generalizations as to how the "outer world" accepts him. They are his innermost generalizations as to the attitude toward himself of the world of things and people and even of sensations *not* under his control. Can he face this world with confidence, or does it forever threaten to thrust him away? Can he assimilate his contacts with this world, or must he resist in self-defense its pressures? As these questions are answered through the experiences of infancy and childhood, the individual builds a whole set of core values which grow in organic relationship with each other to form a unified self-concept. This self-concept is the nucleus around which the entire personality structure revolves in its homeostatic process of maintaining consistency and stability within the individual personality.

QUESTIONS FOR DISCUSSION

1. Give an illustration of a contemporary figure who appears to substitute aggression for leadership.
2. On your campus is aggression considered desirable as a quality for student leadership? Explain.
3. How could a clearer differentiation between mere aggression and true leadership affect democracy?
4. What factors make for qualities of followership? How can an understanding of the importance of this be spread?
5. What is the connection between aggression and totalitarianism?
6. Do you believe that most people consider the motivation behind actions?
7. Do you think that most people reveal their structural characteristics?
8. At what level of personality should charm and good manners be placed?
9. Do you believe that most people judge others by surface behavior?
10. Is friendliness always expressed in the same manner? Explain.
11. Describe the core value from which hostility stems.
12. Describe the hub at the center of confident behavior.
13. What are the similarities in core values of the person who is very hostile and the one who continually tries to please everyone?
14. Armed with the understanding derived from these chapters on personality, are you qualified now to analyze people? What are some of the precautions which must be remembered?
15. In what ways do you believe that more understanding of the growth of personality might help in solving some of the current local and national problems?

ADDITIONAL READINGS

Duffy, Elizabeth: A systematic framework for the description of personality, *J. Abnorm. Soc. Psychol.*, 1949, 44:175–190.

Fiske, Donald W.: Consistency of the factorial structures of personality ratings from different sources, *J. Abnorm. Soc. Psychol.*, 1949, 44:329–44.

Gibb, Cecil A.: The principles and traits of leadership, *J. Abnorm. Soc. Psychol.*, 1947, 42:267–284.

Guthrie, Edwin R.: *The Psychology of Human Conflict, The Clash of Motives within The Individual*, Chap. 12, Peter Smith, New York, 1950.

Macfarlane, Jean Walker: Study of personality development, Chap. 18, in R. G. Barker, J. S. Kounin, and H. F. Wright (eds.), *Child Behavior and Development: A Course of Representative Studies*, McGraw-Hill Book Company, Inc., New York, 1943.

MacKinnon, Donald W.: The structure of personality, Chap. 1, in J. McV. Hunt, *Personality and Behavior Disorders*, Vol. I, The Ronald Press Company, New York, 1944.

McClelland, David C.: *Personality*, Chap. 7, William Sloane Associates, New York, 1951.

Mead, Margaret: Problems of leadership and mental health, *Bull. World Federation for Mental Health*, 1949, 1(6):7–12.

Murphy, Gardner: *Personality: A Biosocial Approach to Origins and Structure*, Chap. 26, Harper & Brothers, New York, 1947.

Schettler, Clarence: Objective measurements of personality traits, *J. Person.*, 1947, 15:292–299.

Sherman, Mandel: *Basic Problems of Behavior*, Chap. 3, Longmans, Green & Co., Inc., New York, 1941.

CHAPTER 10   *The Adjustments of Personality*

The term "adjustment" appears in diverse uses. A very general meaning is the process of living itself, the dynamic equilibrium of the total organism or personality. The healthy person seems to live smoothly, taking things in his stride even when conditions are difficult. Less healthy persons become upset easily and require considerable time to get back into their stride again. The maintenance of homeostasis may be considered the *general adjustment process.*

A second use of the term refers to the state of *being adjusted.* A wrist watch can be adjusted, *i.e.*, put into good adjustment. A watch can thus be thought of as being poorly adjusted or as being well adjusted. And so it is with the human being. If his adjustment is poor, if he is maladjusted, he is immature, having not yet achieved the adjustment appropriate to his age. In either case the reference is to the individual's *type* or *pattern* of adjustment. This is his characteristic way of maintaining his own personality structure; it is evidenced particularly in his scheme of values. This more limited definition of adjustment is the one most used today.

A third use relates to the relative adequacy or *efficiency* of the individual's adjustment techniques. Good coordination in muscle activity means that the opposing members of the paired muscle groups do not pull against each other. When the contracting biceps muscles are pulling the forearm upward, the extensor muscles at the back of the upper arm should not be pulling the forearm downward. To have opposing muscles pull against each other is inefficient; when this happens, neither muscle group is able to function with minimum use of energy and maximum output of work.

Similarly, when motives within the personality pull against each other and *conflict,* and when the individual strives "to have his cake and eat it too," the resulting behavior remains indecisive and thus inefficient. *Conflict-laden* behavior illustrates inefficient adjustment simply because the individual has continued to be unable to learn his way into solving the problems he faces. He is afraid and resists at the same time that he is trying to move assimilatively into the new situation. It is efficiency of adjustment which constitutes the basis of the present discussion.

THE CONCEPT OF ADJUSTMENT

Nonadjustive Behavior

Sometimes it is not possible for an individual to adjust sufficiently within a given situation to indicate that his needs ever will be satisfied. Sometimes the pressures which bear down upon him threaten destruction or serious injury to his personality and then he judges himself helpless. Such a predicament is well described in Maier's famous studies of frustration behavior in rats.[1] The clarity of behavior patterns is much more obvious in rat behavior than in human, but the same fundamentals are present in both.

A laboratory setup was created similar to the one designed for earlier experiments by Lashley. The rat crouches upon a small platform facing a wall which is within jumping distance and contains two openings. Around one opening is a white card marked with a large circular black spot; around the other is a black card marked with a large circular white spot. The rat-subject is first trained to jump at one of the openings, by means of a food reward placed behind it. Thus it will be learned that one opening is preferable; when this opening is covered with a card, that card soon becomes the sign of the food reward.

Through varying the position of this card, with its food reward, the rat can be taught that the card and not its relative position indicates the food. Additional learning incentive can be provided by latching one or the other card, causing the rat to suffer a fall whenever he chooses incorrectly. When it has developed a card preference in this manner, any rat-subject may be said to have established a specific adjustment technique. This technique is efficient, or

[1] Norman R. F. Maier, *Frustration: The Study of Behavior without a Goal*. McGraw-Hill Book Company, Inc., New York, 1949.

"good," adjustment in that it achieves the food reward with predominant success.[2]

Once the behavior pattern has been established, it is possible to follow an irregular order for latching the cards. The latched card causes the rat to fall; the loose card permits him to enter and secure the food reward. This irregularity makes it impossible for the rat to exercise profitably his previously learned card preference. He follows his established tendency to jump, but only by chance strikes the unlatched card which covers the food reward. As often as not, his preferred card turns out to be latched tightly, causing him to fall annoyingly into the net below! He soon restrains his tendency to jump, holding himself in a crouching position on the platform in a hopeless or defiant attitude. His problem situation has become *insoluble*.

From this stage onward the experiment requires some form of *forcing* or *pressuring* to compel jumping. Prodding by a stick might work, but a more accurate control can be achieved through the use of short blasts of air of predetermined length and strength. The rat is thus forced to jump or to endure the painful blasts. This situation, combining an insoluble problem with strong pressure to launch into an established but unsuccessful jumping action, is a *frustration situation*. The rat becomes frustrated in it.

In goal-oriented behavior the organism characteristically moves forward into new relationships with its environmental situations. But when extremely frustrated, the organism seems determined to do nothing useful, to have no goal. It may refuse to act in any motivated way. Or it may compromise by jumping "abortively" toward the preferred goal in an awkward manner which precludes successful goal achievement. Neither of these actions improves the organism's relationship with its environment. They are therefore *nonadjustive* reactions. They serve merely to avoid in a primitive and crude way the threatened overstimulation and failure.

Humans as well as rats experience frustration. During the years of the great depression in America many formerly excellent workers became apathetic and goalless. Similarly, shortly after their discharge from military service men and women commonly experience

[2] *Ibid.*, pp. 25*ff.*

a period of adjustment in which they feel inclined "to do nothing." Their former military goals have been removed and their goal orientations in civilian situations are weak and confused. In some cases these nonadjustive reactions became chronic, *i.e.*, fixated.

The Scale of Adjustments

With the above concept of nonadjustive reaction in mind, it becomes possible to imagine a scale for rating the efficiency of specific adjustments. At one extreme would be the completely nonadjustive act, in which no improvement in the organism-environment relationships is achieved and therefore the behavior does not reduce tensions nor satisfy the organism's needs. At the opposing extreme would be a completely efficient act of adjustment, unrestrained and free-flowing.

Such a scale might be illustrated in the use of a dictionary. If the word sought is found promptly, if it has a simple definition, and if its spelling is known, there is no difficulty experienced in getting directly from the need for clarification to the satisfaction of knowing what the word means. The entire activity moves forward efficiently and successfully, each stage reassuring the individual as to his coming goal achievement. His feeling of impending success is quite the opposite of the frustrating feeling of inevitable failure.

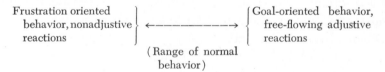

The above scale of adjustments entails an intermediate range of activity. All human activities are complex. Only on rare occasions is a situation completely frustrating or, for that matter, completely satisfying. It is very probable that every ordinary activity combines some elements from both extremes of the scale. Jim, for example, can see his way to an A in the history mid-term examination if he does a thorough job of review and preparation. But on the evening before that exam his girl friend wishes to attend an important reception which requires her to be escorted. No matter which alternative Jim chooses he must accept a measure of failure. He must lose in the exam or lose in love, if not in both. Ordinary behavior, ranging between the two extremes of the scale, draws frequently from each end but often more from one end than from the other. Few activities are hopelessly frustrating and few are entirely without some ingredient of frustration.

Tolerance for Frustration

In Maier's experiments some rats showed the same reaction. Some became permanently invalided. A few, the highly stable ones, continued to exhibit goal-oriented behavior long after the others had resorted to nonadjustive reactions. These few, following their experiences in the frustration apparatus, abandoned their behavior fixations. They maintained their ability to learn through *variation* of their own behavior whenever the situation permitted. Variation is characteristic of goal-oriented, or motivated, behavior. It is essential whenever the route to success has not yet been achieved. As was noted in the chapter on Motivation, motivated behavior shows three such general characteristics: *persistence, exploratory variation,* and *emotional energization.* In the few highly stable rats behavior continued to show all three characteristics. In other cases the rats lost their ability to vary their behavior, or ceased to show persistence in goal seeking. Behavior fixation replaced the variability, and then in some cases an *intense inactivity* replaced activity. A few of the rats launched into acute neurosis, *i.e.,* suffered complete nervous breakdown and were unable to return to normal, goal-oriented activity.[3] Nonadjustive reactions tend in this way to become the *persistent* nonadjustive reactions so characteristic of higher as well as of lower animals who have undergone severe *stress.* When an organism is undergoing stress, it is behaving as it is forced to, not as it would of its own accord.

Withdrawal into a shell, which is the snail's and the turtle's reaction to a forced or unacceptable situation, is literal nonadjustive reaction. With remarkable similarity in function, rats curl up and refuse to act when frustrated. Rabbits, when escape is impossible, cower and remain motionless except for trembling, as does a dog threatened with an unavoidable beating. So it is also with human beings. When the situation appears hopeless to the individual, he

---

[3] *Ibid.,* p. 35.

"How about society trying to get adjusted to me?"

Fig. 10–1. Rigidity can isolate. (*Reprinted by permission from Today's Health, 1951.*)

"withdraws into his shell" by becoming nonadjustive. Unfortunately these nonadjustive behavior patterns tend to become persistent— the individual loses some of his powers for varying even his motivated behavior. He thereafter finds himself more and more easily frustrated, more inclined to resort to stubborn or rigid stereotypes of past behavior. He gravitates toward the frustration end of the scale in his general adjustment pattern, fixates in his specific adjustment techniques.

Although completely frustrated men and animals react by complete nonadjustment, the most important area for the study of personality lies between the two extremes of adjustment. As noted above, human acts are normally complex. They include some stimuli which indicate frustration and some which indicate successful goal achievement. In this way the perceptual field includes vectors of resistance as well as of assimilation, difficult as well as easy possibilities for reconstruction. The attitudes or perceptual sets which the individual brings to a specific adjustment situation thus will cause him to prejudge the situation toward his more characteristic end of the scale of adjustment. Once having become fixated or stubborn in one phase of his living, he tends to develop more rigidity in other phases. This holds true even though the newly developed rigidity is relative rather than extreme. People who become very rigid in the economic phases of their living as a result of failures that have occurred in spite of great effort usually show rigidity in their social and religious living.

A Case of Nonadjustive Behavior

An illustration of the less extreme nonadjustive reactions is available in the life history of William Sidis. His father, a psychopathologist, sought to make him into a child prodigy. He finished eight years of elementary school in six months. At the age of eight he had devised a new logarithmic table based upon the mathematics of the number 12 instead of the usual number, 10. When he entered Harvard College, at the age of eleven, he astonished the faculty by his ability to discuss four-dimensional bodies. He graduated *summa cum laude*. At the age of twenty-one, having gained wide fame as a prodigy and mental wizard, he disappeared.

Five years later he was found working as an adding-machine operator. He refused to take any but petty office jobs, and his usual earnings barely sufficed for a simple livelihood. He had reached the limits of his mental capacity, and, being unable to keep up with his prodigious past record of continually performing new acts of genius, he felt frustrated. His refusal to attempt further achievement on the level of his earlier performances was evident in his complete avoidance of anything difficult or in line with his potentialities. He had "curled up inside his shell" by stubbornly remaining a nonentity. In 1944, before reaching middle age, he died of an intracranial hemorrhage, a fact which suggests prolonged nervous tension resulting in a vascular disorder. Being nonadjustive evidently is strenuous. Maintaining resistance by being insistently nonassimilative involves great and prolonged tension.

THE MECHANISMS FOR MAINTAINING SELFHOOD

Many studies of human adjustment demonstrate that Maier's rats were showing generally fundamental behavior. Of course studies of humans can hardly be so drastic as those of rats, but human beings have a way of obliging research workers inadvertently! Automobile and other accidents often produce brain damage which approximates the deliberate damage done in laboratories on the subjects in neurological experiments. Acutely neurotic patients appear in clinics and hospitals who present all the requisite behavior patterns for demonstrating the results of frustration. Only a case-history investigation is needed to make the neurotic patient a full substitute for deliberately frustrated laboratory animals. Clinical evidence provides in this way a wealth of information which is invaluable to the study of the psychology of personality. Such information must be kept as nearly at the *factual* level as is humanly possible. Thus the psychologist usually makes his own observations of the clinical patient and his own interpretations of case histories.

In the literature of clinical and psychotherapeutic study there has evolved a group of concepts called *adjustment mechanisms*. Frequently it is assumed that these mechanisms are essentially the same as the physiological mechanisms discussed earlier as functional systems and reflexes. The truth is that these are not inborn behavior patterns but are learned. Although such mechanisms are of little scientific use to students of personality, they serve to introduce a deeper level of understanding of the motives which underlie ordinary behavior. Moreover, in every area of study there is an obligation to be familiar with commonly used terms and ways of thinking.

To be recognizable an adjustment pattern must appear in identifiable form again and again. If its pattern is sufficiently defined to recur in this way, its very recurrence suggests that it is a *fixated* type of behavior resulting from difficult earlier experiences which probably were frustrating. Since variability is such an important characteristic of healthful behavior, clearly an excess of such fixated behavior is unhealthful. Mechanisms of adjustment are not only stable patterns of normal adjustment which are identifiable in the actions of very many different people; sometimes they also tend to be *rituals of nonadjustment*. In this extreme form they are readily recognized.

Compensation is an adjustment mechanism frequently found in literary and dramatic contexts. The character of Gloucester in Shakespeare's *Richard the Third* illustrates this adjustment mechanism.

> But I, that am not shap'd for sportive tricks,
> Nor made to court an amorous looking-glass;
>
> . . . . .
>
> I, that am curtail'd of this fair proportion,
> Cheated of feature by dissembling nature,
> Deform'd, unfinish'd, sent before my time
> Into this breathing world, scarce half made up,
> And that so lamely and unfashionable
> That dogs bark at me as I halt by them;
>
> . . . . .
>
> And therefore, since I cannot prove a lover,
> To entertain these fair well-spoken days,
> I am determined to prove a villain
> And hate the idle pleasures of these days.

A stunted and deformed body with narrowly limited possibilities for winning love and importance leads Gloucester to *compensate* by shrewd and loveless striving for power. Followers of Alfred Adler, whose writings stress the importance for every personality of the feeling of mastery, would probably describe Gloucester as evidencing an "inferiority feeling" or "inferiority complex.".

Doubtless many people do respond to negative influences and personal handicaps by aggressive behavior as did Gloucester. Equally important, however, is the fact that such aggressive behavior is often constructive. Social, religious, and political reforms have frequently been pioneered by leaders who obviously were compensating for limitations in their own respective personalities or their life backgrounds. Economic ambition, too, may be interpreted as compensation for economic or other weakness and insecurity. Serious scholarship doubtless has many times served as a compensatory effort put forth by the individual as his personal reaction to some inadequacy.

Identification is another adjustment mechanism that is widely encountered. It serves a more limited application than does compensation, for its immediate fruits are personal. Endless criticisms of "Hollywood movies" as being lowbrow, meaningless, inartistic, and degrading have apparently failed to achieve major reform of any sort. People still flock to the movies, even critical people! On psychological grounds, particularly in view of the many drab routines of house, factory, and office activity, *identification adjustments* make good returns for the price of admission. Witless and plodding persons may, for a brief hour, swell with pride in brilliant banter and meteoric fame as they forget themselves in identification with screen heroes and heroines.

The presence of the audience adds to this vicarious enjoyment a strong note of dramatic reality: laughs and sighs from the audience provide a touch of reality to the dreamlike experiences deriving from identification with the show characters. In a similar way, although more privately, love-starved persons live out their daily needs for romance in the overly tense dramas and relatively uncensored suggestions of consummated love on the screen. In normal living, pity, empathy, hate, rage, and every other specific emotion may be expressive of the identifying personality. Hero-worshiping ambition, too, may be a mechanism of identification, as are "back-fence gossip" and the morbid curiosity exhibited by laymen and professional workers alike.

Substitution is frequently used by adults in dealing with children when an unapproved act is "sidetracked" by presentation of another and more acceptable line of action. An apple—a more healthful and equally interesting or appetizing snack—may be substituted for a lollipop. A trip to the zoo may substitute for a denied visit to the movies. In adult living this process is more likely to appear as replacement of fame by economic gain. The recognition achieved through being noticed in a social group may be substituted for the experience of being responded to by a beloved person. Many of these substitutions are of minor significance and get lost in the daily routine. Important ones, however, are often only half successful. The individual finds himself continuing to want the original goal even after the substitute has been accepted and the matter "settled." Substitutions serve to use up accumulated energy and to release tensions for the time being. They thus pave the way for other mechanisms to work more effectively. It is doubtful whether substitutions are ever adequate to long-term needs, but they are useful in emergencies.

Sublimation, as interpreted by psychologists, relates closely to substitution. But as interpreted by many psychoanalysts the term has to do with the expression of sex drives or interests through such seemingly unrelated channels as art, music, sports, and even religious activities. In the psychological interpretation, when a major interest in life is blocked or frustrated the individual may intensify some of his other activities to such a pitch of effort that he becomes more or less completely absorbed. His earlier, frustrated interests tend to disappear as his new satisfactions broaden and intensify.

When an individual is attempting sublimation he typically launches into his new program of action with increased intensity of effort. Rejected suitors may sublimate through increased application to job, studies, or hobbies or through intensified concern for their other friends. Unmarriageable youths may enter enthusiastically a field involving work with children. Socially uncouth students may concentrate on their studies and eventually become great scholars. Individuals whose verbal competence is slight may find their athletic powers of increased interest, thus avoiding anticipation of poor scholastic records while gaining broader satisfactions. Not all sublimations are successful, but these examples show the possible results of intensified effort which is positively oriented, even though its launching is motivated by failure.

Negativism is a mechanism which serves everyone in one way or another. To be negative is to be "contrary" or "mulish." Suggestions are taken to be commands, and commands are taken as impositions calling for aggressive resistance. Sometimes a negativistic individual even refuses to do things he really would enjoy, merely because these acts have been suggested to him by a person toward whom he feels negative. Such reactions play an important part in late infancy and in adolescence, for during these periods the individual is experimenting with being independent.

This mechanism provides a kind of "retreat" by aggression; inwardly the individual feels that he is making a show of independent strength. That there is a deeper feeling of inadequacy, which is only screened over by this show of strength, is today commonly assumed. Students sometimes feel negative toward their instructors, employees toward supervisors, the poor toward the wealthy, and vice versa. Unions and managements often assume negativistic attitudes toward each other, as do racial groups, religious organizations, and cultural classes. Much negativism is little more than a transplanted parent-child antagonism which has been carried on into the adult years. But negativism serves some useful purposes, too, as in the case of good citizens feeling negative toward criminal persons and other antisocial groups.

Rationalization is a process of devising acceptable explanations for apparent failures. These explanations may be offered in good but superficial faith, merely for the record. They may be believed with sincerity. Face-saving on the golf course, by a dramatic trampling down of the imaginary weed which "misdirected" the rolling ball, illustrates this. If the cause-and-effect process which is thus suggested were factual, the golfer's competence would not be put in doubt. The process of rationalization is also explained as "emotional" thinking, *i.e.,* thinking wishfully instead of objectively or factually. Many of the folkways and mores of every social culture doubtless would disappear promptly if it were not for the support given them by elaborate systems of rationalization. Travel and cultural intermingling soon make many of these cultural rationalizations evident, but they frequently fail to change the individual's daily use of rationalization as a means of evading reality.

Several techniques of rationalization have been given names drawn from mythology and folklore. The "sour grapes" are merely the ones which the fox could not reach. In this way, rejected appli-

"*I'll wait another ten minutes—and if he doesn't show up I'm jilting him!*"

Fig. 10–2. Rationalization is a face saver. (*Courtesy of Esquire Magazine, 1952.*)

cants for jobs sometimes say, "I didn't really want that job anyway." The "sweet lemons" are the opposite of sour grapes: they are second choices or left-overs which must be made to appear as first choices.

Projection is the technique of seeing one's own wishes and ulterior motives as if operative in another person.[4] The gambler justifies his immoral acts by saying that "all life is a gamble," thus projecting his own interests into the entire universe. Blame projections, illustrated by the golfer described above who "blamed" the weed, are common in children and people who are not very sure of themselves.

[4] This use of the term "projection" must be kept separate from the use discussed in the chapter on Perception. The present use is less fundamental, but not in conflict with the other.

Hero-worshiping projections, in which credit is taken for more than one's true accomplishment, form a means of rationalizing oneself into importance. The personification of inanimate objects and of animals is in essence a process of projecting purposes so as to rationalize criticized behavior which we do not wish to change. Rationalization thus ranges from simple but undemonstrated "explanations" to the extremely complex "systematized delusions" of the mentally ill person.

Escape mechanisms are of two general types: *daydreaming* and *regression*. The former, much the same as night dreaming, tends to fulfill the needs of the individual. Daydreams offer momentary but dramatic relief from frustration. Temporarily the individual is removed or "flown" from the conflict-laden situation, with resulting satisfaction and relaxation. Unfortunately, this relaxation is only as enduring as the distraction of the dream, which comes to an end when bodily tensions get strong and when sense receptors demand attention. Daydreams range from these moments of simple escape to the formulation of ideals and utopian schemes expressing true genius. Daydreams are fantasies. They may be provoked by fleeting incidents or profound experiences, by the drama, music, literature, or art, by alcohol or drugs. It is difficult to draw the line between wholesome fantasy and the unhealthy extreme of mere escapism, even in the daydreaming that springs from wholesome stimuli.

Regressions are escapes by return to an earlier-known way of behaving. Usually these regressions are to a simpler form of interpretation of the problematic situation which is pressing. Sometimes the retreat is even to a childish or infantile level. Small children normally want to be "babied" occasionally, indicating that they sometimes feel discouraged by the daily increase of new responsibility which is a necessary part of growing up. Adults enjoy similar regressions when they visit the scenes of their childhood happiness. Adolescent temper tantrums are regressions to the period of late infancy, as are the stubborn spells of many aged persons. Regressive acts are common and useful behavior mechanisms so long as they do not lead to undesirable results of commission or omission. Temporary escape frequently offers a moment for recovery, a refreshing interlude. Perhaps much of the drowsiness and sleep which are enjoyed at times when fatigue is not based upon real exertion is essentially an escape mechanism. Prolonged regressions, however, should be considered as serious indication of need for professional help.

Other behavior mechanisms have been described by various writers. The preceding interpretations would not receive the full approbation of some unusually specialized viewpoints. But in general these are the well-known behavior mechanisms. They do not indicate abnormality except as they may be used in extreme or drastic form. An hour of daydreaming a day, *e.g.*, is quite harmless and may even be advantageous if oriented toward idealizations and plan building. Much time spent in mere mind wandering, on the other hand, indicates quite a different trend and should be carefully watched. The same is true for extremes of any other behavior mechanism, either in the intensity or in the frequency of the individual's dependency upon it. Some understanding of these behavior patterns is a handy tool with which to evaluate one's own adjustment practices as to their degree of efficiency.

WELLSPRINGS OF NEUROTICISM

The traditional behavior mechanisms continue to serve a useful purpose by aiding amateurs to interpret the behavior of their friends and neighbors. By means of these mechanisms, rather satisfying insights into behavior at outer levels of personality structure may be gained. But the deeper and more complete understandings can be gained only by way of a theory of personality. One such theory has been sketched in an earlier chapter and may now be applied to some of the many forms of adjustment which so often puzzle the layman.

Maintenance of Selfhood

Throughout all adjustment activities there is one general pattern, the *maintenance of selfhood*. This general pattern is, it will be recalled, the homeostatic equilibrium of the total personality. It shows generally as the tenacious and persistent following out of the life cycle, interpreted specifically through the individual's life history or biography. All his specific motives will contribute to this general pattern of growth. Each period of his biography will necessarily and unavoidably take important motives from the physiological phases of his make-up. Other phases, also necessary and unavoidable, will come through the sociocultural media. And still other phases will manifest directly his own unique scheme of values. Such a concept of the nature of personality is, unfortunately, difficult to grasp. But then, personality itself is far from simple or static.

"Ugly part of town, ain't it?"

Fig. 10–3. Perceptions develop from past experiences. Unpleasant situations in regard to these various sights have affected the evaluations being made. These youngsters have developed an antagonistic feeling toward anything connected with their unhappy experiences. (*Cartoon by Stan Fine. Courtesy of The American Magazine.*)

An illustration of the maintenance of selfhood appears in a recent incident in which a local college professor was billed by a physician for an office call in which he had seen the nurse but not the physician. The two professional men were unable to resolve their impasse, each feeling that to give in would be to accept a subordinate status which would imply a loss of selfhood. After several months of continual billing and curtly written replies denying the obligation to pay for the office call, the bill was placed in the hands of a collection agency, which threatened to take the usual legal action to enforce payment. To avoid the added expense of such court action, the professor paid the full bill, explaining that he was doing so only to avoid the inconvenience that the unethical means used by the physician would entail.

Thus the professor felt that he was not manifesting his true selfhood in this act of payment, since he did not approve of payment for services not performed. The physician promptly replied, in evident defense and maintenance of selfhood, that he had turned the endorsed check over to a foundation for cancer research. Thus he had "not accepted" money from a disputed account, had not forced payment to himself of money for services which he had not performed. Each man felt that he had been able to maintain his professional ethics, had not lost in selfhood. Both had followed an adjustment process essentially the same, even though it obviously does not appear complete to an outside observer. Each must have retained some small measure of doubt as to the adequacy of such a settlement. In a small way the professor had lost status, and in a small way the physician had acted counter to his concept of himself as an ethical practitioner.

As was described earlier, the selfhood which is maintained is highly complex. The physiological phases of the self are structural residues of the past, including organic conditions achieved through maturation and learning. The self-concept phase is a perceptual pattern which has grown out of the individual's personal history and which expresses his scheme of values. These values are known subjectively at one extreme as *feelings of achievement and adequacy* and at the opposite extreme as *feelings of failure and inadequacy*.

The professor and the physician were maintaining similar self-concepts, *i.e.*, honest and ethical selves adequate to the professional standards of their respective careers. To be adequate to these careers, these selves must be able to resist encroachment by persons and situations which exploit and pressure the individual into unethical or dishonest activities. Each man had to adjust his own self-concept to the external situation of charges and payments and legal conventions. But at the same time each man had to take account of his own self-integration, in this case of his loss of selfhood through having not acted quite as he really felt he should have acted. This residual feeling of loss of selfhood is a *guilt* feeling, or a feeling of *inadequacy*.

Loss of Selfhood

The technically recognized "inferiority feeling" and the popularly known "inferiority complex" show themselves to the psychologically trained observer as admissions of inadequacy. An individual who lacks the power or strength necessary to achieve his own chosen goals has not the ability to carry out his own plans for being himself. His scheme of values implies a competence which he cannot prove either to himself or to others that he possesses. His own worth is thus less than he feels necessary. These feelings of inferiority or inadequacy represent *conflict states* in which the self-concept is threatened—the individual is in danger of having it proved to him that he is not in existence in the manner he thought he was. He is, in this way, perhaps not himself! He therefore struggles to remain himself in accordance with his accepted scheme of values. What shall he do, it being recognized that he is not willing to lose the self that he has been and yet is not willing to change this self as seems to be necessary? Like Maier's rats, this individual is unable to resolve the conflict, cannot evade it successfully, and so launches into frustration behavior.

An illustration of the loss of selfhood just described is dramatically presented in the "old sergeant syndrome" which became well known during World War II.[5] This syndrome was seen only in Army divisions which experienced prolonged battle commitments without relief, and then only when the men were well motivated, previously efficient soldiers. These men were usually described by their officers as the "old reliables" of the Army. Many had received citations, awards, and medals for outstanding conduct and devotion to duty. These excellent soldiers eventually developed abnormal tremulousness, sweating, and a tendency to be the last to leave a foxhole after having been the first to get into it. Once this condition set in,

[5] *Combat Psychiatry*, Bulletin of the U.S. Army Medical Dept., Supplemental Number, November, 1949, 137–146.

they were almost useless to their units and had to be removed from the zone of combat.

When not under fire, these men usually behaved normally. In combat they took a hopeless attitude and were unable to make quick decisions involving the lives of the other men. They were "sweating it out until the one with their serial number on it came along," *i.e.,* they felt doomed to death and there was nothing to do but wait. When assigned to combat duty, these men tried their best but became so fearful that they could not control themselves. Because they "would not send their men in where they could not go themselves," they were useless if not detrimental to the Army command.

Study by Army psychiatrists revealed that these men were usually the sole survivors of groups of men who had seen exceptionally hard and long battle service. Once the facts were placed in order, their breakdowns seemed to follow a clearly discernible pattern. Prolonged and intense defeat, felt each time one of their buddies was lost in battle, if not destroyed physically right in front of them, took its toll. They could not help but feel inadequate, totally unable to help their closest comrades, even though it was comradeship which meant most of all to them in the hours spent awaiting battle. Like layers peeled from an onion, their ideals had been stripped from them.

First to come off was the *remote* ideal, such as fighting to win the war to preserve the "four freedoms." These men lost this ideal after seven or eight months of combat, coming to feel that they "hadn't time to talk about such things when under a barrage." Usually they substituted a form of personal religion and prayer for this distant ideal.

Next to peel off was the *hatred of the enemy* which they had learned through propaganda and training for combat. In place of this original generalized hatred, these men usually developed a specific hatred such as could be traced to the killing of a buddy by the enemy. But these specific hatreds seemed to be inadequate to maintain the personality during combat. Sometimes they even led to feelings of guilt related to the belief that it is not right to hate anyone.

The third layer to peel off was the *short-term goal.* The men often felt that after prolonged combat they would be relieved. Frequently they were heard to remark, "If we take this next hill, we get a rest." Such short-term goals often proved to be boomerangs, for usually the next assignment of these men was to get ready immediately for the next battle. Thus the feeling of exhaustion changed into a feeling of futility and hopelessness or inadequacy.

Next to peel off, after the feeling of futility had developed, was *pride in self*. This was indeed the breaking point for the self-concept, the point at which loss of selfhood occurred. The combat-experienced soldiers were often promoted to the rank of sergeant, and at such times the feeling of futility which had been developing became even more acute. It now involved an enlargement of self through increased responsibilities. Thus the vicious cycle of added responsibility conflicting with the deep-seated feeling of reluctance to face further combat rapidly led matters from bad to worse. Pride now degenerated rapidly.

The last layer, and probably the most important defense against the breakdown of personality, was *loyalty to the group*. This loyalty attached only to the immediate group, such as the platoon to which the individual was then assigned and through which his own actions were determined. Since in combat the individual is dependent for his own survival chiefly upon the actions of his comrades, there is only one way in which this individual can respectably find a way out—by being killed or wounded. Any other way is disloyal to the very men to whom he owes his own survival. But under the individual's very eyes this group is depleted through battle losses. Such an experience is more than man seems able to take, and the individual at this stage is ripe for an emotional breakdown.

When the soldier's special friend, or someone he has admired, is killed or injured, the "straw that breaks the camel's back" is added to his burden. He usually suffers an uncontrollable reaction of weeping and rage, which may last only a short while or may be prolonged. In either case he is not likely to be able to face combat again. His last defense within his own personality has been broken through. Humans, like the lower animals, can stand only so much. As we analyze the old sergeant's syndrome, by watching the soldier as he is stripped of his ideals, layer by layer, we see the inner structure of the personality mercilessly exposed to pressures which inexorably force the self-maintenance to the point of complete inadequacy.

Human Neuroses

Unlike that of the lower animals, however, human frustration behavior manifests itself in many different and often subtle ways. Perceptions structure themselves so that the individual's feeling of inadequacy becomes a vision of impending doom or catastrophe. The pattern of his life appears to be a series of dreadful incidents which cannot be avoided. Because he feels his own inadequacy, he attends to his own subjective experiences instead of attending to the objective stimulus situations. This *egocentric tendency* weakens his chances for learning to manage his environment. He cannot approach these new situations adventurously, wishing to learn, for he is fearfully resisting these same portions of his environment.

A slow but definite trend toward *rigidity of personality structure* marks his relationships with people and things. He becomes increasingly resistant to changing his own ways, even though these ways consistently result in failure. Thus he holds out until pressures upon him accumulate. Then he gives in only to increasingly intense demands and pressures. His life tends to become predominantly a reaction to pressure. This trend entails an almost directly proportionate increase in frustration. For the more resistant he becomes, the more often mere change in his environment becomes pressure upon him to change his way of living. Literally but unwittingly he is "asking for trouble."

Every change in the environment becomes a threat to the stability of the frustrated personality. His adequacy or competence, like that of the "old sergeant" casualty, in the face of a world perceived by him to be increasingly threatening is more and more often placed in doubt. His *tolerance for frustration* lowers. Each new effort at resistance to these dreadful pressures promises to be the breaking point. The individual then finds that his older reassurances no longer seem to work. He becomes "sensitive" and defensively emotional. He is anxious, *i.e.*, he evidences *anxiety*. He seems ever aware of his unstable situation and his impending destruction or loss of selfhood. Eventually, upon meeting an especially difficult situation, he launches into extremely emotional and disorganized behavior. This is the *nervous breakdown,* the *acute neurosis.* It is a *catastrophic reaction,* preceded by a period of anxiety which may or may not have been recognized.

"*Well, I finally saw that psychiatrist you've been pestering me about, and I give you three guesses who's at the root of all my trouble.*"

Fig. 10–4. Defense of self can become the overwhelming preoccupation of an individual. (*Reproduced by permission, copyright 1951 by The New Yorker, Inc.*)

But there are *in-between degrees* of failure as well as in-between stages in the development of a breakdown. Loss of an arm or leg will set narrower limits to an individual's activities and in this way reduce somewhat his possibilities for living out his previous scheme of values. Loss of faith in his own competence, amounting to the feeling that he is inadequate or inferior relative to whatever values he has believed in for himself, results in a narrowing of the limits of living. This narrowing results from the development of nonadjustive and rigid or ritualistic patterns of behavior which have no relation to changing reality. Rigid selfhood is an inferior substitute for normal adjustment by dynamic self-maintenance. Personality assimilation is greatly reduced by fear-laden rigidity. A vicious cycle is set up in which the personality both fails to adapt to circumstances and also fails to grow into improved powers of understanding. Self-maintenance thus becomes increasingly difficult as self-understanding becomes weakened and more limited.

Rigidities resulting from the unresolved frustrations which arise from the individual's value behavior (evaluations) are the *wellsprings of neurosis*. They start in small ways, ways that gain in significance as time passes. They peel off the various outer layers of the personality by destroying outward expressions of the scheme of values. The core value of unacceptability, which had its start in early infancy, predisposes the individual to such rigidities and the attendant frustration experiences. Frustration may appear at any stage of the life cycle and, if severe or drastic enough, weaken the personality structure. This is what, in a life history, is termed "traumatic neurosis," a condition susceptible of relief through psychotherapy and rest. A life history which begins with feelings of unacceptability and which later on shows the neurotic syndrome would thus be called "psychoneurotic."

Psychoneurosis involves an early predisposition to a low tolerance for frustration. The psychoneurotic individual will become nonadjustive and rigid under less severe strain than the individual whose core values include feelings of acceptability. Everyone has a breaking point, but some have greater endurance than others, depending upon the core values with which life starts—a fact which seems hopelessly fatalistic until it is realized that the individual can, if he works at it, develop skills *in* living and values *of* living which will buttress his weakened beginnings. Put into other language, these unresolved frustrations first threaten and then erode away the values from the individual's personality structure until his remaining self-concept is but a thin and weak semblance of what it formerly was. The nature of the task of personality reconstruction is suggested by this simple fact.

PATTERNS OF DEVIATE BEHAVIOR

Definition

Behavior which may properly be called "well-adjusted" tends to lack frustration tendencies. It is typical of the organism which learns to understand its new stimulus situations. This understanding indicates a form of personality change which takes place through *the organism's learning to manage itself successfully in new situations.* By means of success experiences of this sort the organism builds its attitudes toward its own future. Much success is needed to build the feelings of adequacy which are the only known justification for welcoming new experiences with new people, new things, and new ideas. The individual grows through these success experiences. Also the general pattern of these experiences becomes the pattern of understanding which this individual will use in the future to interpret the world and his own place in it. Success begets a feeling of confidence in understanding, of faith in the universe. Failure begets a feeling of inadequacy, of anxious distrust of a threatening universe. And only the individual within himself can be the judge as to what is success and what is failure. Only he is sensitive to the valences in his perceptions which anticipate assimilative acceptance or frustrated resistance to the stimulus.

Deviate behavior is merely behavior in which the organism's activity differs from normal ways of living. It is, of course, normal to develop the earlier described frustration or nonadjustive reactions. But this development is not healthful. Frustration reactions may start in infancy and progress slowly, giving the individual opportunity to develop strength despite the early appearance of conflict. Or they may develop into what Overstreet has called a "pervasive uneasiness in the handling of life." [6] Or, again, they may remain a nucleus of neuroticism which like a festering sore will increase its proportions and become in later years really serious. If the individual merely carries limited and specialized maladjustments onward from infancy, corresponding parts of his living will always remain *infantile*.

Behavior which has become rigid or fixated at the time of some early frustrating experience tends to remain very much as it was. Fears in food taking, fixated in infantile form, remain fundamentally infantile throughout life; in this category are irrational distastes and even specialized tastes. Usually these infantilisms are glossed over by subsequently learned mannerisms such as food fads, overconcern with body weight, and emotional overeating. This is one example of nonadjustive self-maintenance.

Catastrophic Reactions

Oddly enough, fixated behavior seems to be dominant over adaptive behavior. Subjects with varying degrees of rigidity of personality who are given the Thematic Apperception Test make it very evident that in spite of superficial changes in mood the underlying personality pattern of rigidity or fixated behavior remains constant once developed. [7]

Once the rats in Maier's experiments had become neurotic, they showed changes in social behavior suggesting withdrawal. Their ability to stand repetition of the frustration situation also diminished. Socially and experimentally these rats seemed to substitute for adaptive learning behavior various forms of resigned, regressive, or aggressive behavior. Other experiments have found the same reactions to be true for other animals, *viz.*, dogs, cats, pigs, etc. [8] Clinical evidence points to the same conclusion for humans. Once the human individual has been frustrated to the point of fixation of the behavior pattern, he becomes relatively less able to adapt or adjust to new situations. He resorts to the same resigned, regressive, or aggressive behaviors as the lower animals. In this way a *trend of*

[6] Harry A. Overstreet, *The Mature Mind*, p. 23, W. W. Norton & Company, New York, 1949.

[7] Silvan S. Tomkins, *The Thematic Apperception Test: The Theory and Technique of Interpretation*, p. 17, Grune and Stratton, Inc., New York, 1947.

[8] Maier, *op. cit.*, pp. 140–154.

behavior is started which will distort all later experiences. The substitute and the fixated behaviors become parts of the selfhood which he thereafter strives to maintain in homeostatic equilibrium.

Case histories show that major frustrations, those which produce fixated reactions, may occur at any age or period of life. But these extreme, or traumatic, experiences clearly are not the only sources of maladjustment. Drastic experiences on the field of battle, natural catastrophes, and serious accidents do not always lead to traumatic neurosis. Certain personalities in the face of great danger tend to anticipate total and unavoidable destruction of themselves. Reactions of this sort are, in a very real sense, *catastrophic reactions* and therefore greatly disorganizing.

There is much evidence in the files of schools, welfare agencies, and mental-hygiene clinics to support the theory that human traumatic neuroses ordinarily occur only when predispositions are present. These predispositions are the same as underlie the personality structure described as "psychoneurotic." The distinction formerly made between traumatic neurosis and psychoneurosis has therefore ceased to be of fundamental importance.[9] It seems only to suggest the relatively drastic nature of the events immediately preceding the acute breakdown.

Psychoneurotic Disorders

The Veterans' Administration has carried on considerable research on psychoneurotic disorders. Following is a simplification of an outline devised by authorities of this group.[10]

The chief characteristic of these disorders is anxiety, which may be either "free-floating" and directly felt and expressed or unconsciously and automatically controlled by utilization of repression, conversion, displacement, etc. In contrast to psychotics, patients with such disorders do not exhibit gross distortion or falsification of reality, and there is no gross disorganization of the personality.

Anxiety in psychoneurotic disorders is a danger signal felt and perceived consciously. The various ways in which the patient handles this anxiety result in various types of reactions.

[9] Lawrence I. O'Kelly, *Introduction to Psychopathology*, pp. 191*ff*., Prentice-Hall, Inc., New York, 1949.

[10] *Veterans' Administration Technical Bulletin T B 10A-78*, pp. 3–5, Appendix A, Washington, D.C., 1947.

1. *Anxiety reaction:* Anxiety diffuse—not restricted to definite situations or objects as in case of phobias, not controlled by psychological defense mechanisms. Psychological and physiological aspects of anxiety are felt by patient but only the latter observable by physician.

2. *Dissociative reaction:* Anxiety may overwhelm and momentarily govern the total individual in acute cases. In less acute cases, repressed impulses giving rise to anxiety may be expressed as depersonalization, dissociated personality, stupor, fugue, amnesia, dream state, somnambulism.

3. *Phobic reaction:* Anxiety becomes detached from specified idea or situation in the daily life behavior . . . and is displaced to some symbolic idea or situation in the form of a specific neurotic fear . . . , *e.g.,* of syphilis, dirt, closed places, high places, open places, some animals, combat noises, planes, etc.

4. *Conversion reaction:* Anxiety, instead of being experienced consciously, is converted into functional symptoms in organs or parts of body. Ordinarily such reactions meet immediate needs and are associated with "secondary gains."

5. *Somatization reactions:* Anxiety is relieved by channeling through autonomic nervous system into visceral organ symptoms and complaints. The symptom is due to chronic, exaggerated state of normal physiology of the emotion with subjective part partly or completely repressed. Long-continued visceral dysfunction may actually eventuate in structural changes.

6. *Asthenic reaction:* Physiological neuro-endocrine residue of previous anxiety and not necessarily an active psychological conflict appears in general fatigue; also associated with visceral complaints.

7. *Obsessive-compulsive reaction:* Anxiety as obsessional fear of uncontrollable impulses or under apparent control through a mental mechanism. The emotional charge may manifest itself in useless, excessive or repetitive activity. These symbolic acts temporarily protect patient against threat.

8. *Hypochondriacal reaction:* Anxiety shown in obsessive concern about state of health and multiplicity of complaints about different organs.

9. *Depressive reaction:* Anxiety allayed and thus partially relieved by self-depreciation and guilt for past failures and deeds; precipitated by current situation although dynamically the depression is usually related to repressed aggression.

Anxiety Reactions

All neurosis seems to be built upon underlying and prolonged anxiety. This is indeed in line with the theory, described earlier, that personality centers in the building of the self and the homeostatic maintenance of selfhood.

There are many ways in which the individual may defend himself against the continuing changes in his environment. The seemingly unlimited variety of personalities and of ways of thinking and doing suggests that among maladjusted and well-adjusted people alike there will always be great variety of behavior. But a little genius for understanding behavior and a large amount of effort and experience in working with people have yielded a simple interpretation of this seemingly unlimited variety. This simplification stems directly from the concept of adjustment, which places the *feeling of anxiety* at the center of maladjusted behavior.

No matter what the variety of behavior, the psychologist must pierce through to the fundamental layers of personality structure, to the core values. If the core values established in the earliest periods of the individual's life history are laden with fear of the outer world, he is thereby predisposed to develop anxiety as to his ability to cope with that world.

Phobias

For purposes of illustration two classifications in the outline will be discussed briefly: *phobic reactions* and *obsessive-compulsive reactions*. As is noted, phobic reactions are anxiety reactions in which the specific fear has become detached from its original object. Fears thus detached are free to add their impetus to others which may have developed earlier or which may appear later. They may add also to an existing anxiety, strengthening it and becoming powerful but unreasoned fears *attached to some symbol of the breakdown of selfhood*. The American poet William Ellery Leonard vividly describes a phobic reaction to railroad engines in *The Locomotive-God*. He pictures his general feeling of "objectless terror" and his impelling need to find an object for this feeling in order to "understand" it.

Phobic reactions frequently seem to center in acts which are related to the individual's attitude toward cleanliness and safety. The following case illustrates a rather common reaction of this sort.

Mr. J. was a successful salesman whose business deals required him to spend most of his time in downtown office buildings. He seemed to enjoy his work, finding only one aspect of it distasteful. The use of public washrooms worried him considerably and was an increasing problem. He carefully avoided all direct contact between his hands or body and the equipment in these washrooms. He used paper towels as "gloves" whenever he touched faucets or soap dispensers or even doorknobs. At the time of his first psychological interview he was experiencing a feeling of general anxiety each morning as he made preparations for his day's work. This way of starting the day seemed to take much of the "punch" out of his first contacts.

Careful exploration by means of case study and projective tests revealed that Mr. J. was overdependent upon his mother, that he had gone into selling against her wishes, that his early home training had stressed greatly that he be a "good boy," and that he had suffered from general nervousness over a period of many years. He had maintained since childhood a strong interest in a small local religious group which stressed a doctrine of eternal damnation for "cardinal sin." He currently held a position of lay leadership in this group.

Interpretation of this case stressed the long-standing condition of anxiety, the history of nervousness, the near-fanatical extreme of religious faith, and the choice of such a hate-laden doctrine. It appeared that Mr. J.'s choice of religious belief actually expressed a deep-seated hostility probably directed toward his dominating mother. He also felt deeply guilty for each of his acts which went contrary to his mother's opinions and could thus be considered disrespectful or unloving toward her. Sin, meaning to him both the doctrinal taboos related to fornication and his failure to love his own mother, was symbolized in the possibility of venereal infection from the public washrooms and toilets. He actually felt himself to be deeply sinful, *i.e.,* unclean, but was not clear as to why.

His hostility feelings toward his mother must never be faced, for he could not bear to admit such sinful behavior. On the surface he had spent so much of his life being the "good boy" he had been taught to be, that those deeply hidden feelings must be kept hidden, except as they might be brought out through surface-trait activities which did not look sinful. The possibility of infection acquired unavoidably and through circumstances beyond his control in the process of honorably earning his livelihood thus served his needs.

His particular "damnation" for sinful guilt could be expressed in this subtle manner, thus permitting him to act out through his bodily, or functional, systems the tensions which existed within him. His specific fear was merely one symptom of the general phobic reaction.

"Shut up! Who's driving anyhow? I'll go as fast as I please! If you don't like the way I drive, you can get out and walk..."

THE SATURDAY EVENING POST

Fig. 10–5. Hostility can be expressed harmlessly. (*Copyright 1951 by the Curtis Publishing Company.*)

Described in terms of the larger theory of personality, Mr. J.'s case illustrates a core value in which the feeling of unacceptability was established. His early experiences probably involved periods of affectionate approval interspersed with a disciplinarian lack of affection. Thus his core values said conflictingly that he was *worthy* and also that he was *unworthy*. He grew up feeling that he could accept portions of the world around him but that he must fight for his share of things. Such a viewpoint was to his advantage in a selling career. But in his noncompetitive activities he was forever reminded of his conflicting core values, hence his anxiety and his feeling that the world threatened his destruction. His "uncleanness" was merely the way in which he would be punished or destroyed. Fortunately, he had not yet reached a state of maladjustment which was beyond help. Under greatly intensified stress, however, his guilt feelings might be exaggerated. He might then feel obliged to carry out a drastic atonement such as self-destruction. Suicide might even appear to him to be an effective means to reinstate himself in the love of his mother as he had known it on some few early occasions.

Obsessive-compulsive Reactions

Like all the other diagnostic categories, the obsessive-compulsive reactions represent behavior forms which may be found both in everyday living of normal people and in cases of serious mental illness. To avoid later difficulty and suffering, every person develops specific defensive and preventive techniques. Washing the hands before eating serves to reduce the possibility of illness through contagion. Following the local traffic ordinances very exactly reduces traffic hazards. Being so concerned with avoidance of contagion as to spend a total of several hours a day on hand washing, however, suggests that more than literal cleanliness is involved. Overconcern with the pedantic observance of traffic ordinances, too, suggests that the real explanation lies deeper.

In each of the above examples the purpose of the act is avoidance of difficulty and suffering. But, it must be asked, just what type of difficulty or suffering is anticipated? Why does the individual look forward with so much anxiety to the seemingly catastrophic results of deviation from extreme cleanliness or from exact law abidance?

An *obsession* is an idea or desire which may or may not appear reasonable to the individual but which compels him to perform certain acts to avoid suffering painful feelings of anxiety, a sense that something terrible is about to happen. After he performs the particular act or acts he feels somewhat relaxed or relieved. These acts are called *compulsions*. Sometimes compulsions grow into elaborate rituals which have to be exactly and rigidly carried out, even though the individual knows that they are entirely nonadjustive and irrational in relation to his immediate environment.

A GI college student was observed on several occasions in class to perspire freely, flush, and sit very tensely, as if holding tightly onto himself. When an opportunity arose, the instructor discussed this condition with the student. He found that the perspiring and the other signs noticed were not the only evidences of anxiety: on the way home after class this student had to perform a whole series of rituals. Some of these were as simple as childhood games. For example, he had to pace off a square around each tree he passed in the sidewalk. At home he had to perform rituals which were "so horrible they could not be described" to the instructor. Any form of self-evaluation seemed to require him to perform these rituals as a means of reducing his intense anxiety feelings. He had undergone nearly two years of hospitalized psychiatric treatment before his release from military service as a completely disabled obsessive-compulsive psychoneurotic. He knew these actions were irrational, but this knowledge did not help him to act normally.

Obsessive-compulsive tendencies doubtless exist to some extent in every personality; they are of importance only if they get out of control. The overly exacting housekeeper feels relieved when her house has been made spick-and-span. But if the house is spick-and-span to begin with, then the need to clean it up again is a need to perform a *ritual*. Why, when the house is already clean, must it be cleaned again? Why must hands that are already clean be repeatedly washed? Why must some people eat certain foods, such as sweets or fats, which they know do them harm, and then give elaborate "explanations" or "sales talks" to anyone who will listen?

Again, why must the alcoholic and the drug addict persist in the recognizedly irrational behavior which is so often their undoing? These behavior patterns become understandable both as physiological dependence and as obsessive-compulsive reactions. The so-called basic drives, or tissue needs, are easily distorted into ritualistic practices which become fixated expressions of less acceptable motives. It is very easy to assume that any organic phenomenon is beyond the control of the mind. Rigid diets "except as prescribed" often are ritualistic. There are many other irrational behavior patterns that come under the heading of compulsive rituals, *e.g.*, knuckle snapping and muscle spasms such as tics, as well as irregularities of breathing, sexual behavior, and excretion. They give the individual a feeling of release.

Behind the scenes of obsessions and compulsions there is an identifiable personality type—the type that is behind every other one of the nine categories outlined above. This is the *anxiety-laden* personality. The more extreme the neurotic behavior, the greater is the underlying anxiety. To understand this correspondence it is necessary to realize that the obsession itself is a *symbol.* To the individual in question it takes the place of a larger and very important experience having to do with his core values. If the specific symbol of the obsession is a socially accepted one, such as commonly suggests patriotism or piety, there is no cause for the individual to be embarrassed in using it. At the other extreme, symbols which are socially unacceptable cause their users to feel themselves increasingly unacceptable.

Generally speaking, all these symbols are answers to threats and serve as some form of evasion or escape. Compulsive acts are performed as means of evading the intensely painful anxiety feelings. They are not performed as evasions of environmental situations. Therefore they do not seem, to the untrained observer, to make sense or to be reasonable goal-seeking activities.

Phobic reactions and obsessive-compulsive reactions illustrate the fact that deviations from the normal functioning of personality may be classified according to various systems. The system used by the Veterans' Administration is based upon the theory that anxiety develops in both the lower and the higher animals under conditions of extreme frustration. The helpless infant is especially susceptible to frustrations, and they can be drilled into his growing personality continuously as he grows into adulthood. Deviations in behavior manifest the several modes of reaction to anxiety experiences; among these are acceptance of fears into the self or personality, assignment to the non-self or outer world as threat of catastrophe, and attempted reconstruction of the perceptions, which usually results in fantasy. These reactions occur only in an already rigid personality; the normal person adjusts to frustration by temporary concessions.

The normal person will resort to a long-term perspective which permits self-maintenance in the long run even though temporary deviations are made. The nine forms of psychoneurosis outlined above are cited merely for the light they shed on the personality structure and the individual's ways of life. Much of the individual's behavior will be best understood as his habitual way of attempting to manage his environment *as he perceives it.*

PERCEPTION AND NEUROSIS

The place of perception in adjustment can be illustrated by a modification of Fig. 8–1.

1. Primitive stimulus — S
2. Perceptual set to find threat to organism's self-maintenance

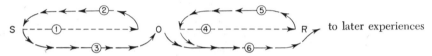

3. Stimulus now is perceived as pressuring organism to behave in unacceptable ways, or to blocking of self-maintenance
4. Established tendency to react to perceived stimulus
5. One or several trial reactions
6. Selected reaction or reconstructed self-environment process accepted as basis for further living experience. This is the "completed transaction"

Such a diagram must be drawn in several stages if it is to show the etiology or the development of the present adjustment pattern. An early stage would describe the individual making almost no perceptual interpretation at all as in early infancy (2). As moment-to-moment experiences combine, stage 2 begins to show previous learnings. Gradually the individual is forming his general and undifferentiated evaluation of his world and his place in it. This childishly simple overgeneralization is the start of his core value; this is his own personal feeling of being fundamentally acceptable and welcome or of being fundamentally unacceptable and unwelcome. Once the personal core value has appeared, stage 2 in perception remains continuously at work, coloring all later experience. Everything this individual perceives will thereafter "look" as this individual feels "at heart," in his core values. Unacceptability will look like threat, and stage 3 then will mark specific threats. The more maladjusted this individual is or becomes, the more drastically and persistently will this stage become a series of threat-laden perceptual habits or fixations.

The Feeling of Rejection

Faced with the threat-laden stimulus, the individual is required to react—he is unable merely to do nothing. If he is healthy, the reaction to threat will be a vigorous problem-solving effort. This will be a process of experimental and persistent thinking which will move through a variety of possible reactions. Each of these proposed reactions will have to be evaluated for probable effects on the individual and on the later situation. If the self-concept held by the individual suggests weakness, even a slight threat will be considered serious. If the self-concept suggests strength, the individual may be able to force a change in the situation, *i.e.*, he may feel able to *manage* it.

Weakness in the core of personality will suggest need for self-defense. If this weakness is the expression of extreme unacceptability, including feelings of inadequacy and utter loneliness, the individual will have a *feeling of rejection*. Because he sees so few possible reactions which promise removal of the threat-laden stimuli and sees no help from outside himself, his behavior becomes anxiety-laden. Continued failure serves to verify the original core value and to apply it to more and more areas of living, making it evident to the individual that there is less and less worth in him. This is the "peeling off" process discussed earlier, which leads to breakdown when continued too long.

As few avenues of reaction are left open to him, he adheres rigidly and desperately to those which, in his weakness, he is able to take. Frustration is now easy, and greater rigidity will develop. Stage 5 thus comes to lack both variety and optimism in the neurotic personality. Stage 6 of perception becomes then merely a generalized or projected fear of the future, an amplification of the feeling present in stage 2. Usually the neurotic personality will "defend his weakness" with his last ounce of strength by enumerating its causes. He *traumatizes* himself, *i.e.*, maintains his weakness, by proving it to be the result of generally accepted causes.

The Feeling of Hostility

Preceding paragraphs stressed the feeling of rejection, of utter loneliness. A similar pattern is present in the *feeling of hostility*. If the child has a core value derived from unacceptability experiences in his family and if his play groups confirm this core value, he will develop feelings of rejection. But if his family stresses the value of fight, rather than overriding his attempts at self-assertion and striking back, he may develop a confirmed belief that he must fight the threatening aspects of his world. Particularly if his play group puts him into the role of the "smartest" or "biggest" or "toughest" in the group, he will learn to feel that all is competitive in this world. He will perceive each person hostilely, judging him to be weak and unworthy or strong and threatening, therefore to be, respectively, used or to be destroyed. Rejection and hostility feelings are alike physiologically in that both are reactions to threat which involve the bodily changes properly called "emotional."

Emotional Illness

Emotionalized living is deviate, or unhealthy, for several reasons. First, it involves a weakening of the more delicate and precise adjustments in behavior at the level of thinking and of action. Second, the presence of emotionalized reactions makes for a reduction of learning reactions. Third, the physiology of emotion does not consist merely in the stronger reactions called the specific emotions; it also includes the mild emotional reactions or tension states which tend to become chronic and fixated.

Mild emotion, continued over a period of many years, results in the general adaptive or adjustment process which is called the "general adaptive syndrome." This syndrome is at the base of, or adds to by aggravating, physiological conditions which seem to have no specific causes. These conditions are *somatizations*, tissue conditions resulting from prolonged emotional tension of a mild degree. Arthritis, heart disease, hardening of the arteries, stomach and intestinal ulcers and malfunctions, many asthmatic and allergic reactions, migraine headaches, and a host of other tissue conditions are frequently of this sort.

There is much reason to believe that *anxiety* is merely a term used by psychologists to indicate the same condition known to physiologists as emotion. In turn, the psychologist studies the misuse of emotion under the heading of "maladjustment." In extreme forms maladjustment is known as "mental illness." The mentally ill individual deviates from normal so far as to be concerned with his own anxiety more than with his environment proper. He is *disoriented*. He becomes unable to manage his own affairs because he is reacting to a world which he perceives to be essentially abnormal, or essentially against him. Given such a world, his adjustment is true to form but inefficient.

QUESTIONS FOR DISCUSSION

1. Explain the relation between an individual's core values and the amount of stress he is capable of standing.
2. List some frustrating situations which typically confront college students.
3. Illustrate the use of the concept of a scale of adjustments in connection with a broken-engagement situation.
4. Has thinking through the mechanisms of adjustment made these tools more or less easy for you to use? Explain.
5. Illustrate from your experience the maintenance of selfhood through homeostasis.
6. In psychological terms what is a person really saying who continually refers to his "inferiority complex"?
7. Describe the development of a phobia in yourself or a friend.
8. Explain how improvement in mental health might affect the incidence of ulcers.
9. Describe the probable origin of a marked antagonism toward others.
10. What may be the developmental reasons behind an individual's complete absorption in music or philosophy?
11. Give some examples of adjustments which should be termed "infantile."
12. Explain the psychological meaning of the line "The lady doth protest too much, methinks."
13. What is happening psychologically when an adolescent engages in temper tantrums?
14. List the systems you use most for the maintenance of your selfhood.
15. In the light of this chapter, do you think punishment is an effective means of ending hostile behavior? Explain.

ADDITIONAL READINGS

Allen, Frederick H.: Aggression in relation to emotional development, normal and pathological, *Ment. Hyg., N.Y.*, 1950, 34(3):353–363.

Allport, Gordon W., and Kramer, B. M.: Some roots of prejudice, *J. Psychol.*, 1946, 22:9–39.

Boardman, Rhea K., and Hildreth, G. H.: Adjustment problems of the gifted, *Understanding the Child*, 1948, 17:41–44, 51.

Dreikurs, Rudolf: The four goals of the maladjusted child, *Nerv. Child*, 1947, 6:321–328.

Hilgard, E. R.: Human motives and the concept of self, *Amer. J. Psychol.*, 1949, 4:374–383.

Hoppock, Robert: Vocational and educational satisfaction, pp. 126–132, in Douglas Fryer and Edwin R. Henry (eds.), *Handbook of Applied Psychology*, Rinehart & Company, Inc., New York, 1950.

Kirkpatrick, Edwin A.: *Mental Hygiene for Effective Living*, Chap. 1, Appleton-Century-Crofts, Inc., New York, 1934.

Kraines, S. H., and Thetford, E. S.: *Managing Your Mind: You Can Change Human Nature*, Chap. 15, The Macmillan Company, New York, 1946.

Lewin, Kurt: Behavior and development as a function of the total situation, Chap. 16, in Leonard Carmichael (ed.), *Manual of Child Psychology*, John Wiley & Sons, Inc., New York, 1946.

McKinney, Fred: *Psychology of Personal Adjustment: Students' Introduction to Mental Hygiene*, 2d ed., John Wiley & Sons, Inc., New York, 1949.

Prothro, E. Terry, and Teska, P. T.: *Psychology: A Biosocial Study of Behavior*, Chap. 7, Ginn & Company, Boston, 1950.

Rokeach, Milton: Generalized mental rigidity as a factor in ethnocentrism, *J. Abnorm. Soc. Psychol.*, 1948, 43:259–278.

Ross, Helen: *Fears of Children*, Science Research Associates, Chicago, 1951.

Symonds, Percival M: *The Dynamics of Human Adjustment*, Chap. 7, Appleton-Century-Crofts, Inc., New York, 1946.

Veltfort, Helene R., and Lee, George E.: The Cocoanut Grove fire: a study in scapegoating, *J. Abnorm. Soc. Psychol.*, 1943, 38(2):138–154. (Suppl.)

Vernon, W. H. D.: Hitler, the man: notes for a case history, *J. Abnorm. Soc. Psychol.*, 1942, 37:295–308.

White, Robert W.: *Lives in Progress*, The Dryden Press, New York, 1952.

Part Four AREAS OF PERSONALITY ADJUSTMENT

Part Three dealt with the inner dynamics of personality. Each individual has to work out a repertory of adjustments to life which will achieve for him the maintenance of selfhood. A healthy personality will be adjustive, able to cope with new situations. The psychoneurotic personality will show a low tolerance for and early predisposition to frustration. Because of his insecurities the psychoneurotic will lean heavily on stereotyped behavior for support. He may suffer from such basic weakness in the core of his personality that for the sake of homeostatic equilibrium he will have to be defensive or hostile. He may find himself in such emotional turmoil that readjustment will be required if he is to live happily and adequately.

Both healthy and unhealthy personalities continue to ascend the ladder of life. Much can be learned from watching the many types of personality structures as individuals go about the business of living. Part Four presents a very typical series of testing grounds. These have been chosen on the basis of their potentialities for affording insight into personality adjustments. The dynamics of personality will be examined in courtship and home and family relationships. Personality will be observed as it is strengthened or weakened by handicap and as it finds negative expression in delinquency. Thus the study of personality will be carried into the laboratory of life.

Seldom in life is there such opportunity for direct application of the study of personality as is afforded by courtship and marrying. Research and clinical studies are unearthing guiding principles. More and more difficulties in marriage are being explained in terms of personality problems. On the basis of much evidence it would seem that it is possible to gain psychological immunization against heartbreak in this phase of life through increased understanding of oneself and the one with whom a successful marriage is built. Courtship can serve as a broad orientation into all the ramifications of this important commitment to a way of living.

This chapter will develop the meaning of readiness for this step in life. It will discuss the strengths and weaknesses inherent in various courtship practices.

READINESS FOR COURTSHIP

Success in moving from one level of life to another depends upon maturation into readiness for new responsibilities and activities. Emotionally mature youths, having passed successfully through all the preceding levels of development, will have lived out the great majority of types of behavior appropriate to the earlier years. To the degree that maturity has been developed during the pre-courtship period, youth may be considered ready for courtship.

Pre-courtship Personality

Each new rung of the ladder of life may be thought of as a test of present and a step toward future personal adjustments. Just how successfully youth progresses in the pre-courtship stage of life will depend upon the personality he brings to this period. It is a time in which heterosexual interests stand high on the priority list. The individual who is ready will have passed the saturation point as regards infantile behavior patterns and will have lost interest in them. He will have attained relative emancipation from parents and become an integral part of his own age group. He will have weighed the major values and aims of life and achieved confidence in himself. Thus he will be inoculated against emotionally immature action and be prepared for successful dating and courtship.

To speak in psychological terms, the personality which is most nearly ready for this new phase of life is the one that comes closest to fitting the description of a healthy personality. The individual with a healthy personality will not have an inner need to dominate or hurt others because of his own inner feeling of rejection. He will not have an insatiable hunger for emotional support, or be over-dependent. Instead he will feel adequate and at ease with others. He will be prepared for the numerous adjustments which each new experience in life requires. He will not be so set in his patterns of behavior or perception that he cannot make the compromises which every intimate social relationship entails. He will not suffer from cultural myopia to such a degree that he is critical of differences in background. In short his personality will not get in the way of successful heterosexual experiences. He will be ready for a relationship which is in every sense cooperative.

Parent-Youth Relationships

Parents and youths must grow together through their respective life cycles. Youth is a transitional period. Sometimes young people find that they or their parents are not yet ready for the transition. The lack of readiness of parents to let their offspring achieve independence is due just as much to their own unwillingness to face the next stage of life as it is to youth's lack of readiness to assume the independence appropriate to this stage. As youths develop more adequacy in handling their own lives, parents become more willing to relinquish their authority. To work out the delicate balancing of just enough guidance and just enough independence requires much understanding on both sides. Even when parents and youths are both well adjusted, successful weaning is a difficult process. The person who faces life realistically will anticipate occasional difficulties. Growth must take place on the part of both parent and youth. The ability of the youth to handle his share successfully is one of the criteria of readiness for courtship.

Fig. 11–1. Discussions often clarify courtship problems. Mothers and daughters need to understand each other's viewpoints if marriages are to be successful. (*H. Armstrong Roberts.*)

The youths who achieve emancipation most successfully are those who have the greatest degree of insight into their parents' personalities. They realize that they have filled an important place in their family's need for affection and belongingness. They understand that much of their parents' motivation in life has been to satisfy their children's desires. Parents sometimes work out a pattern of life in which they are too dependent upon their offspring. Strangely enough, it is much easier for youths to understand the mechanisms parents have used to maintain selfhood than it is for parents to see themselves. A parent with a stereotyped pattern of reaction will find it difficult to accept ways which differ from those of his own youth. A parent who because of a child's poor health has felt it necessary to overprotect him will find weaning a traumatic experience. By looking at their parents through a psychological fluoroscope, as it were, youths ready for courtship will be able to help parents with their own problems and work out a relatively smooth weaning process.

An emancipated relationship with his family is part of a youth's readiness for courtship. Those who carry the child-parent relationship over into courtship will find their role a turbulent one. The continuation of this relationship through the engagement period sets the stage for many in-law problems. This does not mean that parents do not have an important part in youths' lives. Some twenty years of close association must result in a certain understanding of their children. Since parents are further along in the life cycle, they have had more personal experience with many common problems. Often parents or parent surrogates are able to view a specific courtship with more adequate perspective than youth can bring to it. Such resources will be used to their utmost by every well-adjusted youth.

Specific Effects of Immaturities

Many illustrations of the difficulties encountered by those who are not ready for the responsibilities of youth could be given. Immaturities like those which appear in the following typical stories are found in every college and office.

Bill had many inferiority feelings. He had never felt quite sure of himself. When the other youngsters on the block were playing baseball, he would be in his room reading. When parties were planned, he was not included. Now, at college, between classes he would study or walk alone. He felt insecure. He had an abnormal hunger for acceptance, but he just did not belong to his peer age group.

Sally played right up to Bill's neurotic need. She had none of the qualifications of a successful spouse. She had no need of them because Bill was like a drowning man clinging to a raft—one desire was overpowering. He needed ego building so badly that he grabbed at it, blind to everything else. He fancied himself in love with Sally just because she supplied the one ingredient he so badly lacked.

Bill's emotional immaturity plunged him recklessly into a catastrophe which he did not begin to see in its true light until after several weeks of marriage. Sally, too, must now face the unpleasant fact of a poorly planned marriage.

Chris had never been happy at home. She could not remember a time when she had not been in rebellion against her parents. Through her early years she had gritted her teeth, promising herself that she would escape as soon as possible. The first man who asked her for a date was immediately cast in the role of deliverer. She clung to him as her chance to escape unhappiness. She did not realize that she was only adding to her problem until she discovered that she was married to a man who was unable to experience genuine affection.

Art's deep-seated immaturity came from being tied to a "mom." He had become fixated at the mother-baby stage of parent-son relationship. He had never grown beyond the stage of feeling dependent upon his mother. Although chronologically and intellectually he had reached adolescence, he was emotionally still an infant.

When Art's mother was suddenly killed in an accident, he found himself completely helpless. In the only human relationship in which he had become experienced he was overdependent. The first woman he met who took a motherly interest in him tied him up completely. The fact that she was selfishly satisfying her own needs and lived in accordance with a completely different scheme of values from his made no impression. He was putty in her hands, not a husband but a mere son substitute who would need professional help to grow into full adulthood.

Vi had always been antagonistic to her father. She felt that he had dominated and wrecked her life. Although she was completely unaware of it, she projected this attitude onto all the men she met. She was punishing them for the unresolved relationship between herself and her father. She could never feel at home with men and wondered why they did not seem to retain their interest in her.

These youths were not ready for the heterosexual role in which they found themselves cast. They lacked maturity, being childish in their reactions to any show of attention. They had no understanding of themselves or of others and thus were not equal to youth's responsibilities.

Knowing the Other Sex

Individuals who bring to the pre-courtship period a wide experience with people, especially with those of the other sex, are much better prepared than the youths just cited. Large family groups, of course, contribute to this preparation, but there are many other ways to become acquainted with people. One of the essentials for genuine friendship is common interests, preferably so intense as to be absorbing. The classroom, extracurricular activity, and employment bring together people who have similar interests. These opportunities should be grasped to their limit. The more intimate acquaintanceships one has with persons of the opposite sex, the better prepared he is for the rest of life. Experience with people in various situations brings an understanding that can be gained in no other way. It is the immature youth or adult who finds baffling mysteries in the other sex. As youths see their friends in various situations and watch the diverse reactions to common experiences, they become more realistic about themselves and others. On the one hand they will be less easily taken in; on the other, they will be less apt to expect everyone to be ready to take advantage of them. The star dust drifts from their eyes so that the difference between daydream fantasy on the idealistic side and cynicism on the other becomes clear. They are in a position to evaluate the other sex realistically. They are ready for courtship.

COURTSHIP

Heterosexual interests and activities stand high on youth's priority list. Dating predominates in the social life of almost every college. Noncollegiate youth expresses the same behavior tendencies in somewhat different contexts, through church, YWCA and YMCA, business and industrial recreation programs, and many others. Thus an understanding of the whole area of courtship is of prime importance.

Goals of Courtship

College students' questions and activities show that courtship is one of their foremost interests. A Cornell University study found that more than 80 per cent wished to marry within three years of graduation.[1] Mate selection is considered by many students of college culture patterns to be one of the major goals. Just as in other cultures, however, there are minority patterns. Those who are planning for some years of graduate work usually do not take courtship seriously at this period.

Studies tend to show that divorce is more often a failure of courtship than of the marriage years themselves. Too many people are not aware of the important part which the period of courtship plays in successful marriage. A childish attitude is far from ideal. Failure to live this period to its fullest may result in rash action which will be forever regretted. Moreover, missing this part of life is in itself a loss, since it is one of life's most interesting experiences.

Courtship is a golden opportunity for *experimental companionship*. Getting acquainted with as large a number of young people as possible is the first step. No one can really understand a single individual unless he has engaged in various types of activities with all kinds of personalities. Before this period of youth, the individual is closely involved with his own family relationships and with the contacts stemming directly from his home. After marriage complex economic and social relationships make so many demands that there is little place for experimentation. In our culture, experimentation after marriage usually is indicative of immaturity. Thus the individual who wishes to use the courtship period to its utmost will "shop around" as much as possible. He will not take any one person too seriously.

As this period progresses, the individual finds that his interests and likes and dislikes are becoming more definite. It has been sug-

[1] Lemo D. Rockwood and Mary E. N. Ford, *Youth, Marriage and Parenthood*, p. 71, John Wiley & Sons, New York, 1945.

gested that friendships might be visualized as forming a pyramid: the numbers slowly grow fewer until the one top favorite is found. This process usually starts with chumming; in mature personalities it comes to encompass true courtship.

Rating Qualifications

Many lists have been devised to show the characteristics that lead to popularity with members of the other sex. Evelyn Duvall suggests that the three requirements met by the people who get dates are that they are *emotionally mature,* have *social competence,* and *"rate."* [2] The last evaluation, she believes, is worked out in "bull sessions" and is based upon social status, physical attractiveness, personality factors, reputation, and participation in campus affairs.

In a study of more than 1,000 women students at Stephens College it was found that date qualifications and mate qualifications differed somewhat.[3]

Date qualifications	Mate qualifications
Ability to dance	Companionship
Ability to converse	Ability to provide
Good manners	Understanding of wife
Attentiveness	Love
Consideration	Ambition in vocation
Pleasing personality	Intelligence

It is not difficult to see that the mate qualifications reach much deeper into the personality and evidence much more emphasis upon the central values of the self. This difference is well worth checking carefully against one's own "private life."

Some of the local cultural mores of various colleges or business firms have a marked effect upon the extent to which wide acquaintance between men and women is possible. Local customs range all the way from dating anyone at all, regardless of race or creed or economic status, to rigid taboos against being seen with anyone who is not a member of a designated fraternity or social class. In some groups the local folkways encourage much "shopping around,"

---

[2] Evelyn Duvall, Courtship and engagement, p. 33, in Morris Fishbein and Ernest Burgess (eds.), *Successful Marriage,* Doubleday and Company, Inc., New York, 1947.

[3] Henry A. Bowman, *Marriage for Moderns,* p. 155, McGraw-Hill Book Company, Inc., New York, 1942.

while in others the only proper or approved conduct is to "go steady." Both women and men are sometimes rushed by the pressure for gaining status with one's peers into announcing engagements before sufficient evaluation has taken place. Surely experience with, and understanding of, the opposite sex is good insurance for success in the choice of a life partner. Marriage, after all, is far from a "blind date" relationship.

Bases of Attraction

Survey studies indicate that for the most part marital selection is based upon a combination of the following factors: (1) propinquity, (2) conception of the ideal mate, (3) personality need, (4) parental image, (5) homogamy.[4] All five are active in every selection of a courtship or marital partner, but their relative emphasis varies with different conditions and personalities.

Propinquity may consist in either *geographic nearness of residence* or *interaction in a socioeconomic activity*. The importance of propinquity is self-evident. Kennedy's research in New Haven, Conn., revealed that 76.31 per cent of the spouses had lived within 20 blocks of one another.[5]

The concept of an *ideal mate* is in process of psychological formation from infancy onward. Experiences with parents, teachers, and peers all contribute. Individuals are conditioned by movies, radio, television, books, and lectures. The present concept of a desirable mate has been roughed in by all these influences as they added and organized various details. The idealization may range all the way from one simple requirement, such as size or type of face, to a whole series of trait combinations. The individual with minimum requirements may live through a chain of infatuations, while the one with maximum requirements may never find anyone who quite measures up to the idealization. One student in a large metropolitan college described her ideal mate as follows: "He must be tall, handsome, blond, brown-eyed, wealthy, poetic, a sports lover, prefer country life, have many famous friends, dislike bridge, adore cats,

[4] Ernest W. Burgess and H. J. Locke, *The Family—from Institution to Companionship*, p. 415, American Book Company, New York, 1945.

[5] Ruby Jo Reeves Kennedy, Premarital residential propinquity and ethnic endogamy, *Amer. J. Sociol.*, 1943, 48:580–584.

prefer gray cars, be a constant admirer, like the mountains, hate the seashore, and consider Sinclair Lewis his favorite author." Such a description is obviously daydreaming, a fantasy built to substitute for a real and available mate. Experience and improved understanding should help this student to develop a more realizable ideal picture.

"She's got everything! Freckles—muscles—a bicycle—!"

Fig. 11–2. The concept of one's ideal changes. (*Reprinted by permission from Today's Health, 1952.*)

Personality Needs—the Magnet

Personality needs determine one's responses to others, and these needs always have psychological wrappings from the past. Below the level of present awareness are many forces which attract the individual to or repel him from certain people. A person tends to like those who match his own pleasant experiences and to dislike those who match his unpleasant ones. He responds to those who make him feel desired, partly because these people are considered attractive by others and partly because they satisfy his personality needs. He is drawn to people who reproduce former family relationships if these have been satisfying. He normally repudiates those who remind him of his father and mother if his relationships with them have been frustrating. The "reactive value" of a person may lie not so much in his own qualities as in the fact that he resembles in some way a much-hated brother, a beloved uncle, or a "brat" of a cousin.

A psychiatrist and a psychologist describe this unique-personality-need basis of mate selection as love. In their words, it is: [6]

a complicated relationship with another person, built deep into the personalities of both partners. Love is what lovers make it. You cannot accept or reject your feeling for your sweetheart by comparing it with a standard model. One man will find his most satisfying love in a woman who mothers him a bit. Another will fulfill himself in protecting a weaker nature. Still another will work out a comradely, almost brotherly relationship with his wife . . . to mention only some of the most obvious types of marital bliss. But whether the pattern is that of an Apache and his woman or Albert and Victoria, the marriage is founded on true love if it proves a durable combination of the needs of two natures.

Homogamy is the tendency of like to marry like. An individual is drawn to people who like the same things as he does; he is seldom drawn to those who have nothing in common with him. People from small-town backgrounds tend to find satisfaction in companionship with people from small towns. Educational level, economic level, sports interests, religious viewpoints, and many similar factors contribute. "He is our kind of person" is a popular expression of the homogamous tendency.

Predictive Techniques for Marriage

Unhappily, true love does not announce itself with a rash and a fever as does chickenpox. It should be said that a person "grows into love" rather than that he "falls in love." Most people go through a variety of rehearsals in the form of infatuations, or "puppy loves," before they find real love. Sometimes several engagements are tried and found wanting. A few of those who get off at one of the way stations never do reach the final destination of genuine love. There is no need to belabor the point that marriage choices could be more successful.

[6] John Levy and Ruth Munroe, *The Happy Family*, p. 41, Alfred A. Knopf, Inc., New York, 1938.

Considerable work has been done toward developing tests that will serve as guides in the choice of a life partner just as vocational-aptitude tests serve in the choice of a career. This, however, has proved difficult. There are many criteria by which to judge the success of an occupational choice. Amount of production, quantity of sales, salary earned, etc., are measurable standards. But what are the parallels in marriage? Typical criteria applied in the researches are the following:

Permanence of the marriage
Happiness of the members of the couple
Social expectations of the community
Personality development of husband and wife
Degree of companionship of husband and wife
Satisfaction with the marriage
Integration of the couple

Employing one of these standards as a measure of success, various background characteristics have also been investigated. Statistical correlations have been worked out to determine which factors in the background and the personality seem most likely to lead to success or failure in marriage.

Studies in Marital Happiness

Research has uncovered several fallacies in traditional ideas. As factual evidence replaces superstition, new tools for effective marital counseling will doubtless come into common use. Dr. Lewis Terman of Stanford University conducted one of the most inclusive studies of the psychological factors involved in marital happiness. He studied 792 couples representative of the middle and upper-middle classes of urban population in California. Questions used represented two years of preliminary experimental work. Careful techniques were devised to assure complete anonymity. Participants were secured from family-relations conferences, churches, mothers' clubs, parent-teacher associations, social clubs, study clubs, women's clubs, veterans' organizations, and other groups.

A "marital happiness score" was computed for each subject, based upon information regarding community of interests, average amount of agreement or disagreement in ten fields, customary methods of settling disagreements, regret of marriage, choice of spouse if life were to be lived over again, contemplation of separation or divorce, subjective estimates of happiness, direct admission of unhappiness, and a domestic grievance check list.

This marital happiness score was correlated with a personality score based upon some 233 personality-test items including interests, attitudes, likes and dislikes, habitual response patterns, and concepts of ideal marriage. In differentiating subjects of high and low happiness, these traits were shown to be characteristic of the unhappy mates: [7]

to be touchy or grouchy
to lose their tempers easily
to fight to get their own way
to be critical of others
to be careless of others' feelings
to chafe under discipline or to rebel against orders
to show any dislike that they may happen to feel
to be easily affected by praise or blame
to lack self-confidence
to be dominating in their relations with the opposite sex
to be little interested in old people, children, teaching, charity, uplift activities
to be unconventional in their attitudes toward religion, drinking and sex ethics
to be bothered by useless thoughts
to be often in a state of excitement
to alternate between happiness and sadness without apparent cause

Helpful Suggestions from Research

In summing up his findings Dr. Terman says: "A large proportion of incompatible marriages are so because of the predisposition to unhappiness in one or both spouses." [8] This is one way of saying that if either or both husband and wife are "looking for failure" they will probably find it. The potential of a chronically pessimistic attitude to produce failure is probably no greater in marriage than it is in any other area of living. The personality which has as part

[7] Lewis M. Terman *et al., Psychological Factors in Marital Happiness*, p. 369, McGraw-Hill Book Company, Inc., New York, 1938.
[8] *Ibid.*, p. 110.

of its structure, and thus in its perceptual field, the general tendency to expect failure and trouble is evidencing neurosis to some extent. Overidealism in courtship practices and in choice of mate is but a form of the fantasy so typical of neurotic behavior.

Although much research is being conducted in marriage clinics and family-relations courses and by individual counselors, conclusions must be considered as only tentative at the present time. Nevertheless, just as experts in vocational counseling have, over the decades, cut the amount of error in choice of vocation and in employee selection, so in due course by means of valid marriage-aptitude tests the percentage of marital happiness will be increased. Perhaps, as has been said in jest, some day the stock answer to a proposal of marriage will be a coy "What's your score on the premarital aptitude test?" Or, more realistically, perhaps some day marriage requirements will typically include passing such a test as well as a physical examination.

Some of the problems encountered in translating general marriage aptitude into specifics have arisen from individual differences and from varying cultural patterns. Also, in a marriage just as in a vocational field, the *ability to succeed* is meaningless unless accompanied by *adequate motivation in the direction of success*. Marriage ceremonies should be performed only if both candidates, together and individually, have a sincere and dominating desire to make the marriage work. If the individual comes from a background of unhappy home life, this should be especially noted. Adequate motivation and well-informed effort, properly applied, can overcome almost any specific lack in marriage qualifications. There are, in fact, so many intangibles in every marriage that there will always be room for individual differences and adaptations of a thoroughly satisfying nature.

The question is often asked, "How much shall I leave to luck?" Research and counseling experience in premarital, marriage, and divorce problems have shown that there are techniques which are much more reliable than luck or guesswork. Each person has a general happiness aptitude. Specifically, some people are much better risks for marriage happiness than others—*regardless* of who the other partner is to be. Also, when both partners take psychological tests and have them interpreted by a trained counselor, each gains insight into the feelings and aspirations of the other. This in itself helps to develop good attitudes toward marital adjustment. Educational and clinical facilities are offering help in these directions. Some colleges have marriage-counseling sections in their psychological clinics. Resources of this type are becoming more plentiful and efficient as the years pass.

Individual Differences in Marriage Roles

Because every marriage contains a sociocultural as well as a personal aspect, both must be recognized during courtship and throughout the marriage. In twentieth-century America cultural standards for the ideal marriage are changing. Traditions and philosophies are in a state of flux. There now can be no one narrowly fixed pattern for the courtship, the marital, or even the family role. Complexity of personality is demanding recognition in this area of living too.

In the older tradition of marriage in America, roles were fixed, or rigid. The man was the breadwinner, the woman the homemaker. The female was "courted" by the male until marriage. Then she was supposed to revert immediately to a role of inferiority. But today the concept of the family is changing in the direction of the cooperative working relationship. More and more wives are giving up the traditional subordinate role for that of companion or partner.

Cultural patterns defining successful marriage appear to differ according to *social status, local community mores,* and *religious traditions.* The attitude toward equality of husband and wife varies markedly among subgroups. It has been found that the usual attitude in what is termed the "lower-middle class" calls for more assertion of authority on the part of the man.[9] Otherwise he is considered weak or effeminate. College students' mores on the questions of marital roles were polled by Lemo Rockwood and Mary Ford.[10] They discovered that on most questions pertaining to liberalizing established mores the men were more willing to change than were the women. Are college men coming into closer contact with the changing times? Or have they thought more about improving the *status quo?*

[9] Burgess and Locke, *op. cit.,* p. 435.
[10] Rockwood and Ford, *op. cit.,* p. 131.

There is one factor, however, in the above study which shows a more liberal point of view on the part of the women: Whatever condition was stipulated, more college women than men approved of married women working for pay outside the home. Of all the men polled, those in the College of Agriculture showed the greatest approval of the wife working during the early years of marriage. Men in the Hotel School were more favorable to married women working if they could assist the husband in his business than were the others. The Arts and Science students were more inclined to approve married women working if the women possessed special talent or training than were the men in the other colleges. Another interesting finding of this study was that the men who had been most economically favored in their own home life were most desirous of maintaining the traditional roles for men and women. On the other hand the parallel group of women was the one which was most willing to abandon the established pattern.

Many thinkers in the field of marriage relationships have suggested that the most important part for education to play is to aid students in examining the many traditional prescriptions for the masculine and feminine roles and to evaluate these roles in terms of importance and continuance.

Neither men nor women in twentieth-century society can be satisfied merely to perpetuate the marriage roles of the sexes as they have existed for centuries past. They will need to work out their ideas on family and community roles together. Unless this area has been thoroughly explored during their early acquaintanceship, a couple cannot know whether their personalities are really compatible or not. Serious disagreement as to role playing will cause much serious frustration. Just as it is realized that some people have more aptitude for and interest in salesmanship than in accounting, so people are beginning to understand the absurdity of thinking that every man should be the same type of husband and want the same type of wife as every other man. The development of different marriage patterns provides for individual differences. To force people of diverse temperaments, capacities, and education into one rigid mold weakens the attractiveness and stability of marriage in general and prevents the individual marriage from developing into normal goal-oriented behavior.

ENGAGEMENT

Engagement, the interlude between courtship and marrying, has great potentialities for contributing to marital success. In the discussion that follows, various behavior patterns followed by youths today will be evaluated in terms of their positive and negative influence on later happiness.

Premature Engagements

In some colleges engagement is regarded as the great "campus sweepstakes." Senior breakfasts feature coeds who have been "pinned." Coeds not infrequently feel that their best chance to find a marriage partner is lost once they graduate. This motivation for choosing a life partner is hardly a sound one. Short-term achievements do not substitute for long-term goals.

It is difficult to set the exact age at which the individual becomes wise enough and sufficiently settled in his goals to choose a mate. If the marriage decision is made before tastes and attitudes have become well developed, one partner may soon grow away from the other. The findings of interest tests indicate that values and attitudes change considerably during the teen years. Most studies show that there is a greater chance for success in marriage after age twenty than before. Dr. Terman found indications of less happiness in women who had married before age twenty and in men who had married before age twenty-two.[11] A study of 409 couples indicated that those who were under twenty at marriage took longer than the others to work out their adjustments.[12]

Rehearsal for Marriage

Engagement offers a splendid opportunity for a rehearsal of marriage. Thus if it is to fulfill its purpose engagement must be a progressively more familiar and more intensified relationship. It comes to be a proving ground for *marriage readiness*. It should include practice in the many types of situations to be encountered

[11] Terman, *op. cit.*, p. 181.

[12] Judson T. Landis and Mary G. Landis, *Building a Successful Marriage,* p. 110, Prentice-Hall, Inc., New York, 1948.

in marriage. The more natural and down-to-earth the engagement can be in both variety and intensity, the better prelude it is to marriage. Lavish expenditures which must cease at the start of marriage, like Cinderella's festivities at the midnight curfew, are

"I'll be glad when George and I are married
and I won't have to pretend to enjoy this."

JANE SPERRY

Fig. 11–3. Pretense isn't the best policy during engagement. It is well to remember that one is going to have to remain in years of marriage very much what one appears to be during months of courtship. Admitting some difference in interest should enrich companionship. (*Copyright 1951 by the Curtis Publishing Company.*)

indeed poor preparation for everyday living. False fronts of perpetual perfection forecast a jolt after the wedding bells have rung. Engagement must be *real living*, not tinsel-wrapped, or play-acted in evening clothes, or merely copied from the movies and magazine cosmetic advertisements. Some of these glamorized accounts are unhealthful cultural influences, out of line with general standards.

Lovers should try to see each other as personalities, each having strengths and weaknesses. Cry-baby tendencies or "I'll take my marbles and go home if you don't play my way" attitudes should be gauged. Infantile emotional tags and jags will act like sand in the gears of marriage. Experts usually suggest that realistic engaged persons should plan a vacation away from each other for several weeks late in the engagement period, to test whether or not their compatibility and interdependence are genuine.

Engaged couples ought to be together in a wide variety of activities and under a wide variety of circumstances, including business, social, and other types of situations where the couple will meet people with whom they will be associated after marriage. Many a man begins to see his wife encircled by a question mark the first time he introduces her to his work associates! Often a woman feels completely rejected when dancing and night-clubbing, the only common activities of herself and her husband before their marriage, cease on their return from the honeymoon. Common activities and friendships can serve as irreplaceable bracings to keep a marriage steady. Marriage will not thrive in a social vacuum, even if it chances to start in one.

Blueprinting the Future

Some plan of life for the married couple should be roughed out. Certainly details will have to be added at several later times. It would be daydreaming to plan ahead for those phases of life which are dependent upon circumstances subject to change. But to guard against the serious disillusionment of waking up to divergent values after marriage, couples should talk during engagement about their broad ideals and specific plans. Students who plan to do graduate study peruse department offerings in university catalogues to prepare for what lies ahead. Successful businessmen provide for variations in the business cycle. In the same way those on the threshold of marriage can profitably survey the areas in which they may have to make adjustments. Authorities in the field of marriage counseling point out certain areas that research studies have shown to be especially important in building a successful marriage. A list of these areas would include sex relations, family finance, religious life, recreational activities, relationship with in-laws, and child rearing.[13]

[13] See Gladys Gardner Jenkins and Richard L. Jenkins, Building a marriage, *Child Study*, 1952, 29(2):6–8, 30–32.

Many people do not realize that individual differences are real. Some are blind to the fact that there are ways of doing things quite different from their habitual patterns. To face these truths in a practical way, conversations should get down to brass tacks early on budgets. Ideas could differ all down the line from invest-in-a-better-future-drastic-economy-now to the enjoy-it-while-you-can philosophy. Sometimes one member has fantastic notions of how much a budget can be stretched and thus is in line for terrible frustration later on. Discussion and planning are prophylactic in this area.

Religious attitudes run the gamut from enthusiastic participation in all church functions to outright antagonism toward these activities. If compromises between divergent religions are to work, added preparations must be made. If the partners have agreed to maintain their separate religious affiliations, they should try out this solution during engagement to be sure that it will work for them. If they have decided on the conversion of one to the religion of the other, all the ramifications of this step should be discussed with competent religious advisers from both sides in advance of marriage. If they have in mind joining a new church, they should have some experience with this solution before the marriage ceremony takes place.

The problem of social activities and recreation will need clarifying. It often happens that experience in these fields has been limited to activities engaged in during the courtship period. Sometimes after marriage the partners discover that one is interested only in doing things with people while the other enjoys only "lone wolf" activities. Friends, too, can interfere with marital happiness. Any rigid notions of one partner about preferences in types of people must be clearly understood and accepted by the other.

The success of in-law relationships will depend on many variables. Much difficulty can be averted by more interpretation of families. As was noted in the chapter on Culture, the cultural patterns of families are varied. In discussing her unhappy marriage one young woman reported how shocked she had been when she learned that her husband presumed they would spend every weekend with his family. His was a closely knit unit presided over by a rather dominating mother. All the other sons' wives had simply bowed to family tradition. This type of situation should be cleared up during engagement.

The subject of parenthood has many ramifications, including number of children hoped for and when, philosophies of child rearing,

"What did I do today? Not much, dear. Just sat around all day in breathless anticipation of this evening."

FIG. 11–4. Marriage partners need individual and cooperative interests. Too much *courting* and not enough self-sufficiency give both spouses dull days. A man or a woman must have wholesome individual interests even though married. (*Copyright 1951 by the Curtis Publishing Company.*)

standards of parenthood, and religious training. It is very upsetting to the "progressive" member of a couple to find that the other has "authoritarian" ideas about child rearing. No adequate home can be developed for children without considerable unity in philosophy.

Developing Techniques for Adjustment

Psychological preparation for marriage should include an acceptance of the fact that adjustments are necessary in the building of a successful partnership. Compromises, or better, integrations will inevitably be called for. Discussions can and should be laboratory experiences in handling the problems which must arise in the adjustment of any two human beings. The engagement period is an ideal time to develop and to test adjustment techniques.

Some individuals may find that they have been more or less rigid in demanding that people acquiesce to their ideas. Others may realize how weak they have been. The intimacy of the relationship between two engaged people is usually an entirely new experience and highlights any selfish attitudes. Perhaps a beginning can be made in substituting the best interests of the couple for those of the individual. If all this comes in the rehearsal period, there will be less stress and strain than ensue if it suddenly erupts in the early part of marriage. As in every other worthwhile undertaking, time is needed to perfect techniques. Engagement can be a real internship in skills for successful integration. Drs. Burgess and Wallin found that the *measure of success achieved in adjustment to engagement correlated well with later adjustment to marriage.*[14]

Misunderstandings in the Sexual Area

Probably the most misunderstood question that arises concerning engagement as a rehearsal period is that of determining sexual compatibility. The word "sex" is surrounded by a remarkable area of confusion in the American culture. Ruth Benedict has pointed out a discontinuity in conditioning in this important area of life.[15] She notes that the *child* is expected to show *no* interest in sex. Then the adult, to build a successful marriage, must break down carefully developed inhibitions so as to avoid impotence or frigidity or guilt feelings.

Some helpful perspective can be gained from understanding how much less inhibition is built up in many other social cultures. In

[14] Ernest W. Burgess and Paul Wallin, Predicting adjustment in marriage from adjustment in engagement, *Amer. J. Sociol.*, 1944, 49:324–330.

[15] Clyde Kluckhohn and Henry A. Murray (eds.), *Personality in Nature, Society and Culture*, 2d ed., p. 528, Alfred A. Knopf, Inc., New York, 1953.

Samoa the child grows to adolescence without developing any sex fears and is expected to experiment with sexual relationships. This absence of taboo seems to result in an absence of exaggerated interest in sex and to make for happier marriage relationships. It seems to make possible the formation of sex-habits with no attendant hostility feelings.

In the United States culture the whole sex problem bursts suddenly upon the adolescent, causing much worry and conflict. So many different interpretations of his needs in this area of life are thrust upon him and such divergent patterns of conduct are suggested, if not prescribed, that the adolescent boy and girl commonly become confused. Muddled thinking is everywhere apparent. Many people still rely on pseudoscientific information for guidance in this important area of living. Discussion often seems to be affected by a fear of facing reality. When expressing their reactions, both old and young show a great lack of understanding. Some indication of this is evident in the following questions quoted just as they were submitted to one of the authors by members of a psychology class, as a basis for discussion.

Is there any truth in the statement that certain people are sexually incompatible?
Will petting increase chances for a wise choice of a marital partner?
Who is sexually normal?
How intimate should couples get during courtship?
Should one person subject himself to the other during the courtship with the possible idea of better adjustments after marriage?
Is lack of sexual adjustment at the basis of all marriage unhappiness?

Such questions betray a need for more adequate instruction, in home or school, not merely about sex but about the whole field of personality.

False Notions of Sexual Compatibility

One of the students' questions listed above brought up the question of "sexual incompatibility." Experts in the field have pointed out that this is usually an excuse for, or a rationalization of, the lack of all-round marital compatibility.[16] An illustration of how

[16] Levy and Munroe, *op. cit.*, p. 117; Norman E. Himes, *Your Marriage: A Guide to Happiness*, p. 317, Rinehart & Company, Inc., New York, 1940.

this type of rationalization is used by those who wish to have a plausible excuse for terminating a marriage, is the following actual case.

Mrs. E. was referred by a gynecologist who could find no physical basis for her trouble. Her husband had told her that there was nothing to do but get a divorce, that he hated to do this but they were just physically mismated. He was sorry, but their anatomy made physical love impossible.

Mrs. E., knowing very little about the subject, took his words as the complete story and felt terrible. She supposed that he knew what he was talking about and that they were simply victims of fate. The story behind the scenes was that during his Army experience Mr. E. had met another woman with whom he fancied himself in love. Knowing that Mrs. E. was really fond of him, very idealistic, and opposed to divorce, he turned to this organic reason as a way of escaping from his marriage bonds.

This idea of predeterminable physical sexual compatibility or incompatibility is usually merely a scapegoat. It sounds decisive. As has been pointed out, people are much more willing to accept organic causes than psychological ones for their problems. It is easier on the pride to be able to blame something on organic conditions than it is to look within one's personality for the difficulty. The files of psychiatrists and psychologists are full of case reports in which this miscalled physical incompatibility evaporated after psychotherapy had led to improved insight into the real psychological problems. This outworn excuse for maladjustment in marriage belongs with the beliefs that the world is square and that all illness is organically caused.

Growth toward Compatibility

A heartening piece of information is that frequently *it takes considerable time to work out a satisfactory adjustment in the sexual phase of marriage.* Dr. and Mrs. Landis found in their intensive study of 409 couples that more than 12 per cent needed a year and 10 per cent needed six years to develop a physical love relationship which was most happy for *both* spouses.[17] Most experts working in the field of marriage counseling agree that it is a complete myth that on the basis of one "tryout" in sexual intercourse it can be predicted whether sexual adjustment will be happy or unhappy. Books on achieving such happiness in marriage typically make the point that immediate success should not be expected.

It takes time and understanding to develop any complex behavior pattern, such as sex. The type of physical love-making which calls forth the most responsiveness in a partner has to be learned co-operatively with that individual. A sexual relationship that does not include the sense of heightened self-esteem that comes with enjoying friendliness, warmth, and admiration is usually not very satisfying. Sex play without emotional involvement may leave the partners with a feeling of dissatisfaction with themselves, empty or perhaps depressed. Skill in physical love-making approaches perfection only after much experimentation under conditions of security, ease, lack of hurry, freedom from guilt, and mutual concern. Only a marriage based on genuine love can give such conditions, and then only if the physical situation is adequate. The psychological foundation underlying these factors, and making them of inescapable importance, is the undeniable fact that normal sex reactions are processes of the *total personality*.

Dangers in Premarital Intercourse

Two rather typical examples in which premarital intercourse interfered with the development of marital sexual adjustment are described below.

Mrs. M. had been referred by a physician because she was unhappy in marriage. She could not accept the more intimate marital relationships. She still thought she was very much in love with her husband, but the whole physical side of marriage was abhorrent to her. The story behind the story was that she and her husband had lived together before marriage. During this time, they had both felt guilty and fearful that their social status might be jeopardized. Their hide-out had been in unattractive surroundings. In short, their introduction to physical love-making was accompanied by so many

[17] Landis and Landis, *op. cit.*, p. 270.

unpleasant thoughts and worries that they both felt much inhibited. Thus they added unpleasant conditioning to feelings toward sex, acquired during childhood.

Mrs. B. was referred by a gynecologist because she was so unhappy in her marriage relationship. Though there was no physical cause, she was experiencing much difficulty. She feared that she was frigid. She had tried everything she could think of, but nothing seemed to help. She was afraid that her husband was becoming interested in another woman.

A conference with Mr. B., held in accordance with the usual procedure in marital adjustment cases, revealed that he felt his wife was frigid and was quite impatient with her. In the course of trying to determine just why he thought Mrs. B. was frigid, his story came out.

Mr. B. had been living with another young woman just prior to his marriage. His sexual relationship with her was happy; this proved to him that he was "normal." It was his wife, therefore, who was "to blame." She did not respond as had his former mistress.

The fact was that this very fickle woman, who soon left Mr. B. for another man, had been following this procedure all her life. She was entirely different from Mrs. B. She was very aggressive in her sex life and used all her available salesmanship. She had really forced her attentions on him in order to keep him involved until her interest turned to someone new.

Without realizing it, Mr. B. had used his mistress's behavior as a model. Since his wife did not duplicate her behavior, he felt that there was something the matter with his wife.

With a greater understanding of the whole situation and some improvement in love-making technique, Mr. B. turned into a more successful lover. Mrs. B. responded to his new attitude. Not being hampered by the feeling that she was frigid, she was more at ease, and their whole love relationship improved.

Wholesome Attitudes

The cases cited are just samples of the widespread lack of understanding of the whole topic. Couples sometimes do presume to learn of marriage relationships in detailed but oversimplified form before assuming the status and establishing the complex conditions of a home. In some culture groups or subculture groups physical intimacies during engagement are the secret standard, but it is a markedly false presumption that these premarital relationships will compare accurately with established marriage relationships. Habituation to less than the complete sexual relationship results in development of narrowly selfish attitudes toward sex. The exploitation of one person by another in the sex relationship is not essentially different from exploitation of any other type; it represents the tendencies of a personality fixated at the infantile level of being always served by other people.

Maturity in sex attitudes and understandings is an ideal. Some individuals are adult in chronological age but infantile or adolescent in some other aspects of their personalities. These immature personalities are unable to understand, or are unable to assimilate into their own self-concepts, the idea that it is the orientation of sex toward a complete and permanently satisfying companionship of marriage that is the guiding principle for successful marital life.

People who are really fond of each other will feel their love with *all* facets of their personalities. At its height, love is the culmination of intellectual, physical, social, and spiritual harmony. In all their relationships with each other, at all levels, the partners in love will respond with their whole personalities to each other. They will want to express their feelings in affection on as broad basis as their total personalities. Loss of this breadth through overemphasis upon one phase of loving, such as socializing, economic struggle, sex activity, or intellectual strivings, soon leads to the narrowing of compatibility and the development of "incompatibilities" of a more or less radical sort.

Successful Attitudes toward Marrying

Adolescent dreams applied to courtship and marriage problems are doubtless responsible for wrecking many marriages. The idea that marriage is an accomplished fact once the ceremony has been read is mere fantasy. Much of this unrealisticness stems from romantic love propaganda. It is part of the immaturity continually nourished by movies, radio programs, television, and fiction. It makes for an ostrich-like attitude of hiding one's head in the sand. It is, psychologically speaking, in the category with the "flight of fantasy."

"This is the happiest day of my life—no more diet,
no more hairdressers, no more lotions . . ."

Fig. 11–5. Building a marriage does not end at the altar. The marriage altar is like a birthday; it marks a point in the growth continuum for the personality involved. (*Cartoon by Tom Zib. Courtesy of The American Magazine.*)

This attitude is not advocated in other realms of life. Jobholders realize that they must put something into their work if they are to succeed; they don't believe that merely securing a position is their ticket to success. They admit that they must grow on their job if they are to keep it. Job adjustment is known to require motivation, planning, and careful selection of the job situation. Marriage adjustment should follow much the same plan: readiness for marriage, planning, and careful selection of the home situation.

It is trite to say that one receives from marriage in proportion to what he gives to it. This, however, is probably the most useful attitude of approach. No successful intimate relationship between two different personalities just happens. It must be built by both partners. The important psychological tools for this building are (1) the real desire of both partners for the happiness of the couple, (2) a mutual understanding of each other as human beings with certain psychological needs, and (3) a willingness to cooperate in working out necessary adjustments.

Truly desiring the happiness of one's mate is an earmark of mature love. It shows in generous understanding. The immature person, completely involved with himself and his own problems, wishes always to receive and never to give. He will not accept his spouse as a person but will use the spouse to glorify his own ego or as a screen onto which to project his own difficulties. The more a couple can perceive that each member is a bundle of psychological needs, the more valuable they become to each other. A real partner will want to share in building that type of emotional climate which will be most helpful to the other's personality.

Summary

Marriage offers most people vastly greater opportunities for happiness than single life. Modern marriage is complex, offering such a variety of possible husband-wife relationships that the activities leading into it need to be carefully worked out. There is no magic short cut to a happy marriage. All possible resources are needed to bring about success. The pre-courtship period has a distinct bearing on the type of personality which will start the courtship period. During this period the healthy individual will make the most of his opportunities to really learn to know the other sex. He will consider the engagement period as an insurance policy on his choice of partner. Thus prepared, he will be in the best possible position to build a happy marriage.

QUESTIONS FOR DISCUSSION

1. What factors should influence a person in deciding to "go steady"?
2. Must neurotic men or women remain unmarried or marry in the expectation of divorce? Explain.
3. How can one cope with a parent who consistently feels that a prospective mate is not good enough?
4. What has inner dissatisfaction to do with falling in love?
5. Is it wise for a young woman to try to hurry the courtship if the man seems slow in proposing marriage? If so, how?
6. If a man enjoys courting women but loses interest as soon as engagement seems imminent, what steps should he take?
7. If a couple's idea of life is very different from that of the in-laws on either side, how can conflict be avoided?
8. How can young people wean themselves from their families without causing any hurt feelings?
9. How should one member of a couple act when the other is in conflict with his or her family?
10. If members of an engaged couple find that they dislike each other's friends, how should they proceed?
11. Can a couple be really in love if they are continually quarreling and patching up their differences?
12. Should engaged couples read books on marriage or attend marital-relations courses together?
13. If a man has several years of training ahead of him, what should be done about becoming engaged?
14. Can anything be done about a tendency to demand assurances of love?
15. How can an engagement be broken with the least possible hurt?

ADDITIONAL READINGS

Bowie, Carol C.: Psychiatric insight into choice of mate, *Marriage and Family Living*, 1949, 11:68.

Brav, Stanley R.: Notes on honeymoon, *Marriage and Family Living*, 1947, 10:60–65.

Centers, Richard: Marital selection and occupational strata, *Amer. J. Sociol.*, 1949, 54:530–535.

Duvall, Evelyn M., and Hill, Reuben: *When You Marry*, D. C. Heath and Company, Boston, 1945.

Eckert, Ralph G.: *So You Think It's Love!* Public Affairs Pamphlet No. 161, New York, 1950.

Foster, Robert G.: *Marriage and Family Relationships*, rev. ed., Parts I, II, The Macmillan Company, New York, 1950.

Frank, Lawrence K.: Opportunities in a program of education for marriage and family life, *Ment. Hyg., N.Y.*, 1940, 24:578–594.

Leuba, Clarence: *Ethics in Sex Conduct: A Manual on Youth, Sex, and Marriage*, Association Press, New York, 1948.

Magoun, F. Alexander: *Love and Marriage*, Harper & Brothers, New York, 1948.

McKinney, Fred: *Psychology of Personal Adjustment*, rev. ed., pp. 471–526, 527–558, John Wiley & Sons, Inc., New York, 1949.

Nimkoff, Meyer F., and Wood, Arthur L.: Courtship and personality, *Amer. J. Sociol.*, 1948, 53:263–269.

Schmeideler, Rev. Edgar: *Marriage and the Family*, McGraw-Hill Book Company, Inc., New York, 1946.

Strauss, A.: The ideal and the chosen mate, *Amer. J. Sociol.*, 1946, 52:204–208.

CHAPTER 12

Home and Family

The courtship myth, that love will find a way, has been largely supplanted by the more realistic psychological approach. Adequate courtship, as described in the preceding chapter, lays a stronger foundation, upon which the marriage is more likely to succeed. A similar shift in understanding of the home and the family has been taking place during the past few decades. Family patterns are no longer the exclusive territory of the scientific investigator. Housing is being judged as to its efficiency by many people. Life with father has given way to life with the family. Just as mother has become a companion to father, a role established during modern courtship, so children have now become individual personalities in the home.

All these changes are still in process, somewhat unfinished. Growing from youth into adulthood involves the establishment of a new family group in which parenthood replaces childhood. Maturation continues throughout the life cycle, with marriage following youthful independence and family soon following marriage. In order that behavior may be goal-oriented during the years of youth and early adulthood, it is necessary that insight be achieved into the broader basis of home and family activity. The present chapter seeks to build such insight.

THE FAMILY LIFE CYCLE

The home plays an important part in the life cycle. During the lifetime of all its members the family is a continuing influence. It must meet certain biological requirements, obey certain cultural imperatives, and fulfill its members' personal needs.

Meaning of the Life Cycle

The entire span of years from birth until death stands linked with the home and family processes. The baby is dependent upon the nesting situation. The child's world is for the most part limited to his family group. Adolescents are striving to find their own independence at the same time that they continue to cling to parental bonds. Youths are experimenting with an in-between stage, having become relatively free of parental ties but as yet having established none to take their place. Early adult years bring the problems of home and family building. In the years of old age, home and family relationships have not been well defined in modern America.

Stage One

Stage one of the family life cycle might well be called the "Early Married Couple." Adjusting two individual selves to the new status of being a married pair is the initial goal in the home and family history. In realizing this goal the partners will be concerned with these specific steps:

Meshing their respective philosophies of life
Enlarging the emotional attachments established in courtship
Learning to communicate their real thoughts and feelings
Working out cooperative division of home responsibilities
Devising methods of securing and spending family income
Establishing a more broadly satisfying sexual relationship
Balancing their lives between too little and too much independence of spouse
Perfecting working relationships with relatives, peers, occupational associates, the community and its institutions
Accepting the possibility that there may be children

The extent to which these steps are successfully accomplished will determine the family's course of development. Outside stresses and supports beyond the control of the individuals involved will also be influential.

Stage Two

The second stage of the family life cycle will normally be entered with the first pregnancy. The anticipation of the adoption of a child marks this second stage in certain relatively rare cases; in other unusual cases the acceptance of responsibility for the care and rearing of a relative's child serves the same purpose. The important step is *adjusting to the fact of being expectant parents.* Psychological or emotional readiness will be evident in the individual's approach. Ideally this is one of the most fascinating and challenging experiences of life. It is as thrilling as a new romance, but it can be appreciated as such only by the individual who is ready for the experience. The individual who has not yet completed the adjustments of adolescence or of youth will not be prepared for this new rung in the ladder of life. Fearful anticipation, instead of interested growth, will then be likely to prevail.

Some indications of readiness for parenthood will be given by the way in which the new member of the family is welcomed. Practical underwriting of the welcome will take the concrete form of readjustments in the personal life of each parent. There should be a realignment of both affections and arrangements to meet the child's needs. The more this is based upon pleasurable anticipation of new and interesting experiences, and the greater the cooperation between the parents, the better the start for the child.

Stage Three

There is need of another realignment in the family pattern when the children are developing their independence. A slow reversal of parental roles must take place as one responsibility after another is shifted to the emerging adults. Some young people find that they or their parents are not yet ready for the current stage of their own home and family cycles. This lack of readiness of parents to let their offspring achieve independence is due as much to their own lack of readiness to face the next stage of life as it is to a lack of readiness of the offspring to assume the independence appropriate to his age. Youth and early adulthood are the "launching years" of the life cycle. By this time young people are out in the adult world and its responsibilities whether they are ready or not. The more clearly everyone in the family understands the nature and significance of the whole cycle, the more wholesome the atmosphere of the home will be.

Evolving Concept of the Family

The family has been steadily contracting in size, both because of the trend toward having fewer children and because of changed customs of dividing the generations. However, there is some indication that increase in length of life as well as in cost of housing may turn this tendency in the other direction. Much of the traditional material production of the home has been pushed outside its four walls. Many of its prerogatives of training have been turned over to schools and character-building agencies. Its once-rigid internal organization has become more flexible. Changes always seem to confuse traditions and to build frustrations. Some of these feelings are mirrored in the following quotations:

> Our earth is degenerate in these latter days; there are signs that the world is speedily coming to an end; bribery and corruption are common; children no longer obey their parents; every man wants to write a book and the end of the world is evidently approaching. [From an Assyrian stone tablet of about 2800 B.C.]

> The children now love luxury; they have bad manners, contempt for authority; they show disrespect for elders and love chatter in place of exercise. Children are now tyrants, not the servants of their households. They no longer rise when elders enter the room. They contradict their parents, chatter before company, gobble up dainties at the table, cross their legs, and tyrannize their teachers. [Attributed to Socrates (469–399 B.C.) by Plato.]

The mere reading of these expressions of highly emotionalized feelings of frustration gives one a certain perspective in thinking about the home and family cycle. Both physical and psychological patterns change, but the life cycle is a continuing reality.

Tomorrow's Home and Family

Many community activities for promoting the improvement of family life are being sponsored by churches, clubs, and other organizations. Various types of family institutes are being developed by educational institutions. Conferences between groups at different levels of the life cycle are helping to show parents how youth feels and to explain to youth why parents react as they do. Writers are suggesting that both parents and children can be helped by reading material with a more realistic approach to actual feelings. Pollyanna stories in which family relations continually run smoothly make for frustration on the part of all. Films are being developed to interpret the give-and-take between the various members of the family unit.

These endeavors are now reaching into international levels. The International Union of Family Organizations was created by representatives of twenty-seven nations in 1947.[1] The 1948 session was devoted to emotional security in the family and psychological problems of married people. Thus in many different ways the role of the home and of each member of the family group is being shown to be increasingly important to everyone in all parts of the world.

GOALS OF HOME AND FAMILY

The home is the laboratory in which the cohesions within and between individuals are nurtured and strengthened into permanent personality traits. The goals toward which the home strives in the *production* and *preservation* of healthy personalities are the family equivalents of the motives of the individual.

Family Functions

The atmosphere of the home must, if it is to be a home in any true sense, serve the needs of the individual as he strives to act in accordance with his fundamental motives and to maintain his scheme of values. Observation of family situations as these channelize the development of personality brings to light certain common functions. These are to aid the growth of youth and to satisfy the fundamental needs of the adult members of the home. The carrying out of these constitutes the work of the home and family.

Each of the following common functions interacts with the others: (1) provision for rest and reintegration, (2) building self-expression, and (3) developing skills in close human relationships.

Provision for Rest and Reintegration. Security and safety in opportunities to recover from fatigue and discouragement and to regain integration are indispensable to the growth and preservation

---

[1] Robert Boudet, An international union of family organizations, *Marriage and Family Living*, 1951, 13:97.

of personality. These represent not a regression or retreat into the past from momentary pressures but a tissue necessity of life itself.

To meet this need there should be an adequate physical setting, a familiar atmosphere without tension and with opportunity for the expression of *primary feelings*. In our high-pressured, sophisticated culture the home and family is the one oasis. Here the individual should find conditions relatively free from threat even during unguarded moments, the opportunity to interpret his own more primary feelings. Each adult needs a certain amount of permissive freedom and the family is the traditional spot for this.

With the principles of child psychology gaining broader acceptance, the parents' monopoly on complete freedom in the home has necessarily become restricted. The one-time extreme of children being seen and not heard and the home being entirely slanted to the convenience of adult members has more or less disappeared. The opposite tendency—to completely overlook the parents', and especially the mother's, need for freedom—is lessening somewhat. The ideal situation provides a maximum of relaxed, permissive atmosphere for every member of the family circle. Here the individual should find opportunity to consider his plans, to evaluate his recent experiences, and to adjust his efforts anew following the resurgence of hope that comes with relaxation.

When the home and family have met this recuperative need, any move to other environs will act like a tonic to mental health. A child away at a summer camp or an adult on a long business trip may crave this haven. It seems necessary in order to relax and rest that the situation, plus the individual's own imagination, must bring back his intimately satisfying experiences. The stimulus situation may be being with one or more members of his immediate family. A cue could also be found in various objects, whether of antique or ethnic or purely sentimental value. Such an example is the statue of a dog which was used by a young man who was forced to live in rooming houses far from home. This *sign of home* he carried to a new room every few months and placed in a prominent spot. Thereafter, this statue told him with each glance, "This place is now home."

Sometimes the stimulus is a neighborhood or landscape. The hill folk of the South do not feel at home in the valley plains. They love their mountains as the sailor loves the sea. These stimulus objects reinstate the long-established attitudes and feelings of security built in childhood. They bring relaxation and reintegration.

Building Self-expression. The second job which the family can perform for its individual members is to provide opportunity to de-

Fig. 12–1. A pet provides reassurance. Pets are helpful to the child's growth, particularly in the hours when parents have necessary work to do. Also, pets are permissive, allowing the small child to develop his own feelings of affection. (*H. Armstrong Roberts.*)

velop and strengthen feelings of assurance in self-expression. To do this the home must offer a combination of emotional security and positive channels for the utilization of abilities. Without this function well performed in every stage of the life cycle, life will seem futile.

The growing personality of infant, child, or adolescent must have a feeling of room to develop. Critical attitudes on the part of the important people in his universe are cramping to this freedom. Life to the infant and child is much like the communication between two lovers. A negative sign, or even a "poker face," is taken as disapproval, as an indication that the much-desired love is now absent from the beloved's feelings. The great sensitivity which lovers experience to minute details of behavior is a source of constant worry

Fig. 12–2. Family recreation develops skills in human relationships. Informal social life within the family strengthens the feeling of belonging. Happy experiences with family members carry over in later attitudes toward people. (*H. Armstrong Roberts.*)

to many couples. It is also the very foundation of the satisfaction of the state called "being in love." Infants, children, and adolescents are no less sensitive to the actions of their parents and heroes than are lovers to the actions of each other. Only the positive expressions of love can be reassuring.

Warmth of affection is necessary for growth.[2] Many a pediatrician's prescription for an hour of fondling and cuddling a day

[2] Harry Bakwin, Emotional deprivation in infants, *J. Pediat.*, 1949, 35:512–521.

has changed a feeble institutional infant into a well one, thus dramatizing the importance of affectional nourishment. This support must continue, gradually lessening as the life cycle progresses but never quite disappearing.

The adult also needs assurance and encouragement from his home and family. In the mature adult, feelings of confidence are less general than in the infant and child. Some types of activity imply less threat to the individual than others. An individual may have strong feelings of assurance in sports but feel threatened or lacking in self-confidence in academic activities. If he feels insecure in the economic aspects of living, he may readily accept ideas stemming from another culture. Many studies of satisfied and unsatisfied workers show that family ego support is basic. In this competitive machine culture the workman, who before mass production found props for his self-assurance in his creative work, is especially dependent upon the home for this needed support. An intensive study of a cross section of the counselees of the Vocational Counseling Service in Boston from 1934 to 1943 revealed that the family relationship was the most important influence on work adjustment.[3]

Developing Skill in Close Human Relationships. Skill in human relationships entails the development of acceptance feelings plus the opportunity for close personal contact, first within the family and then with outsiders. Through the intimate contacts of members of the family with one another and the familiarity with everyone in this primary group, there develops a feeling that the bodily functions are normal and to be taken in one's stride. The experience of eating together, of sleeping and bathing and dressing under one roof and with the knowledge of the rest of the family, provides the basis for self-evaluation of bodily characteristics. Practice in fondling, roughhousing, and affectionate embraces is the springboard for the development of natural feelings toward oneself. Even sexual functions must be recognized and aired freely through open discussion in a factual manner.

When this process fails for any of the bodily functions, it is usually because an adult expresses his own feelings of guilt and inadequacy.

---

[3] Jeanette G. Friend and Ernest A. Haggard, *Work Adjustment in Relation to Family Background: A Conceptual Basis for Counseling*, p. 47, Stanford University Press, Stanford University, Calif., 1948.

Criticism and censure by adults soon result in similar feelings within the young. Then there develops the false modesty which all too often stands in conflict with the bodily functions. The feeling that these functions must be kept private or secret produces worry simply because the child's voluntary control of organic processes develops slowly. Eating, elimination, perspiring—all the functional reactions, including sexual excitement and release—are *factual*. Outside the family they need not be discussed openly, but if within the intimate circle they are accepted as factual they will seem natural processes to the child. Similarly, the other inward feelings and aspirations of the personalities should be communicated within the sheltering atmosphere of the family until these expressions have gained the strength to withstand the colder reactions of impartial secondary groups.

With this preparation as a basis, the family is the primary atmosphere for practice in the social skills. When these foundations are laid with the family's encouragement, the social horizon can be extended for practice in dealing with diverse types of individuals. The family attitude should be a welcoming one to friends of all its members. Interest in extra-family contacts will aid in broadening the basis of social life. Participation in family recreation groups is important, as is joining hands in community enterprises. The opportunities for in-service training in human relationships are endless. All age combinations gain from this laboratory for experimenting with the social skills.

The Price of Neglect in Family Work

Studies of maladjusted personalities have highlighted the great importance of human relations in home and family. A surprising number of people have very strong feelings which they do not know how to express. A taboo on the tangible expression of tenderness may cause an exaggerated emphasis on the value of substitute satisfactions and lead to lust for power or pleasure or to pathological sex reactions. Drifting away from parental supervision, love-starved individuals learn techniques for personal contact which become abnormally important. Sex thus offers the only channel for personal contacts, and love finds itself narrowed down to the ephemeral tissue processes of hormone reactions. As is pointed out in the chapter on

Delinquency, much sex delinquency can be directly traced to this kind of warping. In reaction to such thwarting, some individuals withdraw into masturbation [4] or seek to attain a feeling of adequacy or power by hurting others. Had these individuals been able as infants and children to express and enjoy affection and other feelings within their own families, they would be able to respond to others in later years. In short, to the degree that the family's work has been well accomplished individuals are able to meet their basic needs in a healthy way and to perceive their fellows as warm and friendly.

INFLUENCES THAT SHAPE FAMILY GOALS

Home and family goals are aided or hindered by various factors. Positive and negative influences lurk in the many situations which make up what is known as the "family climate."

Housing as a Stage Setting

The physical symbol of the home is housing; this is the stage upon which the drama of family life is played. The adequacy of the setting can add to or detract from the success with which the *work* of the family is accomplished. Sociological and social-welfare investigations of housing and psychological studies of maladjustment expressed in school problems and delinquency have highlighted housing weaknesses. This tool with which the family must work affects the entire gamut of home functions.

Freedom for individual development, security, the ease with which members can relax or socialize are affected by the arrangement and esthetics of the home. A functional setting in which various members of the family can carry on their own interests in their own way adds to the recuperative value of the home. Even greater rest and integration can come from actual family participation as a group. It has been suggested that part of the tension and friction at the tag end of the day, when Dad comes home, is due to a poorly planned physical setting. Room for cooperative activities

[4] Margaret A. Ribble, Infantile experience in relation to personality development, p. 646, in J. McV. Hunt (ed.), *Personality and Behavior Disorders: A Handbook Based Upon Experimental and Clinical Research,* Vol. 2, The Ronald Press Company, New York, 1944.

enhances the development of social skills. The general attractiveness and amount of color used in a house definitely influence the morale of its occupants.

The physical setting has a part in giving assurance and encouragement to each member of the family. An individual's self-assurance may be affected if he is ashamed of the physical symbol of his family. The young child is afforded opportunity for manipulation and healthy growth if he has an area for his own use. The adolescent needs a part of the house for social life where his crowd will not upset everyone else. The elder members of the household may feel "in the way" unless they have a more or less isolated section to call their own. For maximum usefulness, houses should be "elastic," built to adjust from couple to expanding family to contracting family. Arrangements for enlarging during the child-bearing and -rearing phases and dividing when the children leave are psychologically important.

Life on a farm with its open spaces, life in a small town with a yard for each house, and life in a jam-packed city apartment afford three entirely different stages upon which to grow. The big house on the hill is the traditional indication of physical luxury and financial ease, but it is also the literary symbol for affectionless living. Neither generalization is necessarily true. Nevertheless, these literary traditions do not err in suggesting that it takes more to make a home than merely a well-built house.

Crowded housing, with three or even four generations in less than that number of rooms, is far below the necessary minimum of equipment and space. Young children raised in such quarters have no opportunity to grow into a feeling of independence. Instead they must be "dumped" upon the street to get along without home and family during many hours of the day, or when in too crowded quarters, they must stereotype themselves to think and act as their parents think and act.

There is need for more consideration of the psychological importance of the physical setting of the home. The work of the family in the production of adequate citizens can be greatly enhanced by a healthier environment. The implications of housing in the development of personality are so far-reaching that they can be mentioned only briefly in this chapter.

Mental Health of Parents

For the most part, children's behavior will be determined by the behavior of the parents and other adults living close to them. Parents' differences in physique or economic class are relatively easy to see. More complicated is the matter of noting and evaluating the emotional conditioning of parents on various levels of adjustment. Par-

"Perhaps, if you would put these on . . . He's an admirer of Hopalong Cassidy."

FIG. 12–3. Immature parents often overprotect children. (*Courtesy of Albert A. Mueller, Parents' Magazine.*)

ents illustrate all varieties of emotional maturity. They have a point of view and a history.

Depending upon how well their own childhood homes succeeded in carrying on their three common functions, parents will be able to achieve their grown-up home and family goals. Some are intrigued with infants and seem to lose interest as they grow. Others do not feel at home with their children until they show interests which they themselves can share. The family is a network of emotionally charged channels or relationships. Much of this is nonverbal in its communication, but it definitely produces feeling. This emotional tone is the result of the dynamic forces within the parents' personalities. Whatever the parent-child relationship is, it will be carried over into adulthood.

Happy parents feel warmly toward their children and tend to radiate acceptance feelings, showing genuine love for them and a desire to encourage development into self-sufficient independence. Postponement of recognition of the independence of one's offspring is, in effect, admission that this independence is not welcome. "Momism" and "popism" paralyze youth by making it difficult for them to cooperate in other friendships. They are also at the root of the in-law problem. The mother whose emotional needs require an exclusive claim on her son will be in competition with his wife. The father who craves his daughter's continued emotional dependency will interfere with her marriage.

Individuals who are not ready for parenthood will incline their infants toward emotional insecurity. They are unready for the initial stage of parenthood, *i.e.*, pregnancy. They resist parenthood at the level of ideas, claiming that they cannot afford children, complaining that the children are not healthy, or finding that the children are unresponsive in some way. Thus the child, to defend himself from his stronger parent, may withdraw into his private world. These rejections of the child are, fundamentally, rejections of the role of parent. Although the child is in fact rejected, this is more unrecognized than deliberate. The same is true of the parent who is overambitious for his child. Any pushing of the youngster beyond his capacities places him in a position of being criticized. This applies to diverse learning processes, from toilet training to reading. Impossibly high ambitions for the child may be needed to counteract the parent's guilt feelings for not really welcoming his own parenthood. These high ambitions may also be an attempt to meet vicariously the parent's own frustrated success needs.

Some fathers regard their offspring as competitors for their wife's attention and services. They reject the infant as a handicap. To them parenthood has "spoiled their life." They may try to escape by being too busy, or by claiming that their responsibility in earning a living requires all their time and energy. Thus the "reasons" for neglecting the role of parent are "the child's own good" or the neglect is due to "circumstances beyond control."

Mothers, too, sometimes reject the role of parent by similar means, usually claiming that at some mythical later date they will be better mothers. From a study of family counseling service in a university community comes this statement: "There seemed to be a great uncertainty regarding the role which women should play. Not only were the women in conflict regarding the most effective way in which to discharge their responsibilities as wife and mother, but the

Fig. 12–4. Father's interest is very important. This father is showing in concrete terms that he enjoys his daughter. Every daughter needs the feeling of being worth while in her father's estimation. (*Courtesy of McCall's. Photograph by Sarra.*)

men also were uncertain what to expect of their wives as well as of themselves." [5]

Parent-Parent Relationships

The parents' adjustment to each other will be the basis of their family relationships. The degree to which they have brought their two personalities into emotional harmony will determine the amount of security in the atmosphere of the home. This means mutual loy-

[5] Margaret Gilbert Benz, *Family Counseling Service in a University Community,* p. 116, Teachers College, Columbia University, New York, 1940.

alty and willingness of each to work for the fulfillment of the other. Mother will have to take over when father's core values show too little self-assurance, particularly if his expression of these feelings is hostile. In this sense, mothers and fathers play the same role in compensating for the immaturities of the other. Each must recognize that the other requires opportunities to express his own feelings in the home and each must give assurance that the other is fundamentally worth while despite occasional lapses.

When the parent-parent relationship is unsatisfactory, there is a projection of this onto the children. All the motives of the home are thwarted. Sometimes this type of emotional conditioning appears as rejection; the following case is an illustration.

Mary, a coed in a municipal college, had always felt left out of group activities. She simply felt unwanted. She realized that she had always been resented by her family, even though they dressed her well, gave her a good allowance, and allowed her more freedom than her peers enjoyed.

This feeling of being unwanted or unloved was explained by the psychologist as a by-product of the following facts. Her mother and father had separated several times, finally arriving at a compromise trial reconciliation just before Mary was conceived. Her appearance in the family caused them to stay together in a somewhat strained relationship. Mary's older sister, also love-starved, resented the care that went to the new infant, so she too made Mary feel unwelcome. The feeling of being unwanted which troubled Mary was in fact far from groundless. She was unable to show friendship, having had no adequate opportunity to develop this skill. This added to the number of times each day that she was stimulated to respond with feelings of unwantedness.

Thus unseen influences in the form of emotionalized parental attitudes are responsible for the relationship between parent and children. The vicious circle of maladjustment continues from generation to generation. In many definite ways the parents' relation to each other adds to or subtracts from the conditions for recuperation and reintegration, for building self-expression and developing skill in handling close relationships.

Pressures from Totalitarian Philosophies

The combination of the emotional adjustment of parents and their cultural patterns determines the type of child management used. Families, somewhat as nations, tend toward totalitarian, laissez-faire, or democratic organizations. Reared in one type of family and having all his contacts with other types of family "interpreted" by the elders of his own, it is usual for the individual to be ignorant of the alternative family philosophies. This indoctrination, which includes strong emotional props, perpetuates the established pattern. The parent who as a child was starved for affection in the maintenance of selfhood often develops an authoritarian personality. He attempts to legislate or administer a narrowly restricted system of life to be followed by the rest of the family. He dominates by direct exercise of force, often through instilling fear of drastic punishment.

Whether mother- or father-controlled, this totalitarian family organization tends to fashion robots. This is well illustrated by the German father-dominated family with its goal of training the child to implicit obedience by the age of five years. It is reflected in the common development of the personality type so well suited for autocratic government.[6] Personalities so indoctrinated cannot make decisions. They are paralyzed as self-starters. Much adolescent difficulty in developing to the point of accepting adult responsibilities stems from this type of family setting. Without benefit of freedom or encouragement toward independence, these groping teen-agers are completely at a loss when it comes to making decisions. The following is an instance of the working of this influence.

Beth could not understand why she was always the first to be discharged in offices in which she worked. She was most conscientious and cooperative. Finally one supervisor told her frankly that she was always asking how everything should be done and showed too little independence. Behind the scenes of Beth's growing personality was a dominating atmosphere of totalitarianism. Her parents had made all the decisions for her. Thus her conception of a supervisor was

[6] Bertram H. Schaffner, *Father Land: A Study of Authoritarianism in the German Family*, p. 23, Columbia University Press, New York, 1948.

someone who should decide every detail. To a busy boss this appeared to be a weakness, a lack of effectiveness on the job.

This type of domination, if it is somewhat inconsistent, will fashion hostility-laden personalities prone to resent authority. The antagonism may develop into such pronounced negativism that all outside suggestions will be fought against. Families based upon this concept of the father or mother as dictator fall easy prey to national dictatorships.

Dictatorships within families are consistently revealed as hierarchies, or "pecking orders," with the small or nonfavorite children at the bottom, and the authoritarian personality of an adult at the top. This pecking order also tends to develop in children's play groups, particularly if the largest or strongest child in the group comes from a dictatorial family. The smallest child has a larger child on his back, ready to strike him, and the next larger child has a larger child, etc. Such pecking orders are not instinctive. Rather, they are direct enlargements of the unhealthy personality structure of the largest or strongest child from the totalitarian family. They exemplify the transfer of hostility behavior from the authoritarian parent to the play group, where the hostility can be "taken out" on the other children. It is safer to express hostility in the play group than in the home. This common reaction to the authoritarian home makes life difficult for one's associates during the early years of emotional and cultural conditioning of the life cycle. The individual tends to expect all human relations to follow this authoritarian pattern.

Typical Conditioning by Totalitarian Philosophy

The following illustration describes a young man who realizes that he has a problem but is not yet ready for therapy.

John was having difficulty in his college activities. His strong efforts and marked abilities failed to bring the success he felt he deserved. Superior intelligence and abundant energy should have resulted in his winning the student-body presidency the year after he had the vice-presidency. But this did not happen, and in addition his scholarship dropped. On the outside he was becoming deeply involved with an artistic group strongly communist in their interests. From the reports of other students, the personalities in this group were much like that of John: excellent ability accompanied by antagonistic feelings of "not being appreciated."

The family background of John confirmed that a strong anti-authority reaction was present. This showed particularly in his relationships with those college instructors and administrators who made assignments of the more exacting type. John's mother was a very strong personality with abundant energy. According to her own interpretations, she "ran" her home and family efficiently. The only way to get along with her was to let her have her own way. So the father spent many extra hours at the office, commonly arriving home after the children were in bed and leaving in the morning before they were awake. The children were thus "little gears revolving around a master gear," the mother.

John had a long history of allergies and enuresis. He was not interested in working with materials; he preferred to deal with ideas and words, which could be manipulated to suit his own emotional thinking. His hostile resentment of his domineering mother was as subtle as her techniques of dictatorship. His interest in the radical group was a form of escape from the stressing of conventionality for which his mother had stood. The talents of the members of this group served to justify or veil this activity, for which he felt guilty. His guilt was his bond of dependency upon his mother. His tendency, which he concealed well, to take an exploitative attitude toward his girl friends was a transferral to all females of his resentment of his mother. These emotional handicaps will certainly interfere with John's success and happiness. In his case, as in many others, the totalitarian philosophy makes impossible the successful achievement of the home and family purposes.

Effects of Laissez-faire Philosophy

Amateur politicians frequently confuse the laissez-faire governmental philosophy with the democratic. In the former no attempt is made to regulate the lives of the people except to the minimum extent necessary for the maintenance of life itself. Within the family organization this arrangement would amount to the mere provision of food, clothing, and shelter, with some related fittings. No effort would be made to lead or to force the members of the family into any given way of behaving. This type of family organization sounds enticing to the individual who has grown up in a dictatorial family. Unfortunately the daydreams and fantasies of frustrated people are sometimes unrealistic in the extreme. A more careful look at the laissez-faire family in operation hardly confirms favorable judgment.

Some of the types of personalities favoring this kind of family organization are breaking away from one very restrictive set of strong national or religious traditions or practices but have adopted no other positive patterns. They are in transition from an unsatisfying past but do not know quite where they are going.

During the great depression of the 1930s many parents lost all ambition. They experienced continuous failure of their traditional ideals of being able to support themselves and their families, of making economic progress, and of believing that there is "always room at the top." The children of these frustrated parents thus in many cases grew up in homes which were without long-term goals. These were minimum family structures—laissez-faire homes. Years later, in college, these children evidenced a sort of helpless and negative feeling of general nervous tension. They seemed to be without well-organized and well-oriented personalities.

Other families reacted oppositely during the depression, pulling more closely together and enjoying each other through inexpensive activities such as picnics, home games, reading library books, and the like. The children of these families did not seem to suffer the weakening of personality that the children of the laissez-faire homes did.

Children show the same generally tense behavior when they have grown up in transitional home and family backgrounds wherein a major shift in religion is involved. Cultural transitions, too, seem to set this pattern. Sometimes "dollar madness" or "social climbing" or merely a generally cynical disillusionment follows the transition. In these various ways the laissez-faire family organization is a phenomenon of transition. It lacks a positive program and thus is a complete abdication so far as the *work* of the family goes.

Definition of Democratic Family Structure

The democratic type of family organization requires more skill than either of the preceding two types. In this organization is found the greatest hope for wholesome personalities, for the steady progress of society which western civilization idealizes. Joseph Folsom, in his book *The Family and Democratic Society*,[7] urges that democratic family organization should be the primary seed bed for national as

Fig. 12–5. Working together makes for family harmony. Cooperative undertakings are helpful in giving each member a share in homemaking. Joint efforts cut down jealousies and tensions. (*H. Armstrong Roberts.*)

well as local democracy. Some have suggested that it should be the foundation for better world cooperation. The growing child needs to try himself out on his own level of ability. Each year he can take part in more activities. Each member should carry the responsibility for certain functions, as his age and ability fit him for these. This does not mean that one member is boss all the time, that being his traditional function. As many persons as possible should have turns

[7] Joseph Folsom, *The Family and Democratic Society*, p. 350, John Wiley & Sons, Inc., New York, 1943.

at being responsible for the coordination of every large activity. In-service training to gain skill in human relationships and self-assurance can be acquired by working with the other members of the family. Each needs practice in "holding office" effectively, from the most lowly chore to the highest executive decision. All members must share in family councils on spending policies, in recreational plans, in regulations for the good of all, and in devising new projects. When discipline is needed, it can be better handled by a skilled family conference than by the traditional "board of education applied at the seat of learning until it hurts."

Positive Results of the Democratic Philosophy

The self-disciplining which comes with the development of leadership-followership capacities is the only solid foundation upon which democratic living can become efficient and enduring. The healthiness of the democratically organized group was well illustrated during the years immediately following World War II. Many so-called war marriages were dissolving, with resultant suffering by all concerned but especially by the small children. A study of 272 successful families which had shown themselves able to withstand this period of stress indicated that both totalitarian and democratic families had survived. In the instances in which the father's dictatorial powers had been removed, the family had usually become disorganized. A greater percentage of democratic families survived.[8]

Decidedly more in the democratic family than in other types of structure will the individual member have the opportunity to develop his own powers of appreciating the interests, needs, wishes, and limitations of the personalities of the other members. This will help him to gauge accurately his working place in later organizations, both primary and secondary groups. He will not be pressured from within to resist every authority.[9] IIis understanding of the need for social controls will be adequate—adaptive but not worshipful. He will have the self-assurance needed to assimilate new experiences, to accept the challenge of living in the world of material,

[8] Reuben Hill, *Families under Stress: Adjustment to the Crises of War Separation and Reunion,* p. 333, Harper & Brothers, New York, 1949.

[9] Kurt Lewin, Roland Lippitt, and Ralph K. White, Patterns of aggressive behavior in experimentally created "social climates," *J. Soc. Psychol.,* 1939, 10:271–299.

social, and intellectual reality. This will cut down on the stress of emancipating himself from the family at adolescence. He will be better prepared to assume the responsibilities of the mature adult.

Summary

There is a powerfully integrating force in the combination of individuals at different stages of the life cycle. If each person is encouraged to contribute and enjoy the full privileges of partnership according to his abilities, the home and family can be most constructive. It is the constant climate in which the personality is produced and preserved. Perceptual patterns which come to be habitual are in large part a duplication of one's own home and family patterns, both past and present.

The importance of the work of the family is everywhere in evidence. More and more as the threads of unhealthy symptoms in individuals and society are unraveled, they lead back to the home and family. The family is being internationally acclaimed as the bulwark against catastrophe. Each individual's development of personality is correlated with the success of the work of the home and family. Each member of a home and family group adds to or subtracts from the healthy personality adjustment of the group. Possibilities for the improvement of the home and family in terms of its contribution to emotional maturity are beyond definition.

QUESTIONS FOR DISCUSSION

1. What are some of the main qualifications a working mother should look for in outside help so that the home and family will not suffer?
2. What can busy fathers do to contribute their part to the home and family?
3. What should the child of divorced parents be told about the parent with whom he is not living?
4. What makes parents overdominating? How does this tendency affect their children's personalities?
5. Why is it that sometimes one child in a family seems to be a problem while the others, who have apparently had the same treatment, are not?
6. When and how should an adopted child be told the facts about his beginning?
7. What methods of coping with grandparents who do not understand the newer approaches to child rearing can you suggest?

8. If a child has been told about sex by older children in an unhealthy manner, what can the parents do?
9. What should be done in the case of a child who never asks about reproduction or sex?
10. How should parents handle the problem of masturbation?
11. What can parents do when a child continually hurts his younger brother?
12. What is the explanation when a child is shy and quiet around his home but rowdy at school?
13. What brings about finicky food habits? How can parents prevent these from developing?
14. Will children develop healthier personalities if parents concentrate all their interests on them?
15. What are the resources in your community for materials on home and family? Are there discussion groups?

ADDITIONAL READINGS

Abrams, Charles, and Dean, John P.: Housing and the family, pp. 299–321, in Ruth N. Anshen (ed.): *The Family: Its Function and Destiny,* Harper & Brothers, New York, 1949.

Anderson, Phoebe M.: What kind of person will your child be? *Childhood Ed.,* 1950, 27:9–14.

Auerbach, Aline B.: What does a child need? *Child Study,* 1951, 28:3–5.

Benedek, Therese: The emotional structure of the family, pp. 209–225, in Ruth N. Anshen (ed.): *The Family: Its Function and Destiny,* Harper & Brothers, New York, 1949.

Benedict, Agnes, and Franklin, Adele: *The Happy Home: A Guide to Family Living,* Appleton-Century-Crofts, Inc., New York, 1948.

Bossard, James H. S.: *The Sociology of Child Development,* Chap. 7, Harper & Brothers, New York, 1948.

Childcraft, Field Enterprises, Inc., Chicago, 1949.

Christensen, Harold T.: *Marriage Analysis: Foundations for Successful Family Life,* pp. 81ff., The Ronald Press Company, New York, 1950.

Colm, Hanna: Do our children's books meet emotional needs? *Understanding the Child,* 1951, 20:117–118.

de Schweinitz, Karl: *Growing Up: The Story of How We Become Alive, Are Born and Grow Up,* 2d ed. rev., The Macmillan Company, New York, 1945.

English, O. Spurgeon, and Foster, Constance J.: *Fathers Are Parents, Too: A Constructive Guide to Successful Fatherhood,* G. P. Putnam's Sons, New York, 1951.

Jenkins, Gladys Gardner: Discipline, what is it? *Parents' Magazine,* 1948, 23 (5):18–19, 80–82.

——, and Neuman, Joy: *How to Live with Parents,* Science Research Associates, Chicago, 1948.

Levine, Milton I., and Seligmann, Jean H.: *The Wonder of Life: How We Are Born and How We Grow Up*, Simon and Schuster, Inc., New York, 1940.

Marmor, Judd: Psychological trends in American family relationships, *Marriage and Family Living*, 1951, 13:145–147.

Ribble, Margaret A.: *The Rights of Infants: Early Psychological Needs and Their Satisfaction*, Columbia University Press, New York, 1943.

Underwood, Virginia Van Meter: Student fathers with their children, *Marriage and Family Living*, 1949, 11:101.

Weill, Blanche C.: *Through Children's Eyes, True Stories out of the Practice of a Consultant Psychologist*, Island Press Co-operative, Inc., New York, 1940.

CHAPTER 13 *Handicap*

"Handicap" is a convenient word used to describe a characteristic which is limiting. Certain physical disabilities are innately frustrating to personality development or behavior in almost all cultures. Some emotional handicaps are not yet so recognized by a large segment of American society. Distinguishing features such as race or nationality are handicaps in certain sections of this country. Some qualities are undergoing a change in cultural definition. The increasing percentage of older people in our society is affecting the traditional perceptions directed toward this group.

In studying the growth of personalities one must consider the cultural influences that are constantly assessing individuals. The social majority endows members of certain groups with limiting characteristics. Each person in such a segment must be thought of as being continually surrounded by these attitudes. Thus the individual may be stereotyped as inadequate by family, neighbors, and society in general.

For the sake of clarity this discussion will deal with the problem of handicap in five sections. In real-life situations these groupings of emotional, physical, mental, social, and age characteristics are not so well defined. Often handicaps in several areas combine in one individual.

THE MEANING OF HANDICAP

A handicap is like an obstruction on an obstacle course; it adds to the difficulty of the growing process. Thus a person with a handicap is one who is challenged by an emotional, physical, mental, social, or age hurdle. The techniques used for running the obstacle race will be a reflection of the individual's personality dynamics. His perceptual sets necessarily will prejudge every situation.

Personal Weighing Scale

People constantly interpret themselves in relation to other human beings. No personality characteristic, physical or mental, can be measured in a vacuum. Always it must be evaluated in its setting. Each person has subjective components which make up what Douglas Spencer terms "fulcra of conflict." [1] These components might be thought of as constituting a filter through which each new experience is strained as it is integrated into the personality. This consists of the individual's idea or concept of what his parents, his relatives, his friends, and society in general think about him, and also what he thinks about himself, or his self-concept. In other words, each person perceives himself and his world according to his own *frame of reference*. Thus many typical characteristics are perceived as handicaps to the degree that the individual's own scheme of values rates them as weaknesses. The weighing scale which determines this evaluation will have been built out of the interaction between the pressures of his environment and his own inner feelings. A handicapped person often feels that because he is handicapped he is necessarily inferior and inadequate.

The same personal difficulty may be overpowering in its effect in one segment of society and quite unimportant in another. Cultural pressures rather arbitrarily interpret certain personality characteristics as handicaps. The cultural pattern is one of the forces in the outer environment with which a personality must struggle in its own integration process.

Constructive Attitudes

When one part of the whole person is handicapped, his development must and will take place in such a way as to allow somehow for this limitation. Liabilities will influence and be influenced by assets in the over-all developmental process. Handicaps must be considered in relation to the other facets of personality structure.

[1] Douglas Spencer, *Fulcra of Conflict: A New Approach to Personality Measurement,* p. 90, World Book Company, Yonkers, N.Y., 1938.

They are examples of traits which may bring about secondary reactions of many types on the scale from nonadjustment to a completely efficient adjustment. The most healthy of over-all attitudes toward handicap would be the attitude which is in effect in certain

Fig. 13–1. Adjustment reflects one's health of personality. This physician, paralyzed by polio, tries to create as normal an atmosphere as possible in his home. Here he is reading to the youngest of his five children. He is also slanting his medical work to those fields in which he is able to function despite his handicap. (*Reprinted by permission from Look Magazine.*)

sports. A personality handicap should be considered similar to a golf or race-track handicap. Whatever victories the individual achieves should be scored in terms of his starting handicap. The greater the handicap, the greater the victory.

The more understanding every person has of the meaning of handicap, the more conducive to healthy growth the surrounding situation will be. Many people complicate life for the handicapped by treating them with oversentimentality or as "different." The fat child almost expects to be the butt of jokes, the racial or religious minority member to be rejected, the blind to be confronted with maudlin sympathy. These fixed role and status expectations are not healthy for personality growth. The enlightened student can help to interpret the role of the person with a handicap. By his own actions and influence he can lessen the psychologically unsound social pressures, can stress the importance of considering the handicapped individual as a personality having some characteristics which are limited. He can aid in opening up additional social and employment opportunities. He can support legislation which will provide resources for diminishing the handicap. In many ways he can use his influence for greater awareness of the preventive and prophylactic possibilities to be found in psychological approaches to the problems.

Handicaps are seldom found in isolation. They intertwine with and influence each other. This linkage should be kept in mind throughout the following discussion even though it is divided for the sake of convenience into five groupings: *emotional, physical, mental, social,* and *age.*

THE EMOTIONAL HANDICAP

Emotional handicaps are not so easily identified as other handicaps. Many are catalogued as laziness, hotheadedness, or merely bad disposition. Others are expressed in psychosomatic illnesses. They may be mirrored in rigidity or so-called "temperament," vanity or excessive modesty, craving for affection or withdrawal from human contacts. They sometimes appear as phobias, paralyzing their victim in some phase of activity.

Development of Neurotic Nucleus

The emotionally handicapped person is emotional because he is fighting too many battles expressing inconsistencies in his integration. The growth process was described earlier as the integration into the personality of the experiences of which the biography is made. The individual either assimilates, resists, or reconstructs these experiences. Assimilating experiences, directly or as reconstructed, is the normal learning process. If these experiences tend toward insecurity and anxiety, the individual develops a "neurotic nucleus" which plays an important part in the underlying plot which is the dynamics of his life history. If a problem is too upsetting for him to face realistically, it may distort or interrupt his learning process. To save face and maintain selfhood, habits of resistance must be built. This is necessary to prevent or avoid new contact with the threat. Thereafter growth proceeds around this neurotic nucleus, which may be at any one of the levels of personality described earlier. Then there

FIG. 13–2. Conflict results in inefficient behavior. This young woman is torn when faced with any decision. This emotional handicap is continually interfering with her business of living. (*Courtesy of McCall's. Photograph by Ralph Steiner.*)

are continual repetitions of this same fixated defensive process. The would-be learner is prevented from insightful learning which might reactivate the upsetting nucleus. Such defense of the neurosis assures its continuance. The further down into the inner layers of personality structure it penetrates, the more difficult it will be to reach. The individual may defend this or use it as a defense of more deepseated evaluations of his outer world.

There are all sorts of combinations of personality illnesses. But always a disproportionate part of the individual's energies must be devoted to the awkward nurturing of his defensive and protective organization. This results in lowered efficiency, lack of energy, and chronic dissatisfaction, all of which limit behavior. These character-istics may be a decided handicap to success in college or on the job, where one is expected to meet general requirements, not those tailor-made to fit individual personality needs. The shifting sands of inner feelings often play havoc with individual progress.

Emotional Handicaps of College Women

Some interesting effects on college women of fixations or rigidities of personality resulting from disintegrative experiences have been described.[2] In overconscientious or "rigid" women a generalized in-hibition has been used as a defense to protect the poorly integrated core values composing the neurotic nucleus. This is shown outwardly in overseriousness, excessive reliability, a pressing drive to excel, and an excessive need to please. Such women seem afraid of their own impulses or judgments. They project their anxiety or personality constriction into the world by amassing much information; in exam-inations they reproduce the professor's lectures exactly. They enjoy lecture courses in which neither initiative nor originality is expected. They must protect themselves, at all costs, from their own conflict-laden opinions or feelings. This then is their emotional handicap. They have "adapted" at the level of surface traits but have not really adjusted in the general meaning of the term, *i.e.*, by gaining insight into their source traits and core values. They must conduct their activities so as to bolster this general inhibition and to guard against the structure being toppled over. If they are required to take sem-inars demanding original thinking or synthesizing, they might break under the strain.

A contrasting group of women is described by the same researcher: the temperamental, or "scattered," students. These rebel against standardization of any kind. They dislike reading assignments or collecting information. They prefer writing papers in which they can use original ideas and autobiographical material. They shift their majors at the drop of a hat. Such behavior seems to be motivated by inadequate satisfaction of their fundamental needs. If their need is for great quantities of affection, they sometimes become very en-thusiastic over poetry dealing uninhibitedly with love and sex. If

[2] Ruth L. Munroe, *Teaching the Individual,* pp. 156–318, Columbia University Press, New York, 1942.

they are waging a struggle against domination, they become propagandists for parent education, a cause into which they can siphon off their feelings against an autocratic father. The results are very one-sided learning and prejudiced attitudes. Thus constricted, the sufferer experiences real trouble in securing a well-rounded education.

Handicap in Close Relationships

An example of an emotional handicap affecting another sector of life is Miss T. She was conscious of difficulty only in her heterosexual relationships. A successful teacher, she belonged to many organizations and enjoyed a wide circle of friendships, including both men and women. But she felt definitely handicapped in close associations with men. She enjoyed men as long as they were casual friends but found herself becoming critical and cynical at any show of warmth from them.

She had no memories of her father, and her mother would not talk about him. She had married the present stepfather when Miss T. was very young. The stepfather had accepted her as a daughter and tried to be a father to her. He had always treated her kindly, but she had never been able to feel close to him. It seemed that the more affection he showed the more hostile she felt.

It was clear that Miss T. was anxious about her real father. She had tried to obtain information from her mother's family. She had written and hunted, but nowhere could she learn anything about her father. She could not bring herself to query her mother any further because any mention of this topic seemed so upsetting. Although Miss T. could not admit it to herself, deep down underneath she felt that she had been deserted by her father, and she had worked out no satisfactory adjustment to this. Thus she projected hostility and antagonism onto every cue which reminded her of her rejection at the hands of her real father. This meant that all men were targets for her hostility as soon as they became more than social friends.

Handicap in Social Life

Mr. M. was a middle-aged lawyer, most successful in doing research and writing briefs. His emotional handicap affected his relationships with clients. Of course he was very busy and did not have time to do very much socially. Most people bored him and were a waste of time. He enjoyed books more than conversations anyway. Also he did not like to take time from his hobbies and important activities. As he expressed it, to succeed in the modern world one must "cut the mustard" morning, noon, and night. And so, on and on, his defenses were verbalized.

The brick-by-brick building of this handicapping neurotic structure showed a rather common pattern. Mr. M. had been the youngest in a large family and definitely unwanted. Thus he withdrew into himself for comfort. As he grew, his older brothers and sisters reemphasized this rejection. They teased him about being the baby and, as such, incompetent. The only attention he ever enjoyed was gained through intellectual accomplishments. On occasion his parents would ask him about some book he had been reading. This gave him the only feeling of nearness to them that he ever experienced. He treasured these precious instances and was continually driven to repeat the stimulus, hoping for further pleasant responses. Intellectual pursuits and hobbies, being relatively free of rejection possibilities, were pushed to the limit. He didn't dare to get close to anyone for fear of receiving the kind of treatment that he had been accorded by his parents and siblings. The cue he would take from any situation involving people was one of rejection.

Effect on Vocation

Madge's personality handicap seriously interfered with her career. She was a talented pianist, but when she tried concert work her hands seemed to freeze. At first she believed that she must have a muscular paralysis; of this physicians could find no organic evidence.

As a child, Madge had been unattractive and unhappy. Her parents' only interest in her was expressed in their ambition that she become a musician. They forced her to practice and discouraged any association with other children which would take time from her preparation for her musical career. They constantly reminded her to be careful not to injure her valuable hands, warning that this would wreck her career.

Although she was fond of music, at times she was bored. Life was dreary. To make up for her lack of satisfaction in real life, she day-

dreamed. She would picture herself as incapable of practicing because of a paralyzed hand. Thus in fantasy she would float off into
space and a fascinating life. Whenever she was especially upset she
escaped into this dream world. She began to escape so often that it
became difficult to keep herself from slipping into this reaction in-
voluntarily.

As she grew older Madge began to be ashamed of her childish
daydreams and suppressed these "silly ideas," as she termed them.
She decided that she wanted to be a great musician and threw herself heart and soul into this quest. She consciously forgot all her
background, about which she felt rather ashamed and guilty. For
some time she was quite successful. Then she reached her limit professionally and saw that the ambition of her life to appear at Carnegie
Hall would not be realized. Unknowingly she reverted to the same
mechanism of escape from an intolerable situation which she had
used in childhood. Her hands became paralyzed. This was much
easier on her self-concept than to admit to herself that she lacked
sufficient musical ability to reach the star to which her chariot was
hitched. But personality illness now threatened even her mediocre
success.

As these illustrations have suggested, college work, occupational
success, social success, even marriage are often restricted by handicaps of personality. The individual and his dependents suffer. Emotional handicaps may have far-reaching effects. Many neurotic
leaders project their abnormalities into all sorts of life situations.
Such a projection is called *ego involvement*. Their maladjustment
plays a part in their leadership. They project their anxieties and
inner insecurities onto other political leaders. They denounce people and causes not because of objective reasons but as an outlet for
their own hostilities. Instead of seeing this behavior in its true light
as an emotional handicap, much of the psychologically unenlight-
ened public seems to catalogue it as outstanding leadership, as great
ambition. Thus democracy is often threatened by the ego involvements and undetected instability of some of its own leaders.

Personality difficulties often interlock with and magnify other
handicaps. Physical or organic problems, mental retardations, social
stratifications, and advanced age are frequently accompanied by

some sort of emotional reaction. Emotional handicaps thus should be thought of as appearing alone or as introducing and setting the frame of reference for each of the other handicaps. Emotional handicap combined with other handicaps tends to produce greatly increased difficulty for the individual.

THE PHYSICAL HANDICAP

The physical condition of an individual is undeniably part of his personality structure. Body size, malformation, musculature difficulties, sense organ limitations cannot be overlooked in personality evaluation. Physique is often one of the bases upon which class and caste distinctions are made.

Conditions Surrounding Handicap

There are many phases of the total situation to be considered in understanding the person with a physical handicap. Physical difficulties run the gamut from the obvious to the subtle. Certain ones are noticeable in some environments and not in others. Some curtail behavior markedly; others operate only at certain intervals or under specialized conditions. Some are permanent with no hope for improvement, others only temporary with a good chance for diminishment. Sometimes a handicap is part of a whole situation otherwise very favorable for personality growth; sometimes it is the last straw in an environment that is burdensome from all points of view.

If the handicap is present at birth, it is immediately part of the constellation of influences molding the personality. It will affect both parental and peer relationships. It may necessitate additional parental care and economic strain. The extra attention required may make the individual very dependent upon his family. Sometimes the handicapping condition engenders tremendous guilt feelings in the parents, who feel personally to blame for producing a defective offspring. Often this generates a tense and anxiety-laden home atmosphere. This parental feeling may take the form of antagonism or of oversolicitude. It offers a mother starved for affection and attention an opportunity to develop a "silver cord" or "smother love" relationship.

If the handicap comes into the picture later in the process of personality development, it may have a very different effect. If it must be superimposed upon a fully developed personality, still other problems will arise. Individuals who have tasted an unhampered life find it hard to accept these limitations on their freedom. The newly handicapped individual will use habit patterns which the cues in the situation suggest as appropriate. The new threat may serve to uncover tendencies which have been dormant in the personality. Like all new experiences, the handicap may be assimilated, resisted, or reconstructed. Not infrequently the handicap serves as a target for all personality difficulties, forming the basis for intensive traumatizing.

Possible Reactions

Any of the mechanisms and modes for maintaining selfhood described in the chapter on the Adjustments of Personality might be used in a traumatic situation of this type. Depending upon the self-concept which has been developed, the individual may withdraw into a smog of self-pity, daydream of a miracle, or use other escapist techniques. In fantasy he may, while doing nothing in the present, plan impossible feats he may perform some day. He may develop added difficulties of a psychosomatic nature to give more outward proof that any constructive activity is impossible. He may regress to a childhood period which was happier, using such props of that period as oversimplified thinking, temper tantrums, and complete dependency. He may suppress the handicap into the background of his perceptions and attempt to live as if it were not part of his milieu. Although completely aware of the strict vocational-school taboos against specific physical deformities, some individuals hide their heads in the sand and attempt to enter these vocations regardless. Some cardiacs refuse to admit their handicap to themselves and thus die in harness much earlier than necessary.

More fighting mechanisms are also used. One young woman, who acquired a very unsightly scar during her teens, met her new limitations by means of hostility. Sensing that her handicap made marriage improbable, she specialized in finding the unpleasant aspects of marriage. She slanted her reading toward unearthing any and all bits of information which would bolster her "sour grapes" attitude by proving marriage undesirable.

Another illustration is that of an injured veteran who threw himself into politics, joining an anarchist group, to rectify the situation he thought had produced his handicaps. In the extreme, this could become negativism approaching fanaticism. He might be almost unconsciously fighting everyone in power, regardless of the fancied enemy's objective guilt. Reconstruction of himself and the situation is the only healthy solution. The technique of starting where one is and going on from there to make the maximum use of the potentials he has is the only psychologically sound approach.

Cosmetic Handicaps

Cosmetic handicaps are usually undisguisable. These must be thought of in terms of their definition by various cultures. In Arabia and Turkey cross-eyedness is considered indicative of organic superiority. It is thought to add to attractiveness and to enhance sex appeal.[3] The individual is conscious of this social evaluation of the handicap as a deviation from the so-called norm. Some societies mark the body with grotesque cuts and tattoos or constrict the growth of the head, feet, or other parts of the anatomy by binding them. Although they add to prestige in certain cultures, these deviations would be considered deformities in the United States.

Body size or proportion is another relative trait. Thin women, although given definite preference in many parts of the United States, are not considered attractive by men in certain other parts of the world. Obesity, which is admired in some cultural patterns, is considered a disturbing handicap in this country. Formerly, obesity was thought to be hereditary or entirely of glandular origin, tending to appear in successive generations of given families. This physical explanation sounded definite and final and seemed to be based upon fact. As research has been piling up, however, it has become more and more evident that in a sizable proportion of cases the cause is overeating and that needs other than physiological are being in some way met by this overeating. Fat may in many cases be termed an "emotional residue." If parents satisfy their emotional needs through overeating, the child finds this behavior a most effective parent-pleasing or attention-getting device. Often the mouth-centered needs of infancy have not been completely satisfied; then overeating or drinking is a delayed continuance of the individual's attempt to meet

[3] A. H. Maslow and Béla Mittelmann, *Principles of Abnormal Psychology: The Dynamics of Psychic Illness*, p. 24, Harper & Brothers, New York, 1941.

this craving. This pattern of behavior has been known to be used as a weapon against a disliked parent or husband.

Extreme shortness in men or tallness in women is socially upsetting to many. Our mores are critical of too much difference in

Fig. 13–3. They make the best use of their potentials. Each client of the Institute for the Crippled and Disabled is evaluated for vocational aptitudes in the Guidance Test Class when he enters. These exhaustive tests take three weeks and form the basis for planning a career in optical mechanics, welding, jewelry, leather goods, art, printing, or office work. This training will go hand in hand with physical restoration. (*Courtesy of Institute for the Crippled and Disabled, New York City.*)

height, particularly if the woman is taller than the man. The rejected or insecure small man or tall woman often withdraws from competition with those nearer the norm. Some seem driven to push themselves into positions in which they will command, on the basis of other successes, the respect that they are denied because of their size. Antagonisms engendered by differences from others are often projected onto the world.

Specific irregularities such as buckteeth, big ears, a large nose, thick glasses, baldness, or any other bodily disproportion or discoloration can be interpreted as handicaps. Yet everyone is able to think of instances in which these have been used as trademarks for "million dollar" personalities of stage and screen. Individuals with traumatizing tendencies, however, concentrate all their anxiety into this one channel. The following case is an illustration:

Example of Emotional Interpretation

Miss A. came to the psychologist because a friend had told her that this particular practitioner knew many plastic surgeons and could refer her to one who would operate on her nose successfully. Her perception of the situation was verbalized as this "terribly deformed nose." It was the seat of all her problems. She was not able to get a job because the interviewers disliked looking at her nose. If by some chance she did find a position, she lost it very soon because the other workers were bothered by the shape of her nose. She could not go out socially because she was an esthetic detriment to any group. She just could not do anything until she was helped by plastic surgery. It was a life-and-death matter, and she was willing to mortgage her entire future to get the wherewithal to have this handicap removed.

If Miss A. had not mentioned her nose, the psychologist would not have noticed it. It was slightly large but certainly within the realm of the normal. However, it was a convenient peg upon which all personality difficulties could be hung. It was physical, and everyone understood that kind of handicap. It would be harder to define inner feelings of insecurity.

Miss A.'s personal history included the usual biographical details of the insecure person—parents' quarreling, family unhappiness with little or no affection for the children and strict disciplining to keep them out of the way. The fact that she belonged to a religious minority group seemed to reinforce her insecurity. All the other problems had loomed so large that she had not become conscious of her nose until she started working. Now it overshadowed the others, was the complete scapegoat for all her difficulties.

It was suggested to Miss A. that she eliminate some of the inferiority feelings which were making her so unhappy and postpone the operation. With the aid of considerable psychotherapy she succeeded in reorienting herself to life, and she lost interest in her nose. It was no longer needed to justify her indefinite feelings of insecurity. In another case, both psychotherapy and plastic surgery might be needed to relieve the inferiority feelings. These two therapies would then have to be used in cooperation.

Orthopedic Disabilities

Many are the orthopedic disabilities (defects of limb or body musculature) which handicap individuals. In one sense these are not so difficult from a psychological standpoint as some of the others. Because they are visible, all the world is prepared to make allowances. In this country the presidential prestige lent to this type of handicap by the late Franklin D. Roosevelt did much to boost the morale of this group. More and more the various possibilities of cooperation between the agencies for physical and psychological rehabilitation are being explored. At the request of UNESCO an international conference was held on these problems in 1950.[4] Sixty-five experts from seventeen countries discussed the following problems: psychology of the orthopedically handicapped child, coordination between medical treatment and education, relations of the orthopedically handicapped child to family and community, problems of employment, training of educational, welfare, and nursing personnel responsible for the care and education of the orthopedically handicapped child.

Much can be done to help these individuals reconstruct their lives. At the 1952 meeting of the American Medical Association, fully automatic kitchens for handicapped housewives were exhibited. The Institute for the Crippled and Disabled in New York City has facilities for helping the individual to evaluate his assets from all points of view and to work out a possible plan. It aids him in reorienting himself to the realities he will find in life both psychologically and physically. The orthopedic patient is supplied, *e.g.*, with life-size models of bus steps, subway steps, street curbs, and various types of chairs. With such help he can develop skill in

---

[4] Conference of experts on educational problems of orthopedically handicapped children, *Int. Child Welf. Rev.*, International Union for Child Welfare, Geneva, 1950, 4(2):52–103.

manipulating his world. Many have successfully reconstructed themselves and the situation.

Cerebral Palsy

Perhaps more difficult than the handicap just described, from a psychological point of view, is cerebral palsy, a condition in which

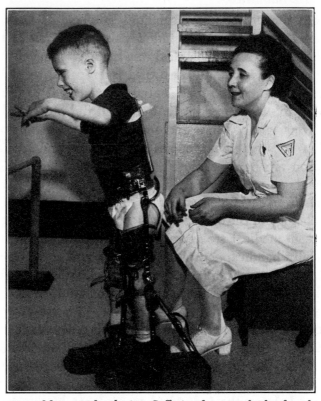

FIG. 13–4. His confidence is developing. Suffering from cerebral palsy, this boy learns to stand in stabilizer, to walk in parallel bars at left, and to climb the mock staircase at the right. (*Courtesy of The National Society for Crippled Children and Adults, Inc.*)

there is difficulty with control of muscles or joints. This delimits exploration by touch, which may slow down learning. This is sometimes mistaken for mental defectiveness. This and other misunderstandings make the lot of these people difficult. Children often make fun of the cerebral palsy victim because they cannot understand why anyone should be so chaotic and jerky in coordination. Adults have been known to confuse this behavior with alcoholism. Some training facilities are being developed, but the possibilities of much improvement depend upon further research.

Epilepsy

A similar lack of orientation on the part of the public greets the epileptic. In fact it has been suggested that since the name causes such unpleasant reactions the term "convulsive disorders" should be substituted.[5] Since his symptoms are sometimes bizarre, many individuals catalogue the epileptic as "queer" or even "crazy." This attitude is often shared by the sufferer, in that he feels that his attacks put him in the abnormal class. There is a common tendency toward feelings of insecurity because of the unexpectedness of the attacks. Many believe that the seizures are a punishment for something that they have done; they feel guilty and constantly berate themselves for some imagined sin for which they are reaping punishment. Emotional and psychological factors probably do contribute to the disease. In this as in other handicaps psychological procedures should be regarded as supplementary to a full use of the resources of medical science.

Heart Difficulties

In contrast to the disabilities just discussed stands heart trouble. The hidden character of cardiac trouble makes it difficult for some sensitive sufferers to limit their activities as they should. Youngsters are apt to be teased by other children if they fail to participate in sports; they are sometimes made fun of if placed in a special "limited exercise" class. Adults are often dubbed uninterested or lazy if they are not ready to accept extra responsibilities. In spite of these problems many cardiac cases make a favorable adjustment to their limited roles.

Visual Disability

When the sense organs are affected, part of the world is closed off. Blindness shuts out visual stimuli. If an individual has this condition from infancy, he has no orientation from which to draw im-

[5] J. A. Resch and Abe B. Baker, The management of convulsive disorders, *J. Ia. St. Med. Soc.*, 1949, 39:503–506.

portant perceptions based upon seeing. Valuable learning tools are thus missing. This handicap makes for a very limited use of the common mechanism of identification, renders the testing of visual reality impossible, throws the sightless person on his own inner world both mentally and emotionally. He must construct or fill in imaginatively

FIG. 13–5. Sightless youth carries on work. This young man, blinded by an accident two years previously, is at his work in public relations. He is writing copy by means of a Soundscriber and typewriter as his seeing-eye dog looks on. (*Courtesy of Volunteers Service for the Blind, Philadelphia.*)

much of what is missing. If blindness occurs later in life some of this orientation of mind pictures, as it were, can be used for building concepts.

The effects of the lack of sight are especially noticeable in the emotional and social phases of life. To counteract the inevitable withdrawal tendency, the sightless person sorely needs the feeling of belongingness afforded by opportunities for close association with his peers.

Hector Chevigny, who has made an excellent adjustment to the onset of blindness in adulthood, reports that there is too great a tendency to interpret the blind in terms of the feelings of the sighted world. He suggests that many sighted people's reactions are strongly colored by the fear, almost amounting to a phobia, which blindness inspires in them. This attitude makes it difficult for the sightless person to enjoy contacts with the sighted world on a normal emotional level.

He reports that in discussion meetings blind groups register complaints that their environment is too saturated with pity; that they are expected to be melancholy and depressed and to have vacant minds. They find that waitresses often ask their companions for their order and that many people raise their voices or talk very slowly to them, as if expecting them to be incapacitated in all areas.[6]

Acoustical Disability

To the acoustically handicapped, also, an important part of the world is lacking. To him life is a silent film; one avenue of communication is missing. It has been found that this handicap is greatest if it occurs before the child has had an opportunity to develop language habits. This is the real explanation in many cases in which reactions are characterized as dull. With neither hearing to understand what is said to him nor speech to express himself, the individual must necessarily be devoid of many common concepts and ideas. Socially, he is largely unconscious of refinements of behavior; he suffers from mental isolation, which lessens his social competence. He may imagine that others are talking about him and build his insecurities into an attitude of distrust of people.

The partially deaf are often thought to be uninterested. They hear part of what goes on, but at any time the barrier may go up because of a speaker's low voice. They may take extraneous loud sounds for anger on the part of a speaker. In trying to make their handicap inconspicuous, they develop all sorts of tricks to fool others. Unwilling to accept deafness, they pivot themselves into untenable positions through trying to take part in conversations on the basis of the fragments they hear. Wallin cites the case of a teacher who, when she finally decided to admit that she was deafened, found herself much more at ease; people responded to her better when she

[6] Hector Chevigny and Sydell Bravermen, *The Adjustment of the Blind*, p. 142, Yale University Press, New Haven, 1950.

abandoned her unrealistic pose.[7] Reconstructing herself proved a more healthy adjustment than escaping into fantasy.

Unhealthy Interpretations

Sometimes tone deafness is erroneously associated with inferior mental ability. Color-blind people also have been found to interpret their difficulty as a mark of general inferiority rather than a specific defect. Other areas of sense perception can become a source of conflict in the sensitive individual. Anosmic deficiency, the lack of ability to smell, might be a source of embarrassment, or it might even interfere with the choice of a vocation. The same is true of gustic (taste) deficiency. For the most part the lives of sufferers from these sense handicaps cannot be considered seriously constricted. A realization of the complete absence of relation of these deficiencies to other areas should help their owners to accept them without self-depreciation. As seems always to be the case, the difficulty is not so much the fact of physical handicap as it is the development of an interlocking emotional handicap. Physical and emotional handicaps tend to accentuate each other, to magnify each other beyond any reasonable justification.

THE MENTAL HANDICAP

Subnormal minds are different in many respects from those considered normal. Greater understanding of individuals with this handicap is important not only on their account but for the best interests of society at large.

It is important to distinguish between the individual who simply does not have the potential for growth and the one who has been thwarted in his growth process. Children experience various degrees of success or failure, of reward or punishment, when they make their initial efforts. They may easily be *conditioned to failure* by a too critical atmosphere, which produces such anxiety that they stop trying. Learning is resisted when it is inconsistent with the self-concept. In inexperienced hands such personality difficulties are often interpreted as lack of ability.

[7] J. E. Wallace Wallin, *Personality Maladjustments and Mental Hygiene,* 2d ed., McGraw-Hill Book Company, Inc., New York, 1949, p. 182.

Training in Terms of Handicap

A differential examination by a competent psychologist will reveal any special abilities and disabilities which might be obscured by general defects. Individuals found to be in the feeble-minded grade are unable to use their experiences and environment independently for their own benefit or that of others; persons so limited are best cared for in institutions. Those whose potentialities would enable them with limited supervision to respond to the advantages of special education should be given this. The supervision must be designed in terms of their handicap. Their reactions are on an affective rather than a cognitive level. Verbal symbols are not very meaningful to them. They lack ability to discover elemental relationships. They neither understand as well nor learn as rapidly as others. They should not be pitted against brighter individuals in family or classroom.[8]

Specifically the training of these individuals should aid them in succeeding at home, in school, and in community life. They need a different type of training from that designed for the more able individual. It must be more practical and it should continue as supervision throughout life. They can be trained to do specific tasks and guided in their nonworking hours to fit into simplified patterns of life.

The social insufficiency of mentally retarded individuals is one of their outstanding traits. This is evidenced by subnormal personal independence, self-direction, self-support, and social responsibility. They do not have the capacity for good social judgment in unusual situations. Various character-building organizations can aid these people by supplying literal solutions to the problems of life. Their perceptive abilities do not make it possible for them to arrive at these solutions on their own. They must have legislation to guard them from exploitation by unscrupulous people who would use them as pawns to purchase liquor or cigarettes for minors, for gambling, and for prostitution. With adequate understanding, training, guidance, and protective legislation, the mentally retarded can become useful citizens.

[8] For an interesting case illustrative of this see Theodore M. Abel and Elaine F. Kinder, *The Subnormal Adolescent Girl*, p. 36, Columbia University Press, New York, 1942.

Projective techniques in testing have shown that retarded persons commonly suffer from fears, anxieties, and inferiority feelings. Various attempts have been made to help these individuals in their adjustment processes. One of the main objectives of this help is to encourage the expression of emotional reactions which interfere with the individual's employment of the limited powers he has. Acting out some of the common problems is a form of group therapy that has been utilized to advantage. Some simple mental hygiene can be taught which will at least help the individual to deal with frustration and understand that there is help available when he is faced with insurmountable problems.

Experience with mentally deficient and retarded school children indicates that here too the greatest care must be taken to avoid the development of an emotional handicap which may magnify the mental handicap. Such a combination of handicaps is ever the hazard. The importance of helping these limited individuals to develop adequate personalities is indicated by the following cases.

Illustration of Importance in Training

Pris was entirely dependent on her family. She seemed without confidence that she could do anything. All her early life her parents had tried to push her into intellectual areas in which success was impossible for her. She had wanted to help around the house, but her mother insisted that she could not take time from her studies, since she was failing. Pris tried to get permission for dancing lessons, but this was granted only on the condition that she make A's. She was continually tutored, with only frustration resulting. Thus she came to believe that she was a complete failure and gave up trying to accomplish anything.

Ned's parents realized that he could not go far in intellectual pursuits; accordingly, they fitted up a workroom for him and encouraged him to try out various hobbies. It appeared that he liked to make furniture, so they found a cabinetmaker who would help him on weekends. When the other families bragged about their youngsters' school marks, Ned's father enthusiastically showed his handiwork. His parents found clubs of mentally limited boys for him to join. In all these ways they helped him to develop a realistic self-concept and a feeling of confidence. Ned is now assisting in a small furniture business. He is just what his boss needs, a dependable, contented, skillful person in his own nonintellectual way.

Specialized Mental Abilities

Just as society often holds up too high a standard for the mentally retarded child, so it does for the one with specialized mental abilities. The tendency is to expect general superiority from an individual who has a phenomenal memory or is a lightning calculator. However, many of these have concentrated every ounce of ability and energy upon mastering the mechanics of their specialities, and they cannot perform in other areas at nearly this level.[9] It is this overrating of the individual who has only limited or specialized mentality which catapults him into situations for which he is not prepared. Socially he may get into difficulties because his mentality, except for one aspect, is really more like that of the retarded individual than that of the genius.

Mental handicap alone, however, is not beyond management. Society can make use of people so handicapped. When the mental handicap is combined with a physical one, the problem becomes more complicated, requiring specialized assistance or perhaps partial financial support, but it can still be handled. The combining of low or specialized mentality with emotional handicap has a much less favorable prospect. Narrow and inhumane activities which exploit self or others are the common result of such a combination when it gets out of control. The social and psychological aspects of this combination of handicaps merit the concern of every citizen.

THE SOCIAL HANDICAP

Operating through historically determined institutions, arbitrary social forces influence the growth process. They supply criteria for self-appraisal. Various cultures arrange their social hierarchies in various ways. The top of the "social heap" is usually defined by tradition. The scale changes according to time and place. An illustration of how such changes can come about is the way in which Hitler by means of a great propaganda system pushed one selected group to the heights and another to the depths of the social order.

[9] Herbert A. Carroll, *Genius in the Making*, p. 194, McGraw-Hill Book Company, Inc., New York, 1940.

Social Evaluation in the United States

Social status is primarily the classification of an individual by his associates. In contemporary United States, race, culture, and economic status appear to affect social acceptance. Certain ethnic groups and those of low economic status are ranked as inferior. Physical attributes such as dark skin, kinky hair, or slanting eyes, which are characteristic of certain races, thus become lifelong symbols of status and stimulate much anxiety. This applies to the Chinese, Japanese, and Filipinos of California, the Spanish Americans and Mexicans of the Southwest, the American Negroes, the Puerto Ricans of New York City, the Scandinavians and the Finns in the Middle West, and so on and on. In many instances these ethnic groups have cultural goals which are different from those of the *host society* and hence are evaluated by that society as inferior. Some ethnic groups are identifiable by *religious participation* or proclamation. They observe different holidays and take no part in certain activities of the host society. Thus they set themselves strenuously apart from the main stream of culture. The identifying accents, gestures, and sartorial characteristics of these "minority" groups are then considered marks of inferiority by the host society which sets the group norm.

The possibilities of range in degree of social stratification show up dramatically in two contrasting California cities. San Francisco continues a rather rigid class system, with the old families in the pivotal position.[10] Los Angeles, having grown faster than any other city in the United States, has had its original social system, with its carriers of tradition, broken down by the onrush of people with diverse cultural backgrounds. This has kept the status system highly fluid. (The new and unstable Hollywood society, with its so-called caste distinctions, does not affect the main stream of metropolitan life. It is more like the occupational hierarchy of an industrial grouping.)

The stereotyping of individuals in terms of economic class or ethnic classification has been shown to be quite automatic. In one laboratory experiment 150 male judges chosen to represent all groups of American adults were asked to rate some college girls as to looks, from their photographs. Two months later this test was repeated

[10] William Lloyd Warner, Robert J. Havighurst, and Martin B. Loeb, *Who Shall Be Educated?* p. 30, Harper & Brothers, New York, 1944.

but with the addition of Jewish, Italian, Irish, or old American names to the photographs. The only changed feature was the name indicating ethnic classification. The changed ratings of the girls clearly showed the influence of the judges' prejudices.[11] The findings of many studies indicate that the person prejudiced against one minority is consistently prejudiced against all minority groups.

Projection of Hostilities onto Minorities

The hostilities of members of the host society and their other maladjustments are expressed against minority groups as a result of economic and social competition, political rivalries, and moral frustrations. The minority conception is a ready-made tool for the insecure person to use in maintaining selfhood. An individual will be most receptive to that ideology which has most psychological meaning for him. The skeleton in the closet of the personality structure of a very prejudiced person is low self-esteem. In fact, research has shown that appeals to sympathy may do more harm than good when directed to these individuals, whose deepest fear is that they might be identified with weakness.[12] The minority idea offers a chance to bully a helpless group which cannot fight back. This "scapegoating" is well illustrated by the larger youngster who takes his hostility out on a smaller one. Thus the minority member is a foil for the insecure person's hostility, an aid in dissolving the projector's own inferiority feelings.

Reactions to Minority Status

The minority member suffers a mass rejection through the phenomenon of role expectation. This intrudes into the situation a cluster of attitudes which tend to mold persons into a role in social life which may remain fairly stable. These attitudes influence the parents' perceptions, and they in turn carry over the minority concept to youngsters. Thus the mass-rejection phenomenon affects, through the parents, the core values of the developing personality. It envelops whole segments of population in a smog of inferiority. These minority ratings are important phases of the emotional climate in

[11] Gregory Razran, Ethnic dislikes and stereotypes: a laboratory study, *J. Abnormal Soc. Psychol.*, 1950, 45:7–27.

[12] T. W. Adorno *et al.*, *The Authoritarian Personality*, p. 973, Harper & Brothers, New York, 1950.

which the personality must grow. Thus the individual's behavior is the enactment of the child's interpretation of cultural expectation.

In this handicapping situation, once again the various possible adjustment patterns can be traced. Often the individual reacts with source traits of rejection and hopelessness. Withdrawal was found to be the most prevalent response of Negro children in a study made in New York and St. Louis.[13]

Sometimes a solution by flight into fantasy is attempted. By this technique the outcast can dream himself into acceptance. A dramatic case of this type was that of a dark-skinned young man who had always lived at the top of the social hierarchy in his own country. In the United States, where he was studying for an advanced degree, he found himself rejected. Insecurity building on insecurity finally evolved the fantasy that he was one of the leaders of this country. He signed checks and ordered a plane to fly him to an important conference, all under the name of a leading public figure. He had found a feeling of belongingness in this dream for so long that he was unable to distinguish it from reality.

Such rejections are also reflected in psychosomatic illnesses. Clinics are identifying case after case of chronic physical disability as traceable to group rejections. These are found especially in sections where the population includes small minority groups which lack status.

Examples of insecurity being overcompensated for by hostility are legion. The rejected person fights back, demanding attention in the only way he knows. Rejection is a perfect setting for the fashioning of the so-called agitator. He may join an extreme leftist organization working toward the overthrow of the system which has so restricted him. It is suggested that in some instances the minority member so discriminated against is motivated to play a double part. Outwardly he must conform to the rigid caste system. However, his natural resentment is somewhat lessened by substitute modes of aggression. These disguised forms of fighting back are seen in the retaliator's use of flattery, humor, secretiveness, and feigned ignorance for outwitting the dominant caste.

In a minority group much aggression is acted out by "preservation

[13] Regina Mary Goff, *Problems and Emotional Difficulties of Negro Children,* p. 84, Teachers College, Columbia University, New York, 1948.

of the cultural group." This really amounts to aggressive resistance to changing one's own fixated behaviors, which often derive from the frustrations of parental figures. Or, there is the aggressive following of leaders such as the frustrated ones just described. Then there is retreat into the purely cultural group, an attempt to solve the problem by refusing to face minority group status. This "peace of mind" may be centered in the religious, the artistic, the nationalistic, or the merely geographic group (*e.g.*, Little Tokyo or Little Italy). This avoidance by persistent nonadjustment of the assimilation process is an outright example of conflict behavior.

Some Healthy Adjustments

Some healthy personalities with social handicaps have reconstructed their situations successfully. The movie *Lost Boundaries*, based upon a true experience, presents popularly some of the psychological problems and possibilities for reconstruction in this type of situation. Genuine assimilation, accompanied by a continuing sentimental interest in "old-country things," is probably the best solution if the individual is to *really live* in the host society. The relatively fluid social system in the United States offers an opportunity for minority groups to change their status. One of the forces most potent in this process is education. The public schools interpret the central core of American life and inculcate skills that make it possible for individuals to become mobile in the class order. There has recently been criticism, however, to the effect that the school system is more or less slanted to keep society as it is. Some have suggested that recruitment of teachers from a wider social range would help.

Politically, the socially handicapped find opportunity for leadership first in their minority groups and then in larger and larger segments of society. Many are the examples of such individuals who have become national leaders. In these instances the public attitude has been analogous to the sports handicap mentioned earlier in this chapter. Their successes have been considered the greater because of the difficulties at the start. As in other forms of personality handicap, the single handicap is not nearly so serious as a cluster of handicaps. Particularly serious is the combination of social handicap and emotional maladjustment.

THE HANDICAP OF AGE

Both extremes of the life cycle present handicaps. Infants are
definitely age-handicapped. The post-climacteric personality finds
its physical processes slowing down and its environment less in tune
with its changing needs. The rapid pace of United States culture
affects the older years particularly.

Changing Concept toward Age

It is impossible to set a specific time at which age becomes a
handicap. Like the other handicaps, age is relative. Its effects de-

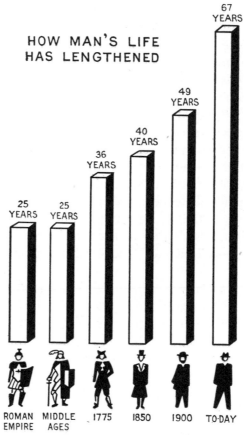

Fig. 13–6. Oldsters are no longer a minority. Adding years to the life span changes
the whole complexion of our population. (*Reprinted from Pageant Magazine. Copyright Hillman Periodicals, 1951.*)

pend upon the particular individual and the attitude of society. In some culture patterns old age is the revered period of life, with elders dominating all spheres of living.

In the United States, with the continuance of the present trend toward a greater percentage of the population in the older brackets, the whole orientation toward age is changing. Political leaders are realizing the voting strength of the oldsters. Economists are alerting the public to the impossibility of so many youngsters and oldsters living off so few "midsters." The need to harness the productivity of the older worker is becoming apparent. Social workers are finding that too many family situations are complicated by the emotional and economic burdens of the older members on the younger. Mental-hygiene workers are uncovering the staggering proportions of personality illness among the aged. The resultant overcrowding of mental-hospital facilities was discussed in the chapter on the Need for Mental Health.

Development of Geriatrics

The study of geriatrics is being pursued on all fronts by economists, physicians, sociologists, psychologists, educators, and many others. Obviously the problem needs the multidiscipline approach if it is to be solved; the present chapter, however, will confine itself to the more central psychological implications.

The problem was approached from the point of view of the older person himself, by means of a questionnaire given to 193 men and women with a median age of seventy-four years. This was answered in an extended interview.[14] The findings were many, but certain ones showed pitch points well known to those who deal in human-relations problems. Two-thirds of the interviewees spontaneously remarked that they felt "unwanted and in the way." Too many still wished to dominate the younger; specifically, one-third expected their grown, married children "to obey them." One-half expected their children "to ask for advice." Thirty per cent thought that they should interfere in the training of grandchildren.

[14] L. Pearl Gardner, Attitudes and activities of the middle-aged and aged, *Geriat.*, 1949, 4(1):33–50.

Unhealthy Personalities

The gap between youth and age is widened by unhealthy personality traits of both groups. The overdominant personality expressed in some of the answers should not have been developed in the first place. More flexibility and adjustability should have evolved instead of such rigidity. Friendships and interests should have been kept in repair. A social consciousness would have prepared the older person with ready-made goals to which to harness his abilities.

Patterns of thinking about age are set early. The child who is unfairly treated may build up a distorted picture of life at the lower end of the age scale. The youngster surrounded by oldsters who use age as an excuse for getting out of doing anything difficult may believe that those past middle age are useless. Those who have smarted under the authority of their own parents not infrequently enjoy turning the tables and penalizing the older person who has not retained kindness and flexibility. Employment interviewers who turn away those past forty may be unknowingly projecting feelings carried over from past wounds.

The earlier discussion of personality growth pictured the continuity of behavior patterns on the ascending rungs of the ladder of life. The basic core values show themselves in trait characteristics appropriate to the respective age levels. Healthy self-concepts do not rust with age. But unhealthy ones soon begin to show their deficiencies. The way one has handled life in the past is the best clue as to how he is equipped to face the post-climacteric era of life. All handicaps are magnified by age. Many inadequate personality patterns come into clear focus as physical breakdown begins. Oldsters are forced to work out personality problems from which they may have been fleeing all their lives. The individual who has been able to escape by changing jobs, by migrating, and by various other means will find that in old age he must come to grips with life. Lessened vigor and fewer opportunities then make adjustments even more difficult.

The basic insecurity which was relieved by overdominant behavior and by attempts at molding others now finds these ready-made outlets less available. The prejudices which could be projected far and wide may be somewhat constricted in the curtailed living of more advanced years. A study of the entire life span of individuals shows that many of the personality inadequacies which stood out in youth were covered over by definite occupational and parenthood roles. As soon as this more or less structured existence, with its many ego props, ended, the personality began to show again the deficiencies it had in earlier years. There is some psychological truth in the old saying that people go through a second childhood. The core values, source traits, and sector traits were built up as the personality grew. Age merely magnifies them. It does not change them fundamentally. The post-climacteric personality is the end result of the growth process.

Mental-hygiene Aids

Possible solutions for easing age handicaps in terms of the psychology of personality involve some reorientation for both the older

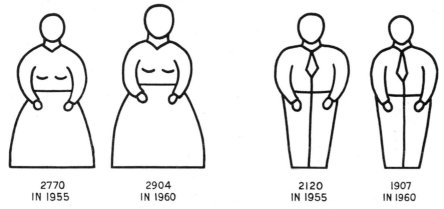

| 2770 | 2904 | 2120 | 1907 |
| IN 1955 | IN 1960 | IN 1955 | IN 1960 |

Fig. 13–7. More and more women are outliving men. Estimated population over age seventy-four shows the increasing number of women who will have to live without men. This problem needs some preparation for successful solution. (*Based upon Statistical Abstracts of the United States, 1951, U.S. Department of Commerce, Bureau of the Census.*)

and the younger group. Many programs are being started for oldsters, and they are showing interest in psychology and other areas of discussion with helpful possibilities. Some industrial organizations have classes for older workers and their wives to help them plan for healthier maturity. More understanding of the developmental nature of life would help the older individual to adjust to his own changing role as the life cycle advances and would also advance his understanding of the ever-growing proportion of the population of which he is a part.

Personality needs for affection and status do not dissolve when one passes life's midpoint. Just as the parental attitude in early life is very important for the child, so the filial attitude is very important for the aged. Many older people feel that the younger members of society want them to be like Whistler's "Mother," satisfied with a rocking-chair existence. Youths often criticize oldsters' attempts to socialize as "not acting their age." They make fun of their new interests or hobbies, expect them to be willing to be put on the shelf. They do not realize that some way must be found to help the age-handicapped reconstruct their lives. Their change of role and loss of status, occupation-wise and parent-wise, break up many of their established habit systems. Since most of the social activities of the church, neighborhood, and club are keyed to the interests of the next generation, new associations and contacts must be made. They need encouragement and freedom for this process of reconstruction.

Example of Improving Adjustment

An interesting illustration of the adjustment potentials of the post-climacteric personality is the following:

Mrs. M. at seventy-five years of age found it necessary for economic reasons to uproot herself from all her associations and move in with a son who lived with his family in a suburban community. She was very unhappy and spent most of the time in her small room for fear of being a nuisance to the younger members of the family. Starved in her contemporary life, she tried to live on the more pleasant memories of the past. When she suggested trying to find some type of work, her son was horrified over what "people would think." Whenever she tried to go out in search of excitement, the family would protest that it was not safe for one of her advanced years. She was completely overcome by unresolved frustrations. A typical case of nonadjustment, she suffered from many physical symptoms of a psychosomatic nature. She was degenerating physically and mentally through a feeling of worthlessness which subjectively and physiologically indicated suicide by slow starvation.

Finally Mrs. M. began to understand what was happening to her. She decided that the family must be educated to the fact that personality needs continue through all the periods of life. She needed purposeful activity and associations. She could not exist physically or mentally on the shelf.

She looked over the field of possibilities and decided that child care was the best opportunity. She marshaled all her former business ability and threw herself into developing a new career. She bought a series of books with which to interest youngsters of various ages and thus added to her popularity. Business boomed, and she had to find an assistant to help her fill the numerous calls. More and more of the people she met in this way were asking her out socially as well. Her personality, which had been on ice for so long, began to flourish again. She joined a past-fifty club, and her activity calendar is one to be envied by young and old. She now feels needed because she has a part in life. She has successfully reconstructed herself and the situation in the direction of effective adjustment.

Importance of Preparation

Increased perspective should derive from experience. The later years offer more time to think, to work out a better philosophy of living. It is the era when pressing problems of the everyday, workaday world recede into the background. It is the healthy personality that grasps this opportunity to put its weight of time and resources into a scheme for the betterment of mankind. Voluntary services are crying for experienced workers. There is much that can be successfully accomplished by the post-climacteric personality. The more the individual is part of life, the more his personality will attract others and the easier it will be to live with himself. There are unlimited opportunities for healthy personalities oriented to the realization that each age should be lived to the limit of its potential. Emotional handicaps need not magnify the feeling of age. The change-of-life, or climacteric, years are the time to plan and prepare for the later years. Such preparation is as important in this period as vocational planning in the years of adolescence and youth.

Summary

The whole subject of handicaps is a study in relationships. To a great extent the cultural pattern determines what constitutes a handicap. In some instances a limitation in one area is misinterpreted by society as an indication of inadequacy in all areas of life. Since the person with the handicap has grown up in the cultural milieu, he will have acquired the common attitude toward his particular minority group.

Outer pressures, combined with the quality of mental health the individual has developed, will determine the type of adjustment he makes. Some individuals will use their handicap as a convenient alibi for failure. Others will project their feelings of limitation onto people and institutions. Some may use their disabilities to gain power over family and friends. Many will organize or reorganize their lives as adequately as possible around the handicap. To certain individuals a handicap is an added motivation for success. Thus in every sense handicaps are a crucial test of the toughness of the personality. They weigh the quality of the mental health.

QUESTIONS FOR DISCUSSION

1. What types of handicaps are apparent? Important but not readily observable? Inclined to go unrecognized?
2. List other handicaps, not covered in this chapter, which might have psychological implications.
3. Does the feeling-of-handicap differ from the feeling-of-unacceptability discussed as a core value?
4. What are some of the reasons why many people feel uncomfortable in the presence of handicapped persons?
5. What facilities does your community have for aiding the handicapped?
6. Should handicapped children go to school together with "normal" children or have separate schools? Why?
7. What solutions can you recommend for prejudice of all kinds—racial, religious, economic, nationality, physical-handicap?
8. How can the general attitude toward the aged be improved?
9. How can youth best ensure itself against unhappy older years?
10. Why do many parents refuse to accept their children's limitations of ability?
11. Give some examples of the protection and citizenship training your community offers for those of limited ability.

12. Give some examples of political leaders who have shown emotional handicaps. How have these affected their constituents?
13. Give examples of common ways of meeting physical handicaps.
14. Which firms in your community employ persons with physical handicaps? Racial? National?
15. Suggest ways in which individuals can prepare themselves for the eventuality of becoming handicapped.

ADDITIONAL READINGS

Bice, Harry V.: Psychological services for the cerebral palsied, *Nerv. Child,* 1949, 8(2): 183–192.

Dai, Bingham: Some problems of personality development among Negro children, pp. 437–458, in Clyde Kluckhohn and Henry A. Murray (eds.), *Personality in Nature, Society and Culture,* Alfred A. Knopf, Inc., New York, 1948.

Di Carlo, Louis M., and Dolphin, Jane E.: Social adjustment and personality development of deaf children: A review of literature, *J. Except. Child.,* 1942, 18(4):111–118, 128.

Foster, Ione Allen: How to cope with teen-age problems, *Crippled Child,* 1948, 26(4):9–10.

Garrett, James F., and Myers, Julian: Clinical psychology in the rehabilitation process, *J. Rehab.,* 1951, 17:3–7.

Gough, Harrison G., Harris, Dale B., Martin, W. E., and Edwards, Marcia: Children's ethnic attitudes: I. Relationship to certain personality factors, *Child Develpm.,* 1950, 21:83–91.

Kuhlen, Raymond G., and Luther, Everett: A study of the cultural definition of prime of life, middle age and of the attitudes toward the old, *J. Geront.,* 1949, 4:324.

Long, Louis, and Roth, Charles: The psychological aspects of rehabilitation, pp. 368–378, in W. H. Soden (ed.), *Rehabilitation of the Handicapped: A Survey of Means and Methods,* The Ronald Press Company, New York, 1949.

Lott, George M.: Mental defectives can become community assets, *Hygeia,* 1949, 27(8):548–49.

McAndrew, Helton: Rigidity and isolation: A study of the deaf and the blind, *J. Abnorm. Soc. Psychol.,* 1948, 43:476–94.

Menninger, William C.: Emotional adjustments for the handicapped, *Crippled Child,* 1949, 27(4):4–7.

Montagu, M. F. Ashley: Some psychodynamic factors in race prejudice, *J. Soc. Psychol.,* 1949, 30:175–187.

Pintner, Rudolf, Eisenson, Jon, and Stanton, Mildred: *The Psychology of the Physically Handicapped,* Chaps. 7, 8, Appleton-Century-Crofts, Inc., New York, 1941.

Pressey, S. L., and Simcoe, Elizabeth: Case study comparison of successful and problem old people, *J. Geront.*, 1950, 5:168–175.

Reeve, George H.: Psychological factors in obesity, *Amer. J. Orthopsychiat.*, 1942, 12:674–679.

Schauer, Gerhard: Motivation of attitudes toward blindness, *Outlook for the Blind*, 1951, 35:39–42.

Stern, Edith M., and Castendyck, Elsa: *The Handicapped Child: A Guide for Parents*, A. A. Wyn, Inc., New York, 1950.

Yepsen, Lloyd N.: Mental deficiency, pp. 413–418, in Douglas H. Fryer and E. R. Henry (eds.), *Handbook of Applied Psychology*, Vol. II, Rinehart & Company, Inc., New York, 1950.

Zeligs, Rose: Children's concepts and stereotypes of Polish, Irish, Finn, Hungarian, Bulgarian, Dane, Czecho-Slovakian, Hindu and Filipino, *J. Genet. Psychol.*, 1950, 77:73–83.

As the young person faces the opportunities of adulthood, release from many early restraints is to be expected. Counterbalancing this release, however, are new responsibilities. Some of these are imposed by society as a whole, some by subgroups or particular social institutions, *e.g.,* governmental units. This societal emphasis tends to make it important for each person to take in his stride these new responsibilities. Adjustments making for a working relation with authority involve conflicting prescriptions which necessitate a reconstructive mode of reaction. Delinquency marks a failure to achieve effective reconstruction. It is indeed the most obvious form of maladjustment.

In this chapter the various types of personalities which tend to use delinquency as a way out will be described. Some of the possibilities for prevention will be evaluated, and some of the strengths and weaknesses in current attempts to deal with the problem will be discussed.

PAST AND PRESENT

The perception of delinquency has been evolving by means of statistical and clinical studies. The cataloguing of delinquency as a behavior apart is being replaced by a conception of it as a symptom of the unhealthy personality.

Who Are the Delinquents?

Generally speaking, delinquency is behavior which stands in opposition to the codes of society. Legally it consists of repeated acts of a kind which, when committed by persons beyond the age handled by the juvenile courts, are punishable as misdemeanors or felonies.[1] The *statutory age* at which juvenile delinquency turns into crime ranges from sixteen in some states to twenty-one in others.[2] There is a growing tendency to drop age differentiations and to use the term "delinquency" to indicate a type of behavior.[3]

Opposition to social codes may be generalized or specialized. It may appear as resistance to all forms of authority—both laws and cultural traditions. Or it may be limited to one of the traditional areas and appear as assault, rape, theft, drug or alcohol addiction, or vandalism. Three very interesting phenomena should be noted in considering delinquent behavior. First, only a small proportion of the behavior which really fits the general definition of delinquency given above is so labeled. Police reports and investigations by sociologists show that social pressures, plus the outside interference on the part of parents in the upper economic and social brackets, keep many of these offenses off police blotters.[4] The social and political powers of the so-called upper class thus provide a protective influence which points up the greater vulnerability of the lower economic and social levels.

Second, some recent studies cast serious doubt upon the long-accepted differences as to delinquency between men and women.[5] The double standard rears its ugly head in this connection. The convention that women should be passive rather than active makes them more often instigators and accomplices than perpetrators. The occupational roles assigned to women in this culture furnish opportunities for much concealed crime in the home and other protected environments. Furthermore, the tradition that women are always pure and noble makes male victims less inclined to bring complaints against them. Police are thus less likely and less able to report them. Conversely, some boys, feeling inadequate, launch into delinquency

[1] Sheldon Glueck and Eleanor Glueck, *Unraveling Juvenile Delinquency,* p. 13, Commonwealth Fund, Harvard University Press, Cambridge, Mass., 1950.

[2] Martin H. Neumeyer, *Juvenile Delinquency in Modern Society,* p. 15, D. Van Nostrand Company, Inc., New York, 1949.

[3] Lawson G. Lowery, Delinquent and criminal personalities, p. 795, in J. McV. Hunt (ed.), *Personality and the Behavior Disorders,* Vol. 2, The Ronald Press Company, New York, 1944.

[4] Lloyd Warner and Paul S. Lunt, *The Social Life of a Modern Community,* p. 427, Yale University Press, New Haven, 1941.

[5] Otto Pollak, *The Criminality of Women,* University of Pennsylvania Press, Philadelphia, 1950.

to prove their own masculinity. One observer has even gone so far as to prophesy that with less exaggeration of the masculine role in the socialization of children and adolescents, with more family and societal emphasis on a common role expectancy, the amount of delinquency for each sex will come to be the same.[6]

Third, there are many culturally accepted patterns of behavior which the general public would label delinquent but which many individual groups do not. Organized racketeers and crime syndicates commonly do not consider their own conduct antisocial. Stock-market rigging, sales of tidewater real estate or worthless securities, and political corruption are certainly opposed to the public good. However, these forms of behavior are not emphasized as delinquent or criminal by the common channels of information such as newspapers, films, etc.

The popular conception of delinquency is largely traditional, a culture pattern. Standards differ widely in various cultures. Thus behavior which is commonly considered delinquent in a particular society is really the type of act which is against the particular mores of that society. It is antisocial in the society in which the individual lives and hence becomes the concern of the law-enforcing agencies of that society. It has been suggested that some day society will consider *all potentialities which are unused or misused* as important instead of merely sorting out the particular type of behavior which traditionally irritates the community. Laymen today are inclined to consider delinquency a unique form of behavior, instead of one of the many indices of maladjustment.

Is Delinquency Inherited?

Since failure to accept culture patterns either in whole or in part has been shown to be characteristic of some individuals in all societies, many hypotheses have been suggested. There is a persistent inclination throughout history to seek simple and single explanations. If blame can be localized in an individual, society can exert vengeance as on a villain in a play. In one sense, offenders serve as psychological whipping boys for those who uphold strongly emo-

[6] James S. Plant, Who is the delinquent? p. 27, in Nelson B. Henry (ed.), *National Society for the Study of Education 47th Yearbook*, Part 1, Juvenile Delinquency and the Schools, University of Chicago Press, Chicago, 1948.

tionalized moral and legal taboos. Antisocial thoughts and impulses in the socially adjusted personality may be felt as righteous indignation toward groups operating against the interests of the larger community. To prove that a delinquent is a thing apart, that he is "bad" and is the cause of his own misbehavior, is much easier for the majority. There is less danger of guilt feelings being developed when the blame can be projected onto a delinquent or criminal. Sharing responsibility for antisocial behavior is an uncomfortable process!

Cesare Lombroso created almost a cult in developing his thesis that delinquents are born and not made. He believed that they were a "throwback" to earlier, uncivilized creatures. He reported that such physical characteristics as cleft palate, scanty body hair, receding forehead, and abnormalities of the external ear were correlated with the predisposition to criminal acts.[7] Later studies fail to prove that specific physical attributes are indicators of a criminal type.

Are Delinquents Feeble-minded?

A similar attempt at projecting the blame for delinquency was the supposition that it is traceable directly to feeble-mindedness, *i.e.,* to mental inability to learn the moral codes. Many reformers suggested that all delinquency could be liquidated if the mentally retarded were rendered sterile and incapable of reproduction. Some states have even passed legislation to enforce this method. However, more recent studies have shown a low percentage of inferior mentality in criminal groups. One study of 10,000 inmates of Sing Sing Prison showed only 13 per cent to be mentally defective.[8] The theory that potentiality for delinquency is inborn and can be blamed on heredity has been proved to be untenable.

Is Delinquency Caused by Poor Housing?

Again, there was a tendency to explain all delinquency as attributable to poor living conditions. Some sociologists described the

[7] Cesare Lombroso, *L'Uomo Delinquente,* 1876, trans. with modification by H. P. Horton, as *Crime, Its Causes and Remedies,* Modern Criminal Science Series No. 3, Little, Brown & Company, Boston, 1911.

[8] Ralph S. Banay, Wanted—an institute of criminal science, p. 117, in Marjorie Bell (ed.), *Social Correctives for Delinquency,* Yearbook, National Probation Association, New York, 1945.

difficulty as due to a combination of poor housing, slum neighborhoods, and lack of recreational facilities. The facts are, however, that more of those who grow up in so-termed delinquency-producing areas take their place in society than turn against it. And, conversely, some individuals in the most favored sections of the population, from the point of view of intellectual capacity and living conditions, find their way into the delinquent group. Large-scale public housing projects may result in reduced delinquency, but there are many forces at work in these project areas in addition to the housing itself.

Thus none of these theories accounts for delinquency. In fact, no simple explanation seems adequate. The roots of delinquency are many, and often the life history of the individual delinquent reveals a unique combination of causative factors.

DELINQUENCY AND PERSONALITY STRUCTURE

Roots of Delinquency

Delinquents show the structural characteristics of their personality more clearly than do those with other types of maladjustments. Delinquency contrasts, therefore, with the emotional disturbances expressed in diet fads, religious fanaticism, psychosomatic ills, etc. In his homeostatic process the psychoneurotic individual reconstructs anxiety experience into fantasy or somatization or he turns his hostility inward as guilt feelings. These techniques for relieving pressures do not directly affect his fellow men. The delinquent assigns these same pressures to the outer world and strikes forcibly against them. Instead of brooding, he explodes. Results of one study indicate that eight times as many non-delinquents as delinquents resolve their conflicts by inner turmoil.[9]

The individual's behavior serves his own needs for personality integration, however inefficiently. Techniques which neurotics and delinquents use to make up for inner inadequacies are a very personal reaction to an individually perceived situation. In the language of behavior both neurotics and delinquents are saying that something is wrong with the personality structure, that homeostasis must be maintained strenuously by some type of unhealthful mechanism. Thus delinquency is the particular way in which the individual tries to maintain selfhood. Why this particular form of activity? What

[9] Glueck and Glueck, *op. cit.*, p. 275.

are the inside dynamics, the plot, of the delinquent's story? In the growth of his personality where did goal orientations get turned against the larger patterns of culture? Why does he perceive the world through hostility-tinted glasses?

One of the most comprehensive researches into delinquency conducted in recent decades suggests some answers in psychological terms. Five hundred delinquent boys were compared by Sheldon and Eleanor Glueck with a carefully matched control group of five hundred non-delinquent boys in respect to age, general intelligence, national origin, and residence in underprivileged neighborhoods. Using many types of social and physical data, of tests and interviews, the Gluecks came to the conclusion that emotional factors in the biography of the growing child were the most important differentiating influences between delinquent and non-delinquent.[10] In an interesting earlier piece of research, Drs. Healy and Bronner studied pairs of siblings, one of whom was delinquent and the other not. They found that although the siblings had grown up in the same home, they responded differently to their environments. The delinquent one had felt unhappy and unloved, whereas the non-delinquent one had felt fairly comfortable.[11] By means of individual case histories and extensive studies of large groups of antisocial individuals the causes of delinquency are being traced further and further back into the psychological structuring of personality. It now appears that the trend of individually delinquent behavior is largely constant once it has developed. It becomes emotionally fixated; this fact suggests origins in frustration experiences.

At the core of the sick personality there is usually a feeling of insecurity and unacceptability. Perceptions structure themselves so that this feeling becomes a sense of inadequacy within and a vision of impending doom or catastrophe in the outer world. The individual is paralyzed by the rigid selfhood which is made necessary by his finding it impossible to work out his dynamic self-maintenance in a threatening world, and his relationships with people and things become definitely distorted. He perceives his world as increasingly

[10] *Op. cit.,* p. 287.

[11] William Healy and Augusta Bronner, *New Light on Delinquency and Its Treatment,* p. 9, Yale University Press, New Haven, 1936.

hostile; his tolerance for frustration is lowered proportionately. He feels an anxious distrust of life. His distrust of himself and of life impels him to act in ways which increase his difficulties, and he does not learn more adaptive behavior. With fewer subjective needs gratified, he is less able to withstand unfavorable outside pressures without becoming deeply emotional. Social behavior in the healthy personality represents a complicated balance between gratifications and renunciations. In the delinquent this balance practically loses itself in instability between core values of acceptability and unacceptability.

Unhealthy Family Influences

The whole emotional atmosphere of the home and family has had a part in structuring the type of negative core value just described. Family relationships have lacked warmth. The pressures of disharmony stemming from sibling rivalries and maladjusted parents have set the stage for frustration. Those who mean most to the child have given him a feeling of being unwanted, rejected. He has been forced to grow into insecurity. His feeling of being unwelcome is mirrored in the statistics which show that by far the greatest percentage of delinquents falls within the middle group of the family, which presumably has a "non-entity status." [12] They enjoy neither the prestige of the first-born nor the attention given to the younger members. Probably for the same reason there are fewer delinquents in the first-born and the only-child categories.

Sometimes parents who adversely affect their children's core values are outwardly very admirable people. Though incapable of warm personal feelings, they are leaders in their own fields. Their own inner insecurities have motivated them to fight in a positive way. They have harnessed their aggressions to push themselves up the ladder of success. They have directed their antagonisms toward competitors or inadequate situations in the environment, fashioning themselves into industrial tycoons or reformers. In these instances identification with a parent, to help the self-integration process, is missing. Twice as many delinquents as non-delinquents do not con-

[12] *Justice and the Child in New Jersey,* p. 95, Report of the State of New Jersey Juvenile Delinquency Commission, Trenton, N.J., 1939.

sider their fathers acceptable symbols for emulation, judging from the Gluecks' findings.[13] Either the youngster attempts to identify and pattern himself after a cold and hostile antisocial parent or he develops very negative feelings toward all parent surrogates, thus toward all authority. Delinquent personalities seem to develop in

"The Joneses got a new car and the Conwells got a new television—and we get this!"

Fig. 14–1. Insecurity fosters hostility. (*Cartoon by Bo Brown. Courtesy of The American Magazine.*)

the home and family situation, reflecting the pattern of parental personalities.

Results of Rejection Illustrated

Jed's story is an illustration of the failure of home and family processes. His parents show the typical rigidity of personality and traumatization that serve as substitutes for objective perceptions. They also manifest the same emotional tendencies as Jed, although more secretively.

[13] *Op. cit.,* p. 280.

Jed at sixteen years of age was seen in an institution for delinquent youth. He had been caught with the goods; the rest of the gang had escaped. He was slight of build and of low intelligence. His over-suggestibility and deficiencies in reasoning made it easier for his peers to exploit him.

His father reported that he had tried everything when he saw "what a disgrace Jed was going to be." Sometimes he wondered why fate had given him "such a poor specimen of humanity for a son— no brawn, puny, a no-good kid." Taking his parental responsibilities seriously, he had used up a lot of energy beating Jed, starting with the first time he misbehaved. He had continually lectured him on the importance of being a good boy. He had insisted that Jed get more education so he "won't have to work as I do. We've never had a professional man in the family and Jed's got to be one. I try to do what I can to get him there by punishing him every time he gets low grades."

Jed's mother explained that she had not wanted another boy. She had prayed for a girl, and what a disappointment when he came! She had had lots of trouble with him every day of his life. He had always been so shy, would not play with other kids the way he should. She had kept telling him what he should do—act less shy— but he was stubborn and would not do anything she told him to, so what could she do? Once she got so disgusted with the way Jed acted that she talked to the teacher about him. Then there were interviews with the principal and finally with some social workers in the child-guidance clinic. But she refused to go back because they began to act as if it was her fault, when she had always done her best. They asked her too many questions and made a lot of everything she told them. They seemed to think that part of the trouble started way back when Jed overheard the family talking about wishing that he had been a girl. "Don't they know better than to blame the parents when they're working as hard as they can to bring up their kids? Why can't they understand that it's the kid's fault, not the parents'?" All their friends knew that she and her husband were good, law-abiding people and had simply had a bad break with this one kid. That's all. . . . The authorities should help punish Jed, not try to find fault with the family.

Influence of Parental Disorganization

Available statistics show a large proportion of maladjustments in the forebears of delinquents. Many of the parents have themselves grown up in families of stress. Studies indicate a greater proportion of criminal background in the parents and grandparents of delinquents than in those of non-delinquents.[14] Their personal failures are evidenced by divorce, remarriage, and abdication of children to the control of courts. Such parents are too involved in their own inner conflicts, expressed as struggle with their spouses and the courts, to be capable of giving their children the acceptance and love they need. They create unwholesome pressures toward delinquency. They seek to justify their own antisocial acts by projecting their own personality rigidity onto the entire universe. They may denounce the neighbor, teacher, or police officer who brings behavior difficulties to their attention. They may stress the value of fight and thus condition the youngster to a confirmed belief that he must destroy all threatening aspects of his world. Thus from the earliest years, when structuring of ideals and symbols of authority are in process, they surround the growing child with unhealthy attitudes, whether the home is actually broken or not.

Reinforcement of Delinquent Trends

Any differences which set a youth apart from his peers will fan the flame of his feelings of inadequacy. Culture conflicts which mirror differences between home and community will be a factor. Memberships in marginal groups suggest and develop frustrations which soon express the child's feelings of hostility toward authority. The various handicaps, discussed earlier, are likely to add confusion to the individual's already befuddled scheme of values. It has been found that delinquent children are conspicuously larger or smaller than classmates of their age, rather than of average size. This unchangeable difference from the other fellow can serve as the last straw added to the burden of inadequacy.[15] Or it may offer special advantage in the "pecking order" of the delinquent gang. Mental

---

[14] Glueck and Glueck, *op. cit.*, p. 279.
[15] Neumeyer, *op. cit.*, p. 69.

retardation, leading to consistent failure experiences in school, increases the inferiority feeling and the break with society.

Shifts in residence make outer security less attainable and inner feelings of acceptability less likely to develop. When people do not have a bond with their neighbors, there are fewer community pressures toward socially acceptable behavior, less cementing of loyalties. The same principle holds for the various minority groups. Migrant laborers flocking to seasonal agricultural jobs pose a similar problem. If the youth finds the sets of behavior norms in his home different from those of his peer culture, he will be in even more conflict. More fundamentally, the parent who feels he has to migrate again and again is running away from himself in seeking escape from his own neurotic tensions.

A paucity of outlets for self-expression in many sectors of our machine civilization plus unwholesome tendencies in the news—such as the publicizing of glamour queens with questionable reputations and of underworld "big shots"—tip the scales somewhat against the social codes. The halos bestowed upon lawbreakers increase the young delinquent's identification with these emotionally immature personalities. Publicity's influence is also marked in the production of psychosomatic ills such as allergies, acid stomach, and functional heart disease. Western culture puts considerable emphasis upon the need for recognition. The traditional American individualistic philosophy of success and the actual possibilities of contemporary life are on opposite sides of a real gulf of conflict.

Thus the individual who has not found his home or community comfortable and adequate for growth will try another solution. Not being able to find a way to solve the frustrating problems he faces, he strikes out. Everything in the world looks to him as he feels at heart. He needs to lash back at the pressures which have hurt him. Thus the inferior-feeling individual can change his rating with himself if he proves his strength. Delinquency is one of the few outlets through which the individual feels he can express hostility against societal and parental pressures to emphasize his own sovereignty. He feels strong as he relieves his tensions by misplaced aggressions such as beating animals, hitting younger children, breaking windows, or wrecking cars. This behavior reinforces his impaired inner prestige. All authority may be lumped together and serve as the target, instead of the parent alone. Laws, police, and institutions are merely parental or authority figures with which he must get even to bolster his self-respect. *This motivates him to seek an antisocial subculture as opposed to more conventional activities and groups.*

Personality Dependency on Gang

With antisocial attitudes as a basis for self-maintenance the individual is ripe for membership in almost any group at odds with the culture patterns. To those in sore need of a substitute for family love and group belongingness, the gang presents itself as just the kind of closely knit unit that will answer the purpose. Recognition achieved through being noticed in a particular group is a good substitute for being loved by a parent. The delinquent may dramatize himself as a hero before his peers in the dangerous enterprises in which they embark. If he lives in a neighborhood in which gangs flourish, he may need one for self-protection. Here he will find the antisocial subculture patterns with which his feelings agree. Research indicates that more than half of the delinquent group are members of gangs, in contrast to less than 1 per cent of the nondelinquent group.[16] It also indicates that the favored companions of delinquents are older. These gangs of older youths act in the capacity of examples, serving for identification or for hero worship. In these delinquently structured elders, the youth on the threshold finds a standard of behavior and a basis for personality integration. His fellowship in the gang during his induction and training period is a parent-substitution process. With these new-found companions he is highly social. He abides by their authoritarian rules and codes of conduct with the same intensity as has marked his unfulfilled need for support from his family relationships. Thus it is not entirely correct to speak of the delinquent as antisocial. Gangs are among the most social of all human arrangements. Fundamentally, gangs are substitutions, compromises, perhaps confusions between the individual's primary and secondary groups. But once he has found his place in this group, his reputation tends to shut him off from his family and from friendships among more wholesome youth. Thus he is thrown more and more on the gang for companionship, cementing his gang tie.

As in war, severe economic struggle, or any other situation

[16] Glueck and Glueck, *op. cit.,* p. 277.

wherein the individual feels inadequate to withstand the pressures, small and closely knit groups are formed. The same impulse is at the root of the "buddy system" of every college campus. Emotionally speaking, all such groups are gangs and psychologically primary. Too much overdependency on either family or gang is unhealthy. These connections exemplify the homeostatic technique expressive of the need for belongingness. Some individuals are never able to outgrow an emotionally fixated dependency. Others try to reform but return to overdependency at their first failure. It has also been suggested that the conflict-laden delinquent finds it much easier to escape from his home problems through groups which engage in exciting adventure than through more quiet types of activity. After this overstimulating experience, school and even other varieties of recreation and association appear tame and uninteresting. Thus the gang connections continue and increase in importance in the life of the delinquency-inclined individual.

The Gang as a Formative Influence

The gang is like a small school or a family as it trains its members. As has been shown in the preceding discussion, emotional blocks have been set up in the personality against learning acceptable social behavior. It must also be remembered that according to the psychological laws of learning the individual will tend to repeat acts from which he gains feelings of satisfaction. Gang approval is a very important antidote to the inferiority feelings of youth. It aids greatly in maintaining selfhood. With the stage all set for learning, the youth is initiated easily into the ways of delinquency. Older members of the gang find the younger followers perfect accomplices for some of their difficult jobs. The usual method of exploiting these boys is to teach them to steal. With their smaller stature they can climb through windows, and they sometimes run faster. Early escapades with a gang form a type of in-service training in which the skills of delinquency are acquired.

Red's story illustrates the place of the gang in the development of personality and training in delinquency.

Red at nineteen years of age was discovered with a gang of racketeers. He was intelligent and capable. The older crooks found him a splendid pawn for their criminal activities. He could be counted on to do the smart thing. He would grow into big-time criminal pursuits some day if he kept up his training with these successful teachers. Until he had joined the gang, he had been a very lonely person with few friends and no recreation. He felt frustrated and

Fig. 14–2. Constructive activities can compete successfully. When youth's interests are met on their own level of growth, they have less need to strike back through destructive pursuits. (*Courtesy Red Feather Service of the Community Chest of Philadelphia and vicinity.*)

was getting nowhere. But now, with these new friends and goals, he felt the thrill of belonging and advancing.

Red had been reared by grandparents who lived on a secluded farm. He was not allowed to leave the place and associate with people lest they turn out to be the kind who had gotten his father into trouble. Red was not going to be like his good-for-nothing father if the grandparents could help it. The father had damaged the family reputation enough; he was still serving out his sentence, and his parents hoped that he would never be "let out."

Red's mother had died when he was born, so that he had known no parental contacts except those with his grandparents. He was not allowed to stay after school or in any way to mingle with his peers because they might be bad influences. To offset his inner feeling of inadequacy, he had tried to find ego satisfaction in intellectual pursuits. He attempted to compensate with school success. However, this met with frustration at home, since his grandparents could not bear to hear him getting away from their old-world accent. They chided him every time he used words of more than two syllables and were always correcting his pronunciation, wanting him to speak the way they did. They made fun of his good marks and said that these only showed that he was capable of more work on the farm and should do this instead of wasting his time on books, which would not bring in any money. The reason that they were so poor now was that his father had been the same way, always getting out of work by keeping his nose in books.

Finally, in desperate longing for some warmth of association, Red started to hang around a "private club" in the town after school instead of going directly home to his nagging grandparents. His inner needs had been waiting for some means of expression. The members of the "club" helped change his self-concept. They gave him friendship and an outlet for his superior ability. He had sorely needed some identification material, and the fact that these new heroes were antagonistic to society did not matter. He had developed no strong idealizations of socially approved personalities, so that he was an easy tool in the hands of this more mature gang. Once indoctrinated into crime, and wanted by the police, his only avenue to success was to use his marked native ability in committing further crimes.

A common beginning in delinquency with a girl is the acceptance of the influence of young women who urge her to trade her sexual possibilities for entertainment or money. Case studies of these so-called delinquents always show great affectional malnutrition in their homes. They have no adult to whom their presence is of special importance. Inferiority and rejection can both be drowned and denied in sexual promiscuity. In sexual response a girl may find outside evidence that she is loved or that she "rates" in the gang. She is also driven by a secondary motive, the enjoyment of adventure and gaiety in restaurants, night clubs, and car trips to offset her colorless home life. Hostility toward her parents is appeased in the mere independent "naughtiness" of her acts. Her feeling of freedom from her parents is a feeling of strength. Repercussions of these episodes can, and often do, embarrass and thus punish the parents, but she really wants to punish them. The more sophisticated older girl slowly becomes an object of identification and is able to make blind dates for the younger girl for hotel parties or trips to motels. This in-service training is a variety of prostitute experience, which society defines and punishes in its more developed forms as being destructive of the very foundations of the home and family. It is met by ostracism from the social groups whose mores frown on it. Thus, to secure affection and a sense of belonging, the delinquent becomes emotionally dependent upon antisocial groups.

Consistency of Pattern

The delinquent is the sum total of predisposing, aggravating, and precipitating causes. His personality has been structured around feelings of hostility and overdependency and given some in-service training in antisocial activities. He is a dramatic example of the truism discussed in the chapter on The Growth of Personality: that neurotic personalities show *consistencies* in patterning; that once the trend of behavior becomes rigid, it continues. Most delinquents have manifested unhealthy behavior patterns throughout their life cycle. Not uncommonly the first indications are present between age seven and age nine.[17] Listening to parents as they describe their children, one hears all the typical personality symptoms of ill health: "always had trouble with him," "wet the bed all his early life," "sassed everybody," "fought all the kids," "always playing truant and running away." Over and over both individual case histories and group studies show truancy and running away from home as common types of behavior for the antisocial individual. That the amount of educational retardation is often greater than can be accounted for by actual mental retardation reveals an active antagonism

[17] Kate Friedlander, *The Psycho-analytical Approach to Juvenile Delinquency: Theory, Case-study, Treatment*, p. 11, International Press, New York, 1949.

to study, the function that both school authorities and parents demand. However, it has been demonstrated that sometimes the same
inner conflicts have led to overinhibited behavior until the breaking
point was reached. The parents' description in such a case history
often runs like this: "Quiet kid, never gave nobody any trouble,
stayed by himself, always did what he was told, never talked back,
. . . mother's pride and joy." In atypical behavior, which can be
either overinhibited or aggressive, the path seems to lead from early
behavior difficulties to juvenile delinquencies to crime. Always the
psychologically trained eye can observe the shaping of the structural
characteristics of personality. History is in the making. There is no
sudden change from a healthy personality to a delinquent one. The
structuring is a developmental process, and a gradual growth in an
unhealthy direction can be detected at many stages. This fact, that
delinquent personalities grow as do all others, is the cue to prevention and treatment.

PREVENTION AND TREATMENT

Ineffectiveness of Punishment

Looking at the individual delinquent as the end product of various inner and outer pressures, the idea of punishment seems as out
of place as if it were being advocated for the treatment of a fever
or an injury. The mainstays of a punitive program are the threat
of more punishment and enforced isolation with other antisocial
individuals. The concept that ideals or judgments of the world at
large uttered in authoritarian terms will be strong enough to overcome inner values derived from ingrained habits is not in keeping
with what is known about the psychology of personality and learning.
It is based upon the erroneous idea that one can be pressured from
the outside to learn a new system of inner values. These values,
which appear as habits and attitudes, are too deeply anchored in the
personality structure to be modified either by kindly talk or by
threats of punishment, up to and including death.

Whatever endangers the individual's way of living, is inconsistent
with his own concept of self, is resisted stubbornly. The more the
individual is blamed or censured, the more his feelings of unworthi-
ness will permeate his entire personality. Thus from within he will

be motivated to find ways to increase his self-esteem. Since the pattern he has worked out to accomplish this is antagonistic to society, added threats to his inner security will only make his delinquent behavior more necessary to him. His gang associations are his value-giving world, his primary group. If society pulls these props out

Fig. 14–3. Early experiences with law enforcement are influential. A youth's attitude toward society is affected by the handling he receives in every encounter with authority. Lack of understanding by parents or police may push him further into crime. (*From The Sniper, Stanley Kramer Co., Columbia Pictures Corp.*)

from under the delinquent and confines him with other personalities which are similarly structured, it actually increases the emotional pressure and causes him to develop stronger ties with another gang.

Each experience which verifies the delinquent's evaluation of himself strengthens his personality rigidity, either by means of successful results or by a renewal of hostilities. Arrests, court treatment, foster homes, reform-school terms, probation episodes—each thing that happens to him will be one more solidifying factor in this molding of a fixated personality structure. Prisoners' personalities are so structured that usually they expect the worst from everyone they meet. Most of them are so fixated and rigid in personality that any attempt to change this trend of behavior seems doomed to failure.

Prevention through Psychological Understanding

Society must become aware of the "time bombs" which are in these personalities *before* it is too late. The earlier this effort at prevention can start, the more effective and inexpensive it will be. It has been estimated that each habitual criminal costs society 50 thousand dollars.[18] Study of the situation will show conclusively that a little prevention will be worth a great deal of cure. The Gluecks' suggestion is especially worth noting here.

"We must break the vicious circle of character-damaging influence on children exerted by parents who are themselves the distorted personality products of adverse parental influences, through intensive instruction of each generation of prospective parents in the elements of mental hygiene and the requisites of happy and healthy family life." [19]

Behind the study of personality is the idea that every individual who is helped to develop skills in healthy emotional living will be a buttress against delinquency. The *preventive* aspect becomes doubly important as it is realized that the same laws of learning apply to parents as to delinquents. There is no short cut to the production of changes in parents, especially parents of youngsters who appear to indicate parental failure. The idea that parents can be forced to go to lectures and learn how they are pushing their children into delinquency is antithetical to the concept of the structuring of personality. The parent's mechanism for maintaining selfhood usually is to project the difficulty onto the delinquent. His perceptions are carefully structured to keep his own inadequate feelings from disturbing him. These cannot be pulled out from under him without more defenses being put up against this threat. This was illustrated in the case of Tommy's father described in the chapter on The Growth of Personality.

The earlier that neurotic deposits in the personality, left by emo-

[18] Melitta Schmideberg, On recidivism, *Amer. J. Psychother.*, 1950, 4:292.
[19] Glueck and Glueck, *op. cit.*, p. 287.

tional bruises, can be detected, the more hopeful is the prognosis. All the resources suggested in the chapter on Approaches to Mental Health will aid in this fight. Many mothers who, without help, are bound to fail as parents could be detected in premarital clinics, welfare centers, and maternity hospitals. If mothers and fathers could learn to understand themselves better and unload some of their hostility before the child arrives, the greatest good would be done at the least cost. Earlier recognition of incipient delinquency traits at the nursery-school level and more adequate psychological facilities in the early school years for both children and parents are part of the answer. Treatment, when needed, all the way along the growth process would cut down the end products of delinquency and save thousands of dollars in the total tax budget.

Constructive Treatment

Special service bureaus and coordinating councils are forming in many areas as the first line of defense against emerging delinquency traits. These are also alerting the public to more psychologically sound ways of meeting the problem. Examples of this more constructive attitude are seen in the creation of the Youth Authority in California, the Youth Conservation Committee in Minnesota, the Youth Service Division in Wisconsin, and the Youth Service Board in Massachusetts. These mark progress toward a modern, positive approach rather than an antiquated, negative approach.

More and more attempts are being made to treat the social offender by means of individual and group therapy. A pilot plan was instigated under the auspices of the College of Physicians and Surgeons in New York City. Social deviates were referred by the Department of Probation of the Court of General Sessions and the Parole Division of the State of New York. Expert treatment brought these individuals to a stability of personality which cut down their needs for finding expression in crime.[20] Various projects in group therapy also have proved successful. These carefully guided discussions give opportunity to delinquency-inclined persons to let off steam and to share their hostilities and tensions. This type of therapy develops understanding of the pressures motivating the disturbed individual's behavior and adds to the feeling of belonging to a group. As the public at large demands improved approaches to this

[20] Banay, *op. cit.*, p. 118.

critical area, as to all others, the democratic processes of government will be able to put more modern scientific psychological viewpoints to work. Adjustment to the critical area of delinquency can be most effectively undertaken by joining in the organized efforts toward psychological understanding and treatment of all delinquents.

Summary

The newer attitude toward the malformation of personality is shown dramatically in the changing cultural patterns concerning delinquency. No longer can the thoughtful person catalogue the delinquent as merely the product of hereditary deficiencies or of poor neighborhoods. The delinquent is a part of the whole panorama of maladjustment of modern times.

As more parents, teachers, and legislators understand the brick-by-brick building of the delinquent personality, solutions will be found. Everything which adds to healthier personality growth will subtract from delinquency. Each dollar spent on readjustment at the first indications of need will save thousands of dollars later on. The development of lesser personality difficulties into serious delinquency does not have to happen here!

QUESTIONS FOR DISCUSSION

1. What type of treatment does your community use in handling delinquents?
2. Why are stories of crime so popular?
3. Can you trace the development of any locally publicized delinquents?
4. Do most people you know understand the reasons behind delinquency?
5. Make a survey of the glamorizing of crime found in contemporary newspapers, magazines, movies, television.
6. In what specific ways does the gang serve to substitute for the family as a primary group?
7. Can recreation programs alone solve the delinquency problem in a community? Explain your answer.
8. Do schools add to the trend of delinquency in any of the instances you have experienced?
9. Would it help the general problem if parents were punished for the delinquencies of their children?
10. What opportunities do parents have in your community to learn more about the psychology of delinquency?
11. How is hostility behavior related to delinquency?
12. Why is it that juvenile delinquents so often come from minority racial or national groups?

13. Why does delinquent behavior become a police problem at the early-adolescence age levels?
14. Why do juvenile delinquents so often develop into adult criminals?
15. What are some of the reasons behind the common attitude that is critical of "coddling the delinquent" and favors punishing him? Have you any suggestions for changing this?

ADDITIONAL READINGS

Brickman, William W.: Juvenile delinquency, *Sch. & Soc.*, 1948, 68:305–311.

Crow, Lester D., and Crow, Alice: *Our Teen-age Boys and Girls: Suggestions for Parents, Teachers and Other Youth Leaders*, Chap. 9, McGraw-Hill Book Company, Inc., New York, 1945.

Deutsch, Albert: *Our Rejected Children*, Little, Brown & Company, Boston, 1950.

Diggs, Mary Huff: The girl runaway, pp. 65–75, in Marjorie Bell (ed.), *Current Approaches to Delinquency*, 1949 Yearbook, National Probation and Parole Association, New York, 1949.

Glueck, Sheldon, and Glueck, Eleanor: What do we know about delinquency? *Survey Midmonthly*, 1944, 80(3):91–92, 103.

———: *Delinquents in the Making: Paths to Prevention*, Harper & Brothers, New York, 1952.

Healy, William, and Bronner, Augusta: What makes a child delinquent? pp. 30–47, in Nelson B. Henry (ed.), *National Society for the Study of Education 47th Yearbook*, Part 1, Juvenile Delinquency and the Schools, University of Chicago Press, Chicago, 1948.

Keliher, Alice V.: Juvenile delinquency: a family affair, *Fed. Prob.*, 1948, 12 (4):26–29.

Merrill, Maud A.: *Problems of Child Delinquency*, Houghton Mifflin Company, Boston, 1947.

Porterfield, A. L.: Delinquency and its outcome in court and college, *Amer. J. Sociol.*, 1943, 49:199–208.

Slavson, S. R.: Group psychotherapy in delinquency prevention, *J. Educ. Sociol.*, 1950, 24(1):45–51.

Spence, Ralph B.: Impact of education on juvenile delinquency, *J. Educ. Sociol.*, 1950, 24(1):3–9.

Teeters, Negley K., and Reinemann, John Otto: *The Challenge of Delinquency: Causation, Treatment and Prevention of Juvenile Delinquency*, Chap. 7 and pp. 707–738, Prentice-Hall, Inc., New York, 1950.

Trow, William C.: Conflicting codes of morality in the life of the child, *Child. Educ.*, 1942, 18:256–262.

Wallerstein, James S.: Roots of delinquency, *Nerv. Child*, 1947, 6:399–412.

U.S. Department of Labor, Children's Bureau: *Understanding Juvenile Delinquency*, Publication 300, 1943.

Part Five PERSPECTIVE FOR
MENTAL HEALTH

Four critical areas of adjustment have been illustrated as proving
grounds for personality. The interaction between individuals and
actual situations helps to clarify the dynamics of personality. Limitations of space preclude the exploration of other areas, such as adjustments between the sexes and adjustments to economic and occupational pressures and needs.

Part Five will suggest ways and means of aiding personalities in
their search for better mental health. Readjustment will be shown
to be regrowth, buttressed by various techniques. The many threads
suggested in earlier chapters will be drawn together into the warp
and woof of the healthy personality. It is hoped that this synthesis
of the characteristics of optimum mental health will help the reader
to define his own goals in the development of personality.

CHAPTER 15 *Readjustment*

In biological sciences the basic concept is *growth*. Throughout the life cycle continuous changes within the organism constitute this growth process. So long as there is growth, there is hope for a brighter future. Careful redirection of growth along wholesome lines is known as the "readjustment process." The need for such readjustment can sometimes be anticipated and even prevented through proper child care, wholesome family life, and courses like the present one. Such educational techniques are essentially mental hygiene. They buttress a personality against potential hazards such as traumatic experiences, restrictions upon freedom, and, particularly, against resistance to psychotherapy.

It is assumed too often that the newest gadget or some trick of biochemistry can repair the maladjusted personality. These have value, for often a patching and repairing job has to be done before a more basic healing can take place. The important thing to understand, however, is that the very first step of readjustment is the realization that only the individual himself can change his own personality. After childhood he cannot evade basic responsibility for guiding his own growth. Without motivation to change one's self for the better, present-day readjustment techniques are of no avail. In other words, the complete process of readjustment must have as its first stage the desire to get well.

Students of personality learn that there are remedial measures which can bring improvement in personal adjustment. When an individual is motivated to get well, *and* when he has come to understand that there are remedial measures, he has achieved *readiness* for readjustment. As in every form of learning, readiness is a necessary condition if the organism is to change its way of behaving.

359

Readiness for therapy or readjustment can be developed most effectively through study of the psychology of personality.

Today the confusion of terms is great, partly because of the rapid strides in research and its applications to man's problems. Some writers, for example, use the term "psychotherapy" to cover every type of effort to assist or to direct the correcting of personality maladjustments. Others prefer to distinguish between "psychological counseling" and "psychotherapy," recognizing these two as adjoining portions of a continuum. Psychiatrists, clinical psychologists, and psychologists specializing in counseling and guidance are the common terms used to describe those professionally trained for this work.

THE GOALS OF READJUSTMENT

False Goals

Many people who feel the need to readjust dream of fantastic results. They long for an escape from their aches and worries, projecting this escape in terms which contrast with their present experience. One Hollywood writer has been having daily conferences for nine years with his "psychoanalyst" in order to "release" his own latent genius! Often the notion of a so-called "block" is used simply to evade reality. No treatment can be really effective except a general and basic change in personality.

Many neurotics hope secretly to become successful in love, art, or business through one or another form of counseling or psychotherapy. As was pointed out at the start of this book, these troubled people are easily exploited. The following escapes are commonly anticipated by such people:

From *boredom* into exciting or "zestful" living
From *gloom* into continuous delight or "elation"
From *worry* and *fearfulness* into perpetual "security"
From *inferiority* and *inadequacy* into "popularity" and "superiority"
From *domination* into unrestrained "freedom"
From *laborious living* into "no responsibility"

It is highly doubtful whether genuine personality readjustments have ever produced such results.

Another false goal is the belief that good mental health can be administered to or injected into a person. Familiar words from medical therapy fall too easily into conversations. Such expressions as "cure," "removal of cause," and even "therapy" and "healing" tend to suggest that readjustment can be passively received. Psychosomatic specialists struggle against this false belief, as do psychiatrists and psychologists. Instead of using terms with medical and surgical connotations, the language of readjustment must be psychological. It must emphasize the total personality, stressing learning and growth as dynamic or active processes. It must check itself continuously in a scientific research program.

Still another false goal encountered in discussions of readjustment has to do with the "finger pointing" or "name calling" tendency. Young students, particularly, are apt to feel that when a person's maladjustments have been identified by name or classification the psychological task has been completed. Along this same line, it is sometimes assumed that counseling is simple and sure. Objective evidence points to the fact that technical understanding of the nature and development of many maladjustments has far outstripped the development of effective treatment.[1]

Some writers maintain that this outstripping of treatment by diagnosis applies to the entire range of maladjustments.[2] There is urgent need today for accurate and scientific measurement techniques or instruments to analyze personalities as to type and severity of maladjustment. Such scientific tools would also be useful in evaluating psychotherapy and counseling, with particular reference to determining the outlook for recovery.[3]

Realistic Goals

The maladjusted personality has *grown* into its difficulties. Consequently readjustment must be understood in terms of growth out of these difficulties. Since no one person can ever understand com-

[1] Harriet L. Goldberg, *Child Offenders: A Study in Diagnosis and Treatment*, p. 184, Grune and Stratton, Inc., New York, 1949.

[2] Joseph Wilder, Facts and figures on psychotherapy, *J. Clin. Psychopath. and Psychother.*, 1945, 7:311–347.

[3] D. O. Hebb, *The Organization of Behavior: A Neuropsychological Theory*, pp. 266–271, John Wiley & Sons, New York, 1949.

pletely how any other person feels, it is not possible for the maladjusted person to appreciate exactly how normal mental health feels. This limitation of understanding doubtless encourages indulgence in the escape fantasies noted earlier. Instead of hoping for normalcy, the maladjusted person dreams of perfect mental health.

There are, however, descriptions of the feeling of mental recovery to be found in statements by people who have undergone readjustment. An engineer who had suffered a variety of physical symptoms was referred by his physician to a cooperating clinical psychologist. After a series of weekly conferences the engineer commented: "Things have happened since I began these conferences. I feel better all over. Today, for instance, I completed a problem on my job in half a day that would have taken me at least five days last year. I hadn't realized how much my work was slowing down because of daydreaming and worrying."

On the matter of formulating the desired outcome of the period of guided growth leading to readjustment, the authors consulted two leading workers in this field. One, a psychoanalyst, suggested that the aims could be stated as follows: the establishment of the capacity for love; the development of social or creative productivity; and the disappearance of troublesome symptoms. The other, a consulting psychotherapist who had formerly been a practicing physician, listed the following: (1) The patient will be understandingly aware of his own motives; (2) he will be objectively aware of his environment; (3) he will have experienced a reduction of symptomatic behavior.

From the viewpoint of the present text, the outcome of readjustment which would apply to all levels of severity and to every area of counseling would be as follows: The client will have achieved (1) an establishment of genuinely goal-oriented living; (2) an acceptance of his own life cycle and rate of growth; (3) a clarified and workable system of values; (4) an acceptance of the role of self in the objective world of things, people, and the passage of time; and (5) capacity for objective perception.

The goals sought through counseling or psychotherapy are the characteristics evident in every strong and healthy personality. The client or patient must *want* to get well and must understand that remedial measures are efficient only as complementing his own efforts. Psychological readjustment techniques known today will not make a superman out of a dullard, nor a perfect body out of defective parts. But like a good tune-up job on a car which is in fundamentally workable condition, readjustment techniques can improve the basic efficiency and can make operation smoother. An early "tune-up" is commonly a preventive of breakdown.

The Larger Goal

Briefly, it may be said that the most fundamental goal of psychological readjustment is the development of insight into the workings of one's own life processes, both physical and perceptual, or mental. Then there must be careful exploration of the objective world of things and people, particularly in the most trouble-provoking area of one's living.

Subjectively, readjustment feels like a renewal of the strength needed to withstand better the stresses and strains of living. The threats of everyday life can now be judged in their true proportions; the body machinery will no longer be mobilized to remove a mountain when only a molehill is on the horizon. The sum of these two— insight into one's own behavior and breadth of perspective on one's own world—form the foundation upon which new and wholesome goal-oriented living can grow. Thus the individual is equipped to develop and to express his productive and creative capacities through progressively achieving new levels of success. As Anthony Sutich has put it, help should be in terms of the "growth-centered attitude." [4]

RESOURCES FOR READJUSTMENT

The Dangers of Advice

All the specific techniques of mental hygiene are mere tools, effective only if used with skill and understanding. Deep insight into the dynamics of personality is essential to the counselor and therapist; no substitute exists. With adequate insight the underlying illness of

[4] Anthony Sutich, The growth-experience and the growth-centered attitude, *J. Psychol.*, 1949, 28:298.

personality can be identified promptly. In many cases the route to improved health will become equally clear. Because he knows this much, the counselor and therapist is frequently assumed to be able to tell other people how to live their lives—to advise them. But personality problems, unlike problems of other sorts, cannot be classified simply. Normal functions cannot be outlined in formulas of advice.

Advice given to help an individual solve a specific problem is often valuable. On the other hand, advice given either directly or by implication to the emotionally upset person is like alcohol or narcotics given to an addict. It soon becomes a part of his disease, enabling him to avoid the necessary corrective steps, which he vaguely knows will require changes in himself that he cannot face alone. Advice, like medication or surgery in the treatment of psychogenic illness, tends merely to fixate the maladjustment and to complicate or hinder healing by delaying the application of appropriate therapy.

A simple situation will serve to illustrate the way in which advice can be harmful. An oversensitive college girl was annoyed by the persistence of a highly neurotic boy friend. He insisted on asking for dates, even though she almost openly despised him. When she refused, he would threaten suicide. Her friends' advice was that she must date him to prevent his suicide! In this particular case, refusal would have caused the boy to suffer the natural consequences of his own neurosis and to seek the treatment he needed. His friends advised him to court her more intensively! Both people need to grow into greater independence of thinking. At best, advice adds weakness to an already weakened personality structure. At worst, advice leads to increased negativism toward treatment and thereby aggravates the underlying mental illness.

The Continuum of Resources

It is becoming common for people to turn to professionally trained psychological counselors—clinical psychologists and psychiatrists. Early contact with such help is desirable and in the long run less expensive than delaying until the maladjustment becomes serious. The problem is to locate the right counselor—one who is highly ethical, adequately trained in a recognized professional school, such as a university graduate school, and established in a professional way. Affiliation with a reputable institution such as an out-patient clinic, hospital, college, or university suggests that the practitioner is competent. Membership in the professional organizations such as the National Vocational Guidance Association, the American Association of Marriage Counselors, the American Psychiatric Association, and the American Psychological Association is important, too.

Generally speaking, psychotherapists tend to become specialized. Dr. Jones prefers to work only with severe mental illnesses, while Dr. Smith prefers to specialize in the behavior problems of children, or perhaps vocational maladjustments. Usually these developed preferences are based upon success in the chosen field. The counselee's symptoms and needs should correspond to the interests and capabilities of the counselor. It sometimes requires two or three conferences to clarify this matching-up process. Then ethical referral to some other practitioner may be indicated. In any event, early contact and prompt referral can save prolonged and expensive shopping for the right type or amount of treatment.

If a person has difficulty in getting along with his fellow workers, he may merely lack understanding of the cultural mores of the group or of social skills. A qualified vocational counselor should be able to guide him. If, however, the counselee's difficulty stems from a serious inferiority feeling based upon anxiety, as was described in the discussion of psychoneurosis, expert therapy will be required. The degree of intensity and comprehensiveness of the help needed will depend upon the depth within the personality in which the nucleus of maladjustment lies. Each area of treatment overlaps the others to form a continuum ranging from brief contact to prolonged therapy.

Stages of Counseling

As an individual begins his readjustment program, he has various expectations. Some of these will have to be swept away, such as the fear that he will become a "case history in a book or an article." One young woman put off counseling for two years, fearing that she would "have to tell everything." A young man carried on weekly

conferences with a psychiatrist for six months before he would cooperate in the effective use of a projective test; his fear was that he
would "expose" himself. These instances illustrate a lack of readiness
for the deeper or more penetrating types of counseling. Most people
react in these or similar ways. It is important to know that it is a
firm principle of psychological counselors and therapists not to force
confidential information from the counselee either in conference or
through testing but to wait until the counselee chooses to describe
inner thoughts and feelings.

The first conferences usually are exploratory. Such information as
age, family background, religious tendencies, occupation, income,
and the like is noted. A medical examination is usually indicated,
particularly if physical symptoms are present.

Supplementary data may be secured through investigations undertaken by a social service worker of the counselee's background and
social relationships. Usually the counselee has questions to ask on
the process, *e.g.*, as to the frequency and length of conferences.
In some types of counseling it is not necessary to probe deeply into
the personality, for instance, when the need is largely for assistance
in making a decision relating to job aptitude or educational plan.

No competent psychological counselor, however, would enter into
an extended series of conferences without having secured the results
of carefully selected psychological tests. Which tests to use and when
to use them are matters for professional judgment on the most technical level.[5] Preference is usually for a battery of tests, including
intelligence, aptitude, interest, personal-adjustment, and others to
serve particular needs. Free-association word lists and projective
tests are widely used to give the counselee more freedom in expressing his own thoughts and feelings. Tests of the latter type may make
use of techniques such as unfinished sentences or cartoons, puppets
on miniature stages, drawing materials, vague silhouettes and pictures, or ink blots. The standardized projective tests most often used
are the Thematic Apperception Test, described in the chapter on
Perception, and the Rorschach ink blots.

Following the preliminary stage of counseling, there begins a
somewhat different process. Conferences consist largely in talking

[5] V. E. Fisher, *The Meaning and Practice of Psychotherapy*, pp. 12–20, The
Macmillan Company, New York, 1950.

about various decisions and experiences the counselee chooses to discuss. In specialized counseling, such as vocational and premarital, it is customary to hold a very limited number of conferences; sometimes group counseling is used, since the information-giving function can be made less expensive on a group basis.

For help in readjustment, of whatever type, the counselee needs to learn to express himself without restriction and without excessive effort. He objectifies his own evaluative feelings and examines his value system through sharing in verbalizations with the counselor. In these conferences he ponders on and acts out aspects of his life values which he has not dared to express under any other circumstances.[6]

Readjustment is a unique growth experience. It begins at the point where the counselee is, and it helps him to draw upon his own potentials to create greater strength and efficiency within himself. It must last as long as he feels there is a troublesome gap between his way of living and his potential to live more wholesomely. When a counselee's strength justifies it, the counselor will usually suggest ways of thinking about specific problem situations, and even trial activities. This constitutes the last and the most technically difficult stage of readjustment.

Areas of Counseling

Sometimes an individual knows that his psychological problem is concentrated in one area of living. This may be one of the critical areas discussed earlier. It may be that he is not ready to admit to himself that he has a genuine personality maladjustment; in this case his readjustment has to be approached by way of special-area counseling. The following chart shows five areas of counseling, although other areas may also be defined. It frequently happens that in a particular locality the specialized areas in which counseling is needed are more numerous than the personnel. Psychological counseling is far from standardized. This chart, emphasizing the variety of problems, also might be taken to illustrate the lack of boundaries for psychological practice.

[6] Norman Cameron, *Psychology of Behavior Disorders*, pp. 576*ff.*, Houghton Mifflin Company, Boston, 1947.

Areas	*Types of problems*
Personal	Social adjustments; appearance in relation to self-consciousness; age and health limitations; minority group attitudes such as **race,** creed, nationality; problems of living.
Marriage and family	Courtship adjustments; premarital testing; parental attitudes; economics of family and home; child and parent guidance; reconciliation and divorce adjustments; readjustments of family patterns following drastic changes; adjustments of newlyweds; in-law problems.
Vocational	Aptitude testing; preference inventorying; information giving; guidance of exploratory employment; job adjustment problems; change of occupation; training and retraining; avocational planning; improvement and objectification of occupational perspective; vocational retirement; health handicaps to vocations; problems of personnel management, selection, and promotions.
Educational	Aptitude testing; preference inventorying; selection of curriculum; choice of avocational or co-curricular activity; selection of elective courses; personal adjustments to campus or to school life; parental understanding of student problems and educational practices; academic standing and requirements for further study.
Rehgious	Interpretation of church organization; understanding of rituals; information giving; assistance in applying approved doctrines to personal adjustments; reassurance; establishment of feelings of belonging in the church. (Choice of church or religion might also be classed here, although it would ordinarily be avoided except if the counselor were employed by a federation of churches.)

Each area interlocks with or overlaps others in every personality and is linked dynamically with the person's core values. Thus the competence of the counselor, regardless of specialty, must be such that his insight into the counselee's personality reaches well beneath the surface traits or even the trait clusters. But, of equal importance, the counselor must know the environmental situation thoroughly if he is to help the individual become objectively oriented in a wholesome manner.

It is impossible to imagine a vocational counselor, *e.g.,* who does not have access to information about thousands of jobs whereby people of many sorts earn their livelihoods. He must know the common relationships between supervisors and employees, the lines of promotion and lifetime earnings for each occupational type. Otherwise he cannot claim knowledge of the reality of working conditions. Matching talents with tasks requires that both be understood. This is not to suggest that advice can solve vocational maladjustments. Rather, the counselor must symbolize reality to the counselee more effectively than does the latter's own experience.

The special area of counseling chosen by any one person is merely the point of environmental pressure or the strategic approach to his own personality in readjustment. Modern psychological counseling has become as complex and as diversified as modern medicine and calls for the same degree of specialization. It needs a background of understanding if it is to be used to fullest efficiency.

PSYCHOTHERAPEUTIC TECHNIQUES

All efforts to correct or to prevent maladjustment must be oriented toward the uniqueness of the given individual's personality integration. To become skilled in the techniques requires both training and practice. Although a variety of specializations has arisen in the field of psychological counseling and psychiatry, to serve the various needs, there is also a rather general approach which is both important and frequently encountered. This will be discussed now as psychotherapy. In some ways it is the oldest of the currently used counseling techniques, having brought together into a common pattern several age-old techniques and given new interpretations to them. The following discussion seeks to give more extensive than profound acquaintance with psychotherapy in its various forms.

Psychoanalysis

Psychoanalysis was first developed by the Viennese physician, Sigmund Freud. Carl G. Jung, Alfred Adler, Franz Alexander, Karen Horney, and many others have reappraised and reinterpreted this technique. Many of the present leaders in the field are advocating ways of shortening the length of treatment, which has usually been calculated in years.

The basic process is complete free association. The patient is encouraged to say everything which comes to mind, regardless of any value concepts he may have about the thought being unimportant, absurd, or unpleasant. Dreams are used as a stimulus to further free association and as objects of interpretation.

The analyst's role may be that of a shadowy screen onto which the patient can project his deep-lying conflicts and feelings. He is sometimes used as father, mother, rival, or whatever is needed in working through the emotional difficulties. Transference refers to the emotional attitudes displayed during the course of treatment. Slowly the "analysand" gains sufficient insight to realize the futility of trying to appease infantile needs in adulthood and works out a better adjustment to the world of reality.

Group Therapy

Groups can be given therapeutic treatment more effectively than individuals in certain limited ways. Sometimes the group process offers a social laboratory for trying out new techniques which the counselee has learned in private session. Social objectification is achieved by discussing feelings in front of other people and by hearing their discussions. Group therapy may be a way of providing richer experiences for the counselee while permitting the therapist opportunity to observe.

Psychodrama

A form of group therapy which in recent years has gained much public recognition is the psychodrama of Moreno. A popular form of this therapy is role playing. Role playing is beginning to be commonly used in industry, where it is applied in dealing with psychological problems between employees, and in many types of classes and conferences. It is also used by hospitals, institutions, and private practitioners for specific therapy. It is a spontaneous drama concerning difficulties; actions supplement words in expressing feelings and in thinking through motivations.

A psychodrama works like this: A dramatic production is started in which each counselee, or patient, takes the part of a particular character. After a certain point he carries out his role by *ad lib* acting and speaking. The role gives him an opportunity to vent his feelings. Since the player is not "playing for keeps," it is easier to let down defenses and release pent-up feelings. The players tend to become so engrossed in the drama of the situation that they forget themselves and are able to live out in the drama their unverbalized and so far unrealized desires and interpretations. This is a sort of catharsis. The first version of the psychodrama may be followed by a repetition with reversal of roles. For instance, a young woman who has played herself in relation to her father, now plays the role of father while someone else impersonates her as daughter. This second stage is a form of action therapy which facilitates the reconstruction of experience and thus produces growth toward a readjusted personality.

To facilitate this process further, sometimes cardboard figures of common characters are supplied. The counselee chooses a mother, husband, child, or whatever, places it in a groove on the cardboard stage and talks for it. Often he does not realize that he is identifying himself with this character. He feels free to express hostility, fear, sorrow, or any other emotion he has not dared to unleash in real life.

Puppet shows are particularly effective with ages six to twelve. Characters and plots are devised to interpret the common emotional problems of children. The youngsters share the daring and aggression against the figures of authority who threaten the hero. They learn that other children about them are feeling the same way. These sessions are used as adjuncts to individual therapy.[7]

A spectator type of dramatic therapy is called "visuotherapy." This entails watching the dynamics of personality adjustment by means of moving pictures and then discussing them. Seeing instances of the development of fears of people through cruel treatment in childhood sometimes speeds up insight into one's own development of crippling attitudes. This method is used to advantage in connection with other therapies.

Play Therapy

Play therapy, both individual and group, is a method of helping disturbed children to help themselves by using toys and constructive materials with which they can dramatize their experiences. It is based upon the fact that play is the youngster's natural medium of

[7] L. Bender and A. G. Woltmann, The use of puppet shows as a psychotherapeutic method for behavior problems in children, *Amer. J. Orthopsychiat.*, 1936, 6:341–354.

self-expression. The setting furnishes an opportunity for the full expression of feelings which might elsewhere be punished. The child who has developed much antagonism against the younger brother who seems to be usurping his place in the family can beat up the boy doll. The child who is afraid of his father can fashion him out of clay and push him around to such an extent that he develops sufficient confidence to meet his father on comfortable terms. In many ways this technique furnishes opportunities to play out feelings and problems. Such play therapy usually lasts for months or longer. Once the emotional action has been completed, the child seems able to return to a less emotionally charged type of play.[8]

Activity Therapy

Some therapists believe that the use of a graded series of activities helps the counselee to come to grips with reality. Some of the psychoanalysts who are advocating a shortening of their technique suggest that the patient be brought up against the specific life situations from which he has withdrawn.[9] These troubled people avoid those types of experiences which are perceived by them as threatening. A prescription of action to be carried out by the counselee will frequently fill this gap. The sufferer may be "punch-drunk" with failure. He needs to be helped to maneuver himself as quickly as possible into successful experiences. Sometimes a simple suggestion serves as the foundation of a start toward growth in confidence. This was the method used with a young woman who was afraid to recite in class. She was helped to volunteer for a few remarks and slowly, with success begetting success, to work up to regular recitations.

Some therapists encourage their patients to lead as full a life as possible and to try to work slowly into those phases in which difficulty lurks. Others carefully figure out specific graded experiences. In some cases occupational therapy or participation in a social group or a small community is used as an exploratory experience. An individual who complains about his symptoms as a means of getting attention may be maneuvered into more healthy attention-getting

[8] For an interesting discussion see Virginia Mae Axline, *Play Therapy*, pp. 30–51, Houghton Mifflin Company, Boston, 1947.

[9] Franz Alexander and Thomas M. French, *Psychoanalytic Therapy, Principles and Applications*, p. 38, The Ronald Press Company, New York, 1946.

devices.[10] Taking a committee chairmanship in a club or doing a favor for an appreciative person may bring the desired ego glow.

Fig. 15–1. Water polo in a mental hospital. The men in this picture are not patients but *merely actors* used in the Veterans' Administration film *Activity for Schizophrenia*, which was based upon real case-study data. Carefully chosen and supervised physical activity is an important part of the general therapy which today serves to return to normal living even severe cases of mental illness. This scene is enacted daily by patients suffering from mental illness which has come to be psychosomatic through weakening of bodily functions. (*Courtesy of Veterans' Administration.*)

Creative Art

Creative art, like play, offers opportunities for catharsis. Talent is of no significance in the therapeutic use of modeling or painting or other art media. Finger painting serves to express the mood of a troubled personality. The painting becomes a means for thinking out the nonverbal but powerful experiences which have been unacceptable to the personality structure. As the painful incidents become more familiar, and the troubled person lives with them and

[10] For a report of a case in which this was used, see Alexander Herzberg, *Active Psychotherapy*, p. 51, Grune and Stratton Company, Inc., New York, 1945.

manipulates them, the fear and strangeness disappear. The therapy can then shift into the more constructive phase of placing these experiences in the value system.

Fɪɢ. 15–2. Painting is an emotional outlet. Transferring feelings to paper is good therapy. No frustrations need stand in the way of complete self-expression through art media. (*Courtesy of Red Feather Service of the Community Chest of Philadelphia and vicinity.*)

Music Therapy

Music therapy works in a similar way. A musical instrument mastered even slightly serves as the vehicle by means of which a feeling can express itself in all its intensity without hurting anyone. When music appreciation is used, the mood created by the music may offer the individual a better opportunity to reconstruct his own memories and to reformulate his scheme of values. Thus overactive patients can be quieted for psychotherapeutic sessions and depressed patients stimulated. This smoothing out of moods can also be done deliberately to encourage participation in the community life of an institution. Like the other supplementary therapeutic techniques, these are only of use in the hands of a skilled and understanding practitioner whose basic interest is in the fundamental psychotherapeutic process.

Hypnosis

Hypnosis is used as a therapeutic tool by both psychiatrists and psychological counselors. Psychiatrists also use drugs to induce a state called "narcosynthesis" or "narcohypnosis." Sodium pentothal is the drug most commonly used for this purpose. Drug therapy is especially well adapted to the treatment of acute traumatic neurosis.[11] This form of neurosis is seldom found in civilian life but is a concomitant of battle; hence the treatment was perfected under military auspices. Under narcosis a repressed horror can be brought to consciousness quickly. It can then be discussed and shorn of the overwhelming guilt or fear which pushed it to such a depth. An instance of this occurs in the movie *Beyond Glory.* A returned soldier, very depressed, seems completely blocked from talking about his past. The drug is administered and induces a state in which he can recall the traumatic experience of his buddy's death, which he blames on his own cowardice. Finally this neurotic nucleus is removed through insight into the true situation—that he had been knocked unconscious by a shell and thus could not carry out orders. Exhuming this trauma starts the readjustment process.

Hypnosis is merely a tool which facilitates the use of psychotherapy by removing specific fears or blockages from the patient's consciousness. He will be able to discuss intimate experiences in detail, without the embarrassment that this would cause him in full consciousness. Post-hypnotic suggestion is valuable in many ways, from the removal of specific symptoms to the promotion of a more helpful and cooperative attitude during the ensuing psychotherapeutic session. In the hands of an able practitioner who understands personality readjustment, it has considerable special utility.

Hospitalization

It is not always realized that the hospital, however complex it may be, is a tool. It is a composite of many supplementary techniques

[11] R. R. Grinker and J. P. Spiegel, *Men Under Stress,* Blakiston, Philadelphia, 1945.

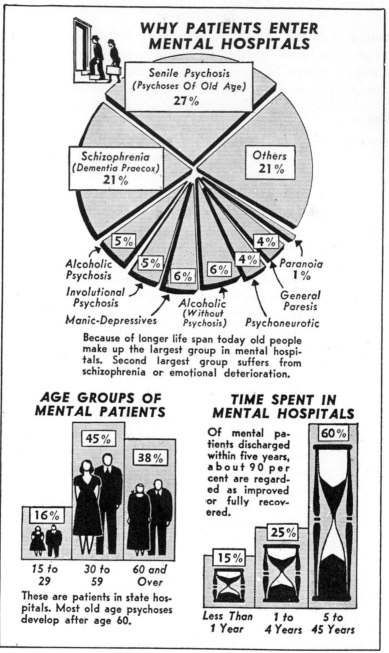

WHY PATIENTS ENTER MENTAL HOSPITALS

Senile Psychosis (Psychoses Of Old Age) 27%

Schizophrenia (Dementia Praecox) 21%

Others 21%

5% Alcoholic Psychosis

5% Involutional Psychosis

Manic-Depressives

6% Alcoholic (Without Psychosis)

6% Psychoneurotic

4% General Paresis

4% Paranoia 1%

Because of longer life span today old people make up the largest group in mental hospitals. Second largest group suffers from schizophrenia or emotional deterioration.

AGE GROUPS OF MENTAL PATIENTS

45%
38%
16%

15 to 29   30 to 59   60 and Over

These are patients in state hospitals. Most old age psychoses develop after age 60.

TIME SPENT IN MENTAL HOSPITALS

Of mental patients discharged within five years, about 90 per cent are regarded as improved or fully recovered.

60%
25%
15%

Less Than 1 Year   1 to 4 Years   5 to 45 Years

Fig. 15–3. Hospitalization is an important tool. (*Courtesy of Chicago Sun-Times based on 1952 Facts & Figures, National Association for Mental Health, Inc.*)

ranging from simple isolation and restful quiet to an intensive clinical approach to the patient's illness. In the hospital it is possible to control social contacts and to remove troublesome social pressures. Moving the patient from his normal habitat also serves to relieve his friends and relatives of the guilt feeling that may arise as they find themselves unable to understand his behavior and needs. This tendency on the part of friends and relatives to feel guilty often leads to their becoming overly aggressive or dominating in a well-meant but nevertheless damaging way.

In the hospital it is possible to carry on full twenty-four-hour observation, to control diet and activity. This is especially important in cases of alcoholism. Medication and other treatments can be assured, as can greater readiness for psychotherapy. Outside the hospital the mentally disturbed patient often is very undependable about meeting his appointments. Certain neurotics are reliable in keeping their appointments only if required to pay fees even though absent. The patient has a greater feeling of progress when his treatment program is fixed and regular. The entire organization of the hospital is so well defined and smoothly operated that it offers a feeling of stability. Moreover, this controlled community can be adapted to the patient's growth in readjustment.

Thus hospitalization can achieve the greatest intensity of the therapeutic approach. Eventually it must be replaced by a return to normal living. Usually a post-institutional counseling program manages this transition. Some hospitals carry on regularly scheduled group therapy for all their alumni, in which the new situations experienced in the laboratory of life are aired. Discussion and interpretation led by therapists, just at the time when support is especially needed, are most important to successful adjustment in the wider community.

Summary

The individual who has developed in a mentally healthy manner is able to carry on the integration processes within his own personality. His perceptual processes lock him effectively into the world of things and people, uniting his values with the likely consequences of his behavior. He launches effectively into goal-oriented activities.

The person who does not enjoy mental health may work toward it through guided readjustment. Establishment of this highly satisfying way of living comes through regrowth. The distance from this goal will determine which techniques will be most helpful in a particular personality reconstruction.

Many clinical and biographical researches have been carried on with the aim of perfecting techniques. As in the development of medicine, new opinions and new discoveries are continually enriching the available types of counseling and therapy. All these contribute to the goal of developing happier and more effective personalities.

QUESTIONS FOR DISCUSSION

1. What do you think is the most common attitude of people you know toward psychotherapy? How derived?
2. Does your community offer counseling in most of the areas discussed in this chapter? Where are the agencies located?
3. Do the psychiatric departments of the hospitals in your community use most of the therapeutic techniques described?
4. What are some of the reasons you have heard given for not securing needed help in readjustment? Evaluate them.
5. To what extent is the public aware of the various psychological and psychiatric associations which list their members and work for the establishment of professional standards? How can public awareness in this area be increased?
6. What would you do if someone asked your advice about a serious psychological problem?
7. What do you believe would be the most helpful attitude a friend could take toward an individual who was undergoing psychotherapy?
8. If you were being helped by a psychiatrist and a relative continually asked you to repeat the substance of the conferences to him, what would you do?
9. One psychologist has told of a patient who brought her child with her and had him wait in the reception room during each appointment so that she could tell her friends that it was her son who was receiving help. Explain the probable reasons for this behavior.
10. List the qualifications and training required for a psychiatrist, a psychiatric social worker, a clinical psychologist, a vocational counselor.
11. Is it the practice of lawyers to refer prospective divorce cases for marital counseling? Why?
12. Can you suggest any reasons why those who are especially in need of help are often the most antagonistic toward psychology and psychiatry?

13. If a couple is unhappy in their marriage and the husband believes that counseling would help, how should he present the idea to his oversensitive wife?

14. If a school physician believes that a youngster needs expert help in handling his personal problems, how would you suggest that he approach the parents?

15. Do you think you would be more ready now to use the available resources for readjustment than before you had considered the subject from the various points of view presented in this book? Should more people be given information concerning treatment possibilities?

ADDITIONAL READINGS

Bach, George R.: Dramatic play therapy with adult groups, *J. Psychol.*, 1950, 29:225–246.

Combs, A. W.: Some contributions of non-directive methods to college counseling, *J. Consult. Psychol.*, 1945, 9:218–223.

Curran, Charles A.: Structuring the counseling relationship: a case report, *J. Abnorm. Soc. Psychol.*, 1944, 39:189–216.

Dollard, John, and Miller, Neal E.: *Personality and Psychotherapy: An Analysis in Terms of Learning, Thinking and Culture*, McGraw-Hill Book Company, Inc., New York, 1950.

Doyle, Kathleen, *When Mental Illness Strikes Your Family*, Public Affairs Pamphlet No. 172, New York, 1951.

Gilman, Leonard, and Paperte, Frances: Music as a psychotherapeutic agent, *J. Clin. Psychopath.*, 1949, 10:286–303.

Hamilton, Gordon: *Psychotherapy in Child Guidance*, Chap. 11, Columbia University Press, New York, 1947.

Karp, Maurice J.: Premarital counseling and psychotherapy: Two cases, Case II: An interfaith problem; Case III: An intercultural problem, *Marriage and Family Living*, 1952, 14:56–75.

Kubie, Lawrence S.: The nature of psychotherapy, pp. 754–764, in Eugene L. Hartley, Herbert G. Birch, Ruth E. Hartley (eds.), *Outside Readings in Psychology*, The Thomas Y. Crowell Company, New York, 1950.

Malone, Thomas P.: Analysis of the dynamics of group psychotherapy based on observations in a twelve-month experimental program, *J. Person.*, 1948, 16:245–277.

McKinney, Fred: Four years of a college adjustment clinic: I. Organization of clinic and problems of counselees, *J. Consult. Psychol.*, 1945, 9:203–212.

Meister, R. K., and Miller, H. E.: The dynamics of non-directive psychotherapy, *J. Clin. Psychol.*, 1946, 2:59–67.

Prados, Miguel: The use of pictorial images in group therapy, *Amer. J. Psychother.*, 1951, 5:196–214.

Rennie, Thomas A. C., and Woodward, Luther E.: *Mental Health in Modern Society,* Chap. 9, Commonwealth Fund, Harvard University Press, Cambridge, Mass., 1948.

Rogers, Carl R.: *Counseling and Psychotherapy: Newer Concepts in Practice,* Chaps. 1 and 7, Houghton Mifflin Company, Boston, 1942.

Schmedeberg, Melitta: Short analytic therapy, *Nerv. Child,* 1949, 8:281–290.

Shaw, Franklin J.: Some postulates concerning psychotherapy, *J. Consult. Psychol.,* 1948, 12:426–431.

Snyder, William U.: A short-term nondirective treatment of an adult, *J. Abnorm. Soc. Psychol.,* 1943, 38(2 Supplement):87–137.

Werner, Simon, and Chevlin, Myron R.: Brief psychotherapy: A hospital program with participation of the social worker, *Ment. Hyg., N.Y.,* 1949, 33:401–410.

Psychologists sense a need to see the entirety of behavior. Similarly, psychologists feel that a complete job of investigation is their contribution to bringing about a more perfect world. Ideals and tissue needs must both be satisfied. Naturally enough, then, the psychological study of personality includes investigation of health. The preceding chapters, discussing several of the most critical areas of adjustment, give examples of the healthy and the unhealthy behaviors which are now well known to psychologists.

Obviously psychotherapy is not the starting point, nor is it the conclusion of the story. Before the need of such therapy arises there is a process of dynamic learning at work shaping the growth pattern and the personality structure of the individual. His functional systems establish rhythms of tissue adjustment which serve physiological, sociocultural, and perceptual needs. His threshold of emotion is established as high or as low in relation to threat-laden situations. The sum total of all these reaction patterns organized into a single unit is his personality structure. Proper learning, *i.e.*, growth, would preclude any need for psychotherapy. Until he can see a completely adequate preventive program applied to the education of all humans at all age levels, the psychologist is not likely to feel that his work is done.

In order to prevent illness and maladjustments which may some day require therapy, standards of health must be formulated. Primitive man evolved elaborate systems of magic to help him avoid suffering. Later stages of civilization continued magic in the guise of traditional superstitions. More modern man has turned to scientific methods of research and developed theories of cause and effect in his search for control of the environment. With adequate control, man need not fear the processes of nature. Psychology is today at work on the mysteries of human behavior. It has contributed much to understanding of growth, of learning, and of the breakdown of personality. The present chapter summarizes these contributions in the form of brief *criteria* of mental health.

UNDERSTANDING ONESELF (CRITERION 1)

Processes and Goals

The contribution of psychology to man is largely improvement of his understanding of himself and his fellows. Understanding the processes of living is comparable to the job of a navigator. If the destination is established, a navigator can use all available geographic information to assure safe arrival. Psychology provides information about the total personality so that an individual may follow an efficient route to the goals established in his living.

Homeostasis and Learning

Breakdown of health is always a breakdown of the processes which maintain homeostasis in the total personality. New experiences are forever testing the homeostatic strength of every individual. Passing the tests is largely a matter of time, however; given a little more time, it is possible to get used to almost any situation or idea. Assimilation of new materials and experiences into the personality may take many years or it may take but an instant. In any event, if time does not permit adequate assimilation and if there is a threat of destruction, anxiety and conflict soon distort homeostasis. The structure of personality then weakens. The individual's behavior becomes emotionally disorganized and his goals confused. Learning, in this condition, fixates and seems only to add to disorganization. Psychotherapy is a means to reorganization after such a breakdown.

Values

Experience entails evaluation, no matter how simple or complex the organism. Values are formulations of the human being's hopes and fears, threat avoidances, and need projections. Some values are worth great effort to achieve. Others are merely fixated reactions which need to be appraised in broader perspective so that they may be reconstructed into the individual's system. This system requires a deeply harmonious matching of one value with all others, permitting compromises only when there is temporary inability to achieve harmony.

Appraisal and reappraisal of one's personal values are necessary to the process of maturation. In the process of homeostasis various values are balanced one against the other so as to maintain a dynamic equilibrium. Thus a unified scheme of values has been developed in the healthy personality.

"We"

The individual personality is not isolated; he is always part of a primary group, a "we." If he has been misguided during early growth he may think of himself in an unhygienic way as a "social atom." But modern psychological study suggests that personalities interlock inevitably into primary groups. Unless an individual does secure satisfactions from his family circle, he will continually attempt to substitute close relationships with secondary groups. He may try to keep the exclusive attention of a small clique or become very possessive in his relations with fellow workers. This type of immaturity reflects the lacks in the primary group process. Thus, only as the primary group process is strong can the child grow hygienically.

Courtship, because it is the keystone of the arch leading from the parental family to the marital family, is a transition from the primary group of the child to that of the adult and parent. It is essentially the maturing of the "we" aspects of personality from one stage of the life cycle to another.

A somewhat similar and later stage appears when the role of parent must give way to the peripheral role of in-law and grandparent. Failure to make the first transition precludes successful marriage and narrows the individual's way of living. Failure to make the second transition precludes success in the younger couples' marriages and narrows the way of living for the older people. Healthy personalities interlock in both hygienic and unhygienic ways; whether the interlocking is to lead to health or illness for all concerned depends on the way.

TECHNIQUES OF INTEGRATION (CRITERION 2)

It will not be possible in this twentieth-century world to bring together into one harmonious unit all that is sought after by all people. Overaggressive efforts to enforce universal unity have created many historically important figures but have thus far been met by equally historic and successful defeats. Some means for living together in peaceful efficiency must be found so that the variety of races, creeds, nationalities, social classes, and even individuals may contribute to one another. This, of course, is an ideal which generalizes the core value of full acceptability. If everyone is acceptable, no one needs to become hostile to prove his worth and no one needs to be rejected and to suffer in utter loneliness.

Sense of Direction

Each individual requires opportunities to assimilate new experiences and thus to integrate his personality continuously. He must feel that his integrations with the larger universe are *right*. This feeling of rightness-in-the-long-run, of proper alignment in this universe, cannot be assumed. Something in every personality requires evaluations to be made which apply to relatively long periods of time. To be accepted today it is necessary to feel that tomorrow will not bring rejection. Anxiety is merely the fear of unacceptability, which entails rejection and destruction of personality.

Relief from anxiety seems to come with the development of a sense of rightness in the directing of one's living; it comes with the development of feelings of proper alignment in the various processes of living. Psychology cannot define ultimate goals, but it can predict probable results upon each personality of various goal-oriented efforts. Psychology can alert the individual to his own motivations, both attended and unattended, and thereby help him to clarify his own values and to integrate or schematize them for more hygienic living.

Reintegration

Every personality is sorely tried at many points in its life history. Some prescription for recovery may be needed after such a trial.

"Take a vacation," "Return to religion," "Get married," "Get divorced," are phrases which point to this need. "Take a vacation" is good advice—if one has not just returned from one. It would be better advice if a careful formula was given as to what sort of vacation it should be. Few people, even among expert practitioners in the arts of healing, are today able to write a prescription defining an adequate vacation for a particular individual. Counseling can usually help in the planning of a vacation, but it cannot write a prescription.

An adequate application of what is known about the basic processes of the primary group would doubtless make most personalities able to withstand the strains of normal living even in periods of difficulty. Achievement of success in these basic personality processes requires, however, that all members of the individual's primary group cooperate fully. Group thinking, such as takes place in a genuine primary group, gives each individual member a feeling of strength and rightness, of unity within and without. Modern living recognizes that the home is the necessary setting for this primary group, or for the family process of integration.

Before the advent of scientific researches into human behavior, man had learned to set aside brief moments at frequent intervals for the purpose of thinking over his progress and his values. Creative artists unite in describing the process of artistic creation as a uniquely integrated experience. Religious specialists seek to define the spiritual experience of unification with the basic causes of the universe. Psychologists study the behavior of people and therefore are concerned with the process of these specialized experiences. More important, however, is the recognition in contemporary psychology that these feelings of completeness and of unity which artists and religionists value so highly are necessary to good health.

It thus becomes possible to recognize a moment set aside particularly for improving one's feelings of unity in personality and with the universe as an "act of prayer." This moment comprises an important process in the reintegration of personality. Without such moments, the integrated personality tends to lose perspective and to become less cohesive. A moment beside the sea, in the forest, or before a shrine—any one, or all, may assist this reintegration.

PHILOSOPHY OF WORK (CRITERION 3)

Artists and Slaves

Since all behavior is motivated, it is fundamental that learning is most efficiently managed through the individual's motives. Perhaps the difference between the attitude of the artist and that of the slave is to be found in their respective motives. If so, the easy fatigue of the slave is merely his inadequate motivation for the task at hand, whereas the boundless energy of the artist to create springs from his overpowering motivation to formulate and express objectively his inspiration.

Goal-oriented Effort

Work may be taken to mean the opposite of *play*, as children have often concluded in reference to household chores. Or, as in an artist's use of the word, work may be the productive activity which fulfills an individual's stronger motivations. This latter meaning of the word is substantiated by studies of goal-oriented behavior in both rats and men. Motives are so much one's own self that each person must formulate and follow through his own motives. A "sense of achievement" is merely the feeling of productive work, of fulfillment of motives which the individual has formulated for himself. When these motives also satisfy the primary group, an even greater motivation can be experienced. An individual who "hates work" is a slave who knows nothing of the freedom of formulating his own motives and the experience of success.

Puddings and Proofs

The proof of the pudding is in the eating, says the adage. Without some evidence of approval, the cook will be in no mood to try again. To each person there must be some evidence of success—his pudding must prove good eating to at least some extent. It thus is necessary for each individual to plan deliberately for success in his living. Beyond this success, he must plan for objective evidence of his effort and skill. Hobbies in sticks and stones and clays and metals are excellent mental hygiene chiefly because they leave such objective evidence. When a man's job deals with intangibles, his hobby should deal with tangibles. The greater a person's need for success experiences, the more carefully he must plan for evidence of his success.

Proof is, after all, a matter of approval and thus touches upon core values. It is efficient in its service to the individual when it takes over the responsibility of describing his worth. He may then proceed to new achievements instead of worrying about past stages in his life history. Realism, in the psychological sense, is merely recognition that the results are going to be evident sooner or later for each act performed. It is a comfort to know that one's achievements are described by objective results, to realize that these results can be seen by all observers and throughout time. The hygienic approach to work is thus a matter of expressing oneself in the work object, as does the artist, so that the end result proves and describes one's worth. This is in one sense a way of "living honestly," because personal secrecy is not needed as a defense.

SOCIAL PARTICIPATION (CRITERION 4)

Variety in Unity

Health is as much a social as it is an individual matter. This has been recognized in a well-known slogan describing the larger goal of mental-hygiene organizations: "a sound body in a sound mind in a sound society." The evident fact is that a great variety of personalities, races, creeds, nationalities, and classes do and must contribute to this larger social process. Psychologically speaking, the most healthy social process is the one which provides freedom for all its members and a variety of stimulation to individual and group action.

The richer the perceptual field, the more every person can find interesting and satisfying activity. Interchange of ideas between personalities of differing backgrounds contributes variety. Every individual needs to structure the highly complex social process into a relatively predictable general pattern. He therefore uses social controls such as institutions, folkways, and mores. He draws upon scientific studies to perceive the social process more objectively and clearly. He uses great art and literature to help him grasp the larger pattern of the social process. In this larger view the criterion of a good art work seems to apply: "variety in unity" leads to interest, excitement, satisfaction, growth.

Adaptive Participation

Successful democratic living requires participation in the social process by everyone. Restrictions upon universal participation frequently represent the efforts of fear-laden personalities unable to tolerate great complexity. Hostile or aggressive persons often struggle desperately to reduce variety and complexity by excluding selected races, creeds, classes, or strong personalities. Rejected personalities often escape into the handicaps of mental and physical illness. If their feelings of rejection are less intense, rejected individuals may withdraw into small but closely knit groups. Such groups soon find themselves discriminated against by hostile people, and struggle replaces more healthy participation.

Handicapped persons, and those who create their own handicaps as defense mechanisms, can learn through appropriate education or psychotherapy that adaptive participation in the richness of the social process is the healthy way of life. Such participation is impossible to the rigid personality which has developed through prolonged living under stress and threat. Participation is a form of adventurous learning. It requires strong feelings of basic acceptability to presume security even during the growth and change of one's own self through reconstructing experiences. Like personality integration, adaptive participation needs to be fostered continuously.

Ends and Means

Genuinely healthy behavior is goal-oriented. Frustration of behavior seems to result in changes known as "emotional," including increased energization but loss of coordination in both muscular and perceptual powers. Maladjustment expresses itself as threat-laden emotion which has come to be known as "anxiety." Sometimes the loss of coordination is compensated for by a rigid fixation or ritualism of activities which temporarily relieves but seldom removes the threat that produced the frustration. This ritualistic tendency in maladjusted behavior commonly appears in the form of being overconcerned with how things are done and losing sight of the goals or end results.

Not uncommonly a maladjusted personality substitutes a secondary-group relationship for a primary-group one. He may use his family group only for a stepping stone to social advancement. He then fails within this group in the necessary primary relationships of affection, self-expression, and reintegration. Eventually he becomes hungry for these basic processes. Since he has not considered his own family as satisfying these needs, he turns to establishing relationships of affection with outsiders.

Alternatively, the emotionally starved person may assume paternalistic if not childlike personal loyalties between himself and his secondary-group associates, *e.g.*, fellow workers, supervisors, or subordinates, or political companions and leaders. Any of these may give temporary surcease, but they never succeed in the long run in replacing the primary-group functions of the individual. The primary group is so much a part of every personality that it is tantamount to an end or goal and cannot be disregarded. Other groups are instruments, means to ends. They are secondary and valuable only as they produce desired outcomes. Confusion of ends and means can be avoided through healthy growth. It can be corrected by readjustment procedures. It can be present in any degree, and the degree is always a vivid index to the individual's health of personality.

LIFE PERSPECTIVE (SUMMARY OF CRITERIA)

Philosophy of Life

Personality is the result of following homeostatically a pattern called the life cycle. Each person sees himself as a given point in a larger pattern—his world. But he also notices that other things change at different rates, some rapidly and some slowly. He sees that life goes on before and after him. He draws upon his capacity to philosophize, seeking to perceive the long-term nature of his universe and to understand his place in it. His life perspective develops as it expresses itself hypothetically in his perceptual projections. Little wonder, then, that leading psychotherapists and scientific students of personality so often evidence a tendency toward philosophizing!

One's outlook upon life may not be well known to him, just as the motives in his behavior are often unattended by him. He often verbalizes one outlook but feels quite another. His real feelings toward life are his self-concept. His scheme of values in actual living comprises his outlook, his philosophy of living. His integration of personality will be achieved and enhanced as his true philosophy of living is better unified.

Growth and Health

All life is a process of growth. Each person can effect changes in his personality. As he grows, his scheme of values grows. He can speed this growth or retard it, in accordance with his deepest wishes. In any case he needs to become aware of his own outlook upon life because this summarizes his larger goals. This awareness is not easily achieved, for it reaches beneath mere words into the depths of his own inner feelings.

The criteria of mental health, as listed above, summarize the salient points of a life perspective. Every step in ascending the ladder of life can be taken with greater security if each of these criteria is reviewed in one's own thinking and feeling at each step. Such review helps to establish whether the basic needs are being satisfied. Healthy growth requires the satisfaction of basic needs, including:

1. A faith that in this universe a person can achieve a happy existence
2. A feeling that one's self is worthy of a place in this universe
3. A feeling of security in a primary group
4. Opportunity to work, *i.e.*, to grow and to express oneself according to one's own motivations

Understanding the psychology of personality provides one means for attaining the health of personality which contributes to a healthy world.

Name Index

A

Abbate, Grace McLean, 171
Abel, Theodore M., 319
Abrams, Charles, 297
Adler, Alfred, 49, 211, 369
Adorno, T. W., 323
Aleck, Adolph W., 144
Alexander, Franz, 20, 71, 369, 372
Allen, Frederick H., 239
Allport, Floyd H., 195
Allport, Gordon W., 60, 150, 239
Alper, Thelma G., 189
Anderson, Gladys L., 144
Anderson, Harold H., 144
Anderson, John E., 60
Anderson, Phoebe M., 297
Anshen, Ruth N., 297
Appel, Kenneth E., 9, 110
Asch, S. E., 144
Auerbach, Aline B., 297
Axline, Virginia Mae, 372

B

Bach, George R., 379
Bacon, F. Alexander, 67
Baker, Abe B., 316, 317
Bakwin, Harry, 281
Banay, Ralph S., 338, 354
Bane, Frank, 20
Barker, R. G., 202
Bartlett, Frederic C., 125
Bartley, S. H., 72, 84, 85
Bauer, W. W., 35, 172
Bavelas, Alex, 192
Beaumont, Henry, 60, 144, 189
Beers, Clifford, 23, 38
Bell, Marjorie, 338, 356
Bender, L., 371
Benedek, Therese, 297
Benedict, Agnes, 297

Benedict, Ruth, 264
Benz, Margaret Gilbert, 288
Berg, Irwin A., 9
Berrien, Frederick K., 60
Bice, Harry V., 333
Binger, Carl A. L., 38
Birch, Herbert G., 379
Birren, J. E., 194
Blair, Arthur Witt, 171
Blake, Robert R., 72, 143, 144, 152
Bloch, E. H., 77
Block, Helen, 144
Boardman, Rhea K., 239
Bossard, James H. S., 122, 297
Boudet, Robert, 278
Bowie, Carol C., 273
Bowman, Henry A., 250
Brav, Stanley R., 272
Bravermen, Sydell, 317
Breckenridge, Marian, 108, 171
Brickman, William W., 356
Brinton, Crane, 38
Britt, Stuart Henderson, 105
Brittain, Horace L., 137
Bronner, Augusta, 340, 356
Brown, Warner, 60
Bruner, Jerome S., 133, 144, 152, 184
Bullis, H. Edmund, 35
Burgess, Ernest W., 122, 250, 251, 257, 264
Burnham, William H., 10
Burton, William H., 171
Burtt, Harold E., 20
Byrd, Oliver E., 92

C

Cameron, D. Owen, 34
Cameron, Norman, 367
Campsi, Paul, 122
Cannon, W. B., 62

Cantril, Hadley, 23, 144
Caplan, Gerald, 39
Carmichael, Leonard, 129, 240
Carrel, Alexis, 73
Carroll, Herbert A., 321
Casterdyck, Elsa, 333
Cattell, R. B., 197
Cavan, Ruth Shonle, 122
Centers, Richard, 116, 272
Chevigny, Hector, 316
Chevlin, Myron R., 380
Chisholm, George Brock, 39
Christensen, Harold T., 297
Chute, E., 72, 84, 85
Colm, Hanna, 297
Combs, Arthur W., 61, 145, 379
Crook, M. N., 194
Crow, Alice, 356
Crow, Lester D., 356
Crutchfield, Richard S., 145
Cunningham, James M., 30
Curran, Charles A., 379

D

Dai, Bingham, 333
Davis, C. M., 65
Davis, W. Allison, 115
Dean, John P., 297
Dearborn, Walter F., 171
De Cillis, Olga E., 97
Deutsch, Albert, 356
Dewey, John, 137, 189
Di Carlo, Louis M., 333
Diggs, Mary H., 356
Dilthey, Wilhelm, 149
Diserens, Charles M., 60
Doll, Edgar A., 171
Dollard, John, 189, 379
Dolphin, Jane E., 333
Dorcus, Roy M., 9
Doyle, Kathleen, 379
Dreikurs, Rudolf, 240
Duffy, Elizabeth, 201
Dunlap, Knight, 49
Duvall, Evelyn, 250, 272
Dysinger, Wendell S., 171

E

Eckert, Ralph G., 272
Edwards, Allen L., 97
Edwards, Marcia, 333
Eells, Kenneth, 115

Eisenson, Jon, 333
Eliot, T. S., 77
English, Horace B., 66
English, O. Spurgeon, 13, 66, 70, 79, 297
Eysenck, Hans J., 193

F

Farwell, J. E., 20
Fishbein, Morris, 250
Fisher, V. E., 366
Fiske, Donald W., 201
Folsom, Joseph K., 122, 294
Ford, Mary E. N., 249, 257
Foster, Constance J., 297
Foster, Ione A., 333
Foster, Robert G., 272
Frank, Lawrence K., 145, 273
Franklin, Adele, 297
French, Thomas M., 71, 372
Freud, Sigmund, 49, 369
Friedlander, Kate, 350
Friend, Jeanette G., 282
Fry, Clement C., 171
Fryer, Douglas, 240, 334

G

Galton, Francis, 143
Gardner, George E., 31
Gardner, L. Pearl, 327
Garrett, James F., 61, 333
Gesell, Arnold, 166
Gibb, Cecil A., 202
Gilbert, Jeanne, 97
Gilhousen, Howard C., 60
Gilman, Leonard, 379
Ginsburg, Sol W., 171
Glueck, Eleanor, 336, 339, 342, 344, 346, 353, 356
Glueck, Sheldon, 336, 339, 342, 344, 346, 353, 356
Goff, Regina Mary, 324
Goldberg, Harriet L., 361
Goldschmidt, Walter, 122
Goodenough, Florence, 158
Goodman, C. C., 152
Gorer, Geoffrey, 101
Gough, Harrison, 333
Gouldner, Alvin W., 189
Grinker, R. R., 375
Guthrie, Edwin R., 97, 202
Gyr, John, 122

H

Haggard, Ernest A., 145, 282
Hallowell, A. I., 145
Hamilton, Gordon, 379
Harris, Dale B., 333
Harris, Irving D., 97
Harris, Robert E. G., 92
Hartley, Eugene, 379
Hartley, Ruth E., 379
Hartshorne, Edward Y., 122
Hastorf, A. H., 145
Havighurst, Robert J., 115, 322
Haynee, Norman S., 122
Healy, William, 340, 356
Hebb, D. O., 89, 95, 361
Henry, Edwin R., 240, 334
Henry, Nelson B., 337, 356
Henry, William E., 115
Hertzman, Jack, 39
Hertzman, M., 144
Herzberg, Alexander, 373
Hildreth, G. H., 239
Hilgard, Ernest R., 152, 178, 180, 183, 187, 240
Hill, Reuben, 272, 295
Himes, Norman E., 265
Hogan, H. P., 129
Hollingshead, August B., 122
Honigmann, John J., 56
Hoppock, Robert, 240
Horney, Karen, 369
Horton, H. P., 338
Huddleson, James H., 79
Hunt, J. McV., 97, 202, 284, 336
Hymes, James L., Jr., 20

I

Ilg, Frances L., 166

J

Jenkins, Gladys G., 35, 172, 261, 297
Jenkins, Richard L., 261
Jenkinson, B. J., 9
Jersild, Arthur T., 34, 176
Jones, Robert, 122
Jost, H., 97
Jung, Carl G., 49, 193, 369

K

Karp, Maurice J., 379
Keliher, Alice V., 356

Keller, Fred S., 61
Kelley, Harold H., 145
Kelly, Janet Agnes, 122
Kennedy, Ruby Jo Reeves, 251
Kinder, Elaine F., 319
Kirkpatrick, Edwin A., 240
Kisker, George W., 18
Kluckhohn, Clyde, 119, 122, 264, 333
Knisely, M. H., 79
Knutson, A. L., 145
Kounin, J. S., 202
Kraines, S. H., 97, 240
Kramer, B. M., 239
Krech, David, 130, 144, 145, 188
Kubie, Lawrence S., 379
Kuhlen, Raymond G., 333
Kunst, Mary S., 158

L

Labarre, Weston, 122
Lambert, Clara, 172
Landis, C., 20
Landis, Judson T., 259, 267
Landis, Mary G., 259, 267
Langer, Walter C., 61
Lashley, K. S., 204
Lazarus, Richard S., 130
Lecky, Prescott, 182
Lee, George E., 240
Leighton, Dorothea, 119
Leonard, William Ellery, 230
Leuba, Clarence, 93, 273
Levine, Milton I., 298
Levy, John, 253, 265
Lewin, Kurt, 49, 61, 240, 295
Libby, Walter, 137
Lindzey, Gardner, 187
Lippitt, Ronald, 36, 295
Locke, H. J., 251, 257
Loeb, Martin B., 322
Lombroso, Cesare, 338
Long, Louis, 333
Lott, George M., 333
Lowery, Lawson G., 336
Lowry, James V., 26
Lucas, C., 93
Lunt, Paul S., 336
Luther, Everett, 333

M

McAndrew, Helton, 333
McCaul, R. L., 189
McCleary, Robert A., 130

McClelland, David C., 202
McDougall, William, 49
McFarland, Ross A., 79
Macfarlane, Jean Walker, 202
McGinnies, Elliott, 133, 180
McGuire, Carson, 122
McKinney, Fred, 189, 240, 273, 379
MacKinnon, Donald W., 202
McLaughlin, James T., 20
Macnaughton, Dorothy, 172
Macomber, Freeman G., 60, 144, 189
Magoun, F. Alexander, 273
Maier, Norman R. F., 52, 176, 183, 204, 210, 227
Malone, Thomas P., 379
Marmor, Judd, 298
Martin, W. E., 333
Maslow, A. H., 58, 59, 61, 310
Mead, Margaret, 113, 122, 157, 202
Meek, Lois Hayden, 172
Meeker, Marchia, 115
Meister, R. K., 379
Meltzer, H., 189
Menninger, William C., 6, 39, 333
Merrill, Maud A., 356
Miller, H. E., 379
Miller, Neal E., 189, 379
Missildine, W. H., 189
Mittelmann, Bela, 310
Mohr, George J., 97
Montagu, M. F. Ashley, 333
Moore, Bernice M., 29
Morgan, Clifford T., 90
Mowrer, O. H., 189
Muenzinger, K. F., 190
Munroe, Ruth, 253, 265, 304
Murphy, Gardner, 132, 135, 202
Murray, Henry A., 49, 58, 138, 264, 333
Myers, Julian S., 61, 333

N

Neher, Jack, 39
Nelson, A. K., 160
Neugarten, Bernice L., 116
Neuman, Joy, 297
Neumeyer, Martin H., 336, 344
Niederland, Wm. G., 20
Nimkoff, Meyer F., 273
Noüy, Lecomte du, 156

O

Ojemann, Ralph H., 35
O'Kelley, Lawrence I., 228

O'Malley, Emily E., 35
Overstreet, Harry A., 20, 227

P

Paperte, Frances, 379
Pennington, L. A., 9
Pepitone, Albert, 145
Perry, J. S., 62
Pintner, Rudolf, 333
Plant, James S., 122, 337
Pollak, Otto, 336
Porterfield, A. L., 356
Postman, Leo, 133, 145, 184
Prados, Miguel, 379
Pratt, Dallas, 39
Pratt, K. C., 160
Prescott, Daniel A., 190
Pressey, Sidney L., 163, 170, 333
Preston, George H., 172
Prothro, E. Terry, 240

R

Ramsey, Glenn V., 72, 144
Rapoport, Lydia, 97
Razran, Gregory, 323
Redl, Fritz, 172
Rees, John R., 20
Reeve, George H., 333
Reinemann, John Otto, 356
Rennie, Thomas A. C., 20, 380
Resch, J. A., 315
Reymert, Martin L., 91
Ribble, Margaret A., 284, 298
Riess, B. F., 97
Ripley, Herbert S., 97
Robinson, Francis P., 163, 170
Rockwood, Lemo D., 249, 257
Rogers, Carl R., 380
Rohrer, John H., 145
Rokeach, Milton, 240
Root, Oren, 24
Rose, Arnelies A., 97
Ross, Helen, 240
Roth, Charles, 333
Rothney, John W. M., 171
Rynerson, Mary Ann, 97

S

Samter, Max, 97
Saul, Leon J., 9, 20, 97
Schaffner, Bertram H., 290
Schauer, Gerhard, 333

Schettler, Clarence, 202
Schmeideler, Rev. Edgar, 273
Schmideberg, Melitta, 353, 380
Schoenfeld, William N., 61
Schwartz, Louis A., 137
Schweinitz, Karl de, 297
Seligman, Jean H., 298
Shacter, Helen, 35, 172
Shaw, Franklin J., 190, 380
Sheldon, William H., 193
Sherif, Muzafer, 145
Sherman, Mandel, 202
Sidis, William, 209
Simcoe, Elizabeth, 333
Skinner, Charles E., 144
Slavson, S. R., 356
Snyder, William U., 380
Snygg, Donald, 61, 145
Soden, W. H., 333
Solomon, Richard L., 145
Spence, Ralph B., 356
Spencer, Douglas, 300
Spiegel, J. P., 375
Spock, Benjamin M., 39
Stagner, Ross, 52, 197
Stanton, Mildred, 333
Steiner, Lee R., 20
Stellar, Eliot, 90
Stern, Edith M., 333
Strauss, A., 273
Sullivan, Henry Stack, 120
Sun, K. H., 160
Sutherland, Robert L., 29
Sutich, Anthony, 363
Symonds, Percival, 240

T

Taba, Hilda, 115
Teeters, Negley K., 356
Terhune, William B., 9, 110
Terman, Lewis M., 255, 259
Teska, P. T., 240
Thetford, E. S., 79, 240
Thomas, W. I., 48
Thompson, Helen, 172
Thorman, George, 20
Tomkins, Silvan S., 136, 138, 139, 227
Torrance, Paul, 39
Torrey, Jane W., 130
Trow, William C., 356
Tuttle, Harold S., 97
Tyson, Robert, 33

U

Underwood, Virginia Van Meter, 298

V

Vance, Rupert, 122
Vanderplas, James M., 143, 152
Veltfort, Helene R., 240
Vernon, W. H. D., 240
Vincent, E. Lee, 108, 171
Vine, D. O., 190

W

W., William, 39
Wallerstein, James S., 356
Wallin, J. E. Wallace, 318
Wallin, Paul, 264
Walter, A. A., 129
Wapner, Seymour, 90, 91
Warden, C. J., 45
Warner, L., 77
Warner, W. Lloyd, 115, 322, 336
Watson, Goodwin A., 168
Watson, John B., 93
Weill, Blanche C., 298
Weingarten, Erica M., 145
Weiss, Edward, 13, 66, 70, 79
Weitz, Robert D., 97
Werner, Heinz, 90, 91
Werner, Simon, 380
Wessel, Bessie, 122
White, Ralph K., 295
White, Robert, W., 240
Whitman, Samuel, 28
Wilder, Joseph, 361
Witkin, H. A., 129
Wolff, H. G., 95, 97
Woltmann, A. G., 371
Wood, Arthur L., 273
Woodward, Luther E., 20, 32, 49, 380
Woodworth, Robert S., 149, 150
Wright, H. F., 202

Y

Yepsen, Lloyd N., 333
Young, Kimball, 122
Young, Paul T., 97

Z

Zeligs, Rose, 333

Subject Index

A

Accident frequency, 13
Acoustical disability, 317
Adaptability, in learning, 175
  of personality, 157
  in social participation, 388
Adjustment, concept of, 204–210
  mechanisms of, 210–217
  motives and, 59
  scale of, 206–207
  sexual, in marriage, 264
  techniques for marriage, 264–265
Adolescent in home, 285, 296
Adolescent dreams applied to courtship, 269
Adolescent period of growth, 161, 164, 165
Adrenin, 83
Adulthood in life cycle, 161, 165
Affection, 281, 282
Aggression, toward competitors, 341
  as dimension, 192
  in parental feelings, 168
  as projection of insecurity, 18
Alcoholics, number of, 9, 92
Alcoholics Anonymous, 30
Allergic reactions, 238
Ambivalence of motives, 200
Ambivert, 193
American Association of Psychiatric Social Workers, 32
American Board of Examiners in Professional Psychology, 31
American Board of Psychiatry, 31
American Psychiatric Association, 24, 31, 365
American Psychological Association, 24, 31, 365
American Theatre Wing, 30
Amnesia, 185

A (continued, right column)

Anosmic people, 134, 318
Anxiety, and cardiovascular system, 79
  as emotion, 238
  expressed as fear, 95
  from ignorance, 37
  in neurosis, 223, 228–236
Anxiety reactions, 229–230
Arteries, 75, 77
Arterioles, 74, 75
Assimilation, 173, 175, 182
Asthenic reaction, 229
Asthma, 71
Astrology, 16, 46
Augustic deficiency, 318
Autonomic nervous system, 87–91

B

Behavior, fixated, 211
  hostility, 200
  motivation in, 35, 52–53
  nonadjustive (see Nonadjustive behavior)
  topological charting of, 50–51
Behavior drive, 47
Behavior patterns, deviate, 226–236
Bicepts, 81
Block, 360
Blood pressure, 76–78
Blood vessels, 81, 173
Brain, 89

C

Canadian National Committee for Mental Hygiene, 35, 36
Capillaries, 69, 75, 77
Cardiovascular system, 72–80
Case study, 155, 350
Catastrophic reactions, 227
Catharsis, 18
Cerebral hemorrhage, 77

Cerebral palsy, 314
Child-guidance clinics, 31, 354
Class patterning, 114–117
Class pressures on child, 115
Cleveland mental health council, 28
Climacteric, 161, 165
Color-blind people, 134, 318
Columbia Obstruction Box, 45
Combat fatigue, 10
Compensation, 211
Compulsions, 233
Conditioned reflex, 47–48, 158
Conflict and learning, 187–188
Conflict-laden behavior, 204
Conflict states, 220
Conversion reaction, 229
Coordinating Councils, 354
Core values, and age handicap, 328
    definition of, 157
    in delinquency, 341
    as infantile generalizations, 200
    in personality structure, 197
    and toilet training, 168
Counseling, areas of, 367–369
    case-studies in, 155
    stages of, 365–367
Counselor, 181, 256, 364
Courtship, 248–259
    cultural influence on, 100
    goals of, 249
    readiness for, 243–248
Cults, 17
Culture, 98–122
    and emotion, 93
    of United States, 106–117
Culture carriers, 102
Culture conflicts, 344
Culture groups, 93
Culture lag, 100
Culture patterning, 98–106

D

Daydreaming, 216
Defense, perceptual, 133
    against threat, 180
Delinquency, core values in, 341
    and culture, 105
    frustration and, 341
    in girls, 48, 349
    hostility in, 350
    and housing, 338
    influence of minority status on, 344
    and inheritance, 337
    mental retardation in, 350

Delinquency, and parents, 341–346
    prevention of (*see* Prevention of de-
        linquency)
    readjustment in, 354–355
    rejection and, 342–344
    rigidity and, 344
    roots of, 339–341
    scheme of values in, 344
    and structure of personality, 339–351
Demagogues, 17
Dendrite, 89
Depressions, 18, 229
Depth psychology, 138
Detroit Clinic for Juvenile Research, 137
Deviate behavior patterns, 226–236
Digestive system, 63–68
Dimensions of personality, 191–194
Discontinuous routes, 109
Disorganization, 185, 229, 238
Divorce, 9, 249
Double standard, 336
Drive, behavior, 47
Dynamic nature of personality, 153–154
Dynamic self-maintenance, 225

E

Egocentrism, 94, 223
Electroencephalograph, 89
Emotion, 91–97
    changing concepts of, 93
    and learning, 176
    prolonged, 78
    in threat reactions, 184
Emotional energization, 53
Emotional handicaps, 304, 305
Emotional illness, 91–92, 238
Empirical approach, 48, 52
Energy, 57
Engagement, 259–269
Epilepsy, 315
Escape mechanism, 216
Escape offerings, 17
Ethnic groups, 322
Ethnic patterning, 110
Ethnocentrism, 105, 118
Exploratory variation, 52
Extrovert, 193

F

Family, compatibility in, 266
    democratic structure in, 293
    evolving concept of, 277

Family, goals in, 258, 278–284
  housing of, 284–286
  in-law relationships, 262
  as integrating force, 106
  unhealthy influences in, 341
Family functions, 278
Family-life conferences, 29
Fantasy, 132
Fatigue, 84
Fear, as channeled emotion, 94
  effect of, on muscles, 86
  in food taking, 227
Feelings, of guilt, 168, 220
  of hostility, 237
  of inferiority, 193, 220
  of mastery or power, 193
  of rejection, 237, 244
Field theories, 50
Figure, ambiguous, 126, 138
  incomplete, 131
Figure-ground organizations, 134
Fixated behavior, 211
Flaccidity, 82
Folkways, in courtship, 250
  definition of, 100
  ethnic, 110
  and rationalization, 214
  regional variations in, 114
Frame of reference, 300
Frustration, definition of, 36
  and delinquency, 341
  as threat reaction, 183
  tolerance for, 207–209, 223
Frustration reactions, 51
Frustration situation, 205
Functional systems, 62–91

G

Gagging process, 65
Gang, 346–347
Ganglia, 89
Gangster, 110
Gastrointestinal system, 63–69
Geriatrics, 327
Gestalt Completion Test, 140
Glands, 81, 83, 87, 90
Goals, and effort, 386
  false, 360
  in family, 258, 278–284
  group, 102
  in motivation, 58
  of readjustment, 360–363

Goals, short-term, 222
  in United States culture, 106
Groups, in- versus out-, 104
  primary, 102
  secondary, 102

H

Habit, as motive, 48
  as organization of perception, 131
  and personality, 151
  stereotyped, 185
Habit systems, 330
Handicap, and adaptive participation, 388
  age, 326–332
  constructive attitude toward, 300
  cosmetic, 310–313
  emotional, 302
  meaning of, 299
  mental, 318–321
  orthopedic, 313
  physical, 308–318
  social, 321–326
  vocational, 306
Hate, 212
Heart difficulties, 315
Hepatic subdivision, 76
Heredity, 155
Heterosexual interests, 248
Hierarchy, occupational, 111
  of ratings, 103
  of roles, 107
  of social classes, 116
Hobbies, 115, 386
Homeostasis, definition of, 56–58
  as equilibrium, 153, 228
  and learning, 382
Homogamy, 253
Hormones, 75, 87
Hospitalization, 376
Hostility, in childhood, 34
  in delinquency, 350
  feeling of, 237
  as projection of insecurity, 18
Hostility behavior, 200
Hunger, 135
Hypertension, 95
Hypnosis, 46, 375
Hypochondriacal reaction, 229
Hypothalamus, 90, 91
Hypothesis, 151
Hypoventilation, 71

I

Identification, 212
Imagination, 137
Immaturity, 227, 246–248
Industrial accident, 13
Industrial Revolution, 47
Infancy, 156, 160, 163, 214
Infatuation, 251
Insanity as legal concept, 6
  (*See also* Psychoses)
Insight, 37, 135, 363
Integration, 106, 384–386
Intelligence, 195, 363
International Congress, on Mental
  Health, 34
  on Mental Hygiene, 22
International Council for the Mental
  Health of Children, 23
International Union of Family Organi-
  zations, 278
Intestinal tract, 64
Introspection, 134
Introvert, 193

J

Judge Baker Foundation, 31
Juvenile courts, 31, 351

L

Lability of perception, 126
Leadership, 17, 192
Learning, adaptability in, 175–179
  and assimilation, 173
  and maintenance of selfhood, 219
  and personality, 173–189
  readiness for, 137
  resistance to, 180–183
  tension in, 176
  unconscious, 158
  visceral phase in, 178
Life cycle, experience of, 159
  family, 274–278
  steps of, in outline, 160–166
Louisiana Society for Mental Hygiene,
  29

M

Macroscopic, 124
Maladjustment, in accidents, 13
  as anxiety, 230
  as continuum, 4–6
  individual view of, 10

Maladjustment, societal view of, 15
Marriage, as continual honeymoon, 109
  cultural influence on, 100, 109
  happiness score, 254
  parent-parent relations in, 288
  rehearsal for, 259
  stages in, 275–276
Marriage counseling, 368
Masochism, 94
Mass activity, 84
Maturation, for courtship, 243
  and maintenance of selfhood, 219
  physiological, 160
Mechanisms of adjustment, 210–217
Mechanistic psychologies, 47
Mental health, 3–40
  in age handicap, 329
  aspects of communications, 28
  coordinated efforts for, 28–30
  and culture pressures, 28
  definition of, 3–4
  National Mental Health Act of 1946,
    25
  of parents, 286–288
  publications in, 32–33
Mental Health Foundation, 24
Mental illness, 6, 9, 233
Mental retardation, 318–321
  in delinquency, 350
Military services, maladjustment in, 10
  old sergeant syndrome, 220–223
  rejectees, 9
Minority, influence of, on delinquency,
  344
  reaction to status of, 323–326
Minority groups, 111
Moods, effect of, on muscles, 85
  evoked by nest situation, 157
Mores, definition of, 100
  foreign, 119
  in marriage roles, 257
  and physique, 311
  and rationalization, 214
Motivation, 43–61
  in behavior, 35, 52–53
  cultural influences on, 100
  definition of, 44
  in fatigue, 85
  and perception, 132
  and structure, 199–200
  tension in, 54
Motives, and adjustment, 59
  ambivalence of, 200
  biosocial, 49
  deeper, 200

Motives, in hierarchies, 58
  and learning, 174
  and philosophy of work, 386
  prescientific, 45
Muscles, in activity, 78
  cardiac, 72
  in digestive tract, 64
  facial, 85
  mass activity of, 83–84
  skeletal, 82
Musculature, 80–87

N

National Association for Mental Health, 24
National Committee for Mental Hygiene, 7, 24, 30
National Institute of Mental Health, 25
National Mental Health Act of 1946, 25
National Mental Health Council, 25
Needs, as basis for marriage choice, 252
  as organization of perceptions, 131
  physiological, 47, 55
  tissue, 85
  (*See also* Motivation)
Negativism, 214
Negro children, 324
Negroes, regional attitudes toward, 113
Nervous breakdown, as acute neurosis, 224
  as failure to adapt, 176
  and traumatic neurosis, 184
Nervous systems, 87–91
Neural pathways and habit patterns, 152
Neuroses, and breathing, 70
  and cardiovascular system, 79
  classification of, 228–236
  definition of, 6, 223–226
  in occupational difficulties, 11
  traumatic, 184
  wellsprings of, 217–226
Neurotic nucleus, 227, 304, 375
Nonadjustive behavior, case of, 209
  definition of, 204–206
Nonadjustive behavior patterns, 225
Nursery schools, 29

O

Obsessive-compulsive reaction, 233–236
Occupational patterning, 111
Old age handicap, 326–332
Old sergeant syndrome, 220–222
Oxygenation, 75

P

Paramecium, 63, 64, 94
Parasympathetic segments, 91
Parent surrogates, 246
Parents, and aggression, 168
  and delinquency, 341–346
  emancipation from, 244
  marital relationships, 288–291
  mental health of, 286–288
  and youth, 244–246
Pecking order, 291, 344
Perception, 123–146
  cultural influence of, 100
  in delinquency, 340
  and learning, 178
  and needs, 131
  and neurosis, 236–239
  use of study of, 134
Peripheral system, 88
Peristaltic action, 64, 82
Personality, adjustments of, 203–239
  analysis of traits of, 194–197
  constancy of, 151–152
  dimensions of, 191–194
  dynamic nature of, 153–154
  growth of, 149–173
  and learning, 173–190
  structure of, and delinquency, 339–351
  structuring of, 191–203
  study of, 32–38
  and values, 154
Perspective, 136, 357–389
Phobias, 230–233
Pierre, the Pelican, 29
Post-climacteric, 162, 329, 331
Prejudices, in aged, 328
  against minorities, 322–325
  as refusal to adapt, 187
  as resistance, 182
Premarital adjustments, 264
Premarital counseling, 254–257
Premarital intercourse, dangers in, 267
Premarital predictive technique, 253–257
Prenatal period, 160
Prevention of delinquency, 351–354
  by improved family relations, 283
  through study of personality, 32–38
  as trend in mental-health effort, 26–31
Projection mechanism, 135–215
Projective tests, auditory, 143
  development of, 136–137
  and mentally handicapped, 320
  in therapy, 137–138

Psychiatric Foundation, 24
Psychiatric social workers, 25, 32, 366
Psychiatry, 21, 30, 149, 221
Psychoanalysis, 44, 369–370
Psychoneurosis (*see* Neuroses)
Psychoneurotic disorders, Veterans Administration classification of, 228–236
Psychoses, 6, 9, 233
Psychosomatics, 62–98
  and cardiovascular process, 79
  and employment, 12
  and illness, 66, 92, 309
  as used by Oriental, 65
Psychotherapeutic techniques, 369–377
  in art and music, 373–374
  in group therapy, 31, 320, 370
  in hospitals, 26–32, 376
  in hypnosis, 375–377
  in narcosynthesis, 375
  in play therapy, 371
  in psychoanalysis, 369–370
  in psychodrama, 370
  in visuotherapy, 371
Punishment, 290, 295, 351–353

R

Rage, 94, 212
Rationalization, 214, 287, 306
Readiness, for courtship, 243–248
  for learning, 137
  for parenthood, 276
  for particular learning, 137, 287
  for readjustment, 359
Readjustment, in delinquency, 354–355
  goals of, 360–363
  readiness for, 359
  resistance toward, 182
  resources for, 363–369
  tests in, 366
Reconstruction, 183, 226, 235
Reflex, conditioned, 47–48, 158
Reflex arc, 89
Regression, 216
Reintegration, as family function, 278–280
  as technique for integration, 384–388
Rejection, of child, 287
  and delinquency, 342–344
  feeling of, 237, 244
  of minorities, 324
Religion, in counseling, 368
  in integration, 385
  in marriage, 262

Repression, 129
Resistance, 180–210
  to learning, 180–183
  and self-concept, 180
Respiratory system, 69–72
Rigidity, and delinquency, 344
  of personality, 126, 223
  as wellspring of neurosis, 225
Role playing, 258, 370
Rorschach test, 140, 366

S

Sadism, 94
Scheme of values, in delinquency, 344
  exposed through perception, 143
  in maintenance of selfhood, 218–220
Security, 48, 191, 280
Self-concept, and age, 328
  in maintenance of selfhood, 219
  and resistance, 180
  and structure, 201
  threat to, 185
Self-maintenance, dynamic, 225
Sensation, 134
Sensory-motor nervous system, 87, 178
Sexual development, 91, 163, 266, 282
Sibling rivalry, 167
Social class, 57, 114–117, 321–323
Sociometry, 103
Somatization reactions, 229, 238
Status systems, individual reaction to, 103
  in social handicap, 322
Stereotype, in evaluation, 116
  of habits, 185
  of leader, 103
  in occupations, 113
  of student, 100
Stimulus-response psychology, 50
Stomach, 55, 64
Subception, 131–133
Subcultures, 102, 346
Sublimation mechanism, 213
Substitution mechanism, 213
Syndrome, old sergeant, 220–223

T

Taboos, 105
Temperament as trait, 195
Tension, from cultural pressures, 108
  definition of, 55
  general, 184
  international, 23

Tension, in learning, 176
  local, 178
  in motivation, 54
Tests, and case studies, 155
  for marriage success, 254
  and perception, 136–143
  in readjustment, 366
Thematic Apperception Test, in counseling, 366
  in exploring of needs, 59
  and perception, 138–143
  and rigidity, 227
Threat reactions, 183–185
Topological charting of behavior, 50–51
Traits of personality, analysis of, 194–197
Treatment (*see* Psychotherapeutic techniques; Readjustment)

U

Unconscious learning, 158
Unemployment effects on personality, 51, 293
UNESCO, 23, 313
United Service Organization, 36
United States, culture characteristics, 106–117
  culture goals, 106
  public health program, 25
  Public Health Service, 30

V

Values, as goals, 134
  in life periods, 163–166
  as organizing factors, 152
  as personality, 154
  in understanding of self, 382
Vasa Order of America, 110
Vascular system, 74–76
Vasomotor system, 87
Vectors, 50
Veterans Administration, on psychoneurotic disorders, 228–230
  and psychotherapeutic techniques, 372
Visceral phase in learning, 178
Visceral reactions, 179
Vocational counseling, 368
Vocational group values, 113
Vocational handicap, 306

W

Withdrawal, 207, 227
World Federation for Mental Health, 22

Y

Yale University Laboratory for Applied Physiology, 30